# THE ARCHITECTURE OF DEATH

*The MIT Press*      *Cambridge, Massachusetts, and London, England*

# THE ARCHITECTURE OF DEATH

*The Transformation of the Cemetery in Eighteenth-Century Paris*

*Richard A. Etlin*

© 1984 by
The Massachusetts Institute of Technology

This book was set in Sabon by The MIT Press Computergraphics
Department and printed and bound by Halliday Lithograph in the
United States of America.

Publication of this book has been aided by a grant from the National
Endowment for the Arts.

Library of Congress Cataloging in Publication Data

Etlin, Richard A.
    The architecture of death.

    Bibliography: p.
    Includes index.
    1. Paris (France)—Cemeteries. 2. Paris (France)—Sepulchral monu-
ments. 3. Architecture, Modern—17th–
19th centuries—France—Paris. I. Title.
NA6165.E84   1984    726′.8′0944361    83–12112
ISBN 0–262–05027–7

To Melissa

# Contents

# II
## THE LANDSCAPE GARDENER AND THE CEMETERY

The Cemetery of Père Lachaise in Paris is perhaps the most famous in the Western world. Although the general public accepts its existence without much questioning, it actually represents a turning point in one thousand years of Western history. From the Middle Ages to the 1780s, such a landscaped burial ground would have been inconceivable. After its opening in 1804, it became equally inconceivable to fashion a cemetery which was not in some way analogous. The entire "rural cemetery" movement in America, for example, which began with Mount Auburn (1831) outside Boston, is greatly indebted to Père Lachaise.

This is a study of the transformations in the image of the cemetery in Paris from the mid-eighteenth century to the origins and early development of Père Lachaise with a postscript on later English and American developments. This book, though, is not a simple architectural or social history. It is an exploration of how a society fashions its physical world to support and sustain its most cherished convictions and deepest feelings. As Leslie Stephen observed, "the doctrines which men ostensibly hold do not become operative upon their conduct until they have generated an imaginative symbolism." One could expand this thought to include emotions with doctrines and to redefine symbolism to embrace architecture and landscape design as well.

In the eighteenth century, Western civilization underwent a radical change with respect to attitudes toward death. A substantially medieval Christian theology was replaced by a pre-Romantic concept of human mortality. This mental revolution, sometimes called a "dechristianization," has been the subject of numerous studies by social and intellectual historians in recent years. My own interest has been to demonstrate the mutual relationships between changing attitudes toward death and the design not only of the cemetery but even of the city itself. Since cemetery design responded to current spiritual needs, one can trace the transformations in existential values and social mores by analyzing the image of death which the cemeteries were intended to foster. In this sense, the drawings and descriptions of proposed new cemeteries are as important documents for the study of *mentalités* as are the quantitative historian's tools, such as wills and testaments, tombstone inscriptions, library inventories, and so forth.

The cemetery, though, did not simply mirror a society's understanding about death. Its architecture or its landscape played a role in crystallizing nascent emotions and ideas. One can talk about a "society" in only the most limited ways. In effect, the story of the reform movement that between 1744 and 1804 sought to replace the thousand-year-old custom of burying the dead inside parish churches and in their adjacent or nearby burial grounds is the story of the interplay between conflicting traditions and ideals.

Furthermore, although the reform movement emerged victorious with the opening of the Cemetery of Père Lachaise in 1804 and with the application of the Imperial Decree on Burials of 23 Prairial, year XII (June 12, 1804), not only to Paris but to all of France, the first reformers would neither have recognized nor understood the new burial grounds that were being fashioned by that time.

In the sixty-year period between the events that unofficially inaugurated the cemetery reform movement in France and the opening of the first true municipal cemetery just outside Paris, the image of the cemetery underwent three distinct transformations. In the first phase, one finds a new Christian burial ground where the traditional features of the cemetery—the peripheral *charnier* or charnel house, mass graves, and Christian symbolism—furnished the basis of the design. New sensibilities, though, along with a new concern about urban hygiene, combined to impart to the cemetery as well as to the hospital, the slaughterhouse, and the prison the taint of impure institutions that had to be banished to the periphery of the city. Simultaneously, the entire infrastructure of the city—its streets, squares, and housing fabric—was to be redesigned to assure the purity of the new Enlightenment urban milieu.

In the second phase of cemetery design, the Christian vision of death ceded to a pantheistic celebration of Nature, conceived as a manifestation of Divinity. Here it is possible to situate the "visionary" architecture of Etienne-Louis Boullée within its proper social context. I have attempted to demonstrate, on the one hand, that Boullée was one of many architects proposing new cemeteries for Paris throughout the second half of the eighteenth century. I have also sought to explain just how Boullée truly was a visionary in the sense that he gave the most complete and, to my mind, the most engaging architectural vision to an eighteenth-century understanding of human mortality.

For the third phase of cemetery design, in which the ideals and imagery of the picturesque landscape garden were impressed into the service of death, I have had to trace the changing role of commemoration through the entire history of this type of garden design. In effect, the memorial or tomb was as much a part of the landscape garden as was the meandering path. Eventually, the tomb took over the entire garden in the form of a cemetery conceived as an Elysium or Field of Rest. The charnel house, along with its reminders about the gruesome aspects of human mortality, had no place in these new Arcadian dreamlands.

Finally, in all three phases, the Académie Royale d'Architecture of France and its successor, the Institut National des Sciences et des Arts, exhibited a consistent commitment to cemetery reform in a way that turns the popular understanding of "academic" upside down. With respect to social issues, in the eighteenth century, academic meant *engagé* rather than reactionary. Not only did the Academy respond rapidly to an emerging vision of the hygienic city; it also questioned the customary use of the cemetery as a mirror of social distinctions according to wealth and class to offer a humanistic alternative based upon personal merit.

The ultimate purpose of this book has not been to provide a specialized study of the cemetery but rather to suggest that standard compendiums of social history include a serious consideration of the design of cities, parks, and cemeteries as an integral part of the story of an age. Both by tracing the broad development in architectural and landscape design and by closely examining the specific features of individual projects, I have sought to demonstrate the degree to which the physical world, whether in idealized descriptions and illustrations or realizations, has played an indispensable role in formulating social and individual values.

## Acknowledgments

It is difficult to select among the people and institutions whose assistance has been invaluable in the preparation of this book. In a sense, this study owes much to my entire education at Princeton University, which began in 1965 with the undergraduate program in French literature and European civilization, continued in the professional graduate program in architecture, and then terminated with a doctorate in architectural history. I am grateful to the numerous fine teachers and scholars whom I encountered at Princeton and particularly to Professor Blanchard Bates, my undergraduate advisor; Professor Kenneth Frampton, my first teacher of architectural history and later, my thesis advisor for the professional degree of Master of Architecture; Professor David Coffin, the second reader for my doctoral dissertation; and Professor Anthony Vidler, my dissertation advisor. At all stages of my education, I was encouraged to pursue the type of interdisciplinary studies that have resulted in this book.

Over the past decade, I have also benefited from various grants. Through a Council on European Studies Pre-Dissertation Grant, I was able to spend the summer of 1971 in Paris, where I studied Etienne-Louis Boullée's manuscript papers and drawings. A Fulbright-Hays Full Grant for France (1973–1974) enabled me to spend the first of two consecutive years doing research in Paris. Subsequent grants from the University of Kentucky permitted me to return to Paris twice again. In the United States, my postdoctoral research and writing was supported by a fellowship from the Design Arts Program of the National Endowment for the Arts and a fellowship at Dumbarton Oaks, Harvard University. I am indebted to Dean Anthony Eardley both for the grants from the University of Kentucky and for the leave of absence that enabled me to accept the fellowship from Dumbarton Oaks.

My year at Dumbarton Oaks, 1979–1980, enabled me to do much more research on the history of the landscape garden and its relationship to the cemetery. It was a pleasure working with Diane McGuire, Acting Director of the Center for Studies in Landscape Architecture, and with Laura Byers, librarian of the Garden Library, who made research with a truly splendid collection a delightful as well as a profitable experience. I am also grateful to Giles Constable, Director of Dumbarton Oaks; Judy Siggins, Associate Director; and Elisabeth MacDougall, Director of the Center for Studies in Landscape Architecture, for having facilitated my work there.

While living in France, I was lucky to find a group of eighteenth-century scholars whose professional assistance and friendship I greatly value: Professor Daniel Rabreau, M. Jacques Guillerme, M. Jean-Pierre Mouilleseaux, Mlle Monique Mosser, and Mme Mona Ozouf. Monique Mosser, in particular, provided me with numerous illustrations as well as important documents. I am also grateful for conversations held with Professor Daniel Roche, M. Philippe Ariès, Mlle Madeleine Foisil, and M. Paul Cailleux, who also provided me with several illustrations.

In Paris, I exchanged ideas with Robert Breugmann, who generously shared material from the dissertation that he was then preparing on hospital design. Several years later at Dumbarton Oaks, David Schuyler showed the same generosity with the dissertation that he was writing on American rural cemeteries, parks, and suburbs. In the United States, I have also been assisted by Professors Thomas McCormick, Damie Stillman, Dora Wiebenson, and Barbara Stafford.

My work in the libraries and archives in Paris was facilitated by numerous individuals without whose assistance it would not have been possible to undertake and to complete this work. I would like to thank, especially, Mme Gestaz and M. Lemagny of the Cabinet des Estampes, Bibliothèque Nationale; M. Léri at the Bibliothèque Historique de la Ville de Paris; Mme Hervier and M. Pérouse de Montclos at the Inventaire Général; M. Gallet and M. de La Vaissière at the Musée Carnavalet; Mme de Garry at the Musée des Arts Décoratifs; Mlle Jacques at the Ecole Nationale Supérieure des Beaux-Arts; Mme Felkay, formerly at the Archives de la Seine; Mme Laffitte-Larnaudie at the Archives de l'Institut de France; and Mme Hautecoeur at the Bibliothèque de l'Institut de France. I am also grateful to the staff at the Archives Nationales for preparing a *demande de recherches* that I requested under the theme, *cimetières et monuments funéraires à Paris, 1740–1820*. This valuable research tool, which seeks to list all of the *côtes* in the Archives Nationales with documents on this subject, is on file at the archives. I am also indebted to the late Dr. Félix Gannal, whose collection of documents in part two of his published study of Parisian cemeteries provided a useful anthology while I slowly tracked down as many originals as I could in the archives. Likewise, Dr. Gannal's manuscript bibliography, conserved at the Bibliothèque Historique de la Ville de Paris, was a useful supplement to the subject headings at this library and to the printed subject catalogues to the collections of the Bibliothèque Nationale.

Finally, to my wife Melissa, who has lived with this book for nearly as many years as we have been married, and to my son David, I owe a debt of gratitude which no words could convey.

# I
## THE ARCHITECT AND THE CEMETERY

# 1
## A New Heaven and a New Earth (1711–1785)

### The Parish Cemetery

The macabre elevation of a funerary chapel by Jean-Charles Delafosse (fig. 1) transports us into a world of death radically different from our own. We are struck by the pile of skulls about to tumble out of the eaves directly over the central portal. This chilling image belongs to the tradition of the *memento mori*, a reminder of our mortality intended to shock the viewer into an appreciation of a Christian eschatology. Beginning in the late Middle Ages, though, the *memento mori* also reflected a most un-Christian terror of man's corporeal end and a fascination with the dead body.

In the late fourteenth and early fifteenth centuries, the *memento mori* entered the public space of the city. At this time wealthy Parisians, in the acts of piety intended to embellish their cemeteries with "beautiful" structures as well as to secure a distinguished place for burial, constructed arcades along the bounding walls. Each bay was a type of private chapel over the sepulchral vault fashioned below. In its physical appearance the *charnier*, as such a gallery was called, was intended as a *memento mori*. At the principal burial ground in Paris, the Cemetery of the Holy Innocents, the *charniers* were arranged so as to display rudely assembled piles of skulls and bones (fig. 2). From their origins until their destruction in 1786, these warehouses of death were intended, in the words of an eighteenth-century chronicler, as "appropriate images to represent the folly of our human vanity."

The walls of the cemetery had pictures and inscriptions that reinforced this moral. In 1408 the Duc de Berry sponsored an illustration of the popular theme of the Three Living and the Three Dead over the main entry to the adjacent church. The scene of three knights encountering three corpses in successive states of putrefaction was accompanied by written reflections on the inevitability of death and of the body's decay and ended with a supplication to pray for the dead duke's soul. Likewise, the earliest known painting of the Danse Macabre, or Dance of Death, was executed in 1424–1425 on the wall of the *charnier* along the Rue de la Ferronnerie. In a series of scenes, a nimble skeleton, representing either the dead person or Death incarnate, compelled an unwilling partner to join him in a dance of death. The entire sequence, including people of all ages, from all ranks, and in varied conditions of health, formed a composite image of society and a global vision of the human condition. The opening lines to the published version of this Danse Macabre reinforced its visual intentions and clearly revealed the contemporary obsession with the physical aspect of death:

By Divine sentence
No matter what your estate
Whether good or evil, you will be
Eaten by worms. Alas, look at us,

1
Jean-Charles
Delafosse, funerary
chapel, c. 1780.

2
Cemetery of the
Holy Innocents,
Paris. View by
Bernier, February 21,
1786.

*A New Heaven and a New Earth*

Dead, stinking, and rotten.
You will be like this too.

Significant changes in burial practices accompanied the appearance of the *charnier*: burying in mass graves capable of receiving up to six hundred cadavers and exhuming the skeletal remains after decomposition. The bones and skulls were stored under the roofs of the parish churches and of their *charniers*. The combined effect of increased population and of recurring plague may have prompted these innovations. In any case, the communal grave and the periodic exhumations were continued through the succeeding centuries to become chief features of the parish cemetery. Like the *charnier*, which served the dual purpose of storage and display, the gaping holes in the earth also taught a vivid lesson about mortality.

Delafosse's architectural fantasy, then, of an open window within the central pediment assimilated the long-established custom of storing bones within this attic space with the traditional aspect of the *charnier* as a display of human remains. Yet true to the spirit of Baroque theatricality, the architect introduced a dramatic element through the precarious arrangement of the skulls. This image recalls the still lifes of the preceding century, many of them in the *Vanitas* genre with a skull as a *memento mori*, in which the entire composition was purposefully arranged in an unstable manner. Lemon rinds, knives, and other objects extended over the edge of the table, threatening the entire composition with imminent destruction. The tension established in the Baroque artistic treatment of death found its most flamboyant aspect in the funeral ceremonies of the royalty and the high nobility. An elaborate cortege through the streets might feature the menacing simulacre of Death as a skeleton triumphant on his chariot. Even more phantasmagoric were tombs that suddenly began to open. The skeleton would make its appearance as a sardonically grinning figure on the huge pyramidal catafalque erected within the church for the funeral and then on the mausoleum erected to perpetuate the memory of the deceased. The most famous of these dramatic images are the tombs designed by Bernini.

The Baroque skeletons owed their existence not only to a continuation of the late medieval tradition of the Dance of Death but also to the more recent sixteenth-century discovery of the cadaver as a subject for anatomy. "Science," writes André Chastel, "almost in spite of itself, placed the mystery of the human organism under the eyes of everybody." A spate of anatomical drawings both popularized the image of the partially dissected body and served as an occasion for frightful speculations on death. The representation of these *écorchés* assumed a surrealistic quality; either a flayed anatomical figure would appear as a quasi living being or a dissected corpse shown in all the horror of precise anatomical detail would be offered as a *memento mori*.

This fascination with the mysteries of life and death through the figure of the corpse had direct ramifications for spiritual life in the Cemetery of the Holy Innocents. One of the most prized treasures there was a statue measuring about one meter tall, executed by the sixteenth-century sculptor Germain Pilon (fig. 3). This statue had the ambiguous appearance of a desiccated body not quite dead. The uncertainty of the figure's condition was heightened by the alabaster stone which, by absorbing light, projected an aura of warmth and hence suggested life. This "skeleton," as it was called in the eighteenth century, was understood to be a figure representing Death. The epitaph on the escutcheon repeated a familiar admonition: "No mortal can escape me: all are destined to become food for worms." This statue, then, not only provided an awesome figure of Death the reaper, but also furnished a mirror to the living of their own putrefaction. Traditionally kept under the Charnier de la Chapelle de la Vierge (Ossuary of the Chapel of the Virgin), also called the *petit charnier* (at the top next to the church in fig. 4), this *memento mori* was shown to the public on All Saints' Day and All Souls' Day, the festivals for the dead.

By the eighteenth century, the appreciation of Pilon's statue of Death in "enlightened" circles had markedly changed. Several chroniclers of the history of Paris celebrated this work as a chef d'oeuvre, thereby reducing an almost mystical figure to the secular status of an artistic masterpiece. Likewise, the architect commissioned to record the Cemetery of the Holy Innocents and its monuments just before their final removal or destruction in 1786 dismissed the moralizing epitaph on the escutcheon as a "most gothic inscription," which he erased in favor of the simple name of the burial ground. Both of these examples reflected a new attitude toward death that no longer savored the horror of putrefaction. This seemingly rational approach to a striking figuration of death should not mislead. It betrayed a desire to banish the image of death from view rather than to live with it in the intimacy of the city.

The novelty of this attitude can be appreciated when one considers that since the seventh or eighth century, Christians had buried their dead inside their parish churches and within adjacent or neighboring parish cemeteries. The faithful were drawn to the church in death through the belief that burial within the sacrosanct ground of the church and more specifically in a location close to a martyr would afford a dual protection to the deceased— security for his body and forgiveness for his sins. Soon burial in a parish church became desired as a mark of social status as well as an expression of piety. This custom had become so widespread by the ninth century that Bishop Théodulfe of Orléans complained

*A New Heaven and a New Earth*

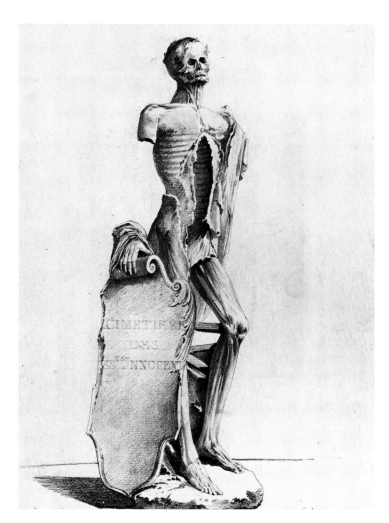

3
Germain Pilon,
statue of Death,
sixteenth century.
Cemetery of the
Holy Innocents.

*The Parish Cemetery*

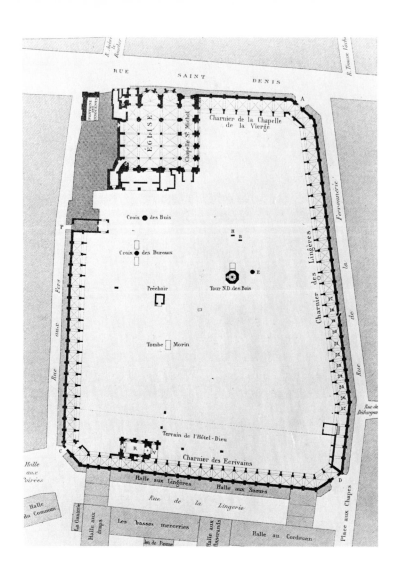

4
Cemetery of the
Holy Innocents,
1550. From
Hoffbauer, *Paris à
travers les âges*.

*A New Heaven and a New Earth*

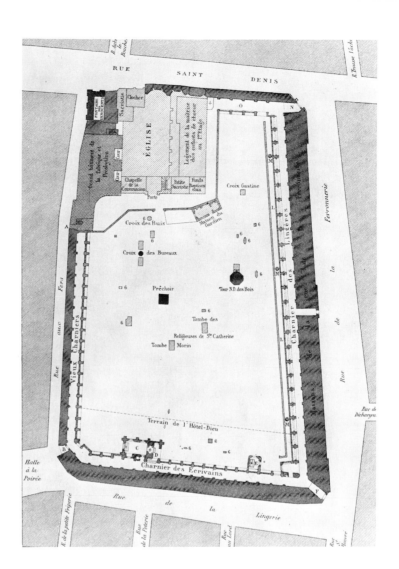

5
Cemetery of the
Holy Innocents,
1780. From
Hoffbauer, *Paris à
travers les âges*.

that the churches had been transformed into veritable cemeteries. With the growth of urban parishes between the eleventh and thirteenth centuries, the city became dotted with places of interment. Amiens, for example had twenty-four cemeteries and Dijon had almost as many. In the eighteenth century Paris had over thirty parish cemeteries.

Traditionally church and cemetery were seen as integrally related. In canon law the "church" included a delimited portion of exterior land in which the cemetery was located. Thus to be buried in the cemetery was to rest within the consecrated precinct of the church. Reciprocally, the *cimiterium* could mean either the space in front of the church destined for interments or more generally a church in which the dead had been buried. The physical presence of the dead at the heart of the parish had a theological significance for the living. Parishioners were reminded each time they came to church of their own inescapable end and also of their obligations to the departed, for whose souls they were instructed to pray. This proximity helped to sustain a spiritual bond between parishioners and their ancestors as well as to direct thoughts toward the ultimate teachings of religion.

Space was not uniformly valued in either the church or the cemetery. In the selection of their place of burial, the wealthy and the powerful sought a sepulcher close to the main altar or alternately within a chapel or under the *charnier*. The parish of Saint-Séverin in Paris (fig. 6) had eighteen chapels around its church as well as a *charnier* around the cemetery. Two large communal sepulchral vaults had been prepared for burials of lesser distinction inside the church. After that came the cemetery, which was divided into two unequal sections by a pathway. The larger sector was called "the cemetery of the poor" and the smaller area was termed "the cemetery of the rich." This physical separation was necessary to establish social distinctions since large mass graves were employed in both.

Unlike most cemeteries in Paris, the Cemetery of the Holy Innocents served not one but eighteen parishes as well as two hospitals and the morgue. The most desirable places for burial here (fig. 5) were the two chapels (the Chapelle d'Orgement and the Chapelle de Villeroy), followed closely by the *petit charnier*, located closest to the church and containing both the Chapel of the Virgin and the revered statue of Death. The three other *charniers* commanded slightly lower fees. Within the cemetery those who could afford an individual grave crowded in a small area by the *petit charnier*. The populace was buried cheaply in the remainder of the cemetery in large mass graves. The farthest portion of the land belonged to the general hospital run by the Church, the Hôtel-Dieu, which interred the poor in charity burials. The cemetery, then, through its hierarchy of places for burial, presented a visual class portrait. Not only were the upper classes separated

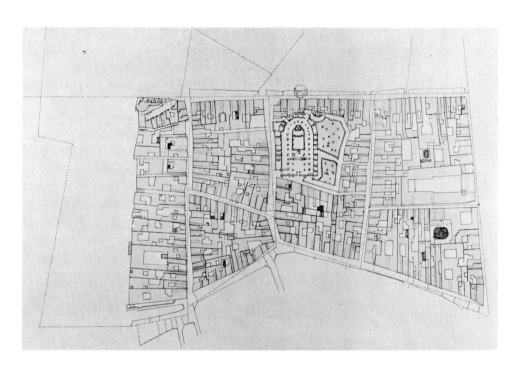

6
Cemetery of Saint-
Séverin, Paris.

from the commoners, but they also were afforded a greater degree of identity through the specific location of their sepulchers as well as from the epitaphs or heraldic seals placed near their graves.

*Urban Hygiene*     The eighteenth century saw the development of a new sensibility for which the old religious values as they pertained to the urban milieu were replaced by a profound concern with public hygiene. Its expression has long been recognized in the writings of the popular satirist of Parisian life and manners, Louis-Sébastien Mercier, whose works exhibited an obsession with the filth and decay found everywhere in the city: the mud covering the streets, the excrement festering in the household latrines that was periodically carted away through the streets, the blood from the slaughterhouses at the heart of the city running over the pavement, the dirty linens from the general hospital washed in the drinking water of the Seine, and the corpses rotting inside the churches and within the cemeteries. To Mercier, writing toward the end of the eighteenth century, Paris was a medieval city with multiple sources of pollution, requiring renewal according to the strictures of the Enlightenment: cleanliness, order, air, light, and sunshine. While Mercier was certainly an insistently vocal proponent of this vision, he was neither the first nor its unique advocate. His concern with urban hygiene was shared by numerous citizens, many of them authors of short pamphlets on the *embellissement* or urban design of a new Paris. The origins of this sentiment have to be sought much earlier in the century; and the subject that figured prominently in the genesis of the new attitude was the question of burying the dead.

Through the course of the eighteenth century, the traditional familiarity between the living and the dead that had characterized the European city since the Middle Ages was fully rejected. This change had been prepared in part in the late seventeenth and early eighteenth centuries when parish churches added new constructions to accommodate the liturgical and pastoral needs of the Counter-Reformation: chapels for communion and confession, an office for the churchwardens, a sacristy, a presbytery, lodgings for the secular clergy, rooms for catechism, and so forth. These additional spaces were added to the existing churches at the expense of the cemetery. As a result, numerous parish cemeteries that were now seriously deficient in land had to be closed and transferred elsewhere in the parish. In 1765, when the English Reverend William Cole made a tour of the churches of Paris, he was suprised to find so many parishes "without" cemeteries. He did not realize that the burial grounds existed, albeit several blocks away.

These new cemeteries constituted a third generation of burial grounds. The first was typified by the Cemetery of the Holy

Innocents, founded over a thousand years earlier according to the Roman practice of burying outside of the city. With the growth of Paris these cemeteries were eventually incorporated into the urban fabric. The second generation included the Cemetery of Saint-Séverin, founded toward 1250 in the heart of the city and adjacent to the parish church. The third generation, as found in the parishes of Saint-Jean-en-Grève and Saint-Gervais, reflected a new spiritual as well as physical distance between the living and the dead.

This change in attitudes permitted the Cemetery of the Holy Innocents, where approximately two thousand people constituting about one-tenth of the annual dead of Paris were buried, to come under close scrutiny in the first half of the eighteenth century. Gradually this cemetery in particular and all cemeteries in general came to be revered less as they were feared more for the dangers that they posed to the public's health. In 1711 the Procureur Général summoned a representative of the chapter of Saint-Germain l'Auxerrois, the ecclesiastical proprietors of the Cemetery of the Holy Innocents, to instruct him "to take all necessary measures to prevent infection within the cemetery." To this end, the Parlement of Paris authorized higher fees for burial at the most popular locations here. Not only was the air found to be "infected" and "corrupted," but the grave diggers sometimes came upon bodies still in the process of putrefaction as they went about their periodical exhumations. Complaints about the cemetery from neighbors prompted visits and reports by the civil authorities in 1724, 1737, 1746, and 1755. In 1736 the chapter of Saint-Germain l'Auxerrois provided its own damning indictment of the burial ground: the soil was worn out and could no longer assist the decomposition of corpses; the overcrowding had forced up the level of the land so that the bodies were piled higher than the level of the neighboring streets; the communal graves had to be made deeper and hence contained too many corpses. Rather than decaying rapidly, the corpses festered in the giant hole and the cemetery emitted foul odors. The chapter cited the widening of the adjacent Rue de la Ferronnerie (figs. 4, 5) by royal order in 1670 as having reduced the usable space by one-fifth, thereby contributing to all of these deplorable conditions.

The widening of the Rue de la Ferronnerie literally and symbolically signaled the end of an era. The circumstances surrounding this event also illustrate the interrelationships between the numerous sources of pollution in the city. The Cemetery of the Holy Innocents had its origins in a burial ground in the open fields along a main Roman road to the north which became the principal way to Saint-Denis. By the Middle Ages, the cemetery, then situated at the intersection of several major routes, had to share its site with the markets developed in the twelfth century by Louis VI and Philip Augustus. These neighboring markets caused the cemetery to become the scene of disruptive and irreverent behavior, as well as serving as a thoroughfare for animals and people.

To protect the burial ground, Philip Augustus had stone walls erected in 1186. Even then, the cemetery was by no means isolated from the surrounding markets. Since the Middle Ages, numerous urban cemeteries had served as communal meeting places where merchants set up shop, livestock searched for food, people of all ages danced, and children played. The Cemetery of the Holy Innocents was no exception. In the eighteenth century, public letter writers and cloth merchants still plied their trades under the *charniers*, that bore their names. Outside in the surrounding streets, the vegetable and herb markets continued to function much as they had for centuries (fig. 7). The problems of crowded streets filled with vegetable debris preoccupied the royal and municipal authorities from about 1630 onward. Ironically, Henry IV had wanted to widen the Rue de la Ferronnerie, whose congested traffic later permitted his assassination in 1610. The street was finally enlarged after Louis XIV ordered the demolition of the old *charnier* for this purpose. As Emile Mâle has observed, the fresco of the Dance of Death disappeared without a protest. This cavalier destruction of a once vital element in the religious life of the cemetery as well as the reduction of available space for burials reflected the loss of prestige suffered by the traditional cemetery.

The hygienic problems of the Cemetery of the Innocents were exacerbated by the poor habits of personal cleanliness of the people living in the surrounding apartments. The residents of these buildings, which generally lacked adequate sanitary facilities, had acquired the habit of throwing their bodily wastes into the cemetery. The drainage ditch constructed expressly to carry away such wastes was ineffective partly because it was often clogged with debris from the markets but also because the refuse was thrown far into the cemetery. The problem became so grave that in 1736 the statue of Death had to be rescued from the *petit charnier*, where it was subjected to a daily barrage of "filth and human wastes." In 1737–1738 the doctors who visited the cemetery in accordance with an Arrêt of the Parlement of Paris concluded that the strong odors there came primarily from the urine and feces and secondarily from the corpses. In the following year, an architect sent to confirm this report could hardly pass through the entrances, so strong had the odors become from the festering refuse. For the people who lived around the cemetery, this site had come to be considered as a dumping ground, a *voirie*, which almost no action could profane. When this practice began is not known. In the eighteenth century, though, it contributed signif-

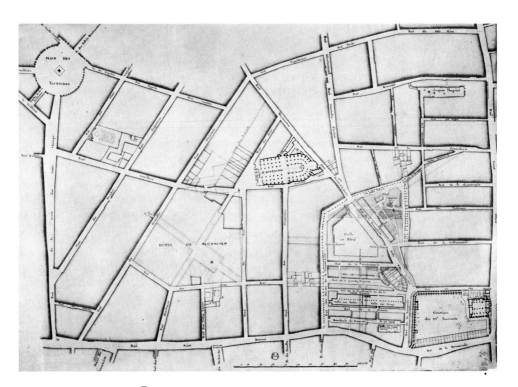

7
Quartier Saint-
Eustache with Les
Halles, mid-
eighteenth century,
Paris.

icantly to alienating the sensibilities of the faithful, who became increasingly concerned with the foul odors in this and other burial grounds and in the parish churches as well.

There are two sides to the Enlightenment's concern for urban hygiene. One might be portrayed as a rational desire to secure a healthy as well as a pleasant physical milieu. In this age of pre-bacteriological science, though, it was thought that disease was spread by the corruption of the air. As Dr. Guillaume-Lambert Godart explained in his "Septicologie" (1767): "Air is our ele-ment . . . we contract mortal illnesses when the air in which we live is corrupted or filled with putrid miasms." From the 1740s onward, corrupted air became a kind of phantasm which haunted the minds of "enlightened" thinkers. Henri Coulet has justly char-acterized this reaction as "a type of new emotion, mixing hatred, horror, and fear and sometimes a certain attraction."

The 1740s were a turning point in the history of French attitudes toward death and toward the cemetery. Historians of *mentalités* or cultural attitudes, such as Michel Vovelle, Philippe Ariès, and Pierre Chaunu have identified this decade as the critical period during which there was a marked decline in the customary rituals directed toward death. The "dechristianization," as Vovelle has termed it, was accompanied by a variety of related fears in which dying and death acquired disconcerting attributes. One was the fear of being buried alive which "exploded" (Pierre Chaunu) in Paris with the publication of Jacques-Jean Bruhier d'Ablaincourt's *Dissertation sur l'incertitude des signes de la mort . . .* (Dissertation on the Lack of Certainty about the Signs of Death and on the Problem of Premature Burials, 1742; second edition, 1749). This terror haunted the capital through the succeeding two decades. The second fear issued from the specter of the corpse as an insidious source of death foolishly harbored within the community of the living. It may not be coincidental that the waning of com-forting religious practices was accompanied by a growing unease and trepidation about death and the dead.

The 1740s also saw the beginnings of a nationwide reform movement to end the custom of burying inside churches and within cemeteries. In 1743 the Abbé Charles-Gabriel Porée pub-lished the first French diatribe against these burial practices. "We are living within an atmosphere of corruption, destruction, and death," warned the Abbé; "we are living there, or rather, lan-guishing and perishing." Porée's arguments appeared to be con-firmed on August 17, 1744, when noxious vapors from a sepulchral vault in a church in Montpellier asphyxiated several people during a funeral. The Intendant for Languedoc summoned a physician, Dr. Haguenot, to investigate the nature of this "murderous vapor." In a paper delivered on December 23, 1746, to a joint assembly of the Société Royale des Sciences de Montpellier and of the

Etats de Languedoc, Dr. Haguenot concurred with the Abbé Po-rée's judgments.

The reform movement gathered momentum over the succeeding decade. The respected surgeon Dr. Antoine Louis warned the public that "putrefaction of the dead is capable of empoisoning the living." Voltaire conveyed the same message more vividly: "What, these people bury their dead in the same place where they worship Divinity? Their temples are paved with cadavers? No wonder that Persepolis [i.e, Paris] is ravaged so often by these pestilential diseases." D'Alembert, in a series of articles in the *Encyclopédie*, reiterated these dangers and recommended, as had Porée and Haguenot, the practice of burying "in a vast cemetery sufficiently far from the city." The *extra muros* cemetery was not merely an ideal, but rather a reality found close to home. D'Alembert reminded his readers of its use in Geneva, thereby providing a model for all to follow.

## The Pure and the Impure

To "enlightened" opinion, the dead were not only dangerous to the living; they also defiled the church. The reformers wanted to separate the two sides of existence not only according to the polarity of the healthy and unhealthy but also along the axis of the pure and the impure. Jean-François Sobry encapsulated the sentiments of the entire movement when he wrote in *De l'Archi-tecture* (1776): "This practice of burying inside our churches is both unhealthy and irreverent." Philippe Ariès is certainly correct in observing that the primary motivation behind the reform move-ment was "the horror and the fear of decomposing bodies, of their formidable chemistry." The hygienic argument, though, was accompanied by a new religious outlook, which saw death as sullying the purity of the church. No longer should the dead have a permanent place there. Coffins, decomposing corpses, and skel-etons inside the parish church now offered a "horrid spectacle" to be removed from sight. Likewise, tombs and mausoleums were thought to clutter the church and sometimes inexcusably to ob-struct the view.

The tendency to order the world through the polarity of the sacred and the profane had a corollary in the minds of those who objected so strongly to the confusion within their churches. The parish church with its numerous functions accommodated in an ad hoc manner was now totally unacceptable. The desire to remove the dead from the church was only one manifestation, albeit the principal one, of an inner need for a clarity of purpose in the physical organization of human activities. The contrast between the Church of the Holy Innocents, as it happened to grow through the centuries, and the ideal parish church as proposed by the architects Jacques-François Blondel (fig. 8) and Claude-Nicolas Ledoux (figs. 9–11) illustrates this point. It is also confirmed by

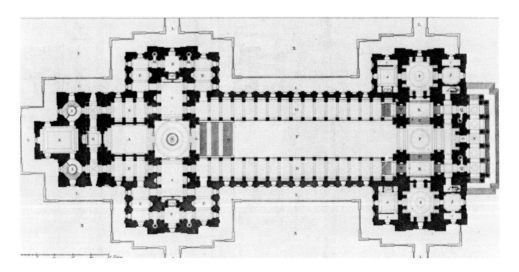

8
Jacques-François
Blondel, parish
church, c. 1766.

*A New Heaven and a New Earth*

the explanatory texts written by both architects, who bemoaned the "distraction and confusion" of mixing different activities together.

Both Blondel and Ledoux predicated their designs for a parish church upon a separation of seemingly incompatible activities achieved through provision for different entrances and exits and patterns of movement as well as through isolation by changes in floor level. The principal division was to occur between the living and the dead. Blondel wished to relegate the dead to cemeteries outside the city; mausoleums, though, would be permitted under the arcades, which would enclose an ample open space around the church. Only the priests were to be buried inside the church, but now in chapels located beneath the raised areas for the choir (fig. 8, A), the altar (B), and the transept (C). In this manner, visitors could come to admire funerary monuments in either location without disturbing the other church activities.

In Ledoux's project, the architect seems to have accepted the presence of the dead within the city. Yet, while Ledoux included burial within the precinct of his church, he excluded most interments from the closed building. Using the residual space of the Greek cross, Ledoux has fashioned four cemeteries, two for each sex divided in turn according to age. A continuous wall around the periphery decorated with bas-reliefs depicting religious processions united cemetery and church.

Ledoux's church was essentially a mechanism for the cortege. Rites of passage associated with celebrating life, such as baptism and marriage, were provided with two opposing entrances along one axis of the cross; funerals were assigned to the other axis. In that way, people participating in functions with "conflicting purposes" would not run into each other at the same door. Ceremonies that called for joy were accommodated architecturally with an ascent into the church beginning with the steps up to the portico and culminating in a flight of stairs leading to the level of the altar and the two naves. In contrast, the funeral procession was provided with a descent into the ground, beginning in front of the church and terminating in the crypt. While the upper church presented an elegant interior whose tall and slender Ionic columns carried four coffered barrel vaults and a central dome, the lower church was provided with a baseless, truncated Doric order whose thick, stubby shafts heightened the sense of claustrophobia in this low, underground space. This compressed order illustrates what J.-F. Blondel termed *une architecture terrible*, the appropriate solution for an underground realm of death.

The upper and lower spaces were further differentiated by the extensive glazing used to flood the upper church with light, contrasted with the somber lighting below. The four cemeteries were

9
Claude-Nicolas
Ledoux, church with
cemetery for Chaux,
c. 1785.

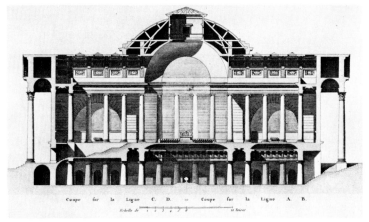

10
Ledoux, church with
cemetery for Chaux,
c. 1785, section.

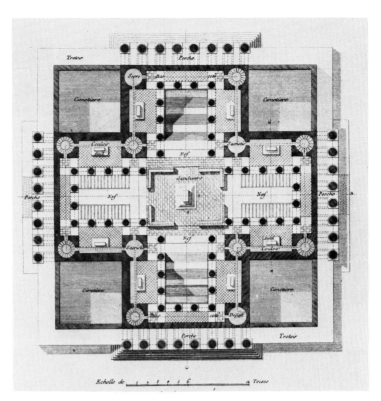

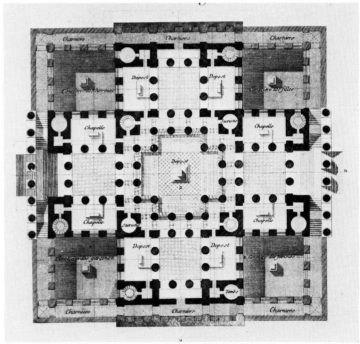

11
Ledoux, church with
cemetery for Chaux,
c. 1785, plans of the
sanctuary and of the
crypt.

*The Pure and the Impure*

characterized by dark cypresses, which extended upward beyond the peripheral frieze. As Quatremère de Quincy reminded his contemporaries, "the ancients used the cypress for the sorrow of the tomb just as they did the rose for the pleasures of love." A further look at both projects would reveal an elaborate compartmentalization of spaces to accommodate separately the other varied church activities. In conclusion, the new parish church classified and separated the different stages of life as well as the varied religious functions according to a physical order that was at once functional and symbolic.

*The Parlement's Intervention*

At the urban scale, the first attempt to separate the living from the dead came on May 21, 1765, when the Parlement of Paris ordered all parish cemeteries to be removed from Paris and severely restricted future burials inside parish churches. This radical break with centuries of church tradition had gradually been prepared over the preceding half century: first an increased attentiveness to the Cemetery of the Holy Innocents (1711–1739), then discussions about the closing of this cemetery (1744–1760), and finally, after two decades of public attention to the question of burials, the Arrêt of March 12, 1763. With this Arrêt, the Parlement, sustained by the opposition of several powerful property owners to the establishment of a new cemetery adjacent to their land in the centrally located parish of Saint-Sulpice, ordered a broad inquiry into the safety of all the parish burial grounds. The preamble to the Arrêt, though, clearly revealed that the Advocate General was already convinced that the old order would have to be abolished. Le Peletier de Saint-Fargeau, like the Abbé Porée before him, saw himself not as a revolutionary but as a reformer. Both men appealed to an older tradition, to the ancient Greek and Roman customs, shared by numerous other early peoples including the early Christians, of forbidding burials within the city. According to these reformers, cemeteries existed within the city because of a deviation from a primitive and natural wisdom abandoned during the "gothic" Middle Ages.

Perhaps the most striking evidence of a profound change in attitudes toward death can be adduced from the clergy's response to the grand inquest of 1763. The curés and the churchwardens were sharply divided in their opinions (see the appendix). Six major cemeteries, including the Cemetery of the Holy Innocents, were condemned by their ecclesiastical owners, who called for a new order in burials. Nine other cemeteries were deemed satisfactory by the parish councils in spite of an adverse judgment by the civil commissioners.

On what basis were these cemeteries evaluated? The reformers believed, in the words of Dr. Godart, that the "corruption" of the air "occurs when matter capable of putrefaction is stagnant

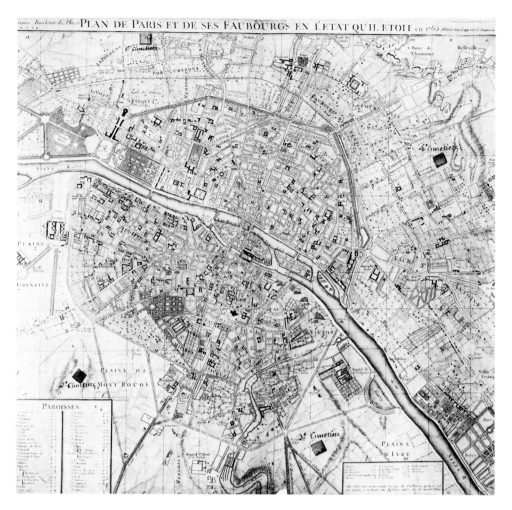

12
Anonymous project
for four new
cemeteries outside
Paris, overlaid upon
plan of 1765.

and when its emanations are retained. Consequently, precautions must be taken to prevent the accumulation of putrid bodies . . . by imparting movement to the volume of infected air." If foul odors were present, then reformers were certain that they were breathing a noxious atmosphere; if tall buildings surrounded the cemetery (fig. 13), then these same observers were convinced that the land could not be properly ventilated. Reports of silver that tarnished, cloth that faded, and soup that turned rancid sustained the belief that the odorous air corrupted both inanimate and animate matter. On this basis and without any recourse to precise epidemiological evidence, the reports by the civil commissioners and several parish councils condemned nearly all of the cemeteries at the center of Paris. Toward the periphery, however, and especially beyond the boulevards, commissioners and churchwardens concurred in finding many of the burial grounds isolated and well aerated.

One can only speculate about the reasons why all the cemeteries were ordered closed. First, archival documents provide evidence that conditions in many burial grounds, especially in the Cemetery of the Holy Innocents, had worsened over the preceding two or three decades. It was only a matter of time before others would be added to the list. Furthermore, if any action were to be successful, it would have to apply to all parties. As the curé and the churchwardens of Saint-Jean-en-Grève warned, partial measures would only give rise to objections about unfair treatment. In deciding to have the parishes themselves pay for the new cemeteries, the Parlement had another reason to include all parties in order to ensure the financial success of the undertaking. This strategy, though, united the outlying parishes that had recently spent considerable sums to open their relatively new cemeteries with the predominantly central parishes that opposed the decree on ideological grounds. Principally for this reason, the Parlement's measure was never applied.

The Arrêt of May 21, 1765, would have broken the traditional intimacy between the parish and its funerals. The dead could not have been carried to the grave, where all participants in the ceremony would partake of the final rites. Rather, the corpse would have to be transported in a type of mortuary carriage either directly from the house or, in the case of the wealthier classes, from the church, to a distant burial ground. While conservatives shuddered at the thought of such a rupture, reformers felt relieved that the dead and the living would have their own separate realms.

The underlying reasons that prompted reformers to separate the cemeteries from the everyday spaces of normal social intercourse were complex. One aspect was expressed by the Abbé Lubersac, who insisted upon "removing from our view the dismal and crushing sights which constantly remind us of our nothingness." The Abbé Porée, on the other hand, as well as the curé for Saint-

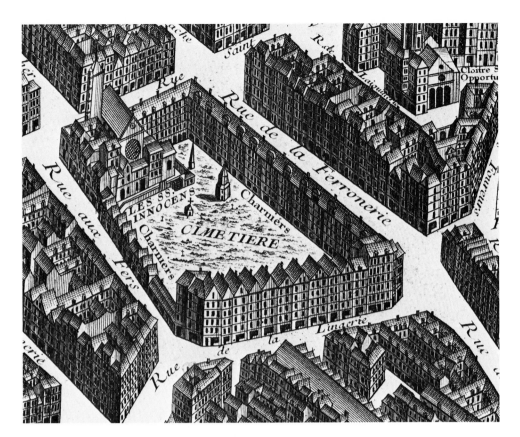

13
Cemetery of the
Holy Innocents,
Paris. Detail from
the Plan Turgot,
1739.

*The Parlement's Intervention*

André-des-Arts, Desbois de Rochefort, welcomed the prospect of teaching this lesson in isolated cemeteries whose silence would be conducive to meditating upon death. Desbois de Rochefort imagined how the mortuary chariot would proceed tranquilly through the night, thereby presenting a "more lugubrious and more religious aspect" than usual. The Abbé Porée, in turn, relished the "unity of purpose" of the new cemetery, where "everything would dispose one toward pious melancholy, source of the most salutary reflexions."

The contrasting attitudes expressed in these statements were not necessarily mutually exclusive. These men did not want to banish death in the twentieth-century sense of stifling both thoughts and discussions about it. Rather the reformers were interested in putting death into what was seen as its proper place. In this *siècle classificateur*, this age bent upon categorization and classification, the mania for rationality was often based upon a fear of the unexplained. One could not fathom the ultimate mysteries of life and death, but one could establish a degree of certainty and control by physically distancing death and by bounding it within closed walls. Order provided assurance if not ultimate knowledge.

*Rethinking the City*

The Parlement's direct intervention into the question of burials must be considered within the broader context of a nascent urbanism based upon the issue of hygiene. The Arrêts of March 12, 1763, and of May 21, 1765, were issued in a certain climate of opinion which they may, in turn, have strongly influenced. Toward 1765 not only the traditional cemetery was called into question but the city itself. The entire urban infrastructure—streets, squares, and houses—as well as particular institutions were carefully scrutinized as to their effect on the quality of the air.

The principal and most comprehensive arguments and strategies can be found in the Abbé Laugier's *Observations sur l'architecture* and the architect Pierre Patte's *Monumens érigés en France à la gloire de Louis XV*, both published in 1765. Together these two texts issued a broad indictment of the insalubrious city. Not only the cemeteries but also the hospitals and the slaughterhouses infected the air and hence belonged "out in the open" at the periphery of the city. Laugier envisaged using the river Seine to transport the sick and the dead to their respective resting places. To provide air, space, and light to city dwellers, Laugier proposed a type of superblock as the unit for urban development instead of the customary crowding of buildings with meager courtyards. Laugier would have capitalized on the existence of vast parcels of open land surrounded by a ring of buildings facing the street. Through slight physical modifications, the unencumbered interior land would be developed with freestanding homes surrounded by courtyards and gardens while the periphery would consist of more modest houses provided with cross ventilation. In 1767, Dr. Léopold de Genneté, who was familiar with the mechanical ventilating systems used in mines and ships, suggested similar solutions for providing the complete gamut of building types, from private homes to public buildings, with a constantly renewed pure air.

While the primary intention of Pierre Patte's treatise was to publish the projects for a square in honor of Louis XV, the simultaneous depiction of all the proposals on one map of Paris (fig. 14) had another effect. The map not only served as a guide for locating the projects and for judging their effect on the particular sites; it also provided an image of how Paris might be transformed into a healthy city. The large squares, with their broad, radiating streets were seen as an indispensable means for securing a pure air. As the Abbé Laugier explained: "Squares are necessary in cities if only to aerate them, to give them sunlight, and to dispel more readily the humidity and bad odors from the street: the larger the city, the greater number of squares needed." When Dr. Olivier from Montpellier dubbed the urban square a "reservoir" for pure air, the phrase immediately became popular.

Since they served as storehouses for fresh air, squares had to be situated at the intersections of several streets where the winds would carry the air deep into the surrounding neighborhood. Looking at the map of Paris, Laugier judged only the Place des Victoires (fig. 7) as worthy of its function as a square. The other famous squares—the Place Royale (now Place des Vosges), the Place Dauphine, and the Place Vendôme—were all too enclosed and too isolated to be effective.

Finally, the square would be complete only if it had freestanding shooting fountains (fig. 15). In this same year, 1765, the architect Marie-Joseph Peyre proposed the construction of these "beautiful ornaments," which had the "even more valuable advantage of contributing to the health of the people who lived there. They purify the air." In this review of the urban fabric, the interests of commodity, urbanity, order, and beauty conflated with those of salubrity into a unified vision. If any one factor, though, provided a sense of urgency to these reforms, it was the fear of a corrupted air.

At this time the projects began to multiply: the competitions for cemeteries sponsored by the Académie Royale d'Architecture (1765, 1766); the cemetery designed by Pierre Patte (1769), the plans for new slaughterhouses by Jean-Charles Delafosse (1766); the cross section of a well-paved street (fig. 16) with elaborate drainage systems to flush toilets, wash courtyards, and clean public thoroughfares by Pierre Patte (1769); and the new design for a well-aerated hospital by Dr. Antoine Petit (1774). In 1769 the city of Paris obtained a royal sanction for the redevelopment of

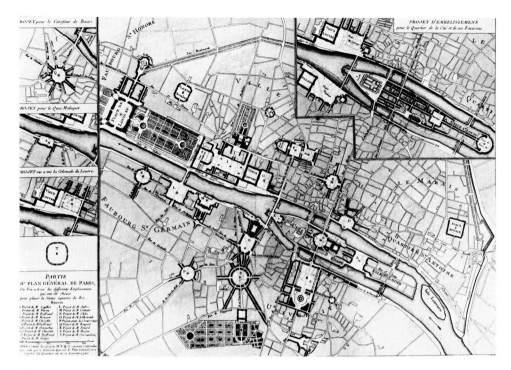

14
Pierre Patte, Paris
with proposed
squares, from the
competition of 1748.

15
Marie-Joseph Peyre,
city fountains, 1765.

16
Pierre Patte, proposal
for street paving and
drainage system,
1769.

the Seine. This project, in preparation since 1762, consisted of a series of public works which would remove obstacles that "intercept the circulation of the air." The houses along the banks of the Seine and on the bridges were to be demolished and wide *quais*, or embankments, were to be constructed along the river. These houses, which had been accepted for centuries as an integral aspect of the urban fabric, were now to be removed both as an eyesore and as an impediment to the most important source of natural ventilation, the air carried through the heart of Paris by the Seine.

Finally, in his *Mémoires sur les objets les plus importants de l'architecture* (1769), Pierre Patte suggested a comprehensive plan for the zoning of Paris. Trades and slaughterhouses would be relegated to the faubourgs. Patte reiterated Poncet de la Grave's earlier proposal (1756) for a navigable canal around the suburbs which would carry off wastes into the Seine at a point below the city. This circumferential waterway would serve another purpose: to isolate the city from the ill and the dead placed in hospitals and cemeteries, respectively, on the far side. Within a few years, then, after the Parlement's Arrêt of May 21, 1765, an entire program for a transformed urban mileu had been outlined. The cemetery was no longer seen as an isolated danger to public hygiene. From this time onward, urbanists incessantly inveighed against its dangers as the most serious of numerous urban ills.

**The Scientific Contribution**

The 1770s saw the development of biological and chemical discoveries that further focused attention on the problems of urban health. Joseph Priestley in England and Antoine-Laurent de Lavoisier in Paris were locked in competition to discover the various sources of the "corruption" of the air. While Priestley made the first advances, publicized between 1772 and 1775, it was Lavoisier who in 1775–1780 read a series of papers to the Académie Royale des Sciences that explained the makeup of the atmosphere, the nature of oxygen and carbon dioxide, and the basic mechanism of respiration. Although these insights had little meaning for understanding the process and dangers of putrefying corpses, they kept the issue under public scrutiny. Furthermore, at this time the question of a dangerous atmosphere vitiated through respiration was seen as a lesser manifestation of the corruption caused by decaying animal matter. Advances in knowledge in one area made reforms in the other seem even more imperative.

Scientific work in the laboratory was undertaken in the spirit of iatrochemistry, chemistry in the service of medicine. The experimenters were primarily concerned with determining the quality of air in potentially dangerous places. In 1775 Felice Fontana toured the capitals of Europe with his new invention, the eudiometer, an instrument to measure the quality of the air. The

French chemist Antoine Cadet de Vaux joined him in Paris, where the pair analyzed the air in the domestic latrines and at the Cemetery of the Holy Innocents. Lenoir, the Lieutenant General of Police, forbade the publication of Cadet de Vaux's findings about the cemetery for fear of alarming the public. Likewise, Lavoisier, vacuum flasks in hand, would sometimes slip into a crowded theater loge near the end of a performance or into a hospital ward early in the morning just as the doors were first opened. In both cases, his purpose was to collect samples of befouled air.

Throughout the 1770s, the reform movement gathered momentum, not only by an accumulation of events but also through their increasing importance. The following chronology must be considered along with the work of the scientists just discussed to appreciate the full extent of the circumstances that led to the closing of the Cemetery of the Holy Innocents and the beginning of the end of the old order in burials.

*1771*

Dr. Olivier published his *Sépultures des anciens* . . . (Sepulchers of the Ancients, Demonstrating that They Were outside of the City . . . and Revealing the Effects of Putrefaction on the Air and on Ourselves).

*1773*

One hundred forty, of whom twenty-seven died, became ill from exposure to a grave reopened for a funeral in Saulieu (Burgundy). This tragedy furnished Dr. Maret, Perpetual Secretary of the Academy of Dijon, the most compelling argument for his *Mémoire sur l'usage où l'on est d'enterrer les morts* . . . (Memoir on the Practice of Burying the Dead inside Churches and within the City).

*1774*

The anonymous *Mémoires sur les sépultures hors des villes* . . . (Memoirs on Sepulchers outside the City, or Collection of Documents Concerning the Cemeteries of the City of Versailles) was issued. This book publicized the recent deaths in Saulieu and also in Nantes as well as recent proclamations against burials within the city by the Empress of Russia and by the towns of Dole and Laon. Its aim was to persuade the king to transfer the cemetery of the parish of Saint-Louis outside Versailles, as he had done for another parish in 1769.

On September 3 the Parlement of Toulouse issued an Arrêt on burials similar to that of the Parlement of Paris of May 21, 1765.

*1775*

On March 23 the prestigious Archbishop of Toulouse, Loménie de Brienne, issued an even stricter ordinance forbidding all burials inside any church building and ordering the removal of all cemeteries within his jurisdiction, even those of mere villages, from within the community of the living.

The Académie des Belles-Lettres, Sciences et Arts of Châlons-sur-Marne applauded this ordinance and published Dr. Navier's prize-winning *Réflexions sur les dangers des exhumations précip-itées . . .* (Reflexions on the Dangers of Premature Exhumations and the Abuse of Burials inside Churches).

July 29 marked the reform movement's most significant accom-plishment to date when Loménie de Brienne successfully addressed the General Assembly of the Clergy of France in the name of the provinces of Toulouse, Tours, and Aix to request a general ruling on burials. As a result of the clergy's decision for concerted action, there were several meetings with the Garde des Sceaux.

*1776*

On March 10 these consultations resulted in the Royal Declaration on Burials. Closely patterned after the Archbishop of Toulouse's ordinance of the previous year, the Royal Declaration was to become the most authoritative pronouncement on burials until Napoleon's Imperial Decree of 23 Prairial, year XII (June 12, 1804). According to the Royal Declaration, all cemeteries deemed insufficient in size were to be enlarged and those located within the community, "which could be harmful to the salubrity of the air will, to the extent which circumstances permit, be removed outside of the community by virtue of ordinances by the arch-bishops and bishops." With the Royal Declaration began the slow process, opposed by the parishes for ideological or economic reasons, of changing the relationship between the dead and the living and between the cemetery and the city throughout France. (Three decades later, the Napoleonic decree was necessary to promote this transformation further.) Paris was made exempt from the Royal Declaration pending reports by the clergy that would enable the king to formulate a special regulation to suit the unique case of so large a city. This promised decree was never given, thereby enabling the continuation of the status quo for several more years.

The Abbé Antoine Lacroix of the Académie de Lyon published his *Réflexions sur les sépultures*, which urged adherence to the Royal Declaration of March 10. On December 7, the Collège de Médecine of Lyon proposed three sites for cemeteries whose merits were publicly discussed in pamphlets by Petetin (1776), Dr. Rast de Maupas (1777), and Willermoz (1777).

*1777*

Robinet's *Dictionnaire universel des sciences* published a scathing indictment of the multiple sources of pollution in the city.

On September 2, Dr. Félix Vicq d'Azyr, President of the progressive Société Royale de Médecine in Paris, read a paper, "On the Dangers of Burials in Cities and inside Churches."

Dr. Vicq d'Azyr, prompted by D'Alembert, published a translation of Scipion Piattoli's *Saggio intorno al luogo del seppellire* (Modena, 1774). The French text, *Essai sur les lieux et les dangers des sépultures* (Essays on the Places and Dangers of Burial), was prefaced by a lengthy preliminary discourse which summarized the arguments of Vicq d'Azyr's predecessors and which was accompanied by an anthology of the principal official decrees.

The Société Royale de Médecine sponsored a prize competition on the role of the air in the transmission of contagious diseases. Dr. Jean-Jacques Menuret de Chambaud's winning essay opened with a condemnation of all sources of a nefarious atmosphere, including the cemetery.

*1779*

Dr. John Ingen-Housz published his *Experiments upon Vegetables, Discovering their Great Power of Purifying the Common Air in the Sun-shine, and of Injuring it in the Shade and at Night, to which is joined, a New Method of Examining the Accurate Degree of Salubrity of the Atmosphere*. This physician was not exaggerating when he wrote: "The common air, that element in which we live, that invisible fluid which surrounds the whole earth, has never been so much the object of contemplation as it has in our days: it never engaged so much the attention of the learned as it has of late years."

The *Fragment d'une correspondance flamande et rochelloise* . . . (Fragment of a Correspondence between Flanders and La Rochelle on the Subject of Removing the Cemeteries from the City) reported that the Archbishop of Tours had established three new cemeteries outside the city.

*1780*

From February into June: At the Cemetery of the Holy Innocents, a mephitic gas from a communal grave in which sixteen hundred corpses had recently been buried filled the cellars along the Rue de la Lingerie. Efforts to contain the gas failed; several people exposed to its effects fell seriously ill. Instructed to remedy the situation, Cadet de Vaux successfully applied a technique utilized earlier in 1778 to obviate the dangers of asphyxiation or of contracting mortal illnesses in the periodic emptying of domestic latrines: quicklime as a disinfectant and fires as ventilators. In separate reports on the salubrity of the burial ground, both Cadet de Vaux and the Faculty of Medicine condemned the air in the Cemetery of the Holy Innocents as thoroughly unhealthy. The cemetery, it was concluded, had to be closed.

On September 4, in response to these reports and sustained by the events of the previous decade, the Parlement of Paris ordered the Cemetery of the Holy Innocents closed as of November 1, extended one month later to December 1.

On December 5, the Lieutenant General of Police, Lenoir, reported that the cemetery had been closed on December 1 and that all but two parishes had secured burial grounds elsewhere. No new cemeteries had been opened, though. The parishes that had used the Cemetery of the Holy Innocents merely transferred their dead to existing cemeteries in other parishes. Finally, Lenoir warned that it would still be necessary to take precautions at the former cemetery to prevent the land from becoming "a continuing source of infection" from the filth and wastes which "contributed significantly to the fetid exhalations" there.

*1785*

On November 5, complaints from the neighbors about the odors that still emanated from the former cemetery as well as from the crowded and noisy surrounding market streets prompted a royal Arrêt du Conseil d'Etat intended to solve both problems. The former Cemetery of the Holy Innocents was to be transformed into a public herb and vegetable market.

*1786–1788*

The Church of the Innocents and the *charniers* around the cemetery (fig. 17) were demolished. Bones from the *charniers* and from the upper layers of the soil were removed to the underground quarries south of Paris henceforth designated as the Catacombs.

**The Fountain of the Holy Innocents**

At the close of the Abbé Porée's *Observations sur les sépultures dans les églises* . . . (Observations on Burials . . . ), 1745, an imaginary interlocutor speculated that the practice of burying inside churches and within the city would continue "until a general conflagration, reducing the earth to a flaming pyre, gives rise to a new heaven and a new earth." At the outset of the reform movement, Porée could not anticipate the degree to which changing sensibilities toward death would affect customary practices over the succeeding decades. The Abbé, nevertheless, permitted himself a dream of a radiant city, which he described as a terrestrial counterpart to the new Jerusalem of the Book of Revelation (21: 1–21). Porée had the prescience to link the future of his cause to the nascent interest in the *embellissement* of the entire city: "The attention today to the embellishment of our cities can include among its aims the cleanliness of our urban centers and the health of its residents."

By the mid 1780s, the groundwork for this city was far advanced. In 1780, the Académie Royale des Sciences issued its report on the hygiene of prisons; on April 20, 1783, a Royal Declaration set building heights and street widths to facilitate the passage of goods and people, to prevent serious fires, and to assure "the salubrity of the air." The publication in 1785 of the architect

17
Sobre, view of the
demolition of the
church and *charniers*
at the former
Cemetery of the
Holy Innocents,
Paris, 1787. The
Fountain of the Holy
Innocents (1550) by
Goujon and Lescot is
shown to the right.

Bernard Poyet's project for a new hospital on the Ile des Cygnes just outside the city to replace the old Hôtel-Dieu at the center of Paris prompted three successive studies by the Académie Royale des Sciences as well as several other alternative projects. Between Dr. Menuret de Chambaud's *Essais sur l'histoire médico- topographique de Paris . . .* (Essays on the Medico-Topography of Paris) and Dr. Mathieu Géraud's *Essai sur la suppression des fosses d'aisance . . .* (Essay on the Suppression of Cesspools and all Types of Dumping Grounds), both published in 1786, virtually no aspect of urban hygiene escaped the vigilant reforming eye. A new Royal Edict given in September 1786 finally prompted the demolition of the homes on the bridges over the Seine. As these impediments to the free movement of the air through the center of Paris came down, Jacques-Antoine Dulaure declaimed against the tax wall being erected around the city by the Fermiers Généraux as an impediment from without. In 1787 the Académie Royale des Sciences prepared a special report on the slaughterhouses of Paris. Dr. Jacques Dehorne, a member of this august body, reiterated many of the reform movement's arguments in his brochure, *Mémoire sur quelques objets qui intéressent plus particulièrement la salubrité de la ville de Paris* (1788). The transformation, then, of the former Cemetery of the Holy Innocents into a market might be taken as an appropriate symbol as well as one further step in the realization of "a new heaven and a new earth."

The contrast between the somber cemetery and the open marketplace was much appreciated by contemporary observers. As early as 1781 Cadet de Vaux had anticipated: "all the neighbors hurry here: this is no longer the rendezvous of death, but rather of young girls. The gaiety of youth distracts us from our lugubrious thoughts. . . . " The market established at this site was more than a place for the sale of produce, for the market reinstituted in an acceptable manner a traditional space of sociability. Instead of the merchants and clients, the scribes and clothiers trampling over tombstones and conducting business while joking about the open graves and the piles of bones, there was now the farmers' market in early morning followed by a flea market for old clothes set up under red parasols. All around this square were markets for fish, fruits, meats, and so forth. Whereas once the Cemetery of the Holy Innocents had housed the most vivid spectacle of death, now it was celebrated as the heart of a cornucopia of life.

The architecture of the site was an equal partner in establishing a refreshing ambiance. The tutelary image of Pilon's macabre statue of Death was replaced by a freestanding, shooting fountain whose tumbling sheets of water still enliven the square today. Once located at the corner of the Rue Saint-Denis and the Rue aux Fers (fig. 17), this fountain was originally a façade with three bays which wrapped around the corner. Voltaire was speaking for an entire epoch when he praised the beauty of the fountain but criticized its inauspicious location. Celebrated by histories and guidebooks of Paris through the century, it was the work of architect Pierre Lescot and the sculptor Jean Goujon, the famous team who had rebuilt the Louvre. Both the Louvre and the fountain were considered masterpieces that signaled the rebirth of fine architecture in France under the Renaissance. Like the Louvre, the Fountain of the Holy Innocents was appreciated for the harmonious integration of its architecture and its sculpture as well as for its fine proportions and graceful lines. With the addition of a fourth side and its relocation at the center of the market, the fountain became an icon for the radiant city, which was to unite hygiene, commodity, beauty, order, and monumentality. The formerly engaged Renaissance façade became a Neoclassical aedicula elevated high upon a podium and transformed into a shooting fountain: "the first," it was boasted, in Paris (figs. 18–19).

As shown by a recent study, directed by André Chastel, of the markets of Paris, the fountain was placed opposite the center of the impressive seventeenth-century façade along the Rue de la Ferronnerie. A passageway through the arcades of this one-hundred-twenty-meter-long edifice framed the view of the fountain. From the opposite direction, the building's façade established an effective backdrop. Bernard Poyet's version of the market as a primitive Greek agora with a stoa to each side supported by baseless Doric columns was in keeping with the utilitarian nature of the project as well as with the modest dimensions of the site. A contemporary observer noted with approval that the two long galleries delimited the poorly contained space around the fountain, which otherwise would have lessened the visual impact of this new monument.

## A New Order in Burials

The Abbé Porée could not have foreseen that a general conflagration would occur in the form of the revolution. Customary burial practices were seriously disrupted as churches were closed and many parish cemeteries sold. The outlying parish cemeteries now became overcrowded as they absorbed the dead from the inner parishes. At the same time, though, the municipal government laid the groundwork for establishing municipal cemeteries at the periphery of the city. This work was consolidated and nearly completed under Napoleon, whose rule combined the dual virtues of an effective administration with a desire to make Paris into a modern city. Perhaps the Napoleonic regime accomplished more for the physical reconstruction of Paris than any comparable period over the preceding century. The program, though, for fashioning a new earth and its ideological acceptance through a new conception of heaven had been prepared over the preceding sixty years. In all stages of this development, the cemetery had figured

18
Bernard Poyet,
Market and Fountain
of the Holy
Innocents, Paris, c.
1790.

19
Maréchal, view of
the Market and
Fountain of the Holy
Innocents, Paris.

prominently, both by preceding other institutions as a subject for inquiry and by appearing as the most ominous of urban dangers.

While the hygienic arguments against existing burial practices were generally uniform from the publication of Porée's *Letters* in 1743 until the opening of the Cemetery of Père Lachaise in 1804, the notion of what a cemetery should be varied. The image of the cemetery changed distinctly over the course of this period as it passed from the traditional charnel house to what was called an Elysium or Field of Rest. The history of these transformations involves the interplay between architectural and landscape design, social and cultural intentions, religious convictions, and commemorative gestures. Like the old burial grounds that they were to replace, the new cemeteries presented in microcosm the totality of an individual's and a society's interests and concerns. The changes in the image of the cemetery were related not only to the cemetery proper but also to the bond between the living and their places of burial. The new cemeteries were to be located outside of the city, but they were not to be shunned. Unlike cemeteries today, they still played an important role in spiritual and cultural life, a function that intensified over the course of the eighteenth and nineteenth centuries.

# 2
## Public and Permanent Buildings (1765–1785)

The new cemetery that the Parlement of Paris envisaged in its Arrêt of May 21, 1765, was a most perfunctory place of burial. The customary places of distinction, the *charniers* and the chapels, were banished in favor of designating only a narrow zone of uncovered land along the periphery for separate graves. The price of these special plots, nearly ten times the price of the most costly sepulchers inside a church under the old system, would have made them prohibitively expensive. Elements of the clergy complained that the Parlement was transforming the cemetery into a dumping ground. Neither the Académie Royale d'Architecture, which almost immediately sponsored competitions to design new cemeteries, nor the entrepreneurs who hoped to win the commission to construct the *extra muros* burial grounds followed the Parlement's example. For both groups, the cemetery was not to be a merely utilitarian structure but rather had to become high architecture. As one enthusiastic proponent of this concept wrote: "Since it is a question of public and permanent buildings, these new cemeteries can be made into veritable monuments of a funerary genre worthy of decorating the capital." In that way the cemetery would be a building type that contributed to the *embellissement* of the city.

The cemetery was a hybrid form which was neither purely architecture nor purely landscape. In searching for design strategies to inform their works, both the Academy and the entrepreneurs turned mainly to Italy, where they found inspiration not only in the famous thirteenth-century Campo Santo of Pisa but also in the reconstruction of ancient Roman baths and gardens as well as terraced gardens of the late sixteenth century. Since each group, though, had its own understanding of what a cemetery should be, the projects diverged to form two contrasting traditions.

## The Academic Tradition

The Academy's vision of the cemetery was established by the terms of the *prix d'émulation* that it sponsored in July 1765, only two months after the Parlement of Paris had ordered all the parish cemeteries closed by the end of the year. (The *prix d'émulation* was a monthly competition introduced in 1763 by Jacques-François Blondel, the new chief professor of the Academy's school, as a regular part of the student's training.) The subject for this particular competition was a cenotaph to Henry IV, one of the most beloved and revered kings of France. This was to be no ordinary place of burial, for "the empty tomb of this prince would be surrounded by vast peripheral galleries for the tombs of the famous men who had made France illustrious." The central monument, then, was consecrated to the symbol of *le bon roi*, the wise and kind ruler, and the *charniers* were given over not to the wealthy but rather to the meritorious dead. Presumably, the intervening space was to serve as public burial grounds.

This type of civic program would inform all of the Academy's subsequent competitions, which it sponsored at each critical moment when it seemed that the government would address the problem of the Parisian burial grounds: in 1766 after the Royal Declaration on Burials of March 10; in 1778 when reformers were placing their hopes in the success of Vicq d'Azyr's *Essai sur les lieux et les dangers des sépultures* to prompt the closing of the Cemetery of the Holy Innocents; in 1785 when the Garde des Sceaux and the Premier Président of the Parlement of Paris were collaborating on a new Arrêt along with a new Royal Declaration on Burials specifically for Paris; and in 1799 after the opening of the makeshift cemetery under Montmartre and at a time when the Department of the Seine was intensely preoccupied with providing Paris with new burial grounds.

With the Academy's program for the public burial ground as the locus of honor and fame, the Parisian cemetery emerged as an heir to the humanist conception of death and commemoration. The Renaissance humanists offered an alternative understanding to the Christian eschatological idea of death as a humiliation from which the good would be saved on the Day of Final Judgment. Now death offered the possibility of immortality through the high esteem of future generations. Since the Renaissance, though, as Hugh Honour has explained, "the honors of civic statuary had been reserved almost exclusively for dynastic rulers." Now in the eighteenth century this practice was to be expanded to include people of all professions and classes. The cemetery was seen as an ideal place to accord these honors through lasting memorials.

At the turn of the eighteenth century, the social theorists Pierre le Pesant de Boisguillebert and Sébastien le Prestre de Vauban had helped to foster these values by arguing that the monarch derived his power and dignity not through Divine Right but from the welfare of his people. Likewise, the wealth of any nation came from its productivity and not from its accumulation of gold. The idea of the worth of ordinary citizens gained further ground through the succeeding decades to the point where at mid-century it vied with the Christian vision in the conception of the new cemeteries.

The Abbé Porée, for example, author of the first cemetery project under the reform movement, combined both orientations. On the one hand, Porée called for a cemetery whose architecture, plantings, sculpture, and graves would offer evidence of the "inevitable shipwreck which menaces us" all. The architecture would have to reflect the "humiliation" of death and to convey a sense of the "annihilation" which awaits us. Conflating the traditional distinction between the three types of architecture (civil, military, and naval) with the different genres of scenes in theater and landscape painting (tragic, comic, and pastoral), Porée called for the invention of a fourth type of architecture, *une architecture fenèbre*, a funerary architecture that would present its own manner of "tragic scene." At the same time Porée insisted that the cemetery honor all those who had exhibited some distinguishing virtue. All classes and all conditions were included in this vision: the good father, the just magistrate, the brave soldier, the exemplary citizen, the zealous priest, and so forth. Finally, these epitaphs and memorials were not only intended as expressions of homage to the dead; they were also conceived as vital elements in the character formation of the living. They were to be "a source of emulation for posterity" to inspire visitors to the cemetery to equal or excel the deeds or accomplishments of their predecessors. The cemetery, then, was to become a school of virtue.

*Balancing Christian and Humanist Ideals*

The coexistence of these two traditions, the Christian portrayal of death and the humanist celebration of worthy accomplishments, is evident in Louis-Jean Desprez's design for a cemetery for one of Paris's largest parishes, which won a *prix d'émulation* in 1766 (figs. 20–23). While placed under the aegis of traditional Christian symbolism, Desprez's cemetery followed the model of the earlier academic project by consecrating the central chapel for royal sepulchers and the circumferential arcade for the tombs and statues of great men. To satisfy both intentions, Desprez drew from several sources of images and design strategies, which, in their newly synthesized form, interwove architecture, landscape, and symbolic statuary into a convincing statement about death, commemoration, and salvation.

The underlying basis of Desprez's design appears to have been the ancient Roman walled garden, the Horti Bassiani Antonini, as depicted in the late sixteenth-century reconstruction by the architect Jacques Androuet Du Cerceau (fig. 24). This garden provided Desprez with his overall design strategy: the quadripartite field surrounded by a gallery with pavilions in the middle and at the corners. The four quadrangles in both examples are separated by broad paths and surrounded by a row of trees. To the exterior, the wall is rusticated and provided with arched openings; to the interior, the gallery's roof is carried by freestanding columns. The principal additional feature found in Desprez's design is the central chapel, whose importance had been established by the program for the preceding *prix d'émulation* of 1765.

With the Roman prototype providing the framework for his design, Desprez then proceeded to accommodate it to a Christian vision of death. Presiding over the cemetery is a statue of Death that rises above the entire complex. This image is clearly analogous to the emblem for Death (fig. 25) in the Hertel edition of Ripa's popular *Iconologia*, for nearly two centuries a standard handbook for artists and writers. In the *Iconologia*, the skeletal figure of

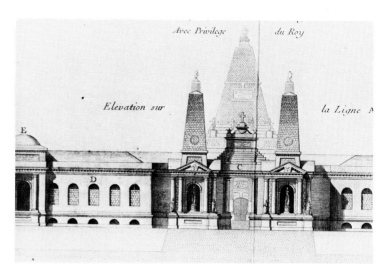

20
Louis-Jean Desprez,
parish cemetery,
Paris, *Prix
d'émulation*, 1766.
Detail of the
entrance.

21
Desprez, parish
cemetery, Paris, *Prix
d'émulation*. Plan
with interior
elevation.

*Public and Permanent Buildings*

22
Desprez, parish
cemetery, Paris, *Prix
d'émulation*. Detail
of central chapel.

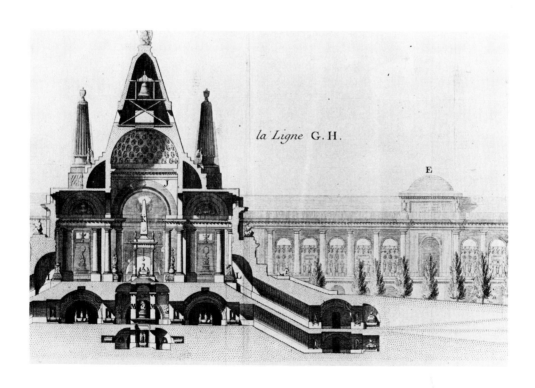

*Christian and Humanistic Ideals*

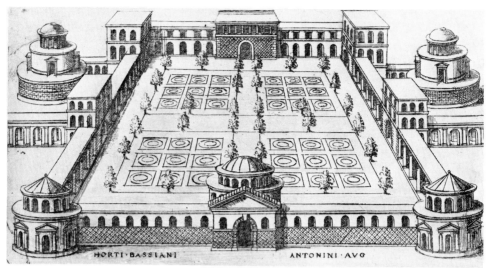

24
Horti Bassiani
Antonini. From
Androuet Du
Cerceau, *Livre des
édifices antiques
romains* 1584.

25
"The World." From
the Hertel edition
(1758–1780) of
Ripa, *Iconologia*.

Death stands in the middle of a labyrinth which presents a visual allegory of the stages of human life.

Desprez, though, eschewed a direct representation of Death the reaper in the form of a skeleton in favor of an alternative Baroque characterization of Death as Chronos or Father Time. This latter figure was often depicted as not quite alive but not fully withered into a skeleton (fig. 26). In Desprez's cemetery such a figure straddles a globe on top of the central chapel. The message here, as in the illustration from the Dance of Death, is a reminder of fleeting time and of human mortality. The combination of this harbinger of death with the crosses over the main portal and on top of four obelisks inside the cemetery constitutes a symbolic equivalent to the pictorial narrative shown on the *charnier* in the German engraving. The story begins with the Fall, depicted in the lower panel, whose consequences are shown through the pile of skulls in the *charnier*, but whose final resolution is portrayed in the upper panel, where Christ reigns in the heavens.

To characterize his design further, Desprez orchestrated the movement through the cemetery as a sequence of descents into the earth. The wide paths in the Roman prototype have become causeways with a broad flight of steps leading down to the level of the tree-lined promenade. Each quadrant of land destined for burying the populace sinks further down to the central point where the obelisks rise. In adopting this strategy, Desprez was following the advice of his teacher, Jacques-François Blondel, who had advocated such a use of the powerful effects of kinesthetics to convey an intimation of the "terrible but inescapable realm which we must inhabit when we die." The living were to be physically shocked into a realization of their inevitable end.

To complement the descent into the earth, Blondel had also recommended fashioning an architectural genre similar to what Porée had imagined as an *architecture funèbre*. In that way the cemetery would reveal its identity to the visitor and would inspire strong emotions to teach the Christian moral of death. For the *charnier* Blondel advocated the use of flattened arches carried by piers finished with a heavy rustication. Just as Porée had chosen the Tuscan order because it was the simplest and most humble, so too were the low arches the least noble form of arch construction. Even more important, the low arches, like the primitive and rough-hewn bosses on the piers, were to suggest a sense of compression and of claustrophobia. The bosses themselves were to be rendered with vermiculation, a pattern carved into the surface of the stone that has the appearance of worms or of a body eaten by worms. Here was a type of ornamentation "analogous to the destruction of matter." As was traditional, the bones exhumed from the cemetery were to be thrown pell-mell into the ossuary under a somber slate roof. Blondel's ideal cemetery had been the

26
Conrad Meyern,
"Triumph of Death,"
1650. From *Die
menschliche
Sterblichkeit unter
dem Titel Todten-
Tanz*, 1759.

public cemetery of Orléans by the cathedral of Sainte-Croix. Here Blondel admired the "deep graves . . . and pyramids of bones intermingled with cypress trees as well as the ossuaries whose high slate roofs presented the disorder so suitable to this genre of monument."

While Blondel praised Desprez's design as a successful interpretation of his prescriptions, it was not nearly as macabre in its decoration. The entire feeling of the *charnier*, with its freestanding Doric columns, its full arches, and its elegant proportions was totally different. The numerous vertical accents with their major and minor rhythms of ascending and descending elements, the addition of other chapels not found in the Roman prototype all contributed an architectural grandeur to the project that stressed the humanist ideal of glory and renown.

Each of these visual features, moreover, designated a particular function. Not only were the arcades intended as "galleries of great men," but the chapels that subdivided them into segments demarcated zones to honor different virtues. The four magnificent corner chapels were consecrated to great men not of the Catholic religion who died in France. In this cemetery, the space of emulation fully counterbalanced the Christian message of humility. Desprez accordingly dedicated his project to Voltaire, not only as a great writer but also as a champion of funerary honors awarded to merit. "I am certain," Voltaire had written in his *Lettres philosophiques* (1734) after visiting the tombs of outstanding British citizens in Westminster Abbey, "that the mere view of these glorious monuments has inspired more than one soul and has formed more than one great man."

In fashioning a new image for the cemetery to combine Christian and humanist ideals into a great work of architecture, Desprez turned toward the only cemetery of international renown, the famed Campo Santo of Pisa (fig. 27). Built in the latter part of the thirteenth century to house the sacred earth brought back by the crusaders from the mount of Calvary, the Campo Santo combined a majestic architecture in two tones of marble with floor-to-ceiling frescoes by some of the greatest masters of the late Middle Ages and the Renaissance. A guide to Pisa of 1751 was not exaggerating in boasting that "perhaps no other people in Italy or in all of Europe had ever conceived of making such a sumptuous and magnificent structure" for Christian burials. Desprez looked to the Campo Santo's restrained articulation of blind arches on the external walls and to the graceful arches of the interior to establish the overall ambiance for his galleries. True to the Palladian spirit of mid-century French architecture, Desprez fashioned a composite image that visually combined the trabeated system of freestanding columns and beams on the first plane with a secondary infill of walls with arched openings behind.

27
Campo Santo, Pisa,
begun 1278. From
Martini, *Theatrum
Basilicae Pisanae*,
1705 (second edition
1728).

*Public and Permanent Buildings*

The Campo Santo of Pisa was celebrated not only for its visual splendor but also for the renowned citizens of Pisa buried there. While the populace was buried in the cemetery proper, wealthy and distinguished Pisans were interred in the more than six hundred sepulchral vaults opened under the patterned marble floor or in the ancient Greek and Roman sarcophagi gathered under the galleries. Monuments along the walls and coats of arms set into the pavement provided a "who's who" of the Pisan social, ecclesiastical, and intellectual elite. By making overt reference to the Campo Santo, then, Desprez was able to associate its artistic, theological, and civic fame with the new Parisian cemetery.

Finally, in his cemetery design Desprez combined the aesthetic and civic purposes of a space of emulation with an attention to the hygienic and well-policed burial ground desired by reformers. The strategy of the arched openings along the outer façade adapted from the Roman garden would facilitate the circulation of the air. The orderly division of the parterre with four sectors to each quadrant would permit different funerals to take place at the same time. Each obelisk had four altars oriented to the corresponding wedge of space. These clear demarcations would also enable the grave diggers to use the land in a systematic fashion and thereby avoid reopening a grave too soon. In conclusion, Desprez's design was an amalgam of different intentions and models which yielded a grander vision of the cemetery than the French were used to in their local parish burial ground.

### The Ascendancy of the Humanist Vision

The next cemetery project sponsored by the Academy, the *prix d'émulation* awarded December 14, 1778, once again for a cenotaph to Henry IV, further developed the image of the cemetery as a magnificent example of architectural design. The winning project by Léon Dufourny (figs. 28–29) succeeded in realizing the types of architectural expression that Jacques-François Blondel termed *une grande architecture* and *une architecture sublime*. The purpose of a grand architecture was to achieve a noble effect through few divisions of a façade with carefully arranged flat surfaces, colonnades, and limited ornamentation in a relatively severe composition. A sublime architecture would be endowed with similar visual characteristics in order to move the viewer profoundly: "it elevates the spectator's mind, it seizes his imagination, and astonishes him." The untutored eye might be misled by the severity of the work, but the connoisseur would understand that the regularity was not monotonous but rather the source of the building's aesthetic force. A sublime architecture, explained Blondel, was appropriate "to the sepulchers of great men and in general to all monuments raised to remind our citizens of the high deeds, the remarkable exploits, and the valor of our princes, heroes, and great generals." Dufourny's cenotaph to Henry IV

28
Léon Dufourny,
cenotaph to Henry
IV, *Prix d'émulation*,
1778.

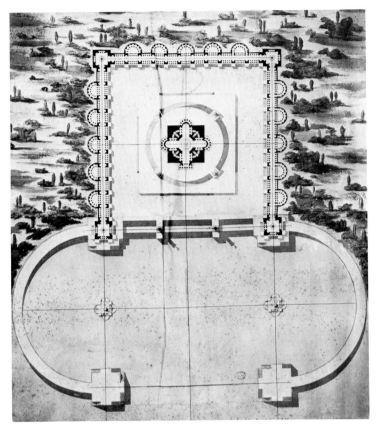

29
Dufourny, cenotaph
to Henry IV, *Prix
d'émulation*, 1778.
Plan.

was the first cemetery project in eighteenth-century France which responded to this challenge.

As an example of a sublime architecture, Dufourny's cemetery continued the tradition that Blondel had found in Claude Perrault's east façade of the Louvre, at J.-H. Mansart's and André Le Nôtre's orangery at Versailles, and in François Blondel's triumphal arch at the Porte Saint-Denis (fig. 30). All of these monuments were praised by Blondel for "the beauty of their mass and the unified relationships of their parts." This characterization is obviously vague when considered by itself, but it assumes a definite meaning when considered in relation to these buildings.

Dufourny provided a Neoclassical rendition of this type of architecture by linking all the galleries with a unified horizontal plane. Into this primary wall surface, the architect cut a subsidiary and segmental horizontal columnar screen. These open spaces are accentuated by a sequence of corresponding friezes that visually stop the vertical movement of the columns. Sculpted into the wall, these friezes define a type of entablature that the columns appear to carry and that is scaled to their size. All three elements—columns, frieze, and implied entablature—also read across the entire length of the gallery as secondary horizontal bands. The intervening wall surfaces are punctuated by isolated obelisks reminiscent of Blondel's treatment of the Porte Saint-Denis. Not only do these obelisks frame each opening, but each one appears successively to frame first the figure to the left and then the one to the right. The result is once again to make both the obelisks and the framed spaces appear as one continuous, uninterrupted horizontal sequence of elements. Finally, a continuous entablature across the top of the entire wall restates the unity of the surface as well as providing a foil to the more complex rhythms established below.

The feeling that this architecture inspires might be described with the words Jacques-François Blondel applied to François Blondel's Porte Saint-Denis: "... this is a monument of great beauty. The firmness expressed in its architecture and the proud lines of its profiles merit the highest praise. One might even suggest that perhaps there is no building in France which displays a more virile character. ..." In searching for an architectural character appropriate to the purpose of commemorating the memory of great men, Dufourny looked closely at Blondel's triumphal arch, erected in 1672 to honor the military victories of Louis XIV. François Blondel's basic design strategy was to establish a block with "male," "firm," and "virile" proportions, which he opened at the center and built up along the sides. J.-F. Blondel was very sensitive to the relationship between the bas-relief cut into the center of the block and the corresponding passageway, which he described as having been cut out of the primary mass. The arched portal was seen as inserted into this aperture.

Dufourny took Blondel's arch as the basis for modulating the façade of his gallery. The changes in the detailing were intended to strengthen the "male" character of the monument. Dufourny replaced the inset portal with the freestanding columns that became the preferred means both of support and of articulating an opening in the second half of the eighteenth century. The sphere crowning the obelisk was eliminated and the *amortissement* simplified into a single stereometric form, used also on the pyramid of the central chapel. The doors in the base of the obelisk, which Blondel had reluctantly fashioned to provide pedestrian passageways, were suppressed. The decoration on the obelisk was reduced to a simple statue to heighten the power of the naked surface. Finally, the horizontality of the entablature was reinforced by adding the deep brackets under the projecting cornice. Like Blondel, Dufourny used martial decorations for his ornamentation, including the rostra, which François Blondel had included in his initial project. Ironically, François Blondel had been criticized by his contemporaries for applying pyramidal obelisks, deemed appropriate only to a funerary monument, upon a triumphal arch. Thanks to this amalgamation of disparate types, Dufourny was able to associate commemoration with triumph in the new cemetery.

The grandeur and sublimity of Dufourny's design also came from the overall development of the plan. In place of a closed quadrangle, Durfourny designed the cemetery as an open form that is extended into the surrounding landscape. The gallery is still present, but it has been opened along one side, where it is preceded by a field in the shape of a vast hippodrome. The cenotaph and the galleries to great men occupy the quadrangle, whose entrance is flanked by two winged figures of Fame, one with a trumpet, the other with a wreath of immortality. The cemetery for the populace presumably has been transferred to the large forecourt.

Rather than sinking into the ground, the cemetery now rises with each successive element. The result is a portrait of society conceived according to merit. The masses lie, so to speak, at the base of the elevated field of honor. To the center and on the highest level is the cenotaph to *le bon roi* Henry IV.

Dufourny's design owes much to the work of Marie-Joseph Peyre. A student of Jean-Laurent Legeay and J.-F. Blondel, Peyre had won the Grand Prix in 1751. While in Italy, Peyre was strongly infuenced by the great baths of Caracalla and Diocletian (fig. 31). Peyre's publication of these plans along with his own projects for the academies and for a cathedral (fig. 32), which in turn derived from these Roman prototypes, set the stage for Dufourny's cemetery.

First Peyre and then Dufourny was fascinated with the isolation

31
Baths of Diocletian,
Rome, A.D. 298–306
From M.-J. Peyre,
*Oeuvres
d'architecture*, 1765.

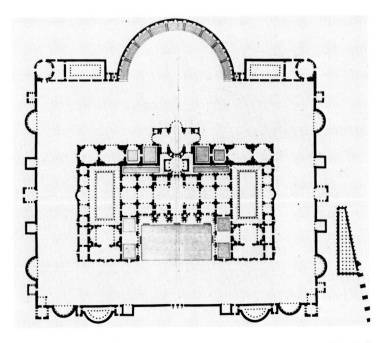

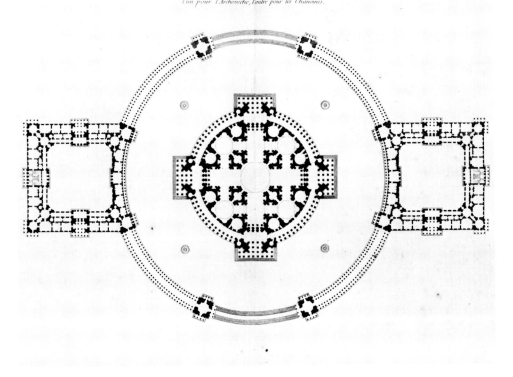

PLAN D'UNE ÉGLISE CATHÉDRALE
*ET DEUX PALAIS,*
*l'un pour l'Archevêché, l'autre pour les Chanoines.*

32
Marie-Joseph Peyre,
cathedral with two
palaces, 1753.

of a central monument within a vast *enceinte*, or precinct. As Peyre explained in describing his cathedral project: "The colonnade which forms the magnificent enclosure distances the church from any noise, thereby preparing, after the manner of several ancient temples, the respect which one had upon entering them." The arrangement of the peripheral elements in Dufourny's cemetery follows the strategy of Peyre's palace for a sovereign (fig. 33), where the open square of the palace is preceded by an amphitheater consisting of wings to either side of the main building. Dufourny's use of the elevated platforms as a base for the buildings as well as the vertical accents owes much to Peyre's design for a cathedral. As in Peyre's architecture, the triumphal columns and flaming cassolettes here further define a special zone around the central monument. This cemetery project, then, is a collage combining the main features of Peyre's two building complexes into a unified vision. Dufourny internalized the design philosophy of the master, which he then applied in his own manner.

In studying Peyre's architecture, Dufourny also returned to its source, the Baths of Diocletian. The chapels along the periphery of the cemetery, with their exedralike projections along the exterior and their columnar screens to the interior, issue directly from similar spaces at the bath. Both the caldarium and the central hall, with their cruciform plans, may have suggested the *parti* that Dufourny adapted for his own central chapel. Nevertheless, whatever the similarities in plan, the elevation of Dufourny's project unmistakably shows it to be a cemetery and not a bath.

The relationship of Dufourny's architecture to the landscape, though, surpasses any lessons that the student might have culled from Peyre's cathedral or from the Baths of Diocletian. To understand fully the sources of inspiration for this project, we must turn to the most neglected influence on eighteenth-century French Neoclassical architecture, the Italian Mannerist and Baroque architecture of the late sixteenth and early seventeenth centuries. Marie-Joseph Peyre, for example, was not only enamored of ancient Rome; he also was fascinated by the work of Giacomo della Porta, Domenico Fontana, Carlo Maderno, and Girolamo Rainaldi. Here Peyre found suitable forms for the shooting fountains that he designed to beautify and cleanse Paris. Peyre also admired the retaining walls in Mannerist gardens, which combined "perron, grotto, cascade, and terrace wall" in one. These works, too, provided the inspiration for Peyre's own project for a garden terrace with niches and fountains that rivaled the designs of the acknowledged Italian masters.

Dufourny, no less than Peyre, looked toward the Italian terraced garden. On an ostensibly flat site, the young French architect went to great trouble to terrace an ensemble of spaces. One notes, for example, that the stairs oblige an ascent at the beginning of the

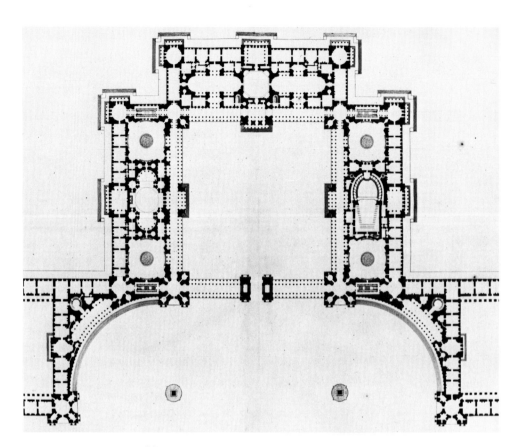

33
Peyre, palace for a
sovereign. From
*Oeuvres
d'architecture*, 1765.

curved ramp in order to provide a descent back to ground level at the middle before climbing upward once again. The purpose of this ramp, of course, is to define a volume where there is no natural terracing of the land. Whereas the Italian garden architects could cut into a hilly site, Dufourny had to create his own enclosing elevations. Dufourny's cemetery, in short, is more than a cloister or a quadrangle opened to one side with an appended hippodrome. It presents a coherent design strategy by which architecture and landscape have been integrated through terracing after the manner of late sixteenth- and early seventeenth-century Italian gardens. There even appear to be fountains located in the hippodrome, either shooting fountains with cascading water like Peyre's or basins with a central obelisk like Dufourny's own *prix d'émulation* of 1772 (fig. 34).

Dufourny's design for the Henry IV cenotaph seems to have been patterned upon the magnificent gardens of the Villa Aldobrandini at Frascati (figs. 35–36). Like Desprez before him, Dufourny was faced with the question of what basic image, what architectural *parti*, what cultural model should inform his design and control all decisions. Both the popularity of Italian garden architecture and a changing perception of the spiritual and cultural role of the cemetery permitted Dufourny to turn to the design strategy of the Villa Aldobrandini.

The garden and villa of Aldobrandini combine two organizational systems: a linear, axial system proceeding directly up through the site and a complementary lateral system composed of three main elements—a hippodromelike space formed by the horseshoe-shaped ramped stairways, or *cordonate*; the villa proper; and the rear terrace wall. Both systems intersect at various points where changes in land level are used to integrate them in a complex manner. While Dufourny adopted an analogous tripartite system of laterally developed spaces, he reduced the force of the linear, axial movement to establish a more balanced Neoclassical equation.

In adopting the lessons of Peyre's grandiose conception of a public complex, of its Roman prototype as found in the Baths of Diocletian, and of the magnificent terraced spaces at the Villa Aldobrandini, Dufourny developed a new image for the cemetery. In Dufourny's design the balance between a Christian understanding of death and a humanistic vision of fame has been tipped wholly in favor of the latter. Dufourny's design strategy, seconded by his Neoclassical style, yielded an architecture in harmony with an emerging secular ideal of glory and immortality.

**The Space of Emulation**

The eighteenth-century conception of the cemetery as a school of virtue and achievement fostered through memorials differed from the practice of erecting an isolated monument to a hero in

34
Léon Dufourny,
obelisk with
fountain, *Prix
d'émulation*, 1772.

35
Giacomo della Porta,
Villa Aldobrandini,
Frascati, 1598–1603.
View of the rear
terrace between the
villa and the
fountains.

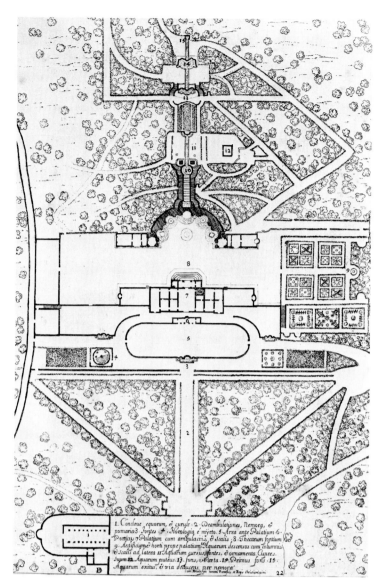

36
Giacomo della Porta,
Villa Aldobrandini,
Frascati, 1598–1603.

*The Space of Emulation*

a church or to a king in a public square. Not only were the honors to be broadly extended to all classes but they also were to be assigned a specific space consecrated to this purpose. While the cemetery might seem to be the most logical place for honoring the dead, it was neither the first nor the only one.

The notion of a space of emulation as found in the academic projects for cemeteries developed out of proposals in the 1740s, which began to envisage the entire city as an appropriate subject for instilling virtue. The competition of 1748 to design a square for the equestrian statue of Louis XV provided the occasion for two such projects. In one, the architect and scenographer Jean-Jérôme Servandoni proposed an amphitheater to be located just outside Paris to accommodate the customary public festivals that were usually held in public squares or along the banks of the Seine. The round form of the amphitheater would not only serve the utilitarian purpose of providing a secure and commodious facility for viewing the spectacle; its geometry could be exploited as well to give a civic lesson. With the statue of the king at the center, other statues of worthy Frenchmen were to be placed in distinctly marked spaces around the periphery. The message, as Pierre Patte explained, was that the monarch "would appear as the source from which everything issues and the center to which everything leads. The statues of great men, distributed methodically in this superb monument, have been placed there to announce the influence of Louis XV's power over their emulation and the conjoining of all talents to illustrate his reign." The crowd seated along the circumference was to identify with its heroes. Several places for statues were expressly left vacant as if to beckon the living to attain these honors. The Academy's image of the cemetery adopted this relationship between the center and the circumference, which was likewise intended to impart a message about the nature of the French state.

Such a program, though, was not to be limited to building types destined for the periphery of the city. In the same competition of 1748, Pierre Patte envisaged an analogous project for the Pont Neuf, the bridge over the Seine at the heart of Paris. This bridge had semicircular exedras which projected out over the water. Patte proposed to provide them with bronze statues of the great men of France. The figure of Louis XV would be placed at the center of the Place Dauphine facing the existing statue of Henry IV, with whom he would now be associated. Once again the king would be seen as the center of the glorious achievements that characterized his reign.

In 1765, the Abbé Laugier extended this idea by proposing that each public building in Paris be given its hall of "illustrious men." This notion had been inspired by the example of several provincial capitals that had busts of their great men in a special room of their city hall. Over the course of the century other authors took up the theme of a public space of commemoration to inspire greatness as it became an integral aspect of the image of the city.

This dual appreciation of a space of emulation for the city of the living and for the city of the dead could also be found in the work of Nicolas-Henri Jardin, *pensionnaire* at the French Academy in Rome by virtue of winning the Grand Prix of 1741. In 1747 Jardin designed a "sepulchral chapel" (fig. 37) and in 1748 a "triumphal bridge," which were both dedicated to this theme. While the two structures were to be located at the junction between the city and the country, the bridge was to welcome a returning hero and the cemetery to honor the worthy dead. The sepulchral chapel for the graves of the "great men who had rendered useful service to their country" was to be placed at the center of a vast square at the periphery of a city. From the country, a broad avenue lined with mausoleums, also accorded to the worthy dead, would lead to the chapel. The outer half of the circular *place* was defined by a semicircle of cypresses, the ancient Roman funerary tree, which encircled a row of magnificent sarcophagi, obelisks, and commemorative columns. In contrast to this pastoral scene, the inner half of the circle toward the city was given an urban aspect with covered promenade crowned with statues. Jardin's grand route lined with tombs of great men was an Enlightenment version of the magnificent Via Appia, with its mausoleums of Roman patricians, just as his chapel was modeled on the pyramidal tomb of Caius Cestius (c. 12 B.C.), then included within the Aurelian walls of Rome (fig. 53). By combining the city gateway and the public square with the triumphal way and the cemetery conceived as a space of emulation, Jardin provided one of the most suggestive interpretations of the popular Enlightenment theme of heralding a community's grandeur at its entrance. The expressive force of all of these architectural types combined to convey the value that the community accorded to noble deeds and great achievements.

## The Speculative Tradition

The architects working independently of the Academy pursued a vision of the cemetery more closely tied to the features of the existing burial grounds. The primary concern evidenced in these designs, other than an attention to hygiene, was a care for clearly maintaining the social distinctions customary in contemporary burials. The various teams of entrepreneurs and architects hoped that their cemeteries would be socially acceptable to the "better" classes. Even the reformers who mocked the pretentions of the rich and the powerful in matters of burial recognized that the success of their cause depended upon making the new cemeteries desirable according to existing mores. One of the principal reasons for the failure of the Parlement's Arrêt of May 21, 1765, was

37
Nicolas-Henri Jardin,
square with
sepulchral chapel,
Rome, 1747.

the harsh rejection of the traditional cemetery. In the name of hygiene, there was to be no gallery for privileged burials in the new cemeteries, nor were tombs or mausoleums allowed. The new cemetery would consist of an undifferentiated plot of land surrounded by mere walls. A narrow space adjacent to the peripheral wall was to be reserved for individual graves. Any memorial had to be attached to the wall itself. The remainder of the land was given over to communal graves. The only structures were to be a chapel and lodgings for the concierge. Toward the summer of 1782, the Parlement relented. A draft proposal for a new Arrêt included provisions for an arcade around the cemetery with private and institutional sepulchral vaults. The Procureur Général conceded that it would be necessary to preserve "the customary order which differentiates our burials."

## The Modest Cemetery

Since none of the official decrees precisely described what the new cemeteries should look like or how they were to be arranged, architects working independently of the Academy also had to determine their own solutions. The earliest designs were also the most modest. Only with the passage of time would there be a growing awareness of the possibilities afforded by the cemeteries to respond to the social and cultural values of the people whom they would serve. One of the first projects came from the architect Pierre Patte in the late 1760s. Patte modeled his design on the traditional cemetery surrounded by a *charnier*. The principal difference between this design (figs. 38–39) and the Cemetery of the Holy Innocents (figs. 2–5), other than the regularity of the plan, was a comprehensive concern for hygiene and a strong conviction, rare at this time, about a decent and honorable burial for everybody. Until the 1780s, Patte was nearly alone in condemning the mass grave not only as unhygienic but also as an affront to human dignity. In place of these communal graves for hundreds of corpses, Patte proposed shallow and smaller graves for a dozen bodies.

The sepulchral vaults under the *charnier* were also designed for safety. Rather than digging graves directly into the earth under the pavement of the *charnier* or even constructing separate sepulchral vaults here, Patte proposed a subterranean gallery much like an ancient Roman cryptoporticus. In this way a continuous passageway, well lit and well ventilated, could be substituted for any of the enclosed structures against which the reformers constantly inveighed. When filled, the coffers dug into the walls would be hermetically sealed. To secure the identity of a family's or a corporation's area, the space would be divided by locked grills which would not intercept the movement of the air. Coffins were to be lowered into the cryptoporticus through one of the numerous openings in the floor of the *charnier*.

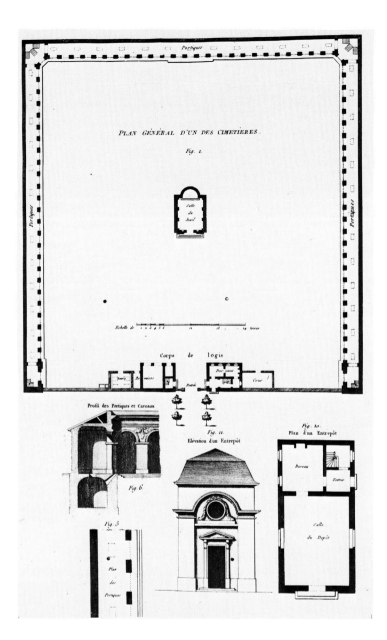

38
Pierre Patte,
cemetery, Paris,
1769. Plan with
section through the
*charnier* and plan
and elevation of a
mortuary depot.

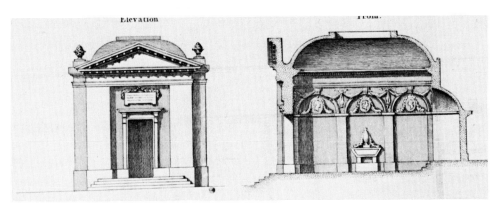

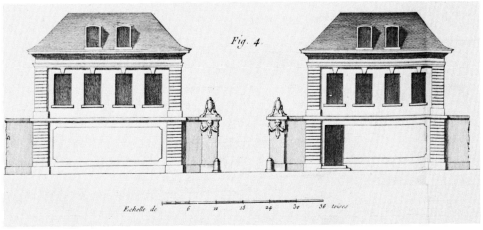

Fig. 4.

Echelle de     6     12     18     24     30     36 toises

39
Patte, cemetery,
Paris, 1769.
Elevation and section
through the central
chapel and cemetery
entrance.

The simple architecture and restrained decoration in Patte's design reflect the idea that a cemetery was a place to bury the dead with respect but with little else. In general, Patte looked toward the architecture of the Parisian Cemetery of the Holy Innocents rather than to that of the Pisan Campo Santo for the example of a suitable ambiance. In the hierarchy of building types, the cemetery remained at the low end of the scale. To Patte it did not even merit a Tuscan order but rather only a system of piers and arches. This manner of construction was traditionally associated with utilitarian structures not worthy of the more noble ornamentation of the architectural orders. This solution accorded well with the Christian view of the humility of death.

Even the entrance to Patte's cemetery used the image of a utilitarian structure in the design of the porter's house, located to the right, and of the stables, to the left. The simple decoration flanking the entrance, a skull and an urn, mirrored traditional models. The parish cemeteries of Saint-Sauveur and of Sainte-Marguerite, for example, each had a black doorway with paintings of white skulls and bones. Not only did Patte follow this model in its imagery, albeit in a more classicized fashion, but he also reserved his decoration to the limited zone of the entrance. The contrast with the splendor of Desprez's entire front elevation could not be more striking. In its visual characterization as well as its organization of space, Patte's cemetery remained true to the tradition of the parish burial ground.

If visual splendor were to enter the space of death, it would occur in the private memorials that traditionally filled the parish churches. These Patte welcomed with relish for the galleries of the new cemeteries. He and the other architects who followed him speculated that these works of art would entice visitors to the cemetery and would spur the development of sculpture through the masterpieces housed there.

The other model for a cemetery was the burial ground without a surrounding gallery. Many of the newer cemeteries, such as the cemetery opened in 1634 for the parish of Sainte-Marguerite (fig. 40), lacked the traditional *charnier*. This burial ground was bounded by the church on three of its sides and by a wall along the street. In 1763 the civil commissioners had cited the cemetery as exemplary. Well-aerated and well-policed, the land here had been divided into thirty-four equal squares measuring slightly more than five meters to a side to permit orderly burials in mass graves dug slightly more than four meters deep. A sufficient amount of space between the rows prevented the bodies in a neighboring grave from tumbling into a newly opened hole. The area around the cross and the residual space adjacent to the two distant walls was reserved for individual graves.

The cemetery proposed by the architect François-Victor Pérard

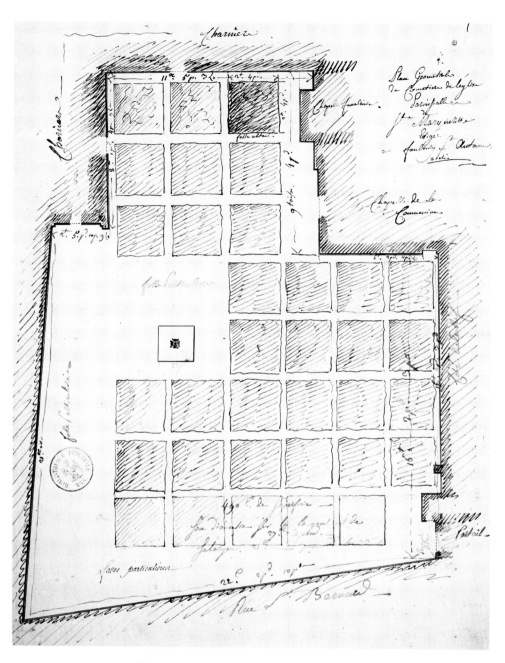

40
Cemetery Sainte-
Marguerite, Paris.
Plan of 1763.

de Montreuil and his business associates (fig. 41) adopted the general features of this second type of burial ground. The land is bounded by a high wall rather than a covered gallery. Private tombs line the periphery to either side of the alternating circular and rectangular forms. These are probably shelters, like chapels, to house family and corporate sepulchral vaults. The center of the cemetery has a modest chapel surrounded by evergreens. The remainder of the terrain is given over to large communal graves, which Pérard has shown as circles.

Pérard's cemetery retains all the principal components of the traditional *cimiterium*, that is, the combination of church and cemetery, but has turned them inside out. In the parish of Sainte-Marguerite, if one elected a sepulcher inside the building, one had the choice of the church itself, the funerary chapel, or a special room where children were taught catechism, which was also called a *charnier*. Pérard's plan presents analogs to these interior spaces in the form of freestanding, well-aerated pavilions within the walls of the cemetery. Pérard's concern with tradition was evidenced not only in his design but also in his provision that parishoners would be free to transfer the remains of their ancestors to the new cemeteries as well as to erect crosses, tombs, or other memorials there.

*A Mirror to Society*

The hierarchical order both in the relative degrees of pomp for the funeral and in the place and manner of burial were reflected most clearly in the two designs for cemeteries proposed by the architect Jean-Charles Delafosse. In 1776, after the Royal Declaration of March 10, and then in 1780, after the closing of the Cemetery of the Holy Innocents, a group of entrepreneurs with Delafosse as the architect presented their first design (figs. 42–43). This project was modified and made more rigorous in its graphic delineation of class distinctions (fig. 44) in 1782, when it appeared once again that the public authorities were about to open new *extra muros* burial grounds.

Like Desprez before him, Delafosse looked toward the late six-teenth- and early seventeenth-century hypothetical reconstructions of ancient Roman architecture for the basic strategy for his design. These he found in Jacob Lauro's engravings of the Baths of Titus, the Baths of Alexander Severus (fig. 45), and the Horti Lucullani (fig. 46). All three examples presented a regularly defined precinct with pavilions at the four corners and an exedra to the rear. The closest visual analogy can be found in the Baths of Alexander Severus, where the exedra is a closed, self-contained unit and where the central monument is isolated within its own set of walls. Under Delafosse's pen the peripheral galleries have been transformed into a *charnier* with a series of separate sepulchral

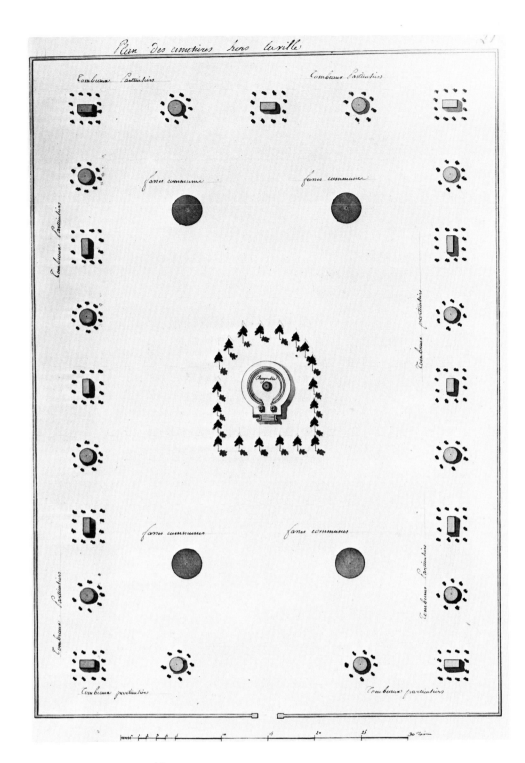

41
François-Victor
Pérard de Montreuil,
cemetery, Paris, c.
1775–1776.

*A Mirror to Society*

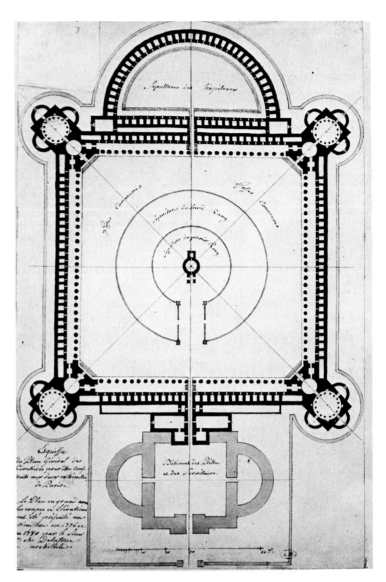

42
Jean-Charles
Delafosse, cemetery,
Paris, 1776.

43
Delafosse, cemetery,
Paris, 1776. Section
through the central
chapel.

*Public and Permanent Buildings*

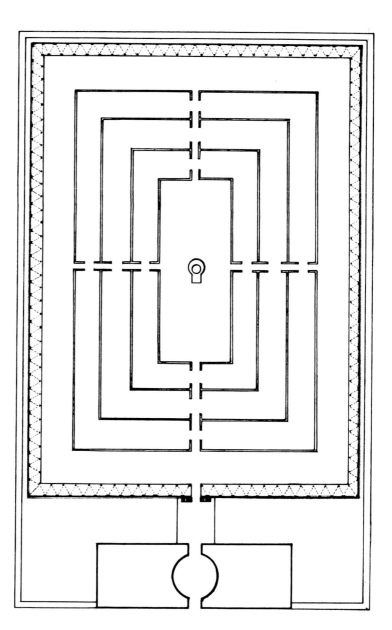

44
Delafosse, cemetery,
Paris, 1782. From
Gannal, *Les
Cimetières*.

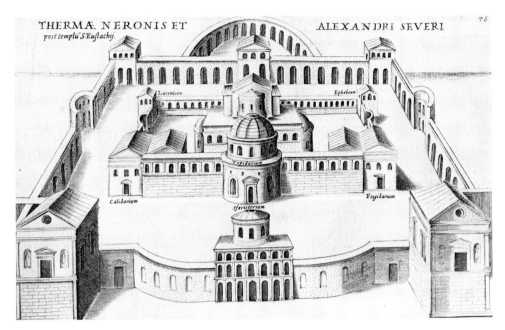

45
Baths of Alexander
Severus, Rome, A.D.
227. Reconstruction
from Lauro,
*Antiquae urbis
splendor,*
1612–1628.

46
Horti Luculliani,
Rome.
Reconstruction from
Lauro, *Antiquae
urbis splendor,*
1612–1628.

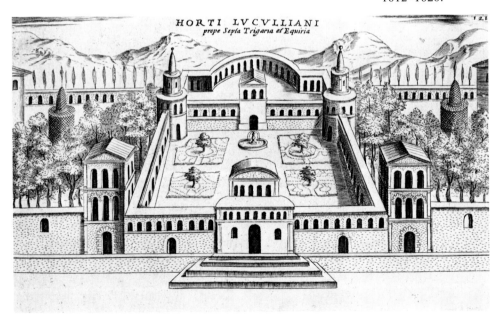

*Public and Permanent Buildings*

vaults. The corner pavilions are probably chapels much like the Chapelle d'Orgement and the Chapelle de Villeroy at the Cemetery of the Holy Innocents. The domed monument at the center has become the focal point for privileged burials within the cemetery proper. The two concentric rings separated by a low wall are labeled "sepulchers of the first and second orders," respectively. The remainder of the land was given over to the communal graves for the populace. To the rear of the cemetery the exedra was assigned to the dead from the hospitals. Since these were the poorest people, who were buried through charity and who had generally died of some disease, the separate zone for the hospitals constituted a hygienic and social isolation. The buildings in front of the hospital were to lodge the carriage drivers, the grave diggers, and the priests who ministered to the souls of the dead.

In this cemetery design Delafosse has substituted a geometric clarity for the vague topological distinctions found in existing cemeteries, whose visual confusion resulted from a disorderly allocation of space. In the old cemeteries certain places had been consecrated through tradition. As we have seen, in the Cemetery of the Holy Innocents (fig. 5), the dead crowded together in separate graves in the small unmarked corner by the *petit charnier*. The much-sought-after chapels were located at the opposite end of the cemetery within the band of land for the Hôtel-Dieu. In the remainder of the cemetery various corporations and families had burial privileges marked by some manner of monument. The result was like a "crazy" quilt where social distinctions followed no evident spatial pattern and where the grave diggers had a difficult time using the land efficiently.

The chapel at the center of Delafosse's cemetery was designed expressly for its function. The large, covered vestibule was intended to protect the arriving carriages in times of inclement weather and the crowning lantern doubled as a beacon to light the cemetery at night. The *lanterne des morts*, or the lantern for the dead, had been a traditional feature of the late medieval cemetery, serving both a pragmatic and symbolic purpose. It was believed that the tower named La Tour Nôtre Dame des Bois had served this purpose in the past at the Cemetery of the Holy Innocents. The interior of the chapel was also suitably characterized. Thick Ionic columns appeared to carry a low dome and a heavy entablature with an appropriately decorated frieze.

In his second project, Delafosse abandoned any pretense to architectural distinction in the design of a cemetery. The Roman prototypes were jettisoned in favor of a modest sequence of concentric spaces. The desire for clarity and order even led to the substitution of rectangular for circular zones. Now more rings were possible, as they all fitted together neatly within the outer gallery.

The hierarchical organization of space in Delafosse's second project responded even more closely to the existing order in burials. The central zone around the chapel was destined for ecclesiastics. Then came a ring for the more elaborate funerals, those with *grands ornements*, and another ring for the lesser distinctions, called *seconds ornements* and *troisièmes ornements*. The fourth ring was for the dead from the hospitals and all others buried by *demi-charité* or *charité*. The zone that immediately preceded the gallery was for individual graves and the gallery itself for privileged burials that could be commemorated with memorials. The sponsors of this project described their cemetery as displaying "a noble and imposing simplicity" and the chapel as being "as simple" as the cemetery itself.

Delafosse apparently could not refuse himself one architectural gesture: the volume removed from the buildings at the front to form an entry has been displaced back into the cemetery to become the central chapel. In this manner the circular space first experienced at the entrance as an exterior courtyard is encountered again at the point of destination in the interior space of the chapel. To protect and to characterize this precinct properly, the entire cemetery was to be surrounded by a dry moat as well as an avenue with four rows of poplar trees.

*An Archeological Fervor*

In 1778 the architect Jean-François de Neufforge published two designs for a cemetery as part of the numerous supplements to his *Recueil élémentaire d'architecture* (figs. 47–48). Neufforge's principal goal was to impart monumentality in a limited space to the parish cemetery. Each of his plans could be fitted into one of the four quadrants of Desprez's project (fig. 21). True to the spirit of the *Recueil*, which investigated the primary permutations of various architectural motifs or types, Neufforge took the circle and the square and explored the possibilities of each through an analogy between the form of the central chapel and its surrounding *enceinte*, or precinct.

The square design owes much either to the same ancient Roman sources that inspired Desprez and Delafosse (figs. 24, 31) or to the contemporary designs themselves (figs. 21, 42). The round variant also looked back to ancient Rome. The theme of four principal quadrants, semicircular in shape, with exterior porticoes establishing entry and with minor circles in the intervening spaces, could have been adapted from Du Cerceau's reconstruction of an ancient naumachia. The distinctive alternation of concave and convex forms could be found in Piranesi's interpretation of a circular covered walkway at the Campus Martius in ancient Rome or more particularly in the hall at the end of the Golden Square at the Emperor Hadrian's villa at Tivoli (fig. 49).

In this circular design, Neufforge has used his complex geometries to provide a variety of places for distinguished burial. One could imagine, for example, that the small circular *charniers*, which appear almost like chapels, would have been more special than the larger semicircular galleries. Likewise, the semicircular land areas near the entries could have readily lent themselves to individual graves, while the four rectangular quadrants in the center of the cemetery could have been used for mass graves.

Neufforge executed a series of designs for funerary chapels or mausoleums which exhibits a great variety in the combination of forms (figs. 50–52). In general the chapels are characterized by a simple Doric architecture, and most of them use the motif of the pyramid to show their purpose further. The entry to the cemetery (fig. 52), with its tall obelisk, is similar in spirit to Desprez's earlier design (fig. 20) and shares with Dufourny the evocation of the funerary triumphal arch adopted from François Blondel's Porte Saint-Denis (figs. 28, 30).

During this first period of cemetery design, French architects preferred the pyramid as the form most suitable for a funerary chapel or a grand mausoleum. In general, the designs were adaptations of the tomb of Caius Cestius or of the legendary tomb of Mausolus at Halicarnassus in Asia Minor, known only through literary descriptions such as that in Pliny the Elder *Natural History*. Engravings by Piranesi (1756) and Barbault (1761) popularized the Roman pyramid (fig. 53), while Giuseppe Galli da Bibiena's stage set, or *capriccio* (fig. 54; 1740) gave convincing form to the tomb of Mausolus, described as having "a high base, a temple-like structure, and a pyramid." While the chapel by Jardin (fig. 37) and the anonymous royal mausoleum (fig. 55) are derived from the Roman model, the chapel by Desprez (fig. 22) as well as the earlier chapel (figs. 56–57) by Jacques Rousseau (1755) and the mausoleum (fig. 58) by Pierre-Louis-Philippe de La Guêpière (1757) present a modified version of the Galli da Bibiena design. In effect, one can trace a sequence of gradual modification of the tomb of Mausolus from Galli da Bibiena to Desprez. First Rousseau transformed the open and round lateral bays into closed, rectilinear chapels while also eliminating the attic that separated the pyramid from the main structure. In addition, he substituted a more modest order, the Ionic, for the majestic Corinthian. The pyramid too was broadened in imitation of the tomb of Caius Cestius to make it correspond to this simpler character. While La Guêpière eliminated the side bays and flattened the top of the pyramid, he also returned the design to the Corinthian mode. Desprez followed La Guêpière's lead by leaving off the end bays and by truncating the top of the pyramid. On the other hand, he returned to the attenuated profile of the pyramid as found in the original model. Finally, Desprez abandoned the

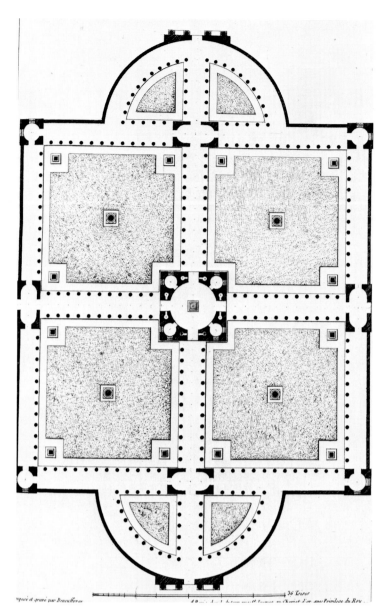

47
Jean-François de
Neufforge, cemetery,
1778.

*Public and Permanent Buildings*

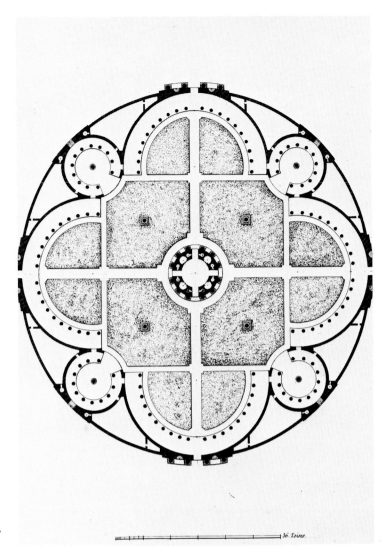

48
Neufforge, cemetery,
1778.

49
Golden Square
(detail), Hadrian's
Villa, Tivoli,
125–135 A.D.

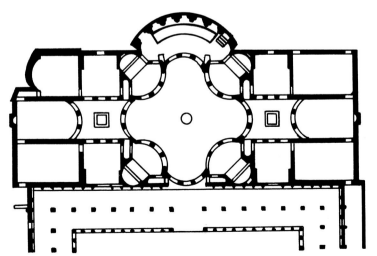

*An Archeological Fervor*

50
Jean-François de
Neufforge,
mausoleum or
funerary chapel,
1777.

51
Neufforge,
mausoleum, 1777.

52
Neufforge, cemetery
entrance, 1776.

*Public and Permanent Buildings*

53
Pyramid of Caius
Cestius, Rome, c. 12
B.C. From Barbault,
*Les plus beaux
monuments de Rome
ancienne*, 1761.

*An Archeological Fervor*

54
G. Galli da Bibiena,
*capriccio* from
*Architettura e
prospettive*, 1740.
Detail.

*Public and Permanent Buildings*

55
Anonymous, royal
mausoleum, c. 1780.

*An Archeological Fervor*

56
Jacques Rousseau,
sepulchral chapel,
third prize, Grand
Prix of 1755.

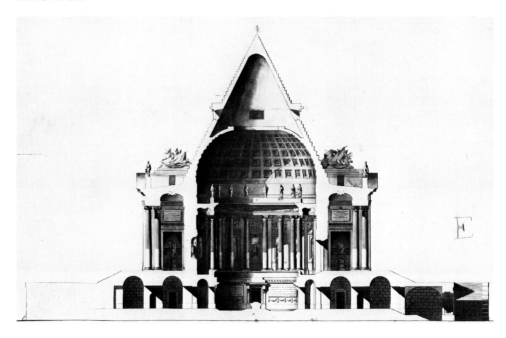

57
Rousseau, sepulchral
chapel, third prize,
Grand Prix of 1755.
Section.

*Public and Permanent Buildings*

58
Pierre-Louis-Philippe
de La Guêpière,
mausoleum, 1757.

*An Archeological Fervor*

Corinthian order in favor of the more severe Doric. Here Desprez was following the advice of his teacher, J.-F. Blondel, who had taught that a cemetery should have a central chapel designed as "a large pyramid of a rustic order."

Whether the pyramid was used as a crown or as the major volumetric piece, it was employed in these eighteenth-century designs as the exterior envelope of a chapel. These pyramids were hollow shells used to create a spaciousness inside the monument that one would not expect from the horizontal compartmentalization of the exterior. In all three interiors, the central room is crowned with a semicircular dome with an open oculus. With this arrangement, the architects were able to design small windows into the pyramids so that light from this source, hidden from the observer below, would mysteriously illuminate the space above the dome. In this way, daylight was transformed into a heavenly aura.

The space below the dome was also treated in a manner expressive of the building's purpose. Desprez, for example, used circular windows to light the baldachin dramatically, which he designed in the form of a catafalque and which was to be used for this purpose. Rousseau, on the other hand, opened the floor of the chapel to reveal the crypt below. A circular promenade on the upper level surrounded a ring of columns treated as a temple open to the sky. From this position, the visitor would look down through the columns into the crypt. From below, the dome would appear to hover over the circular temple, with "heavenly" light entering the darkness as if miraculously from on high.

## The New Catacombs

The closing of the Cemetery of the Holy Innocents in December 1780 did not solve the problem of overcrowding in the Parisian cemeteries. Those parish burial grounds deemed insufficient in 1763 were worse now, and those judged adequate were losing this status as they absorbed approximately two thousand annual burials fom the Cemetery of the Holy Innocents. Toward the summer of 1782, the Parlement of Paris was ready to issue a new version of the Arrêt of May 21, 1765, which would be accompanied by a supplement to the Royal Declaration of March 10, 1776, now directed specifically to Paris. Both of these documents reveal that the Parlement and the king had learned in the intervening years the importance of respecting traditional social distinctions in the cemetery. Thus, as mentioned earlier, the Parlement would now permit the traditional covered gallery with sepulchral vaults around the periphery of the cemetery; and the king would also allow individual graves in a strip of land adjacent to this gallery. The provisions of these draft proposals correspond closely to a cemetery project proposed by a group of entrepreneurs whose architect was a certain Capron. Had the new decree been issued, it seems likely that Capron's four cemeteries would have become the first set of new *extra muros* burial grounds to serve the city of Paris.

Whether Capron and his associates had more favor with the Parlement than their competitors has not yet been determined. Judged on the merits of the design, Capron's cemetery exhibited greater simplicity than projects such as Delafosse's, with its labyrinth of four-foot walls. In effect, Capron's design presented a circular variation of the Pisan Campo Santo: a simple and regular gallery with a chapel engaged at the head of the enclosure (figs. 59–61).

With only a modest obelisk in the center and with no dead corners to entrap the air, Capron's cemetery most satisfied the hygienic concerns of the times. Over the preceding decade, doctors and architects had been attempting to derive the form for a hospital that would most fully facilitate the circulation of the air. One solution, conceived in the early 1780s for hospitals and cemeteries, was the streamlined vessel that presented no angles to entrap the air. In 1780, for example, the architect Soufflot made drawings according to a description by Dr. Maret of the Academy of Dijon for an elliptical ward with no corners and with no projecting or recessed elements. The ellipsoidal shape of both the interior walls and the ceiling, as well as the smooth, uninterrupted surfaces were intended to permit the total renewal of the air. In a project probably designed for the Grand Prix of 1784 and attributed to Lahure, the architect made the wards of his lazaretto circular for the same purpose (fig. 62). Walls and roof were also made continuous by the use of a dome. Capron's cemetery, designed in the intervening years, was an analogous solution conceived according to the requirements of a different but related program.

Capron organized the space in his cemetery in a traditional manner. There were to be four concentric rings of communal graves in the center and a peripheral gallery with underground sepulchral vaults. The two rings shown in the plan adjacent to this arcade were to have lesser sepulchral vaults built deep enough under the surface so that individual graves could be dug above. Slight changes in land level would distinguish these privileged zones from the communal graves in the center.

In spite of the architectural modesty of the plan, its promoters spoke of their burial ground as "catacombs," thereby attempting to associate the project with the famed underground burial grounds of the early Christians in Rome and elsewhere in Italy. This new name referred primarily to the sepulchral vaults that would await the wealthy. Perhaps the entrepreneurs were attempting to capitalize on the recent publication of two highly favorable views of the catacombs of Naples drawn by Desprez for the Abbé de Saint-Non's luxurious edition of *Voyage pittoresque* . . . (A Picturesque

59
Capron, cemetery,
Paris, December 28,
1782. Detail of the
entrance.

60
Capron, cemetery,
Paris, December 28,
1782. View of the
chapel with section
through the *charnier*.

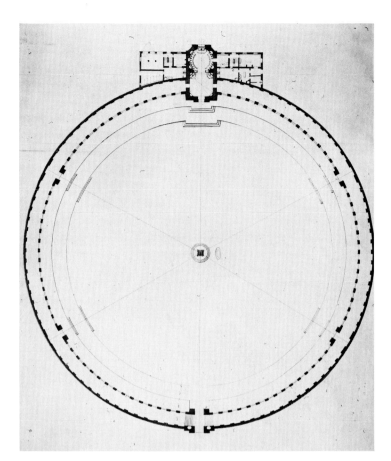

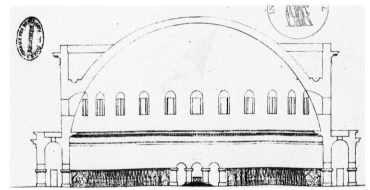

61
Capron, cemetery,
Paris, December 28,
1782. Plan.

62
Lahure (attributed
to), lazaretto. Design
for the Grand Prix of
1784 (?). Section
through a circular
ward.

*The New Catacombs*

Voyage or Description of the Kingdoms of Naples and Sicily, 1781). Desprez may have whetted the public's imagination with his dramatic depiction of Saint Januarius preaching to the first Christians, many of whom are shown attired very much like the elegant lords and ladies of Paris.

Capron dressed his cemetery in an austere architecture which conveyed a traditional Christian understanding of death. To determine a suitable characterization, Capron seems to have turned to the great pattern book of architectural modes published by Neufforge. Perhaps no other architect in the eighteenth century explored so thoroughly the possibilities of varied expression according to the Doric, Ionic, and Corinthian styles. In one such exercise, Neufforge designed three different niches for each of these architectural orders. The third type of niche had a memorial theme. Capron's portal was strongly reminiscent of Neufforge's rendition of the funerary Doric (fig. 63). Both designs featured broad piers, rustication with bosses, a low, rounded pediment, and a prominent keystone. In Capron's project, the outer wall as well as the chapel exhibited a corresponding rusticity. The image of the skull and bones crowned by a star along with the Latin inscription—*Nascitur ad Mortem. Moritur ad Vitam*—was a common emblem used to convey the seemingly paradoxical lesson that we are born to die and that we die to be reborn to eternal life (fig. 64).

One striking feature of all of these designs for cemeteries, from Patte to Capron, was the restrained presence or total absence of macabre imagery. In a sense, the mortuary chapel by Delafosse with its theatrical *memento mori* (fig. 1) would have been out of place in these burial grounds, even in those designed by Delafosse himself. At this time the dramatic Baroque spirit was tempered in favor of a more restrained characterization of death. The atmosphere in these new cemeteries was somber rather than horrific.

## The Naked Cemetery

The sobriety of these designs derived not only from their architecture. The walls which bounded the open land of the cemetery enclosed a terrain generally devoid of trees. These were naked cemeteries whose lack of vegetation said as much about Christian humility as did the rusticated architecture. The cypress walks advocated by Porée and Blondel and the peripheral ring of poplars in Delafosse's design were intended to introduce in a limited manner trees that, through reference to the burial practices of the ancients as well as their somber foliage, would characterize the cemetery.

In general, though, the cemetery was to be free of trees and bushes. This attitude came in part from adherence to longstanding tradition and in part from the official Post-Tridentine Church proscription against planting vines, trees, and grass in the cemetery.

63
Jean-François de
Neufforge, niches,
1757.

*The Naked Cemetery*

64
"And, whilst I living
am, to sinne so dye,/
That dying, I may
live eternally." From
Wither, *Emblemes*,
1635.

*Public and Permanent Buildings*

The third and most compelling reason in the minds of the designers was the hygienic argument. Trees and bushes, it was feared, would intercept the cleansing winds that were to sweep away the dangerous exhalations. The Parlement's Arrêt of May 21, 1765, expressly forbade plantings for this reason. So, too, did the Ordinance of March 23, 1775, by the Archbishop of Toulouse, the Royal Declaration of March 10, 1776, and a ruling in 1776 by the city of Troyes. Dr. Maret (1773), Dr. Navier (1775), and Dr. Vicq d'Azyr (1778) all argued vehemently against the presence of trees in the cemetery. Dr. Maret dismissed Priestley's claim that trees remove putrid emanations from the air as only conjecture. Even Vicq d'Azyr, while convinced that Priestley's findings were sound, nevertheless favored the mechanics of forceful movement over a more subtle chemistry. The physical renewal of the air seemed both simpler and more effective in restoring the "purity" of the air.

While the efficacy of Priestley's findings that living plants renewed the atmosphere by "imbibing the phlogistic matter" was contested by these prestigious French doctors through the 1770s, Dr. Ingen-Housz's study, published in 1779, provided further evidence in Priestley's favor that was readily welcomed in the succeeding years. In clarifying Priestley's work, Ingen-Housz demonstrated that living plants in the presence of sunlight "pour down continually . . . a shower" of purified air. In other words, through photosynthesis plants absorb carbon dioxide and produce oxygen, which they release into the atmosphere. For his contributions to bettering the environment, Ingen-Housz was celebrated as the Lavoisier of the vegetable kingdom.

The first cemetery design to apply these insights came from Jacques-Denis Antoine (fig. 65), architect of the celebrated mint, the Hôtel de la Monnaie. On the one hand, Antoine welcomed the planting of trees throughout the burial ground to foster the proper ambiance. His horticultural palette covered virtually the entire range of traditional funerary trees, such as "the Italian poplar, the sycamore, the plane tree, the yew, the cypress, the laurel, and others," all deemed "analogous to the character of the place." For Antoine these trees were doubly important because, he argued, they also restored the purity of the air. Trees, then, had their place in the cemetery for hygienic reasons as well as sentimental and religious ones.

The trees in Antoine's cemetery project, while greater in number and variety than in designs by his contemporaries, were still restricted to the borders of the galleries and to the pathways. In the division of space and in the use of vegetation, Antoine was following the formal mode of designing gardens that had been popular since the late seventeeth century. The figure of the circle in the square was common to the gardens of the great country

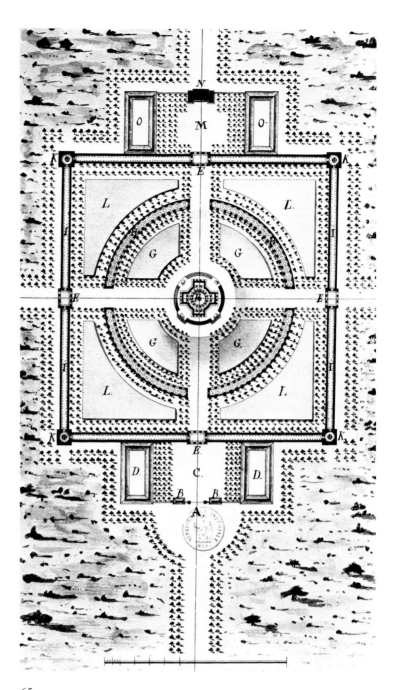

65
Jacques-Denis
Antoine, cemetery,
Paris, 1781(?)–1782.

*Public and Permanent Buildings*

seats of Britain in the late seventeenth and early eighteenth centuries, which were popularized through Kip's engravings.

Antoine's cemetery presented marked similarities to the gardens of the Palais Royal in Paris as they appeared through much of the eighteenth century (fig. 66). Both cemetery and garden employ parterres shaped in response to the circular geometries of the center and to the rectangular form of the periphery. In both designs, the parterres and walls are outlined by trees, while parallel rows of trees are also used to create a promenade. Finally, trees are planted in repeated parallel rows to form a dense mass with a recognizable outline around the periphery as well as a regularly shaped clearing at the center. Antoine-Nicolas Dezallier d'Argenville's standard treatise on garden theory recognized this as a set type: "a woods, planted in quincunx with a room" at the center. If the gardens of the Palais Royal can be considered as providing the prototype that Antoine then adapted to a different program, then one could conclude that the mortuary chapel replaced the fountain, the parterres were transformed into land for graves, and the outdoor room in the formal bosquet was made into a courtyard.

The similarities between Antoine's cemetery project and formal garden design are even more extensive. The overall pattern of pavilions distributed at the top and bottom of a square plot with a circular element in the center is strongly reminiscent of Lauro's early seventeenth-century view of the Villa Lante at Bagnaia (fig. 67). In this popular engraving, the Italian site is shown to be much flatter than it is and as such may have provided a design strategy for Antoine. In the cemetery, the architectural constructions became the service buildings (fig. 65, D), ossuaries (O), and the administrative and religious headquarters (N).

Perhaps the most striking feature of Antoine's design is the circle within the square arranged to form a cemetery within a cemetery. Here again, late sixteenth-century Italian gardens such as the Villa Lante or the Villa d'Este at Tivoli (fig. 68) had similar arrangements of a self-contained central space placed within a square linked to cross-axial paths. At Lante, it is the circular island and fountain reached by one of four bridges across the water; at the Villa d'Este, it is the round cypress theater where the vegetation forms an enclosing wall.

Finally, having seen that the cemetery designs by Desprez and Delafosse appear indebted to the depiction of ancient Roman gardens as found in Androuet Du Cerceau or Lauro, one should not be surprised to discover a close affinity between the compressed dimensions of the galleries, corner pavilions, and entrances to Antoine's cemetery and the Septa Curiata as shown by Du Cerceau (fig. 69). The underlying geometric affinities between all of these

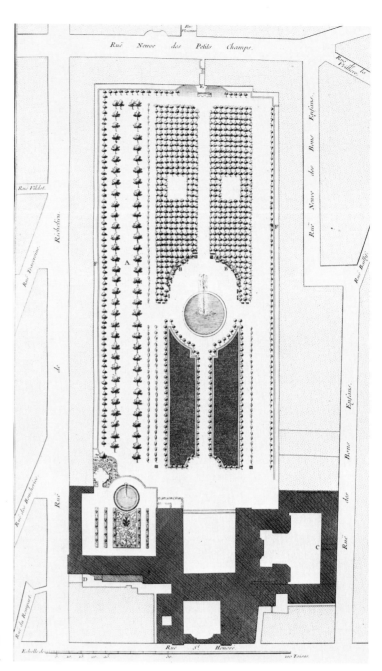

66
Desgots, Palais Royal
Gardens, Paris, 1730.

*Public and Permanent Buildings*

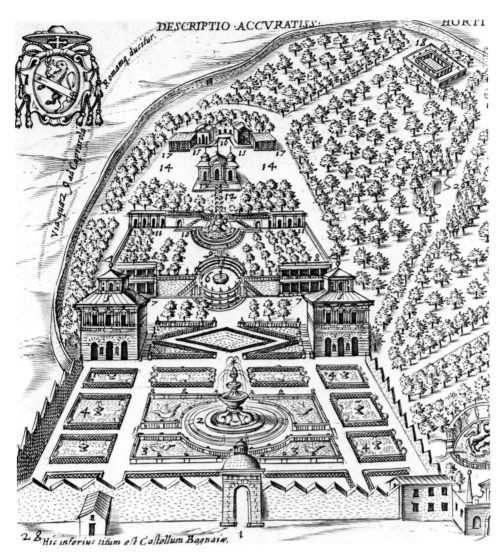

67
Giacomo Barozzi da
Vignola, Villa Lante,
Bagnaia, 1560s.
From Lauro,
*Antiquae urbis
splendor*,
1612–1628.

68
Villa d'Este, Tivoli.
Gardens by Pirro
Ligorio, begun 1560.
View of the Cypress
Theater, from
Venturini, *Le
Fontane . . . di
Roma*, c. 1690.

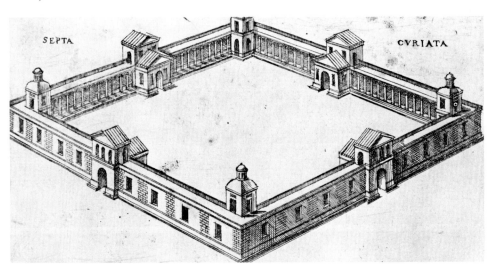

69
Septa Curiata. From
Androuet Du
Cerceau, *Livre des
édifices antiques
romains*, 1584.

models enabled the architect to combine his different sources successfully to achieve a desired end.

In effect, Antoine's cemetery presents a world within a world. Through its geometry, this burial ground becomes a clear mirror of the social hierarchy of the three estates. The central zone is defined by the circular gallery, which is closed along the outside but open toward the central chapel. This inner sanctum was destined for the first and second estates: the four quadrants (fig. 65, G) around the chapel for the clergy and the gallery (H) for the nobility. In this way, even in death, the better classes would turn their backs to the commoners, who were buried outside of the central zone. For those "citizens of a lower order" who wished to escape the mass graves for the poor (L), there were sepulchral vaults in the square gallery around the outer edge of the cemetery (I).

As in the schemes by Capron, the entrepreneurs who worked with Antoine also spoke of offering glorious "catacombs." These businessmen were competing with those curés of Paris who wished to keep the new cemeteries within the control of the parishes. Thus the "catacombs" were heralded by their promoters as superior to the mere "cemeteries" being proposed by the clergy. According to the entrepreneurs, each class in this type of cemetery would be provided with the appropriate degree of dignity in burial. Nobody would be slighted because even the poor would be given adequate land to rot comfortably in mass graves without being exhumed until they were fully decomposed. When, in November 1782, the leaders of the Parlement objected that a ten-year interval before reopening these graves was dangerously inadequate, Antoine hastily recalculated his figures and immediately wrote back that actually one could wait a full forty-five years before reusing a grave. This was a prospect that the Parlement was happy to entertain.

It is difficult to assess the degree to which the notion of proper distinctions between classes as fostered by those in control offended the sensibilities of those who were slighted. If we are to believe the testimony of a departmental Arrêté given toward the end of the revolution on 28 Germinal, year VII (April 17, 1799), these prerogatives were deeply resented. Before the revolution, it was explained, "the pomp of the funeral insulted the poor; and it is well known that this difference in Paris greatly contributed to embitter the indigent against the wealthy. At the time when the National Assembly began to deal with religion, people were saying out loud, now the rich will be buried like the poor without any difference." The cemeteries proposed by the speculators, unlike those envisaged by the Academy, would have perpetuated these distinctions. The designs not only responded to the existing hierarchical order in burials; they would have reified them through their implacable geometry.

# 3

## The Sublime
## (1785)

Sublimity, Boileau had written in his preface of 1674 to Longinus's treatise, "is that extraordinary and marvelous quality in a discourse which enraptures and transports" the reader or listener. Toward the middle of the eighteenth century, through the work of John Baillie (*Essay on the Sublime*, 1747) and Edmund Burke (*A Philosophical Enquiry into the Origins of Our Ideas of the Sublime and Beautiful*, 1755), sublimity became an aesthetic quality not limited to literature but found throughout the material world. This new sensibility had been prepared by the speculations of Henry More, who in 1646 identified God with the infinite space of the universe. In his masterful study of the "natural sublime," Ernest Tuveson has traced the evolution of both the idea and the exalted feelings associated with this concept through the subsequent work of Samuel Clark, John Locke, Sir Isaac Newton, Thomas Burnett, and finally, Joseph Addison, whose "The Pleasures of the Imagination" (*The Spectator*, nos. 411–421) were to influence the next generation of writers on the subject.

Diderot's observations in his account of the Salon of 1767 revealed both the range of subjects that were considered to be sublime and the types of feelings that they produced: "Everything which astonishes the soul, everything which imparts a feeling of terror leads to the sublime. . . . Poets, speak endlessly of eternity, infinity, infernal depths, darkened skies, deep seas, somber forests, thunder, lightning which tears through the clouds. . . . In all these things there is something terrible, grand, and somber." In the 1780s, this new concept of sublimity, which went beyond Jacques-François Blondel's more "classical" understanding of the term, became the basis of a wide range of cemetery designs. In the field of architecture, mausoleums, cenotaphs, catacombs, and cemeteries emerged as privileged themes by which the thirst for the sublime could readily be satisfied. Conversely, given this intense interest in the sublime, it would have been difficult to conceive of a cemetery without being touched if not thoroughly inspired by its purposes.

## Sublimity and the Academy

Pierre Fontaine's cemetery design for the Grand Prix of 1785 (figs. 70–72) was a plastic and pictorial rendition of the essence of Burke's theory: "Whatever is fitted in any sort to excite ideas of pain and danger, that is to say whatever is in any sort terrible . . . is a source of the sublime; that is, it is productive of the strongest emotion which the mind is capable of feeling." While the program called for a sepulchral monument for the rulers of a great empire with a peripheral gallery for the graves of the nation's great men, Fontaine left behind the image of martial valor and heroism expressed in Dufourny's earlier design (figs. 28–29) in favor of a somber and awesome spectacle of death. As Fontaine explained years later in his *Journal*, the principal monument was

70
Pierre Fontaine,
cemetery, Paris,
second prize, Grand
Prix of 1785.

71
Fontaine, cemetery,
Paris, second prize,
Grand Prix of 1785.
Section through the
central chapel.

72
Fontaine, cemetery,
Paris, second prize.
Grand Prix of 1785.
Plan.

crowned with "a circle of galloping horsemen" commanded by the central "figure of Destiny, scythe in hand." To set the proper atmosphere for this scene, Fontaine imagined a thunderstorm with lightning piercing through the rain and dark storm clouds to illuminate only momentarily the summit of his "circular pyramid."

In his choice of theme, Fontaine may have been influenced by two recent renditions of Death as the Fourth Horseman of the Apocalypse as found in the Book of Revelation. In 1775 John Hamilton Mortimer exhibited his drawing "Death on a Pale Horse," published as an engraving on January 1, 1784; and in 1784, Benjamin West exhibited his own painted version of this theme at the Royal Academy in London. In all three versions, a dramatic light breaks through the dark clouds from the upper left to throw the scene into strongly contrasting zones of light and darkness. Benjamin West's rendition even depicted the horseman as controlling the storm, with lightning bolts shooting out of his raised fists. Perhaps adapting this interpretation to the cemetery, Fontaine had the figure of Death preside over an awesome burial ground whose sober forms, devoid of surface ornamentation, and whose vast dimensions made it seem as much a part of the natural landscape as the storm itself.

Adhering to the precepts of J.-F. Blondel, Fontaine dug his burial ground deep into the earth. After passing first through two alleys of evergreens and then through the outer gallery, the visitor was to descend beneath an inner terrace and then down again into the cemetery to reach the central monument. Unlike earlier designs for mortuary chapels, in which the architecture adhered to human scale, here the building has assumed the dimensions and the aspect of a large natural outcrop. The form is not really that of a pyramid but rather a tumulus. In a sense it was a primitive version of the Mausoleum of Augustus (figs. 195, 198) without the terracing. All of the architectural elements in Fontaine's design, moreover, were the most primitive: the baseless Doric columns, the pure pyramids without the picturesque additions of windows or *amortissements*, the obelisks, as well as the tumulus itself, derived from piling a mound of earth upon a corpse. These forms, then, were primitive in the double sense that they were historically early types as well as plain, geometric forms. This architecture was intended to harmonize with nature, depicted as a timeless, chthonic, chaotic, powerful, and mysterious entity to which man must return in death.

The academicians were not prepared to accept such a unified vision of landscape and architecture. Fontaine was denied the first prize and awarded instead the second Grand Prix. The student was chided for paying attention to drawing to the detriment of the essential matter of architecture. One can only speculate as to whether the chilling rendition of sublimity here made the members of the jury uneasy. The other students, though, openly revolted at the Academy's decision and created a scandal by jeering the academicians as they left their meeting room.

The first prize was given to a competent but less daring design by Jean-Charles Moreau (figs. 73–75). True to the spirit of Dufourny's earlier project, this cemetery presented an elevated field of honor. Unlike Fontaine, whose cemetery was an immense complex stretching across the landscape, Moreau adhered to the program, which called for a cemetery no larger than the one designed by Desprez (figs. 20–23). Moreau's image of the cemetery is like a pale reflection of Fontaine's sublimity. The austerity of the plain walls of the interior gallery articulated by niches capped with a portico in the shape of a cover to an ancient sarcophagus contrasts strongly with the earlier academic designs. Likewise, the opposition between open and closed forms occurs here in relatively sweeping gestures: three closed galleries and one side transformed into a type of hall of lost steps. The central monument itself has a simplicity and a grandeur that make it quite different from Dufourny's cemetery, with its play between the porticoes and the pyramid. Finally, Moreau's theme of immortality through lasting fame is conveyed by elevating the statues of either virtues or great men upon a ring of columns around an immense dome with cosmic connotations.

A *prix d'émulation* of 1788 soon afforded another possibility to explore the relationship between architecture and its landscape. The program called for a cenotaph to honor the lost explorers who died with Jean-François de La Pérouse on their voyage of discovery around the world. In calling for a monument on a desert island, the Academy set the stage for an interpretation of the sublime. Vien's first prize (fig. 76) impressed the rude stones into service as a type of natural architecture both for the base of the principal monument and the backdrop for the amphitheater. Five tombs have been placed in sepulchral chambers dug into the rock above the amphitheater and two occupy the interior space of the central cenotaph. The sublimity of this design derived from the minimal and austere quality of the man-made architecture, which served as a strong visual magnet to pull the surrounding, stark landscape into the composition.

Dumannet's second prize (figs. 77–78) more closely resembled the spirit of Fontaine's cemetery, both in its form and in its highly dramatic presentation. In contrast to Vien, Dumannet chose a small island or a sizable shelf of rock by an island, which he nearly covered with an amphitheater crowned by seven pyramids. Empty space, with water lapping into this memorial port, provided an eloquent and appropriately characterized center to the composition. The light breaking through the dark clouds from the

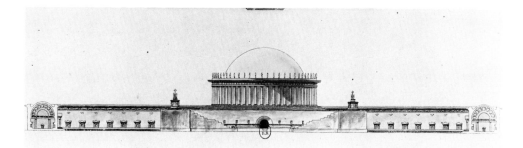

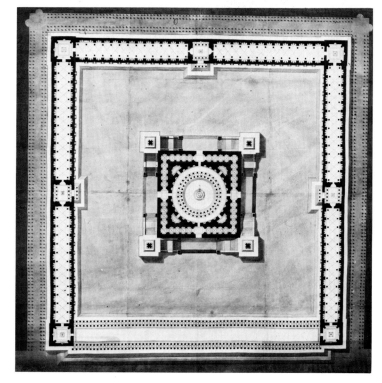

73
Jean-Charles
Moreau, cemetery,
Paris, first prize,
Grand Prix of 1785.

74
Moreau, cemetery,
Paris, first prize,
Grand Prix of 1785.
Section through the
central chapel.

75
Moreau, cemetery,
Paris, first prize,
Grand Prix of 1785.
Plan.

*Sublimity and the Academy*

76
Vien, "Cenotaph in
Honor of the
Explorers Who
Perished in the
Voyage of M. de La
Pérouse," first prize,
*prix d'émulation*,
1788.

*The Sublime*

77
Dumannet,
"Cenotaph in Honor
of the Explorers
Who Perished in the
Voyage of M. de La
Pérouse," second
prize, *prix
d'émulation*, 1788.

78
Dumannet,
"Cenotaph in Honor
of the Explorers
Who Perished in the
Voyage of M. de La
Pérouse," second
prize, *prix
d'émulation*, 1788.
Plan with section.

*Sublimity and the Academy*

left fills this area with a bright illumination symbolic of the dead but immortalized explorers. Inside each pyramid, a sarcophagus rests under the dome, representing a return to nature.

*From the Creation to the Creator*

Sublimity, with its shudder of horror that provided a delicious thrill, was not an end in itself. As the cenotaphs to La Pérouse show, the architects were concerned with conveying a vision of death that joined man to the stark forces of the natural world. The theme of explorers lost at sea certainly lent itself to such an interpretation. More generally, though, this intention was shared by numerous architects at this time who used the sublime, in the words of Paul Van Tieghem, to pass "from the creation to the creator." The funerary architecture of the 1780s was imbued with a pantheistic fervor that sought to make palpable the presence of divinity through the magnificence of the Creation. Architecture, accordingly, was given grandiose proportions which placed it in a more intimate relationship with the largest features of nature within the domain of human experience: the sky, the earth, the sun, the night. Each of these aspects of the physical world was appreciated as conveying the grandeur of nature or as making its spirit manifest to mankind.

The most complete treatment of this theme came in the work of Etienne-Louis Boullée, architect and member of the Académie Royale d'Architecture, who, in 1782, virtually withdrew from the world of private practice to devote himself to his work as an academician, theoretician, and educator. From that time until his death in 1799, Boullée made over one hundred beautiful ink and wash drawings on a large format for the entire gamut of public buildings which preoccupied the advocates of the *embellissement* of Paris. The majority of these drawings were complete by 1793, and the ones which concern us most directly date from about 1781 to about 1785, the first years of Boullée's turning inward to explore the path by which architecture could lead from the creation to the creator. By the time Boullée was finished with designing projects for public buildings, as well as writing an inquiry into the nature of architectural experience, he had left a legacy of dual cities of the living and of the dead. These were complementary worlds, diametrically opposed but inextricably linked, both through their forms, which mirrored each other but in a reverse manner, and in the understanding of the human condition that these forms conveyed.

The inspiration for Boullée's funerary architecture was a deeply moving experience through which the architect had come to understand the relationship between his own mortality and the seasonal "death" of nature. Walking beside a woods in the moonlight, Boullée was struck by the sight of his shadow, which in this instance caused him an "extreme sadness." At this moment and through this scene, Boullée received an intimation of his mortality and of his return in death to the darkness of a primordial nature. As he looked around, he noticed the shadows of the trees and felt that all nature was "in mourning." Profoundly affected by this experience, he immediately applied himself to transfer this understanding to architecture. The result was a vision of the cemetery that might be called an Egyptian wasteland (figs. 86–87). Here a gigantic pyramid, like the embodiment of nature, occupies the center of the precinct to offer the "image of immortality." All around is a vast desert, and along the periphery the low and somber walls of the ossuaries and the funerary chapels, with their austere forms and somber shadows, recreate the ambiance of sadness which Boullée had felt that night in the forest.

While these drawings are undated, it has generally been assumed that they were done toward the time of the Grand Prix competition of 1785 or slightly before. Boullée's interest in comparable themes, which he developed in the Métropole (metropolitan church) (1781–1782) and the cenotaph to Newton (1784), his resignation in December 1782 from his official charges as Controlleur des Bâtiments for the Hôtel Royal des Invalides and the Ecole Militaire to devote himself to such projects and the Parlement's renewed attention to the cemeteries of Paris in 1782–1783 make this dating even more plausible.

## The Egyptian Wasteland

Boullée's fascination with the Egyptian pyramid, which expressed the timelessness of Nature through the simple majesty of its mass and its success in withstanding the ravages of time, owed much to the engravings of Fischer von Erlach. Boullée's use of these images, published in 1721 as part of Fischer von Erlach's depiction of the Seven Wonders of the World (figs. 79–81), represents the most thorough reinterpretation of these scenes, which had earlier fascinated other French architects who were pioneering the new Neoclassical style. Boullée's projects, the most mature expression of this style, served an architectural and cultural vision broader than that of any of his predecessors.

One of the earliest views inspired by Fischer von Erlach's pyramids was executed by Charles Michel-Ange Challe in 1747 while he was living in Rome after winning the Grand Prix of 1741. His *capriccio* (fig. 82) is indebted to the engraving of the twin Moeris Pyramids, which Challe freely interpreted as a vast funerary precinct replete with numerous monuments, colonnades, arcades, and sarcophagi. The drawing suggests a central zone with a central mausoleum surrounded by four pyramids, which, in turn, have peristyles and arcades passing through them. This latter arrangement may have been inspired by the situation of the Pyramid of Cestius, which had become engaged in the Aurelian wall (fig. 53). Several years later, in 1752, Jacques-François Blondel ornamented the

79
J. B. Fischer von
Erlach, "Egyptian
Pyramids." From
*Entwurff einer
historischen
Architectur*, 1721.

80
Fischer von Erlach,
"Moeris Pyramids."
From *Entwurff einer
historischen
Architectur*, 1721.

*The Sublime*

81
Fischer von Erlach,
"Theban Pyramid."
From *Entwurff einer
historischen
Architectur*, 1721.

82
Charles Michel-Ange
Challe, *capriccio*.
Rome, 1747.

title page of his *Architecture françoise* with a vignette by Jérôme-Charles Bellicard, winner of the Grand Prix of 1747, whose stay at the French Academy in Rome coincided with the last years of Challe's period of tenure. Like Challe, Bellicard combined Fischer von Erlach's engravings of the pyramids of Egypt with the Roman tomb of Caius Cestius into an architectural fantasy depicting a vast cemetery (fig. 83). Of the two, Challe's vision was that of a distilled geometric purity where primitive stereometric forms combined with Hathoric capitals and hieroglyphs to evoke a timeless setting.

Toward the middle of his ten-year sojourn in Rome at the French Academy, the painter Hubert Robert reinterpreted Fischer von Erlach's engravings, infusing them with a grandeur that far surpassed the funerary visions of Challe and Bellicard and perhaps even of Fischer von Erlach himself (fig. 84). By placing the pyramid close to the picture plane and thereby truncating its form, Robert brought the viewer up close to a monument which soared high above the clouds. Far away across the landscape one glimpses a second pyramid whose presence suggests an immense cemetery set within the desert. Robert's undated variant of this painting in the Smith College Museum of Art exploits both of the features more fully by shifting the viewpoint to make the near pyramid occupy over half the canvas and by distancing even further the pyramid to the rear. Finally, Robert has added a dramatic entrance to the pyramid on ground level in the form of a low, arched opening.

The force of Robert's painting derives as much from his treatment of the pyramid's mass as from the striking composition. Matter, whether as stone or clouds, has a palpable quality in Robert's work that is missing in Fischer von Erlach's engravings. One could say of Robert what Mario Praz, following Valerio Mariani, wrote about Piranesi, that the architect had a passion for "stones *as stones*." Like Piranesi, Robert also was able to convey what Mariani termed the "hallucinatory fixity in these objects which, completely still and inactive as they are, are laden with mysterious energy." With Robert, the pyramids of Fischer von Erlach's engravings reached a sublimity capable of sustaining a pantheistic celebration of nature.

Boullée's debt to these earlier works for both the general theme and many of the specifics is clear. The clustering of pyramids in Fischer von Erlach's "Egyptian Pyramids" (fig. 79) found its counterpart in Boullée's "Cenotaph in the Egyptian Genre" (fig. 85) as well as in his two depictions of a vast cemetery (figs. 86–87). From the "Moeris Pyramids" (fig. 80) Boullée culled the scissor ramps; and from the Theban Pyramid (fig. 81), the horizontal terracing with aedicula cut into the mass of the pyramid. The latter two engravings also provided the theme of the aedicula or tempietto as a crowning feature. Challe and Bellicard, on the

83
Jérôme-Charles
Bellicard, *capriccio*.
From J.-F. Blondel,
*Architecture
françoise*, 1 (1752).

84
Hubert Robert,
*capriccio*. Rome,
1760.

85
Etienne-Louis
Boullée, "Cenotaph
in the Egyptian
Genre." c. 1785.

86
Boullée, cemetery,
Paris, c. 1785.

87
Boullée, cemetery,
Paris, c. 1785.

other hand, provided the model for aligning a series of pyramids and connecting them with low galleries. The similarities between Robert's vision of the Egyptian wasteland and Boullée's subsequent work (fig. 85) extend not only to the general composition and to the similar rendering of clouds and sunlight but even to the appreciation of the stone as laden with the "mysterious energy" that permeates all of Boullée's cenotaphs and mausoleums.

## An Architecture of Life and Death

Boullée's funerary architecture derived from a comprehensive vision of the human condition understood as a reflection of the larger cosmic order. This understanding of man's place in the universe had, in turn, to be given architectural expression. To a pantheist such as Boullée, the order of the universe could be seen most readily in the course of the seasons. Since 1730, when the poet James Thomson published the first complete cycle of *The Seasons*, along with his "Hymn to the Creator," the seasons had been celebrated throughout Europe in poetry which made them into a corollary of the first principle of the universe, which was gravity. If gravity was the single bond to the cosmic order, then the seasons demonstrated its amazing variety, extensive but regulated according to a recurring cycle.

Poets' panegyrics found a profound echo in the development of the landscape garden in England and France and in the treatises on this subject published in the 1770s. One of these books in particular, Morel's *Théorie des jardins* (1776), seems to have had a direct influence on Boullée's vision. Jean-Marie Morel, the "patriarch of gardens," brought ten years of experience to the writing of what was to become one of the most influential treatises on the landscape garden. In Morel's work, Boullée found an enraptured celebration of the spectacle of nature, which he paraphrased in his own essay on "the art of architecture." Both architects characterized the course of the seasons as the transformation of simple stereometric forms seen under different conditions of light.

Unlike Thomson or Morel, though, Boullée did not understand the seasons as truly cyclical. For Boullée, Nature did not bud in spring to flower in summer with a decline in autumn continuing on into winter. Rather, he saw the seasons as a bipolar opposition of life and death. The first three seasons each embodied a different aspect of resplendent life: the grace of spring, the majesty of summer, and the variety of autumn. Winter, on the other hand, was the season of death. Death was apparent everywhere in the forms of nature and was accompanied by its own characteristic somber light. For Boullée, winter was the "black" season:

What sad days! The celestial torch has disappeared! Darkness envelops us! Frightful winter comes to chill our hearts! It is brought by time! Night follows as it spreads its somber veils over the earth, which it covers with shadows. The brilliant glimmer of the waves is already tarnished by the cruel blowing of the cold winds. The delightful shelter of the woods offers us nothing more than its skeleton. A funerary crepe covers nature. The ravishing image of life has vanished; that of death has taken its place! Objects have lost their brilliance and their color; forms are no longer vibrant, their contours are angular and hard; and the denuded earth offers to our eyes nothing but the vast expanse of a universal sepulcher!

The seasons, then, were like human existence, an alternation between life and death. To characterize death properly and to put man in harmony with nature, the cemetery, too, would have to present the aspect of a universal sepulcher. To this end, Boullée developed the cemetery as a stark landscape reminiscent of the depiction of awesome Egyptian pyramids sitting in the desert. To characterize the cemetery further, Boullée developed a typology for his funerary architecture, calling its forms a buried architecture, an architecture of shadows, and a naked architecture. The buried architecture used forms which appeared to be partially buried under the ground. The architecture of shadows was obtained by incising images into a stone surface so that the dark shadows would become ghostly black figures seen in the pale moonlight. Naked architecture was characterized by the absence of applied decoration and large, unbroken surfaces of unpolished stone that would absorb rather than reflect light.

In designing a funerary architecture on these principles, Boullée returned to the teachings of J.-F. Blondel, who had advocated a rustic architecture for a cemetery whose entrance would lead down into the earth. Boullée not only adhered to the specifics of this vision, as can be seen by the sharp descent into the cemetery at the gateway (fig. 88), but also elaborated on its premises to fashion complementary worlds for the living and the dead. Here Boullée accepted the challenge of Nicolas Le Camus de Mézières's essay, *Le génie de l'architecture, ou l'analogie de cet art avec nos sensations* (1780), which ended with the promise of discussing the relationship between architectural expression and aesthetic response in the realm of public buildings. Le Camus de Mézières never completed this task, but Boullée spent the next two decades exploring this issue through analytical texts and designs.

In a sense, the entire program for Boullée's funerary architecture as well as his *Architecture, essai sur l'art*, can be found in Le Camus de Mézières's discussion of the effect on feelings of simple geometric shapes seen under different conditions of light and shade. Inspired primarily by the theoreticians of the landscape garden, for whom each scene was intended to evoke a different emotion—gaiety, majesty, sadness—Le Camus de Mézières attempted to explain how the same effect could be achieved in architecture. In this way, he extended the notion of *caractère*, or architectural expression, as postulated by Germain Boffrand and

J.-F. Blondel, from a quality that permits the viewer to identify a building's purpose by its appearance to evoking an appropriate feeling. This emotive aspect of character was to become the basis of Boullée's designs for public buildings and cemeteries as well.

While Le Camus de Mézières may have provided Boullée with insights into the relationships between form and feeling, Boullée far surpassed his predecessor by applying and further developing the precepts into the complementary worlds of the living and the dead. The opposition that Boullée created depended upon the customary image of the triangular pediment or the dome carried upon a row of columns. While the architecture for the city of the living was given its basic configuration with round, freestanding columns suitably proportioned to the pediment or dome above, the architecture of the dead transformed this relationship in a manner expressive of its purpose. One can judge both Boullée's debt to Le Camus de Mézières and the degree of his originality by considering how he seems to have applied each of the older architect's principles.

In his discussion of creating the feeling of sadness, Le Camus de Mézières recommended focusing the view into the darkness, where no object could be seen precisely. This Boullée achieved in his architecture of shadows, which he applied to the mortuary chapels along the periphery of the ossuary or located just inside. His forms, however, have such precision that one (fig. 89) appears as a negative image of a pediment whose columns are buried under the earth, while the other (fig. 90) presents a negative image of an entire portico where the pediment seems to hover over the ghostly colonnade. In the first of these examples, the forms appear not only to be partially buried but also to be sliding down into the ground.

The second design illustrates Le Camus de Mézières's other principle, that of employing "tight" or "enclosing" forms. Repeating an observation by Jean-Jacques Rousseau, whose reflections upon "le sentiment de l'existence" were instrumental to both architects' appreciation of aesthetic experience, Le Camus de Mézières remarked: 'In effect, we are made such that, when we are happy our heart expands and loses itself in immensity." Sadness, on the other hand, prompted the contrary feeling, a tightening up inside. Architecture, Le Camus de Mézières argued, could foster such feelings by the qualities of its forms. In his funerary architecture, Boullée reversed the usual relationships between the elements of a building to achieve this effect; thus, in the funerary chapel in fig. 90, the negative image of the pediment is totally enclosed within the larger surfaces of the main body. These surfaces are simple, unadorned, and even "monotonous," after the manner of another of Le Camus de Mézières's prescriptions. The same is true of the columns engulfed within the large, unbroken wall

88
Boullée, cemetery
entrance by
moonlight, c. 1785.

89
Boullée, "Funerary
Monument
Characterizing the
Genre of a Buried
Architecture." c.
1785.

90
Boullée, "Funerary
Monument
Characterizing the
Genre of an
Architecture of
Shadows," c. 1785.
Detail from fig. 87.

*The Sublime*

surfaces forming the interior of the central pyramid (fig. 91).

A corollary to the principle of enclosure was that of giving excessive length to forms, which Le Camus de Mézières cited as favoring sad feelings. Boullée reformulated this principle in his own *Architecture* by observing that low forms which seem to hug the ground have the same effect. Both aspects of this idea Boullée applied to his *Cenotaph in the Egyptian Genre* (fig. 85), where the horizontal terraces taken from the pyramid at Thebes have been given an inordinate length. The long colonnades seem to be almost carved within the mass; the low and sinking pediment cannot begin to balance the extended colonnade; and the lowest level is imagined to be virtually sunken under the ground.

If Boullée integrated his experience in the forest with his reading of Le Camus de Mézières and J.-M. Morel, was he inspired by any specific images in transforming the visions of the Egyptian wasteland of Fischer von Erlach and Hubert Robert? If Desprez, Dufourny, Delafosse, Antoine, and Neufforge were looking at reconstructions of ancient Roman architecture to assist them in designing modern cemeteries, then one might suspect that Boullée was doing the same. In effect, the funerary monument (fig. 90) that appears at regular intervals along the outer terrace of Boullée's square cemetery plan appears to have been adapted in both its form and situation from the Septa Tributa in Androuet Du Cerceau's book on Roman antiquities (fig. 92). Likewise, the entry to the Monumentum Tam Philiorum Liber (fig. 93) may have suggested the disproportionate relationship between the pediment and the colonnade. As for the idea of a buried architecture, Boullée may have drawn inspiration from Challe's catafalque for the funeral of the Dauphine on September 3, 1767, where the piers supporting the arch appear truncated to indicate that they extend below the level of the podium (figs. 94–95). Boullée did not merely borrow these images; he transformed them into integral elements of a total architectural conception.

**Intimations of Immortality**

The ossuary around the periphery of Boullée's cemetery (fig. 87) retained its traditional role of *memento mori*, intended not as a Christian reminder but as a prelude to a union with Nature; and the majestic pyramid at the center furnished the second component of the message. Here Boullée was following a French tradition which, since the late seventeenth century, depicted the triumph of immortality over death through deeds of enduring fame.

One of the most striking renditions of this theme was conceived by the painter Charles Le Brun for the funeral of the aged Chancellor Séguier in 1672 (fig. 96). Contemporaries were deeply moved by the "rare distinction and appeal" of the catafalque, which Le Brun separated into two parts. The lower portion, with its four

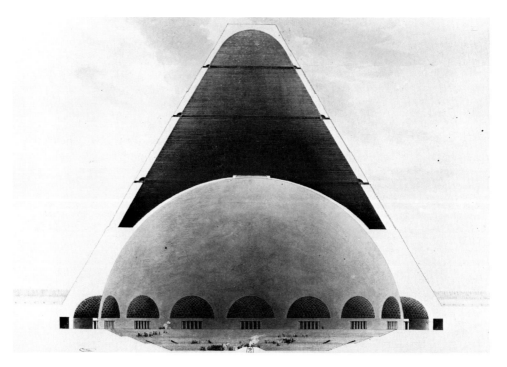

91
Boullée, cenotaph to
Turenne, c. 1785.
Section.

*The Sublime*

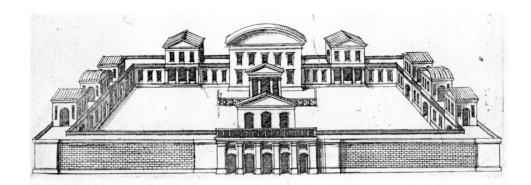

92
Septa Tributa. From
Androuet Du
Cerceau, *Livre des
édifices antiques
romains*, 1584.

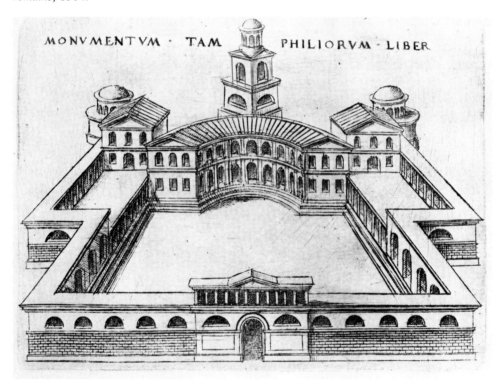

MONVMENTVM · TAM PHILIORVM · LIBER

93
Monumentum Tam
Philiorum Liber.
From Androuet Du
Cerceau, *Livre des
édifices antiques
romains*, 1584.

94
Charles Michel-Ange
Challe, catafalque for
the funeral of the
Dauphine de France,
Notre-Dame, Paris,
September 3, 1767.

95
Challe, catafalque for
the funeral of the
Dauphine de France,
Notre-Dame, Paris,
September 3, 1767.
Section.

*Intimations of Immortality*

96
Charles Le Brun,
catafalque for the
funeral of Chancellor
Séguier, Eglise de
l'Oratoire, Paris,
May 5, 1672.

*The Sublime*

figures of Death flanking the sarcophagus, presented the image of mortality. The upper part used a luminous pyramid, seemingly suspended in the air by four angels to represent immortality.

What Le Brun achieved in a vertical sequence, Boullée applied in a horizontal or temporal progression from the ossuary at the periphery to the pyramid at the center. The portal (fig. 88) provided the link between the two forms as well as between the two ideas. Shown in the moonlight, it glows in the shape of a luminous triangle. As Alexandre Lenoir would soon explain in his history of Freemasonry, the triangle was an ancient, sacred symbol of the elements. The Freemasons had adopted the image of a radiant triangle as a symbol for Jehovah, the great architect of the universe. Whether Boullée, like so many other Parisian architects, was a Mason is of less importance than the fact that Masonic imagery had become inseparable from the wider culture of the Enlightenment. Whatever the specific intention of Boullée's radiant triangle, it presented an intimation of immortality at the initial point of entry along the axis to the central pyramid.

Boullée's project for a conical tower (fig. 97) suggests still another link to Masonic ideas. Possibly modeled upon an ancient Near Eastern sepulcher (fig. 98), this monument is inscribed with what might be interpreted as the Masonic "chain of union" or "mystic chain." Boullée's chain of souls, formed by deep shadows filling the silhouettes incised into the stone, spirals upward to give concrete form to the Masonic rite, which Lenoir would interpret as "symbolizing a sacred tie between the earth and the sky as well as the divine harmony between human life and the universe." Of all the possible images, though, for some manner of apotheosis, the pyramid was Boullée's preferred monument to grace the center of the cemetery.

The antiquity of the pyramid made it a prime candidate for a monument to convey the immortality of the meritorious dead. When the Académie Royale d'Architecture devoted a session in 1765 to reading parts of Norden's *Voyage d'Egypte et de Nubie* (1755), it concentrated on the description of the Egyptian pyramids, whose absence of hieroglyphs and situation on a sandy plain attested to a most venerable age. Having thus proved its permanence, the pyramid seemed to Boullée to furnish an ideal "image of immutability." As the architect Sobry would express it, in the pyramid, "immortality . . . is visible and palpable."

On the one hand, Boullée's pyramids are cenotaphs to personal greatness; on the other, they are incarnations of nature itself. The two themes are combined in the great man, who is considered to have reached a status commensurate with the grandeur of divinity. As Boullée explains: "The homage which we enjoy giving to great men comes from feelings inspired by the height where

97
Etienne-Louis
Boullée, funerary
monument, c. 1785.

*The Sublime*

98
Ancient Near Eastern
sepulcher. From
Maundrell, *Voyage
d'Alep à Jerusalem*,
1705.

our mind places them. We like to find in one of our fellows that eminent degree of perfection which deifies, so to speak, our nature." Few people would reach such heights, but at least through the contact with the colossal pyramids, they could momentarily partake of the so-called divinity of their heroes.

The choice of hero to whom Boullée dedicated the central pyramid in one of his cemeteries (figs. 87, 99) was doubly significant. Maréchal Turenne was not only a great seventeenth-century military hero who had given his life for France after twice bringing peace to his country; he also was the subject of the most "allusive" *castrum doloris* ever seen in France and, according to Tapié, perhaps in Italy as well (fig. 100). The catafalque for Turenne, designed by the masterful Jesuit, Claude-François Ménestrier, was an early instance of an *architecture parlante*, whose fortified tower, taken from Turenne's coat of arms, was invested with numerous levels of symbolic meaning. From this funeral, then, Turenne was already associated with the idea of a monument whose form was expressive of its subject. Boullée, though, eschewed such specific imagery in favor of assimilating Turenne's valor to a more universal form that could also embody the spirit of nature.

Boullée's pyramid, as Jean Starobinski has observed, rises as a *puissance*, a vital force. The pyramid is Nature incarnate, timeless, chthonic, primitive, fertile, and crystalline. In his musings, Boullée had illustrious company in the person of Buffon, the celebrated naturalist who, in his *Histoire naturelle des minéaux*, published starting in 1783, indulged in animistic reveries about the formation of the crystalline shapes of the mineral world. Such imaginings were also shared by contemporary travelers and explorers who invested natural outcroppings of rock with an animistic spirit. In the same year, Romé de l'Ile published his pioneering *Cristallographie*, which established primitive crystalline forms as the basis for the study of minerals. In this work, Boullée may have found a confirmation of his own conviction that perfect geometries were the underlying forms of a universal order. Just how far such speculation could go is illustrated by Samuel Simon Witte's proposition that the pyramids of Egypt were not man-made, but were natural forms. At first Witte wrote that the pyramids had been formed within the earth and then pushed up to the surface. Later he revised this opinion to conclude that they were the result of volcanic activity at the site itself. In his *Cenotaph in the Egyptian Genre*, Boullée joined the idea of a return to the bosom of the earth through death with the image of this same *natura naturans* rising out of fertile chaos as a pure crystalline form.

In the late eighteenth century, Boullée was not alone in identifying death with the fertile darkness of the earth, a darkness that was also associated with the spectacle of the planets and stars in the

99
Etienne-Louis
Boullée, cenotaph to
Turenne, c. 1785.
Detail from fig. 87.

100
Claude-François
Ménestrier,
catafalque for the
funeral of Maréchal
Turenne, Notre-
Dame, Paris,
September 9, 1675.

*Intimations of Immortality*

nighttime sky. Ledoux, for example, imagined the cemetery for the town of Chaux as vast catacombs fashioned in the town's open quarries. With the city of the dead physically occupying the empty space excavated to provide stone for the city of the living, the complementary relationship between life and death was given material form. At the center of Ledoux's cemetery was a spherical cavity half buried in the earth (fig. 101). Here, explained Ledoux, was the image of the awesome chaos before the Creation, a chaos to which man returned in death. To complement this design, Ledoux provided his famous "Elevation of the Cemetery of the Town of Chaux" which was actually a scene of the planets (fig. 102). For Boullée and Ledoux, the bosom of the earth and the immensity of the sky were two faces of a primitive and universal nature.

*The Cenotaph to Newton*

Nowhere do the simultaneous themes of immortalizing the illustrious dead and celebrating the immensity of nature come together more completely than in Boullée's project of 1784 for a cenotaph to Sir Isaac Newton (figs. 103–105). Newton was the one mortal who, in discovering gravity, the single unifying law of the universe, had risen to the level of divine intelligence. In honoring Newton, Boullée was also worshiping the cosmic order with which Newton had, so to speak, identified himself. Hence, Boullée chose to bury Newton in the center of a spherical cavity representing alternately the irradiating sun or the nighttime sky. The former effect was to be achieved by illuminating, presumably with fireworks, a giant armillary sphere; the latter, through holes punctured in the dome that would allow sunlight to enter, giving the illusion of shining stars. The exterior of the monument suggested a sphere whose perfect form Newton had determined to have been the shape of the earth before it was deformed through rotation. In a double sense, then, Boullée could boast that he was burying Newton within his own discovery and hence, within himself.

If Boullée's decision to design a cenotaph to Newton reflected the preoccupation of the period with finding a suitable form for the cemetery and its inspirational monuments, it was also related to the scientific activity of the early 1780s, which captivated the contemporary imagination. In 1783 and 1784, just after Bailly and Laland had published their important treatises on astronomy, the Montgolfier brothers and Pilâtre de Rozier made their first balloon flights. Barthélemy Faujas de Saint-Fond's illustrated narrative of this startling conquest of the skies was immediately translated into German, Italian, and Dutch.

With these balloon flights, man entered into a new relationship with the world around him. Not only could he now understand

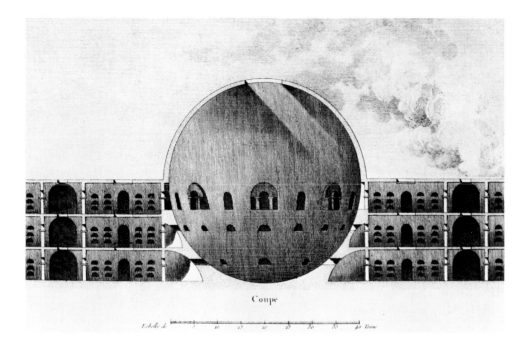

101
Claude-Nicolas
Ledoux, cemetery for
Chaux, c. 1785.

ÉLÉVATION DU CIMETIÈRE DE LA VILLE DE CHAUX.

102
Ledoux, "Elevation
of the Cemetery of
the Town of
Chaux." c. 1785.

131                    *The Cenotaph to Newton*

103
Etienne-Louis
Boullée, cenotaph to
Sir Isaac Newton,
1784.

104
Boullée, cenotaph to
Sir Isaac Newton,
1784. View of the
interior with
armillary sphere.

105
Boullée, cenotaph to
Sir Isaac Newton,
1784. View of the
interior with
nighttime sky.

*The Cenotaph to Newton*

the workings of the universe, he could also experience the immensity of the sky and view the expansiveness of the globe. Boullée, it should be remembered, worked under the portraits of Newton and Copernicus. He owned and used Bailly's treatise in his design for the cenotaph to Newton. He reflected deeply upon the significance of the balloon flights for imparting the experience of the sublime through architecture.

The visit to Newton's tomb, where one would learn about "the expanse of his enlightenment and the sublimity of his genius," would also be a voyage into immensity. Here people would gather to have their "spirits elevated to the contemplation of the Creator and to experience celestial feelings." In the recent balloon flights, Boullée found new possibilities for using a domed space to reach the sublime. Edmund Burke and other British theorists had stressed that the uniformity and vastness of a perfectly circular dome presented an uninterrupted and unlimited view that expanded the mind out into infinity. Working with this idea, Boullée placed his spectators not merely under a half shere but within a fully spherical enclosure. By analogy to the experience of the balloonists, or *aérostats*, as they were called, Boullée announced that in this cenotaph "the spectator would find himself transported into the sky as if by enchantment and carried on the clouds into the immensity of space." As the visitor ran his eye around and around the sphere, he would come to know the immensity of Nature. With curved surfaces to every side and with the tomb as the sole object, the visitor would be frozen at the "center" with the tomb as a type of mental anchor. At the height of this ecstatic experience, the spectator would become both the center and the circumference. At the same time, he would feel united with the tomb (Newton) and with an ever-expanding immensity (the cosmos). As a memorial, then, the cenotaph to Newton was simultaneously a temple to Nature and a means of experiencing the sublime.

Intended as a funerary monument, the cenotaph to Newton was the obverse of the metropolitan church (fig. 106). There Boullée applied the other aspect of Burke's "artificial infinite," which consisted in multiplying the number of columns to impart an ever-expanding sense of self. As one moved through the temple, Boullée explained, "it seems that these columns move with us and that we have given them life." The result would be union with Divinity such as Rousseau recounted in the *Reveries of a Solitary Walker* and in the "Third Letter to Malesherbes:" ". . . my heart, constrained within the limits of its human frame, wanted to bound into infinity." "In my transports I cried out several times, 'Oh Great Being,' and could not think or say anything more."

The primary difference between the metropolitan church and the cenotaph to Newton resided in their belonging respectively to the worlds of the living and of the dead. In the church, sublimity

106
Boullée, metropolitan
church (*Métropole*),
c. 1781–1782. View
on Corpus Christi
Day.

The Cenotaph to Newton

was reached through the safe and reassuring impression of expanding outward by reference to the columns, which, Boullée explains, anchor the self securely. Without such points of comparison, one would be like the balloonist floating so high above the earth that no objects at all were visible. In such a position, one would lose all sense of self. "Wandering in this manner in immensity, man is annihilated by the extraordinary spectacle of an inconceivable space." In the cenotaph to Newton, Boullée brings the celebrant within one step of such an experience of psychic annihilation. As the visitor is drawn into the ever-expanding circumference, his only security is Newton's tomb, with which he merges in the same manner. In the church, at the moment of transcendence, the observer identifies with the circular colonnade, which seems to hover miraculously within the light-filled dome. In the cenotaph, the culminating experience would take one beyond the need for such security into a state of pure immensity, thereby vanquishing the annihilation of death as well.

Boullée's cenotaph to Newton brings together numerous iconographic traditions that used the celestial sphere as a symbolic form. One might be characterized as an architecture of pleasure. The illustration of an imperial bath near Budapest published by Fischer von Erlach (fig. 107) may have provided Boullée with the idea of puncturing the dome so as to achieve the effect of a planetarium. Another example of this genre would be the pleasure palace of the Chinese emperors, whose starlit dome was described by William Chambers. Closer in theme to Boullée's own intentions was the tradition in medieval and Renaissance representations of the seven liberal arts of portraying astronomy as a figure holding a celestial sphere. In this spirit, J. M. Rysbrack conceived his tomb for Newton in Westminster Abbey (1737) with a sphere displayed on the surface of the customary obelisk. Finally, from Campanella's *City of the Sun* (1602) onward, the literature of utopia drew heavily upon the symbolism of a temple of the sun which united worship of Divinity, scientific knowledge, and a well-regulated social order. In Campanella's text, the round temple at the center of the city had a cupola painted with stars and an altar on which there were terrestrial and celestial globes.

The immensely popular eighteenth-century counterpart to the *City of the Sun* was the utopian romance, *The Memoirs of Signor Gaudentio di Lucca*, by Simon Berington. Between 1737 and 1784, the date of Boullée's cenotaph to Newton, there were at least four French as well as ten English editions of Berington's story of the Mezzoranians' blessed country, whose capital city of Phor was built "in imitation of the sun and its rays." The temple of the sun at the center of the city consisted of "three hundred and

107
"Imperial Bath" near
Budapest. From
Fischer von Erlach,
*Entwurff einer
historischen
Architectur*, 1721.

*The Cenotaph to Newton*

sixty-five double marble pillars, according to the number of the days of the year, repeated with three stories one above another, and on the top, a cupola, open to the sky for the sun to be seen through." Paintings of the sun, moon, and stars showed the "different motions of the heavenly bodies." In the middle of the gilt dome was "a golden sun, hanging in the void. . . . The artificial sun looks down as if it were shining on a globe or earth, erected on a pedestal altar-wise, opposite to the sun . . . in which globe or earth are enclosed the urns of their deceased ancestors." This temple of science, then, was also a funerary monument. Religion, science, and commemoration were joined in such a manner that Boullée's cenotaph to Newton would not have been out of place in such a setting.

Jean-Louis Viel de Saint-Maux added science to Berington's fantasy with the publication in 1779 and 1780 of the first two *Lettres sur l'Architecture* . . . (Letters on the Architecture of the Ancients . . . Which Explain the Symbolic Genius Which Presided over the Monuments of Antiquity). As the Court de Gébelin for architecture, Viel de Saint-Maux interpreted the architecture of early peoples and primitive societies as symbolic structures that celebrated the Supreme Being while explaining the workings of the universe. The first letter presented the architectural order as a symbolic form for temples that symbolized the cosmogony. In the second letter, Viel de Saint-Maux reminded his readers of what Vitruvius had taught, that classical temples to Jupiter Lightning, the heaven, the sun, and the moon were open to the sky. In the third letter, he reiterated Kempfer's account of the Japanese custom of observing the solstices and equinoxes in a temple of the sun in which celebrants passed through a giant armillary sphere that indicated the positions of the heavenly bodies.

Perhaps the influence of various sources on Boullée's design for the Newton cenotaph is of less importance than the cultural ambiance in which it was conceived and appreciated. Boullée's was not the only such project. The Académie Royale d'Architecture sponsored a *prix d'émulation* in 1785 for a cenotaph to Newton whose program called for an "ingenious and analogous allegory" that would suitably characterize the monument. Pierre-Jules Delespine's prize-winning design presented a half-buried dome whose interior was decorated as a star-filled sky. For the *prix d'émulation* of November 21, 1800, whose subject was once again a cenotaph to Newton, it was stipulated that the architecture include "a hollow sphere in the middle of which will be a globe representing the sun and the urn which would contain Newton's ashes." All of these projects, from Boullée's onward, express Alexander Pope's figure:

Nature and Nature's laws lay hid in night:
God said, let Newton be! and all was light.

| *From Alchemy to Pantheism* | While Pope could epitomize the sublimity and the profundity of Newton's accomplishment in a couplet, the architects who used his image were not content with reducing their work to a single statement. Rather, they seem to have drawn inspiration from the complex visual language of alchemy. The symbolism of the alchemical quest for ultimate wisdom and immortality lent itself readily to the pantheist's desire for a comparable enlightenment and spiritual plenitude. |
| --- | --- |

Boullée's cenotaph to Newton presents striking analogies with *The Philosophic Work* from Libavius (1606; fig. 108), which Diderot reproduced in the *Encyclopédie*. Both figures employ a sphere set upon a broad horizontal base. In the case of the cenotaph, the sphere is set within the base but is allowed to read as a complete form. In both designs, the sphere is also divided into three horizontal segments. A comparison between Libavius's explanation of the meaning of these forms and divisions with those of Boullée's monument suggests comparable intentions.

In the case of *The Philosophic Work*, Libavius describes the base as "a pediment or foundation, like the earth." At the center of the sphere there is a "picture of a wind (god) blowing into the sea and a sort of mountain" emerging out of "an expanse of black water, as in chaos," which signifies putrefaction. Boullée too uses the bottom drum as a platform suggestive of the earth. Here a funerary portal announces the abode of death, in which Newton's tomb has been placed. Above this underworld, a stylized mountain rises to precisely the same central point, where a sacred fire is substituted for the wind or god of the alchemical image. Above is the zone of immortality, where Boullée reveals the surface of the sphere untrammeled by the earthly base. In the alchemical figure, the narrative leads "from the black (putrefactive) to the white stage of the Great Work." Likewise in Newton's tomb, the pictorial sequence leads from burial in the bosom of the earth to depictions of Newton's immortality (the eternal light on the mountain) and unity with the cosmos (the dome).

Just as the cenotaph to Newton had its obverse in the realm of the living for the purpose of experiencing the sublime, so too did it have a comparable monument for relating the message of universal wisdom. The atlantes, or giants that stand at the entrance to Boullée's library project and support the celestial globe covered with the symbols of the zodiac (fig. 109), are the same type of figures that appear in *The Philosophic Work* and carry an analogous meaning. To Boullée, the library was the repository of man's knowledge about nature. Whereas Newton had discovered the unity of the cosmos, the great minds whose works were housed in the library had divulged its multiplicity and variety. These people were immortalized by portrait medallions in the garland hung along the top of the façade. Adapting this garland from the famous

108
*The Philosophic
Work.* From
Libavius, *Alchymia,*
1606.

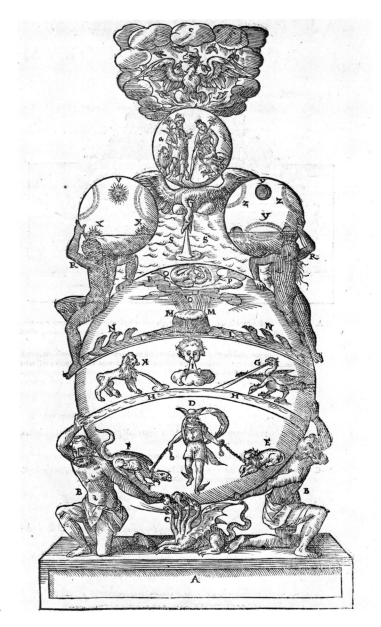

109
Etienne-Louis
Boullée, proposed
entrance to Royal
Library, Paris, 1788.

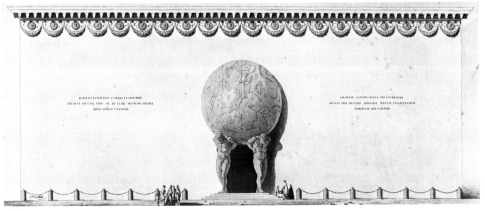

tomb of Caecilia Metella on the Via Appia, Boullée substituted for the bovine skulls in the original the profiles of the greatest thinkers. The library, like the cenotaph, was a memorial to genius. The former commemorated the many; the latter commemorated the one.

The similarities between C. Gay's prize-winning design (1800) for a cenotaph to Newton (figs. 110–111) and *The Bath of the Philosophers*, also from Libavius (fig. 112), are just as striking as those between Boullée's earlier design and its alchemical analogue. Here, numerical symbolism assumes the importance it had in temples of the utopian tradition and in those of ancient and primitive societies popularized by Viel de Saint-Maux. Like Boullée, Gay used the symbolism of alchemy to serve the theme of pantheism.

Both the philosophers' bath and Gay's cenotaph to Newton are organized around a stepped pyramid representing accession to an understanding of the fundamental principles of the universe and, through that, attainment of immortal life. In the alchemical diagram, the seven steps, symbolic of the five planets along with the sun and moon, lead to the Tree of Universal Matter, which crowns the pyramid. Each planet symbolizes one of the "base" metals, as do the five lions on the steps. At the top is the Tree of Universal Matter, with its golden apples, the alchemist's Holy Grail obtained from a transmutation of the base metals into gold. The ultimate metals of gold and silver are symbolized by the sun and moon respectively; above them sit the king and the queen with their feet in a "cleere fountaine," symbolic of purification and revivification.

In Gay's design, the pyramid's steps represent the earlier astronomical chronologies depicted by images incised into the surface. Although deemed incorrect, these systems were appreciated for their ingenuity and are presented here for their role in leading up to Newton's discoveries. At the top of the pyramid, the alchemical figures of the king and queen have been replaced by a colossal bronze statue of Newton sitting majestically on a throne as he pensively determines the "system of the universe." The great scientist is crowned with an aureola of seven rays, one for each of the "primitive colors," which he "discovered" by diffracting light through a prism.

With the theory of a universal gravitation, Newton had discovered the scientist's equivalent to the alchemist's gold. Here was the single, unifying principle of the cosmos. Moreover, under Newton's perceptive gaze the alchemist's sun had become diffracted into the seven colors which form his irradiating crown. Just as the philosophers' bath led to rejuvenation (as indicated by the golden stars, signifying "multiplication and increase") so too did the colors of light vivify the pantheist's world. Poets celebrated the "gorgeous train of parent colours" which issued forth from

110
C. Gay, cenotaph to
Sir Isaac Newton,
*prix d'émulation*,
1800.

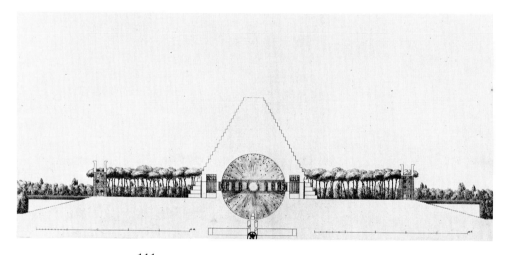

111
Gay, cenotaph to Sir
Isaac Newton, *prix
d'émulation*, 1800.

112
*The Philosophers'
Bath.* From Libavius,
*Alchymia*, 1606.

the prism to enliven the surface of the globe. The sunrise was likened to a cosmogony and the world was celebrated for its robe of many colors.

Like a utopian temple of the sun, Gay's monument is linked symbolically to the cosmos in all of its features. The four approaches and four entries are oriented to the four cardinal points of the compass. The Egyptianate portals are covered with hieroglyphic images of the instruments of astronomy as well as with inscriptions explaining their use.

The pyramid houses a representation of the cosmos, a vast, spherical room painted azure blue and decorated with stars in their true positions. A promenade around the middle is decorated on the outside with twenty-four winged figures representing the hours. Each statue holds a flower, which blooms at its designated hour to form a "botanical clock." On the other wall of this gallery, Newton's complete works are seen engraved on marble plaques. The entire scene is vivified by a luminous globe hanging at the center of the spherical cavity. Newton's ashes are kept below in a small sphere set upon a metal cylinder. This building, then, is at once a cenotaph to Newton and a temple to Nature, a personal archive and a museum of astronomy. Here Newton lives through his work as well as in the memory of the living.

Both the Boullée and Gay cenotaphs can be compared with other alchemical figures in which the imagery is organized according to the theme of a symbolic death and a descent into the earth to become purified in order to discover the Philosopher's Stone. Such is the significance, for example, of the illustration portraying Atlas carrying the celestial globe in Basile Valentin's *Azoth ou le moyen de faire l'or caché des philosophes* (1624, 1659), an image that could also be compared to the entrance to Boullée's library. Likewise, the "Cosmic Vision" (fig. 113) depicted in Mylius's *Tractatus Secundi* (1620) and then republished in Grasshoff's *Dyas chymica tripartita* (1625) presents a close parallel to Boullée's Temple to Nature, in which the larger dome of the sky is placed over the smaller inverted "dome" or hemispherical cavity symbolizing the bosom of the earth (fig. 114).

Finally, the *Sanctuary of the Coniunctio* in Michelspocher's *Cabala, Spiegel der Kunst und Natur in Alchimia* (1616, 1654) shows a stepped pyramid carrying a domed temple with a phoenix on top and the sun and moon under the dome, an image analogous in form and meaning to Gay's cenotaph. The domed temple in the *Coniunctio* is placed before a mountain in a way that also reappears in Boullée's *Monument to the Supreme Being* or necropolis (fig. 202). Boullée's design, like the alchemical precedent, makes the domed temple, to borrow Van Lennep's characterization of the earlier drawing, "a veritable cosmic omphalos," a "foyer to the universe."

113
*Cosmic Vision*. From
Mylius, *Tractatus
secundi seu Basilicae
chymicae*, 1620.

114
Etienne-Louis
Boullée, Temple to
Nature, c. 1793 (?).
Section.

*From Alchemy to Pantheism*

By way of conclusion, all of Boullée's funerary projects—the cenotaph to Newton, the giant pyramids, and the terraced necropolis—employ alchemical themes and images suggesting a return in death to the fertile center of the world in order to join the immensity of the cosmos, which is identified with Divinity. The abstraction in Boullée's architecture, by which the alchemical figures have been significantly altered, suggests that the transfer from alchemy to pantheism is complete. One is less sure, for example, of the intentions behind Ledoux's cemetery project for Chaux (figs. 101–102), where the alchemical symbols may represent a recasting of the alchemical theme of the five planets symbolizing the base metals, along with the moon and the sun, symbolic of the final transmutation to silver and gold, or wisdom and immortality. Ledoux himself presented this scene as an ambiguous image, epitomizing both a return to a primordial chaos and the birth of a new world: "Is this a new world arising from the disorder of chaos or are these the catacombs of the universe?" Perhaps the answer resides in the recurring cycles of death and creation, to which the alchemists gave a symbolic formulation that their pantheist successors found well-suited to express their beliefs.

Boullée's cenotaph to Newton could easily have substituted for the conical pyramid at the center of his cemetery in the form of a circle (fig. 86). Gay's cenotaph, on the other hand, was intended for a park. While it is unclear whether the site was to be Saint James's Park in London or the Folie Saint-James by the Bois de Boulogne in Paris, what is certain is that the building was conceived as an architectural folly set within a luxuriant and diversified vegetation. The trees in Boullée's design, like those around the pyramid in his cemetery, are aligned like columns and function as a funereal equivalent to the architectural order. Beyond the monument, one presumes there is nothing but barren earth. By 1800, though, the idea of the proper setting for a mausoleum or commemorative monument had changed. Now the cemetery was to be a picturesque landscape garden which conveyed a radically different understanding of death. Before Paris was given such a garden cemetery, it received its only realization of a sublime landscape, the Catacombs.

**The Neoclassical World of Death**

While Boullée may have been the most prolific and, in the eyes of some critics, the most talented designer of funerary architecture, he certainly was not alone in formulating the Neoclassical vision of the sublime funerary landscape. Both Boullée and Fontaine, in combining the pyramid with a vast *aula sepocrale* (figs. 71, 91), may have been indebted to Pierre-Adrien Pâris, who designed such an interior hall within a pyramid as a stage set for *Numitor*, which was played at Fontainebleau in 1783 (fig. 115). For the vast rotunda, all of these architects drew upon the model of the Pantheon (fig. 116) and may also have been looking at the Church of the Holy Sepulcher in Jerusalem (fig. 117). Sometimes the outer form of the monument reflected its origins as well as its internal space, as did the Pantheon-like façades of Etienne-Eloy de La Barre's sepulchral chapel (fig. 118) and Delafosse's numerous designs on the same theme (fig. 119). Perhaps the most dramatic interpretation of the sublime came from Desprez in a series of drawings and subsequent aquatints of a necropolis presided over by a skeletal figure of Death (fig. 120). Desprez's King of Death appears as an Egyptianate version of Death from the Hertel edition of Ripa's *Iconologia* (fig. 121), where all estates kneel in homage. In Desprez's version, the rigid feet shown in the arcosolia add a chilling note to an architectural setting that suggests a timeless realm. By juxtaposing such features, Desprez joined the macabre with the sublime.

The French Neoclassical vision of death was continued by Italian artists, mostly scenographers, in the late eighteenth and early nineteenth centuries. Pietro Gonzaga's city of the dead (fig. 122) is reminiscent of Challe's earlier fantasy, with the seemingly endless rows of tombs and intersecting arcades. Both Challe and Gonzaga were indebted to Piranesi, whose engavings taught generations of French and Italian artists about the dramatic effect of galleries crossing on different levels and seen from an angle. Perhaps the closest complete Piranesian rendition of a total architectural realm of death can be found in an anonymous drawing that suggests a world with no center or end (fig. 123). The *aula sepocrale* was also a popular theme with Italian designers, who enriched their interiors with columnar screens (fig. 124) or hypaethral temples (fig. 125) inspired by Piranesi's so-called Temple of Vesta.

These Italian designs covered the extremes of the Neoclassical vision, from the cemetery conceived as an Egyptian wasteland to the awesome monument set in a park, reflecting the new vision of death which was beginning to supplant its austere predecessors. Of the first type, there is a series of drawings attributed to Giuseppe Barberi or his son, Paolo Emilio (fig. 126). This project was probably related to the Concorso Clementino of 1795 at the Accademia di San Luca in Rome, where the project for the first class was a sepulchral chapel in the center of a vast piazza. Both the winning design by Giovanni Campara and the drawings by Barberi resemble La Barre's undated sepulchral chapel with its Pantheon-like central monuments and flanking pyramids. The difference in scale, though, between Barberi's funerary precinct and La Barre's compact monument brings to mind the vastness of the cemeteries envisioned by Fontaine and Boullée. At the other end of the scale, drawings by an anonymous Italian architect of a mausoleum for a French

115
Pierre-Adrien Pâris,
stage set for
*Numitor*, performed
at Fontainebleau,
1783.

116
Pantheon, Rome,
118–128 A.D.
Interior view by
Francesco Piranesi.

*The Sublime*

117
Church of the Holy
Sepulcher, Jerusalem,
restored 1045–1048.
From Le Brun,
*Voyage au Levant*,
1714.

118
Etienne-Eloy de La
Barre, sepulchral
chapel, 1780s.

119
Jean-Charles
Delafosse, sepulchral
chapel, 1780s.

120
Louis-Jean Desprez,
*The Kingdom of
Death*, c.
1777–1784.

121
*Death*. From the
Hertel edition
(1758–1780) of
Ripa, *Iconologia*.

*The Neoclassical World of Death*

122
Pietro Gonzaga,
necropolis.

123
Anonymous,
necropolis, late
eighteenth century.

*The Sublime*

124
Giuseppe Borsato,
*aula sepocrale*, 1799.

*The Neoclassical World of Death*

125
Anonymous, *aula
sepocrale*, early
nineteenth century.

126
Giuseppe or Paolo
Emilio Barberi,
cemetery, 1795 (?).

*The Sublime*

sovereign reflect a transitional period when architects still conceived of the funerary building on a gigantic scale but placed it in nature, surrounded by trees (figs. 127–128). By showing the building during the day and the night, the artist has been able to use nature to complement the message of his architecture. Death is the subject of the moonlit nighttime scene, which shows the entrance into the lower crypt. The other view speaks of immortality, as the mausoleum, with its pure, geometric forms and crowning dome, rises nobly against the daytime sky.

In contrast to these varied interpretations of interior and exterior spaces of death built above the ground, there was the fascination with catacombs. In 1782 an anonymous writer reminded Parisians that the practice of burying the dead in underground catacombs was an ancient custom. Travel accounts told of the vast catacombs of Memphis and Thebes, of Rome, Agrigento, Catania, Palermo, Syracuse, and even of Peru. Paris had extensive underground quarries, which seemed to await a similar use. To transform the quarries into catacombs, it was argued, would not only solve the problems of burials, but would also ensure the regular maintenance and policing of the precarious underground world of abandoned quarries. At this time, Parisians were haunted by the threat of a cataclysmic cave-in of their city. Rumors of this grave danger gained credence with several serious incidents in 1774. After an inspection of the quarries in 1776, the authorities declared "that the temples, the palaces, and most of the streets in the southern neighborhoods of Paris were ready to tumble into this immense abyss." The king's Conseil d'Etat, after consultation with members of the Académie Royale d'Architecture, established a special commission on April 4, 1777, to oversee the operations necessary to protect the city against further cave-ins. On the recommendation of the commissioners, a permanent Administration Générale des Carrières was formed under the direction of an inspector general.

Although the abandoned quarries were not immediately used for burials, a portion under the Plaine de Montrouge was employed as an ossuary to receive the bones from the *charniers* of the former Cemetery of the Holy Innocents. The transfer of bones began in December 1785. With the subsequent demolition of the Church of the Holy Innocents and the *charniers*, the funerary monuments were also moved to this site and were apparently grouped around the entrance. The Catacombs were officially opened with a Church benediction on April 7, 1786. In 1789, the reporter to the Société Royale de Médecine described the opening of the Catacombs as a re-creation of primordial chaos: "The appearance of this subterranean place, its thick vaults which seem to sever it from the realm of the living . . . the profound silence, the frightful din from the crashing bones thrown in here and rolling with a clamor which echoed far away: everything in those moments recalled the image

127
Anonymous, royal
mausoleum, 1780s.

128
Anonymous, royal
mausoleum, 1780s.

*The Sublime*

129
Anonymous,
catacombs, 1780s.

*The Neoclassical World of Death*

130
Catacombs of Paris.
View by Cloquet
from Héricart de
Thury, *Description
des Catacombes de
Paris*, 1815.

131
Catacombs of Paris.
View by Cloquet
from Héricart de
Thury, *Description
des Catacombes de
Paris*, 1815.

of death and everything presented the spectacle of destruction." Originally the bones were simply dumped into the quarries. During the revolution the Catacombs were used to bury the dead from various massacres as well as to transfer the bones from churches and cemeteries which were then being closed.

The somber but majestic underground world of intersecting and seemingly endless corridors fascinated the contemporary imagination. Artists drew inspiration from this theme (fig. 129) while Quatremère de Quincy relished in describing the streets and piazzas of these veritable "subterranean cities" of the dead. Writers appreciated the symbiotic relationship of catacombs to a city, as an underground void corresponding to the mass of buildings for the living. Ledoux, as has been seen, based his cemetery design for Chaux on this idea. In 1810–1811, under the direction of the Prefect Frochot and the Inspector General of Quarries, Héricart de Thury, the Catacombs of Paris were put in order (figs. 130–131). Walls were constructed with skulls and bones to provide a macabre decoration reminiscent of the Capucine chapels in Rome. The Catacombs, in their visual ambiance and through their inscriptions, had the last word in Paris on the relationship of death to the sublime: "Silence, mortal beings! Nothingness." "Vain grandeur, silence! Eternity."

# II

*THE*
*LANDSCAPE*
*GARDENER*
*AND THE*
*CEMETERY*

# 4

## The Arcadian Landscape (1712–1781)

In the third quarter of the eighteenth century, the cemetery as peaceful landscape garden became the preferred alternative to the macabre burial grounds that were rooted in the theology of the Middle Ages. This new conception of the cemetery had its origin in the landscape garden, which originated in England in the early eighteenth century and later spread to the continent. It is tempting to say that the landscape cemetery naturally evolved out of the landscape garden. Not only did such gardens depart radically from the aesthetics of their predecessors; they were also intimately associated with death and commemoration. With the beginnings of the picturesque landscape, the tomb entered the garden. As the landscape garden developed, so too did the tomb acquire an increasing claim to its space and its meaning. The history of this development will be discussed in the following two chapters: first the emergence of the landscape garden in England and its interpretation on the continent and then the literary and landscape influences in France that crystallized the vision of the cemetery as an Elysium or Field of Rest.

### A Natural Gardener

The origins of the landscape garden can be traced to a new world view in which the boundless prospect was appreciated aesthetically while it was identified with God's immensity. Ernest Tuveson explains that it was Joseph Addison who joined the experiential and theological components of a new understanding of both divinity and the physical world that had been in preparation since Henry More's identification of God with the infinite space of the universe in 1646. Newton's definition of space as the "sensorium of God" and Locke's explanation of our ideas of God as issuing from the contemplation of infinity were features of this development.

Just as the new concept of sublimity derived largely from the enthusiastic contemplation of the awe-inspiring features of the natural world, so too did this new orientation produce a longing for uninterrupted views and extended prospects in the design of the country estate. Timothy Nourse, a preacher whose *Campania Faelix* (1700) was reissued in 1706 and 1708, probably reflected an emerging frame of mind as much as he influenced it in advocating an eminence as the only acceptable site for a country seat for just this reason.

Stephen Switzer's *The Nobleman, Gentleman, and Gardener's Recreation*, first published in 1715 and then expanded and accompanied by illustrations in 1718 as the *Ichnographia Rustica*, crystallized many of the developing attitudes toward the landscape into a coherent design. Drawing heavily on Addison's counsel to "throw open" an entire estate to become a garden, thereby uniting lawns and fields with walks, and planting mounds and marshes for profit as well as for pleasure, Switzer took the creative leap by furnishing a plan for what before had been only a general literary formula. Like Addison, Switzer admired the expansiveness of the French gardens. Both the visual evidence of Switzer's "forest or rural garden" (fig. 132) and the supporting commentary in the text reveal that Le Nôtre's garden at Versailles provided Switzer with a point of departure (fig. 133).

Switzer's improved version of Versailles posited a model, to borrow Addison's phrase, of "artificial rudeness" to replace the "neatness and elegancy" of the comparatively smaller and delimited Dutch gardens so popular in England. The clipped hedges and tonsured trees shaped like geometrical figures and animals, which Pope had ridiculed in a celebrated essay of 1713 in *The Guardian* (no. 173), would have no place here. Having trained with the royal gardeners London and Wise, Switzer was no stranger to "La Grand Manier" [*sic*] of the French garden. The engravings of *Britannia Illustrata* (1709) and then the *Nouveau Théâtre de la Grande Bretagne* (1714–1716) show how popular the expansive formal garden modeled after Le Nôtre's work and propagated in England by London and Wise had become. Switzer's aim was to take this development one step further to break down the barriers, both conceptual and physical, between the garden and the estate and between the estate and the countryside.

As at Versailles, Switzer's landscape is organized about a major axis that begins along an esplanade in front of the house and which continues across a terrace to the rear and then through the entire property as an organizational spine. In the intermediate zone between the house and the beginning of the "canal," there are a series of minor cross axes with various formal landscape features adapted from the French example. Also as at Versailles, beyond this zone and to either side of the elongated canal are diagonal allées that extend through forest areas and fields. The principal difference between the two plans resides in the "many twinings and windings"—as many as an estate could accommodate—that cover all parts of Switzer's garden. These "serpentine meanders" were to add an element of surprise and variety to the garden by affording new views at all times.

The most radical features of Switzer's design are not apparent in his plan. Switzer welcomed the sight of gentle breezes blowing through the "loose tresses" of the trees, which would not be shaped into artificial walls. Watteau's drawings and paintings of this time, set in the magnificent parks by Le Nôtre whose formal lines were yielding a softer edge through lack of maintenance, well illustrate the "tall, stately and bold" effect that Switzer anticipated. Furthermore, beyond the terraces around the house, Switzer's garden welcomed and accepted the natural undulations of the land. Why go to great expense, he asked rhetorically, to fill up dales and to level hills, when they were "the beauty of

132
Stephen Switzer,
"Forest or Rural
Garden," 1718.

*A Natural Gardener*

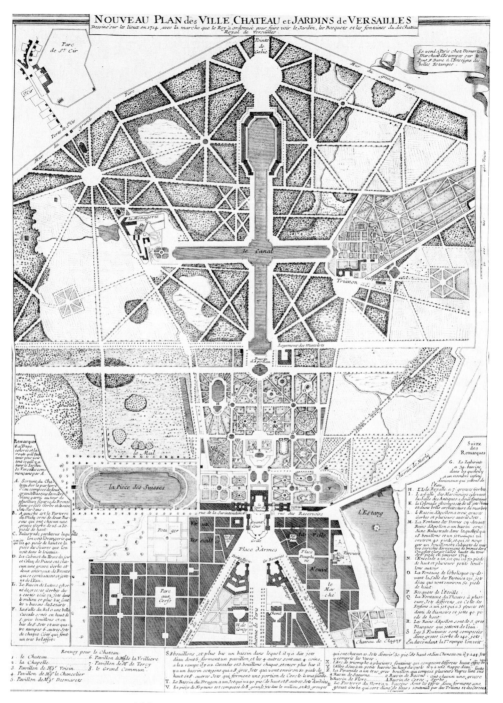

133
Versailles. Château
and gardens in 1714.

*The Arcadian Landscape*

nature?" At the perimeter of the estate, the traditional bounding wall which enclosed the property was to be replaced with raised terraces constructed with the earth removed to form an outer ditch. The effect would be visually to unify the garden and the countryside so that the latter would appear to be an extension of the former (fig. 134).

Switzer's landscape garden achieved unity through the application of a particular type of terrace. Whereas Dezallier d'Argenville's treatise on gardening of 1709, recently published in English as *Theory and Practice of Gardening* (1712), stressed the terracing of the land into stepped levels after the manner of Le Nôtre, Switzer introduced the notion of slightly elevated promenades.

To Switzer there were four types of terraces. Any garden lacking them was sorely deficient in design. The first, or "great," terrace was a broad platform around the mansion to dignify its setting and to provide a plinth from which it could be viewed. The garden itself was to be crisscrossed with flat elevated terraces two to three feet above the ground bordering the parterres and the lawns. A variant of this type of terrace was the walk cut into a side of the hill. Finally, there were the terraces that encompassed the garden. In all four cases, the terrace itself was regarded as an object of beauty and its aim was to provide a panoramic view.

Switzer's designs for a circumferential terrace are particularly important, for they are early versions of the English ha-ha, a device that revolutionized the design first of the garden and then of the cemetery. One type was fashioned by digging a trench and banking the earth to the inside. The counterscarp or outer wall would be gently sloped and planted; the inner side would be provided with a seven-foot-high masonry wall that would extend about two and a half feet above the level of the terrace to form a low parapet at the height of a seat. Switzer credited Sir John Vanbrugh with having introduced the dry ditch manner of terracing into England and hoped that it would become more popular. To Switzer, though, an even more beautiful way to bound the estate was to precede the terrace with a canal or watercourse in lieu of the masonry wall. In this way, the connection with the outer landscape would seem even more natural.

Historians have noted that the French already employed a limited form of this type of ditch, which they termed a *haha*. A brief comparison with this continental gardening feature is instructive, for it reveals that the English and French versions served very different conceptions of garden design. In French gardening, a series of parterres or a long allée was used to establish an enfilade, providing a long, uninterrupted view. This device had an architectural counterpart, the alignment of open doors through the principal rooms of a mansion to create an analogous effect. For

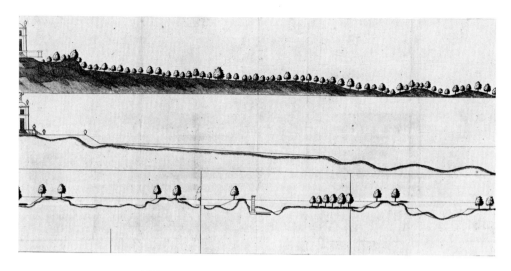

134
Stephen Switzer,
terraces and ha-ha,
1718.

*The Arcadian Landscape*

both garden and house, the enfilade was an organizing axis as well as an element of beauty and pleasure.

The principle of the enfilade being unlimited extension within an otherwise closed system, the axial views through a house would be extended through windows and out into the garden, across parterres to the rear, and through allées to the sides. In the city, when there was no possibility of opening up the walls with side windows, either mirrors or paintings of outdoor scenes were employed to create the impression of extended space. In the country garden, the bounding walls were open with a *claire-voie*, which was closed for reasons of security with a metal grill. This grill was sometimes eliminated in favor of a deep ditch, limited to the opening in the wall and shored up with a vertical masonry wall on both sides, to prevent access from without but to prolong the view from within. (The name "ah ah" or ha-ha derived from the exclamation of surprise as the stroller suddenly came upon this hidden boundary.) Neither Dezallier nor his translator wished to use the ha-ha to throw open the entire estate. To Dezallier, it merely permitted a better view through the opening in the wall. To John James, his English translator, the ha-ha was to be preferred to the traditional grill only "on some occasions." Perhaps the owner had to weigh the benefits of a better view with the loss of an impressive metal grillwork. Clearly the French ha-ha was a means to effect the limited opening of a contained outdoor room.

Switzer's version, then, was radically different. Its intent was to enable the stroller to "look either forward or backward, and view with pleasure the rude and distant scenes of nature, as well as the more elaborate works of art" within the garden. Even the detailing of the counterscarp contributed to the effect as the planted slope visually married the garden to the countryside.

Finally, to complement the boundless prospect, the estate would be provided with smaller features designed to convey a sense of intimacy within the landscape. Inside the garden there would be statues placed on a slight eminence and in small clearings in the woods, seats and arbors of honeysuckle and jasmine, coves, and, most important, water, especially as "little natural cascades and grotts of water." Using all of these elements together, Switzer felt justified in calling himself a "natural gardener."

**Paradise Regained**     Switzer's published work was important not only because of the new vision of the garden which it provided, but also because its author identified the extended garden fashioned in a more "natural" manner with the classical philosophy of the happiness found in country life. Throughout the seventeenth century, poets and essayists, in turning to Horace, Virgil, and a score of other ancient writers, had reformulated this *beatus ille* creed after their own needs. Abraham Cowley, whose enormously popular essays (published posthumously in 1668 with eight editions by 1693) were to find an important echo in Addison and Pope, had stressed both the scenery and activities of rural retirement as the basis for inner peace and happiness. Maren-Sofie Røstvig remarks that Addison was indebted to Cowley when he wrote: "True happiness is of a retired nature, and an enemy to pomp and noise." "It loves shades and solitude, and naturally haunts groves and fountains, fields and meadows." In the early eighteenth century, life on the country estate was considered not as a total withdrawal from the world but rather as a contribution to the public welfare through the improvement of the land. These dual themes of finding peace of mind and of reclaiming the land for agriculture and forestry were to characterize the philosophy of the landscape garden throughout the eighteenth century.

Switzer's text fully reflected these two orientations. This "gardenist" was lavish in his praise of the "seraphic" Cowley, who, along with Addison and Pope after him and with Horace and Virgil before him, provided numerous sources for citation. Switzer supplemented these sources with his own interpretations. To Cowley's praise of the simple contented life in the humble cottage, Switzer added the virtues of views across "distant woods and meadows."

Wherever Switzer looked, observed Røstvig, he seemed to find a classical precedent for the expansive landscape garden. According to Switzer, this orientation was only natural, for "of all the works of the creation, none calls for our attention more than the superficies of the earth, the work of the third day, the beautifulness there is in the prospect of it [,] the excellent uses and variety therein are studies and speculations that excel all others." To organize a country estate was to effect "a kind of new creation," imparting harmony to the inner man as well as profit to his family and dependents.

The expansive garden was the setting par excellence for spiritual life. Switzer speculated that if Adam and Eve had been allowed to remain in the Garden of Eden after the Fall, "it would have in some measure alleviated the dismal thoughts of mortality and that uncertain future state to which they were by their disobedience destined." In Milton's *Paradise Lost*, Switzer noted, Eve regretted the loss of an inner peace that she had found in "those happy walks and shades"; Adam lamented the loss of God's presence, which he had found in the trees, the wind, and the streams. In the final pages of his work, Switzer accepted death because he had attained his own inner peace through knowledge of Divinity afforded by a wondrous nature as found in the garden. The book ends with lines from Cowley in which the poet chooses to retain that harmony even in death by being buried in the garden.

Sweet shades, adieu! here let my dust remain.
Cover'd with flowers, free from noise and pain.
Let winged birds my epicedium sing
And murm'ring echoes distant tidings ring.
Let ever-greens the turfy tomb adorn,
And roscid dews, the glory of the morn,
My carpet deck; then let my soul possess
The happier scenes of an eternal bliss.

Here the modest tomb in the garden surrounded by the gently
moving features of the natural world is invoked as an intimation
of a heavenly paradise.

## The Elysian Fields of Castle Howard

Lest readers dismiss his treatise as mere fiction, Switzer insisted
that there were numerous estates where his principles were beginning to be applied. The importance of one example, to which
he so frequently and so enthusiastically returned, the sixty-six-
acre Wray Wood at Castle Howard, has led Christopher Hussey
to suggest that Switzer very likely played a major role in its development. The history of the gardens at Castle Howard in the
first three decades of the eighteenth century is instructive, for
here one finds the pioneering of the new aesthetic in gardening
joined with a new attitude toward death and commemoration.
In effect, this union amounted to a new purpose for the garden.
Castle Howard provided one of the first pastoral landscapes of
commemoration developed in the arcadian mode.

A poem, *Castle Howard* (1733), presumed to have been written
by Lady Irwin, daughter of the proprietor who created the gardens
at Castle Howard, Charles, Earl of Carlisle, explained the philosophy underlying the development of what Christopher Hussey
terms estate planning on the scale which Switzer was to advocate.
According to Hussey's account, the poem explains the conception
of the landscape garden at Castle Howard as an Elysium which
was to furnish "peace of mind" through a retirement from the
city to "innocent" rural activities. The term Elysium referred to
two types of classical landscapes. One was the Elysian Fields sung
by Homer, Hesiod, and Virgil as the abode of the worthy who
live eternally in a landscape of arcadian bliss:

In groves we live, and lie on mossie beds,
By crystal streams that murmur thro' the meads.
(*Aeneid*, 6, trans. Dryden, quoted in Switzer, 1715, p. 15)

In classical literature, this type of pastoral wonderland soon became
identified with a lost stage of human existence, the Golden Age,
in which material needs had been easily satisfied. This was the
other meaning of Elysium that Lady Irwin's poem evoked. To
restore the landscape of the Golden Age, along with its luxuriant
productivity, would be "to make those happy who on you de-
pend." Lord Carlisle and his gardenists translated this literary
vision into a landscape where

Buildings the proper points of view adorn
Of Grecian, Roman and Egyptian form
Interspersed with woods and verdant plains
Such as possess'd of old th'Arcadian swains.

Hence the traditional *beatus ille* theme was to be rendered as an expansive and informal landscape with classical buildings. Thus constituted, the garden was intended to evoke the arcadian setting of the classical sources. This setting, in turn, would unite the two versions of Elysium, the shady grove of the Elysian Fields for the worthy dead and the fruitful plains of the Golden Age. The main landscape and architectural features arranged to this end were the labyrinth in Wray Wood and the mausoleum and pyramid built out in the fields of Castle Howard.

Toward the second decade of the eighteenth century, Wray Wood was arranged with a series of irregular walks described by a visitor in 1732 as a "tangle of secret paths that rose and fell, twisted and crossed, leading from one circle to another." The northwestern edge of the property was bounded by a raised terrace and a wide ditch. This was the type of "forest or rural garden" that Switzer was advocating in his theoretical texts.

The destruction of the parish church occasioned by the Howard family's extensive building program created the need for a new structure to house the family's dead. This problem was solved by the construction of a classically inspired rotunda on a slight eminence in the open fields to serve as the family mausoleum. Plans for the design and siting of this mausoleum were followed in 1728 with those for the Howard pyramid, to be erected in honor of the earl's ancestor, the Elizabethan William Howard, whose marriage had resulted in the founding of the Howard estate. These two structures gave physical form to the image of Elysium that would soon be celebrated in Lady Irwin's poem.

The use of a garden to commemorate one's ancestors, to celebrate a noble lineage, and to identify a family's glory with a beautiful piece of property was by no means new. The method by which this was done, though, constituted a significant departure from the customary realizations. In the Italian Renaissance garden at the Cardinal d'Este's villa at Tivoli, for example, one finds a mythological landscape of beatitude where the cardinal's virtues and ancestry are celebrated by the statue of Hercules. The garden itself, with its formal, terraced design circumscribed within discrete boundaries, was conceived as a modern Garden of the Hesperides, the mythological equivalent of the Garden of Eden.

The contrast between this Italian example and the later Castle Howard could not be more striking. On the English estate, the pyramid commemorated a real person rather than a mythological ancestor, just as the mausoleum was erected to serve the actual family. Their siting in the rolling countryside made these fields an expansive landscape garden whose aspect evoked the Virgilian Elysian Fields while its harvests realized the Golden Age.

| The Cypress Grove | If Castle Howard represented the new spacious version of the |

**The Cypress Grove at Twickenham**

If Castle Howard represented the new spacious version of the landscape of the *beatus ille* creed joined to a dynastic conception of commemoration, Alexander Pope's garden of five acres at Twickenham by the Thames exemplified the traditional classical notion of finding inner peace on a more modest piece of property. In 1719, Pope, who as a Catholic was forbidden land ownership in England, rented the house whose garden he developed and embellished until his death in 1744 (fig. 135). In a sense Pope's garden embodied the ideal expressed by Horace in his sixth *Satire*: "This is what I prayed for!—a piece of land not so very large, where there would be a garden, and near the house a spring of ever-flowing water, and up above those a bit of woodland." Pope's garden was framed to either side by these two elemental, necessary, and sufficient components of a rural retreat.

The English poet, though, went even further than Horace's prescriptions, for he transformed his garden into a landscape of personal resonances. Both thematically and physically, this personalized garden began at the grotto and ended at the obelisk in honor of Pope's mother. Between the two, the garden was organized as a miniature version of Switzer's artificially "rude" landscape with a casual symmetry about an organizing axis.

The grotto was a convenient solution to having to tunnel under a public road to connect the lawn and house with the garden. Giving further purpose to this space, Pope developed the grotto as the opening feature in what Maynard Mack has termed a garden of "memory and meditation." Just as Pope's house was filled with pictures of close friends, so too was his grotto covered with geological specimens sent from all over the world by friends and admirers. As he dreamed and meditated in his "Grot," Pope was surrounded by glittering mementos of friendship.

Between the grotto and the memorial to Pope's mother nestled in the trees at the far end of the garden, Pope orchestrated a sequence of open and partially closed spaces that gave variety to the landscape, made it seem both larger and longer, and built to a climax. This was achieved largely by adumbrating a formal, axial organization that is always partially denied. The plantings to either side of the main promenade are almost but not quite identical; the quincunxes are not fully regular; the *rond-points* are not always complete; and the irradiating paths do not all intersect the center. While pairs of statues and urns help reinforce the axial nature of the progression as well as mark entry to the next space, they shift to the left or right of center; and the mount with a spiral path blocks the major line of sight. Furthermore, there are isolated straight and winding paths that provide further variety

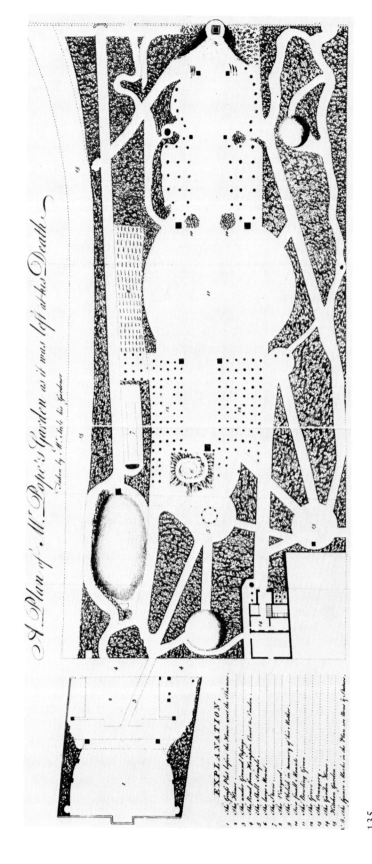

135
Alexander Pope's
garden at
Twickenham. Plan of
1745 by Serle.

*The Arcadian Landscape*

and contrasts. Whichever way one proceeded through the garden, whether along the central axis or through the thick plantings along the sides, the principal paths focused on the obelisk.

To make the garden seem more varied and less enclosed than it was, Pope dissimulated the edges with thick plantings and contrasted the dense vegetation with sudden clearings that gave the effect of suddenly expanding the vista. There is a deceiving simplicity to this plan, whose visual interest consisted largely in the successive compression and expansion of space along with the alternation of porous and hard edges through the use of widely spaced or densely clustered trees. This rhythmic succession of narrow and wider spaces was even more complex than a mere alternation of contrasting features. When, as at Twickenham, an open space such as the bowling green is placed between two more constricted allées, the narrow passageways tend to read together and the intervening open space to "disappear." As a stroller reaches the bowling green, the space suddenly opens in two directions, not only with a lateral expansion but also in length, as the full surface area of the clearing can then be ascertained and appreciated. At the end of the sequence, Pope sought to prolong the garden even further. The obelisk was placed upon a slight eminence flanked by screens of evergreens that came inward as they proceeded up the slope toward the monument. As Pope explained to Joseph Spence: "You may distance things by darkening them and by narrowing the plantations more and more toward the end, in the same manner as they do in painting, and as 't is executed in the little cypress walk to that obelisk."

Horace Walpole understood very well how the landscape and commemorative themes were fused. Pope's garden provided a carefully considered spatial sequence culminating in the obelisk: "the passing through the gloom from the grotto to the opening day, the retiring and again assembling shades, the dusky groves, the larger lawn, and the solemnity of the termination at the cypresses that lead up to his mother's tomb." As Mack has observed, Walpole's description corroborates exactly what the plan suggests: "that the poet's obelisk to the memory of his mother was in fact the point of visual and emotional climax for the observer in the garden." Through the obelisk nestled within a cypress grove, Pope sought in some manner to "repossess" his mother, to keep her present.

Both in England and abroad the elegiac character of Pope's garden was widely and deeply appreciated. In the third volume of the masterly *Théorie de l'art des jardins* (1781), Christian Hirschfeld credited the English with having introduced what had become a universal practice of erecting memorials in the form of urns, columns, and buildings in the garden. Hirschfeld recalled with pleasure that one of the first such monuments had been the obelisk erected through filial piety by Pope in his garden at Twickenham.

**The Elegiac Shenstone**

Perhaps no gardenist did more to popularize the memorial than the poet William Shenstone at his garden, the Leasowes (fig. 136). Just as Pope's gardening activity was paralleled by his literary work of the 1730s in the *beatus ille* tradition, Shenstone devoted much of his literary and landscape activity to the elegy. Once, in contemplating the publication of his elegies, Shenstone imagined that they would be accompanied by scenes of his garden. The connection between the elegiac sentiment and the landscape could not be made more explicit. As if to satisfy the poet's wishes, Robert Dodsley preceded the elegies in the posthumous publication of Shenstone's works with a vignette showing a "solemn" funerary urn in a grove (fig. 137). Shenstone's elegies were plaintive laments in which the poet regretted some loss—a loss of youth, friendship, love, or life.

In Shenstone's circle of literary friends, it was common to refer to the Leasowes, as well as to other gardens, as Arcadias. These were landscapes of illusion, conceived according to the *beatus ille* tradition and intended to evoke the mythical realm of Arcady. While Arcadia actually had been a rugged area of Greek countryside identified with Pan, Virgil had promulgated an engaging myth when he transplanted the bucolic scenes of Sicily, which had been sung by Theocritus, to an idealized Arcadia, land of perpetual spring. As Erwin Panofsky points out, Virgil may very well have erected the first literary tomb there, when, in the *Fifth Eclogue*, the friends of Daphnis engage in an elegiac remembrance as they raise "a lasting monument" to his memory.

This dual aspect of Arcadia, the pastoral amusement and the solemn meditation at the memorial, informed both the design and spirit of the Leasowes. Joseph Heeley captured the sense of the contrasting scenes and accompanying moods as he described the juxtaposition of the statue "of a piping Faunus fancifully glancing within a break of the trees" with "the soft murmurs of a rill, and a lone urn in a solitary nook." The first scene called forth feelings of "festivity" and the second inspired a "solemn meditation . . . those tender feelings of which we are susceptible when any circumstance recurs to revive the memory of a lost friend." In borrowing terms from Milton's twin poems, contemporaries would often refer to such scenes as stimulating "allegro" and "penseroso" moods. This pairing of cheerful and solemn scenes was to become an underlying feature of the English landscape garden.

The Leasowes was actually a farm—a "perfectly Arcadian farm"—which Shenstone embellished as a highly evocative landscape. The entire property was organized as a sequence of spaces

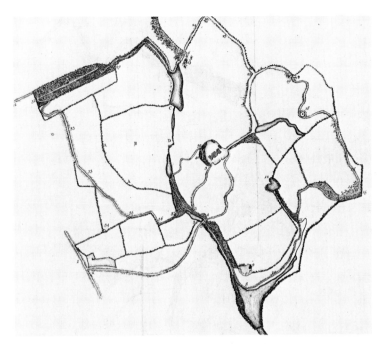

136
William Shenstone,
the Leasowes, plan
of 1764.

ELEGY I.

137
Shenstone, vignette
to *Elegy I*. From the
posthumous edition
of Shenstone's
works, 1764.

*The Elegiac Shenstone*

alternating between groves and fields. The openings between the enclosures were varied to include circumscribed views directed inward and expansive prospects extending out into the neighboring countryside. In general, the groves at the Leasowes—"each consecrated grove"—were commemorative in nature. Water, in the form of ponds, streams, or rills, accompanied the stroller through much of his course and helped to determine the mood. In contrast to the "twinings and windings" of Switzer's plan (fig. 132), which appear as arbitrary patterns, the meandering lines at the Leasowes seem to have followed the natural contours of the land. In a sense, the aesthetics of this landscape, marked by a gentle serpentine of paths, landforms, lines of trees, and waterways, reflected the natural and easy wanderings of the mind. At the Leasowes the visitor was encouraged to open his heart and to yield himself to the sweet nostalgia of the elegiac mode.

In this landscape, elegiac sentiment found expression as one aspect of a more general desire to commemorate friendship. Hence, as in other English gardens toward the middle of the eighteenth century, there were urns, seats, and little buildings consecrated to the memory of living as well as deceased friends. Like Pope's garden at Twickenham, the Leasowes was developed as a garden of remembrance. While they lived, the writers Richard Graves and Richard Jago, both close friends of Shenstone's, were each honored with a seat intended as a token of Shenstone's affection and esteem. There was also a seat in a clump of stately beeches inscribed to Joseph Spence. In a valley, there was a "handsome urn" dedicated to Shenstone's brother. The urn by that murmuring rill so much appreciated by Heeley was inscribed:

To the genius and friendship of William Somerville,
William Shenstone erected this urn
Sprinkling with tears the ashes
Of his poetical friend.

One of the most special places at the Leasowes was Virgil's Grove. It was situated in a small, deep valley described by Dodsley as "opake and gloomy." A stream with mossy banks flowed through the declivity, which was bordered on the sides with thick undergrowth and filled with lofty trees rising from the valley floor. Upon entering through a wicket, Heeley found the "illusion" of a perfect Elysium. A small obelisk to one side under the shade of several old oaks was inscribed to Virgil. Farther on there was a seat inscribed to James Thomson, commonly celebrated as "the English Virgil." Thomson's memorial was doubly apt because nearby was the fountain that he had so much enjoyed during his visits to the Leasowes. The seat thus marked the place that had once given pleasure to a friend and, in a manner of speaking, evoked his presence.

At Hagley, the neighboring gardens developed by Lord Lyttleton, this method of honoring a friend's pleasure in a garden, of conjuring up his presence, and, in a sense, of summing up his character with a landscape, was developed even more thoroughly. As at the Leasowes, Heeley felt himself transported to Arcadia: "and you cannot help fancying yourself, as you recline on a screen, under a bush of laurels, near the old oak, to be within those happy regions of the rural deities, which the classic muse so sweetly sings." Heeley was in this mood as he came upon an urn along the way that Pope used to call "his walk." Pope had actually chosen the setting for this piece; and accordingly, upon the poet's death, Lord Lyttleton dedicated it to his memory. Likewise, farther along the walk there was a Doric portico, called Pope's building, which was inscribed, "To Quiet and the Muses."

Thomson also had been a friend who visited Hagley. The "handsome" octagonal building erected to the poet's memory was situated at the very spot "which when living he delighted in." Since this was also the scene of greatest variety in the park, it served as a fitting memorial to the character of "the ingenious and descriptive Thomson," poet of the seasons. Shenstone too had his place at Hagley in the form of an urn situated in a deep glen with tall oaks.

To the memory of
William Shenstone, Esq.
In whose verses
Were all the natural graces,
And in whose manners
Was all the amiable simplicity
Of pastoral poetry;
With the sweet tenderness
Of the elegiac.

**Et in Arcadia ego**  This outpouring of elegiac sentiment was, as Panofsky has observed, out of proportion to the isolated reference in Virgil's *Fifth Eclogue*. Rather, these many urns reflected a deeply felt sentimental orientation in the English gardenists, which was sustained by their misreading of Nicolas Poussin's second and more famous painting of the theme *Et in Arcadia ego* (fig. 138). In Shenstone's time, this painting of four people at a tomb in the countryside seemed to capture the essence of Arcadia in a wistful meditation over the grave. Actually, Poussin's painting was a highly subtle classicized rendition of the traditional *memento mori*.

We have seen how in the late Middle Ages the Cemetery of the Holy Innocents in Paris and the Campo Santo of Pisa were painted with reminders of mortality such as the Legend of the Three Living and the Three Dead. Likewise, beginning in the fifteenth century, the still life, either in marquetry or on canvas, was sometimes conceived as a *Vanitas* with a skull representing the presence of death within the fragile and fleeting pleasures of life. Toward

138
Poussin, *Et in
Arcadia ego*, c.
1635–1636.

*The Arcadian Landscape*

1621–1623, Giovanni Francesco Guercino painted a variation on this theme in the earliest pictorial rendition of Death in Arcadia. Here two shepherds suddenly come upon a skull on top of a pedestal inscribed "Et in Arcadia ego." The skull is a death's head, that is, the personification of Death, which speaks through the inscription: "Even in Arcadia, I hold sway." "In short," writes Panofsky, "Guercino's picture turns out to be a medieval *memento mori* in humanistic disguise—a favorite concept of Christian moral theology shifted to the ideal milieu of classical and classicizing pastorals."

Close to a decade later Poussin painted his own first version of this theme. Although the meaning of his depiction was basically the same, he introduced several changes. First, he altered the emblematic character of the landscape. Guercino's skull is viewed against a desolate prospect with a broken tree echoing the other symbolic images of the fly and the mouse, which were commonplace emblems for death. Poussin, on the other hand, set his scene in a softer landscape. He replaced the base of rough stones with a large, classicized sarcophagus. The two shepherds, dressed not as the seventeenth-century peasants of Guercino's painting, but rather as true inhabitants of Arcady, have been joined by a woman. Thus, Poussin introduced a disjunction between the peaceful Arcadian scene and its jarring message about death.

In Poussin's painting, the attention of these Arcadians is riveted on the inscription, which they have almost finished reading. They do not seem to notice the dark skull, which the viewer sees sitting on the lid of the tomb above their heads. Whereas in Guercino's painting the country swains are absorbed in their unexpected encounter with death, in Poussin's rendition the startled Arcadians have not yet grasped the meaning of what they have suddenly found. In Guercino's painting both the real viewer and the figures in the canvas reach the same understanding at the same time. In Poussin's painting, though, there is a discrepancy, a tension between what the Arcadians are about to discover and what the viewer already understands. The dramatic character of this scene is reinforced both by the figures' surprise and by the diagonal and perspective arrangement of the composition.

Poussin's second painting (fig. 138) develops this temporal discrepancy between the Arcadians and the viewer in a subtle way. Everything about this composition conveys a deceptive serenity as the meaning gradually unfolds to the Arcadians while revealing itself fully only to the viewer at the end of the visual narrative. The composition is presented almost frontally with a simple tomb replacing the Baroque curves of its predecessor. The shepherds are not seen suddenly discovering the tomb but rather as engaged in a careful and perhaps lengthy consideration of the inscription. Finally, even the diminished death's head has disappeared.

Having ascertained these features, the viewer is prepared to follow the gestures and faces of the shepherds as the painting shows itself to be orchestrated according to a sequence of increasing knowledge. The shepherd to the far left reflects uncomprehendingly upon the puzzling inscription as he leans casually on Death, which is represented here as the tomb itself. The second figure kneels to come closer to the words and hence to the meaning. As he points to the inscription that he is about to decipher, he also points unwittingly to his shadow thrown against the tomb. The shadow of his head falls exactly across the inscription. This shadow is a representation of the spirit or soul: the classical shades, or manes. The third figure has already begun to understand and is about to convey his partial realization and perhaps question the placid goddess who, while resting one hand on his back, appears absorbed in the deepest reflection. Her wisdom is shared only with the viewer, who completes the cycle with the full realization that death is even in Arcadia.

While Poussin's friend and biographer Bellori realized that the message "Et in Arcadia ego" was another way of saying, "Death occurs in the very midst of delight," subsequent viewers radically altered the meaning. Thirteen years later, in 1685, Félibien, Poussin's second biographer, supposed there to be a person in the tomb whose death, nonetheless, conveyed the same lesson. Although the meaning of the tomb had been changed, the menace remained. The full transformation into an elegiac reading of the scene came with the Abbé Dubos's popular *Critical Reflections on Poetry and Painting*, first published in French in 1719, which went through numerous editions and translations throughout the eighteenth century. In Dubos's description of the painting, the sarcophagus became the tomb of "a young maid snatched away in the flower of her age." To Dubos, the Latin inscription referred to this young woman. Thus, for Dubos, "Et in Arcadia ego" meant "Je vivais cependant en Arcadie," or, in the words of Dubos's translator, "And I was once an inhabitant of Arcadia." As Panofsky points out, this rendition is grammatically incorrect but possible to a mind that wishes to find an elegiac theme.

Dubos speculated that the young people, whom he describes as two couples, are at first saddened by the thought that death "spares neither age nor beauty." These feelings, though, soon change into an elegiac mood as they make "affecting speeches" to each other. At this point, Dubos suggested that the reader too would reflect wistfully about the death of dear ones. This interpretation of Poussin's *Et in Arcadia ego* would resound throughout the eighteenth century as the major poets of nature and the champions of the elegiac landscape, such as Shenstone, Hirschfeld, and the Abbé Delille, found in it the epitome of man's relationship to the dead.

Upon reading Abbé Dubos's description of Poussin's painting, Shenstone could not wait to use the inscription in his garden. "The *idea* of it is so very pleasing to me, that I had no peace till I had used the inscription on one side of Miss Dolman's urn, 'Et in Arcadia Ego.' " The Lover's Walk at the Leasowes was situated on a slope deeply shaded by trees and accompanied by "a small bubbling rill." The "very soft and pensive scene" was "terminated" by Shenstone's urn to Maria Dolman, described by Dodsley as "a beautiful and amiable relation of Shenstone's" and by Heeley as a young woman "whom [Shenstone] much loved, and whose death he most sincerely lamented" (she had died of smallpox toward the age of twenty-one). In her memory Shenstone had nestled a gilt urn among the shrubs and inscribed it:

Ah Maria!
The most elegant of maidens;
Alas! snatch'd away in
The bloom of beauty,
Farewell!
How much less pleasure there is in surviving
Than in remembering thee!

What Dubos had observed of Poussin's *Arcadia* was to be true of the garden: each scene was intended to prompt reflection. Gardens like Hagley and the Leasowes were landscapes of meditation. For their owners, a walk through these pastoral settings was like a journey through an externalized portrait of the mind and a record of the heart. After Shenstone's death, his contribution to the elegiac sentiment of the garden was repaid in the following lines, left anonymously on a seat at the Leasowes:

O Earth! to his remains indulgent be,
Who so much care and cost bestowed on thee!
Who crown'd thy barren hills with useful shade,
And chear'd with tinkling rills each silent glade;
Here taught the day to wear a thoughtful gloom,
And there enliven'd Nature's vernal bloom.
Propitious earth! lie lightly on his head,
And ever on his tomb thy vernal glories spread!

Like Virgil and Thomson, Shenstone took his place in the memorial groves of the garden. The conviction that the friend of nature deserved above all others a tomb or memorial in the garden was to become a commonplace in the latter half of the eighteenth century. Eventually, an influential group of French intellectuals and statesmen would insist upon the same treatment for their own friends and family. In the 1790s, an entire society would see itself as the friend of nature and wish for the same communion with the departed in a garden that Pope, Shenstone, and Lyttleton had found decades before. Shenstone and his friends not only changed the meaning of *Et in Arcadia ego* to signify that the deceased had once known the felicities of a beatific life; their memorial urns also suggested that in death, the spirit of the departed remained, in some manner, in the garden. Therein resided the more profound alteration of the painting's inscription. Soon the memorial would be replaced by the actual tomb in the garden. Likewise, Poussin's inscription would undergo a further metamorphosis of meaning to suggest that in death one passed directly into Arcadia.

## The Elysian Fields at Stowe

While the Leasowes provided the model for the personalized elegiac memorial, the garden at Stowe, in Buckinghamshire, popularized the ideal of honoring public virtues. Its most renowned feature, known as the Elysian Fields, was not only intimately associated with this theme but also introduced a new aesthetic into the "natural" design of gardens. After the creation of the Elysian Fields at Stowe in the mid-1730s, the estate was expanded and the earlier garden revised so that the softer contours of the Elysian Fields were extended over areas originally laid out with a certain formality (figs. 139–140). The Elysian Fields at Stowe, perhaps more than any other British landscape garden, were to affect profoundly the French idea of what a cemetery should be.

The history of Stowe is inseparable from that of the evolution of the landscape garden. The first house and gardens, created by Sir Richard Temple, father of Lord Cobham, both reflected the new appreciation of the extended landscape. Toward 1675–1683, Temple constructed his house on the crest of a hill to secure a magnificent prospect twenty-five miles long that culminated in the steeple of a medieval church. A formal garden terraced into three levels of parterres descended down the slope. To the west, past an old walled kitchen garden, there was a kind of wilderness, an informal area with "crisscross paths and only private walks." This portion was terminated with a mount upon which one could take in an extended view. While Temple's garden did not last long beyond his death, the house on the hill became the basis for future additions and still stands as the core of the present building.

If Lord Cobham's first attentions to his gardens dated from 1713–1714 when he and other Whigs were forced into retirement, it was his ambitious building and gardening program of 1720, when he had regained power and had acquired new wealth, which presented the first decisive development of the estate. The garden that Charles Bridgeman designed at this time was in every respect a skilled application of the principles of Switzer's "rural garden." Working with a real site as opposed to Switzer's ideal estate, Bridgeman used the long axis, *rond-points*, formal basins, open fields, winding paths through bosquets, and elevated terraces to secure emphasis and hierarchy where Switzer had allowed repetitious detail to vitiate his overall conception. Moreover, the addition of Vanbrugh's buildings, which terminated the vistas, added

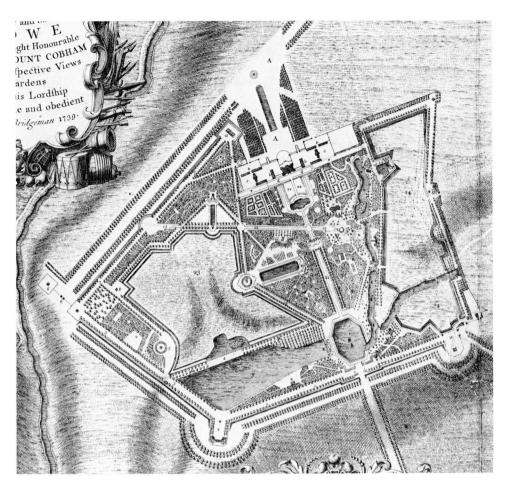

139
Stowe, 1739.

*The Elysian Fields at Stowe*

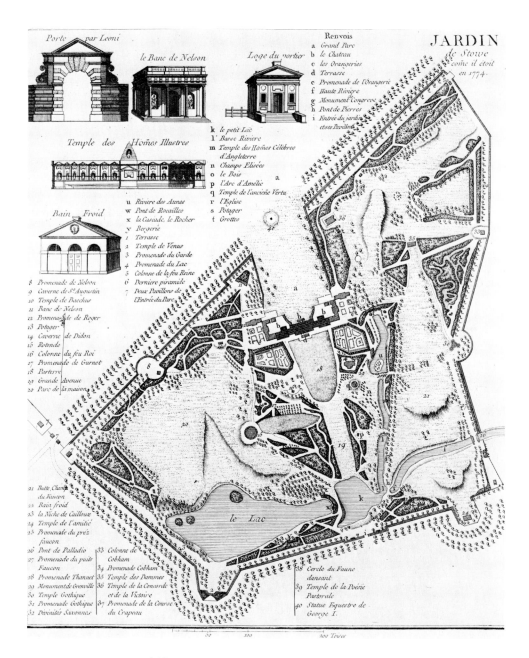

140
Stowe, 1774. From
Le Rouge, *Nouveaux
jardins anglo-chinois
à la mode*, 1776.

an element absent from Switzer's plan and were a capital feature that married art to nature in a way that Switzer had not anticipated. The garden buildings also provided the occasion for an emblematic reading of the landscape.

By the time of Gilbert West's poem about Stowe (1731), in which he likened the gardens to the Elysian Fields, the principal iconological themes had been firmly established. There were pastoral monuments with either benign and lofty or bawdy and playful messages, monuments to civic virtue that sustained the Whig's anti-Stuart, anticlerical, and pro-"1688" convictions, and funerary memorials erected as expressions of friendship and esteem. One of these memorials was an obelisk to the Reverend Robert Coucher, who had been the chaplain to Cobham's Dragoons. The other was a sixty-foot-high "pyramid" (fig. 142) constructed by Vanbrugh and consecrated to the architect by Lord Cobham after his death with the engraved epitaph: "This, sacred to thy Memory shall stand: Cobham, and grateful Friendship so command." Both memorials were located along the elevated terraces around the open area known as Home Park.

Of particular importance to the future development of the Elysian Fields were the eight memorial statues placed around James Gibbs's building toward the southwest corner of Home Park. Here, among the "darksome green" of tall firs and "mournful yews," a "sacred band of princes [Queen Elizabeth and William III], bards [Shakespeare, Milton] and sages [Bacon, Locke, Newton]" constituted, along with the martyred patriot John Hampden, a national Elysium. This Whig ensemble of statues was accompanied by a Latin inscription from Virgil's account of the Elysian Fields:

Here is the band of those who suffered wounds, fighting for fatherland; those who in lifetime were [priests and pure—omitted], good bards, whose songs were meet for Phoebus; or they who ennobled life by truths discovered and they who by service have won remembrance among men—the brows of all bound with snowy fillet.
(Aeneid, 6: 660–664)

With the completion of the western approach road to Stowe house in 1731, Lord Cobham was free to develop the eastern portion of his gardens. He could now take over the old approach road, the Hew Way, which wound through a narrow valley along the eastern edge of Bridgeman's gardens. Shortly after Gilbert West visited Stowe, Cobham's designers, generally considered to be William Kent and Bridgeman, flooded this valley to make a meandering river and developed a glade around it under the name of the Elysian Fields. Farther east and much like the Home Park to the west, an area called Hawkwell Field was surrounded by terraces dotted with garden buildings. When Bridgeman's wife published a plan of her husband's design for Stowe in 1739, two years after his death, the Elysian Fields were virtually complete,

141
Stowe. Monument to
William Congreve,
1736.

142
Stowe. View of 1739
by Rigaud showing
Home Park and the
pyramid dedicated to
the memory of
Vanbrugh (detail).

*The Arcadian Landscape*

as were the terraces, if not the buildings at Hawkwell Field.

These two eastern portions of the garden were dominated by the political themes established earlier in the western sector. The statues of those Britons "who by merit purchas'd lasting praise" were transferred to the Elysian Fields in the mid-1730s to become part of an elaborate allegorical landscape. Likewise, in the early 1740s the statues of the Saxon gods, placed around a "sylvan temple," were moved to Hawkwell Field to be recast in a new symbolic setting.

Whoever was responsible for the design of the Elysian Fields seems to have taken Virgil's description of its landscape quite literally. Here was "a land of joy, the green pleasaunces and happy seats of the Blissful groves" (*Aeneid*, 6: 637–639). Here were "the shady groves," the "cushioned river banks," and the "meadows fresh with streams" (ibid., 673–675). Already in the seventeenth century, as John Dixon Hunt has pointed out, there were images of a naturalistic setting for a paradisiacal abode, as found in Zacharias Heyns's emblem of Tempe and Milton's description of the Garden of Eden in *Paradise Lost*. At the Elysian Fields of Stowe, the literary and visual precedents were translated into a new vision of landscape. Several unlabeled drawings of garden designs by William Kent, in which he experimented with arranging trees in clumps and screens across a rolling landscape, probably convey the type of landscape first created at the Elysian Fields.

In recasting the political allegory previously centered on Gibbs's building, Lord Cobham and his associates drew inspiration from an allegorical dream related by Addison in *The Tatler* of January 1709 (nos. 120, 123). The translation of this text into an actual garden merits a brief consideration because it provided the inspiration for the building program as well as a new way of viewing architecture within the landscape. Both were to have important consequences for the future development of Stowe and then for its appreciation by continental observers who admired the elegiac aspect of its Elysian Fields. Although first conceived as a political satire, the Elysian Fields rapidly became the model for a new mode of burial.

Addison's "dream" presented an allegory of the human condition through the means of a garden or woods whose paths and buildings led the dreamer to an understanding of the nature of human motivations and actions. In the landscape of middle age, the dreamer found himself walking down a straight road bordered with laurels that sheltered trophies, pillars, and statues of lawgivers, heroes, statesmen, philosophers, and poets. This path terminated at a Temple of Virtue, which hid a Temple of Honor directly behind it. Access to the Temple of Honor was gained through a triumphal arch, which led to a room in the shape of a giant zodiac. At the center and seated on a globe was the figure of Eternity radiating light. Upon leaving the Temple of Honor, Addison espied another building "raised in imitation of it upon the very same model." Approaching this building, the dreamer discovered that it had been built without mortar and, furthermore, that it stood upon "so weak a foundation, that it shook with every wind that blew." This was the Temple of Vanity.

At the Elysian Fields the Temple of Virtue became the Temple of Ancient Virtue (fig. 143) just as the Temple of Honor was transformed into the Temple of British Worthies (fig. 144). The Temple of Vanity was made into a Temple of Modern Virtue (fig. 145). Rather than design the latter as a copy of the former, the architect drew upon the Vitruvian and Serlian distinction between tragic, comic, and "satyric" scenes, and the painters' distinction, as codified by Roger de Piles, between the heroic style and the rural style. The tragic scene was composed of Renaissance buildings, just as heroic painting required noble edifices. Hence the Temple of Ancient Virtue was placed on a slight eminence and made into a rotunda, a perfect and self-sufficient architectural form that since the Renaissance had been universally approved as the most noble of all building types. In contrast, the rural style presented "Gothick . . . or partly ruinous" (Roger de Piles) structures. To this end, the Temple of Modern Virtue was made into a rusticated ruin.

The Elysian Fields at Stowe, though, were not conceived as an abstract reflection upon human destiny but rather as a political allegory. The Temple of British Worthies represented the cause of the Whigs against the crumbling Temple of Modern Virtue, which was a commentary upon the shoddy ethics of the present government. A headless statue of the Prime Minister, Sir Robert Walpole, stood by the ruin to emphasize the point. Each of the sixteen niches in the Temple of British Worthies had a bust that carried a particular meaning in the controversy with the government that once again in 1733 had forced the most influential Whigs into retirement. The means of access between the Temple of Virtue and the Temple of British Worthies was not the triumphal arch of Addison's allegory but rather the river Styx of Virgil's *Aeneid*. From the steps of each monument, the other building could be seen mirrored in the water.

The landscape relationships between these two structures differed not only from the dream but also from those of the earlier monuments at Stowe. In contrast to the direct views at Home Park, the Elysian Fields introduced partial and oblique angles. The Temple of British Worthies was located obliquely downstream and across the water from the Temple of Ancient Virtue within a more "natural"-appearing landscape than had been seen before in a British garden.

*The Arcadian Landscape*

143
Stowe. Temple of
Ancient Virtue.

144
Stowe. Temple of
British Worthies.

145
Stowe, Temple of
Modern Virtue.

*The Arcadian Landscape*

In private diaries and correspondence as well as through published descriptions, the Elysian Fields of Stowe rapidly became the most celebrated part of the garden. The intricate political allusions, though, were lost to most observers. Horace Walpole exclaimed that he had no patience for "building and planting" a satire. In 1744, Lady Elizabeth Montagu appeared to find no ulterior significance. She spoke for an entire epoch when she characterized the monuments of the Elysian Fields and of the adjacent Hawkwell Field as an apolitical and idealized landscape that stirred the visitor to noble thoughts about civic virtue, genius, and friendship: "At Stowe you walk amidst Heroes and Deities, powers and persons whom we have been taught to honour, who have embellished the world with arts, or instructed it in Science, defended their country and improved it. The Temples that pleased me most for the design to which they were consecrated were those to 'Ancient Virtue,' to 'Friendship' and to 'Liberty.' "

With the death of Lord Cobham in 1749 and the subsequent work at Stowe by Richard Grenville, who became Lord Temple in 1752, the character of the Elysian Fields changed in such a way that visitors could be even more inclined to ignore its political message. By moving the rostral column to Captain Grenville (1737; fig. 146) from the Grecian Valley to the Elysian Fields, Lord Temple opened the closed story of the allegory, thereby implying that other monuments could be placed there in the future. Such individual memorials, moreover, added a personal and elegiac element to the Elysian Fields to complement the morally august nature of the temples. The inscription on the column for Captain Grenville lamented the death of so young and so engaging a person. At the same time, the character of the entire landscape at Stowe was changing as softer contours replaced the hard edges. In this way, the entire garden began to resemble the Elysian Fields, which themselves sustained comparable transformations (fig. 140).

Aesthetically and pragmatically, then, the Elysian Fields were no longer an isolated event. Memorials in other parts of the garden seemed to participate in the spirit of this area. The inscription on the obelisk for Congreve (1736; fig. 141), just below the Elysian Fields, explained that this was a monument of sadness that could never fully console its sponsor about the death of his friend. At the far end of Hawkwell Field was the one-hundred-fifteen-foot pillar, constructed as an observatory in 1747 but soon afterward consecrated to the memory of Lord Cobham, that could be seen throughout the gardens (fig. 147). Farther away and located in the park northeast of the gardens was the obelisk erected by Lord Temple to the memory of General Wolfe (fig. 148). By the 1770s, Stowe, it seemed, was becoming an outdoor Westminster Abbey.

The commemorative nature of Stowe, with the striking match

146
Stowe. Rostral
column to Captain
Grenville.

*The Arcadian Landscape*

147
Stowe. Lord
Cobham's Column.

148
Stowe. Obelisk to
General Wolfe.

*The Elysian Fields at Stowe*

between its memorials and its new realization of the Virgilian landscape, was much appreciated by Thomas Whately in his influential *Observations on Modern Gardening* (1770) as well as by François de Paule Latapie, whose translation of Whately's book was published in France in 1771. Whately had the highest praise for the Elysian Fields, where those "most distinguished for military, civil, or literary merit" found a worthy tribute. To this observer, the expressive features of nature created a mood "of delight and joy" appropriate to the theme. The lively stream flowing down the winding vale, the glimpses of the other stream that joined it to the south, the "sprightly verdure of the greensward," the reflections of the British Worthies in the water, and the variety of the trees along with the lightness of their foliage made the Elysian Fields a successful realization of its antique literary model.

So inspiring were the monuments at the Elysian Fields that De Latapie put aside his general aversion to sculpture and statuary in the garden. At Stowe, in contrast to Versailles, for example, architecture and landscape fit well together. In effect, for De Paule Latapie, the monuments constituted the heart of the scene. Nothing was more splendid than the busts of the great men of Britain viewed "in perspective under the laurel trees." What a pleasure, wrote De Paule Latapie, to wander through a grove and suddenly to discover a monument such as the obelisk erected by Lord Cobham to his friend Congreve. How inspiring was the rostral column constructed by Cobham in honor of his nephew Captain Grenville, who had died a naval hero while combatting the French. No natural scene, no matter how picturesquely disposed, could equal the impression of these monuments on the "sensitive" observer.

To the garden literature of the 1770s and early 1780s, the Elysian Fields at Stowe presented a new way of considering death along with a new landscape to sustain it. Rather than dwell upon human mortality, De Paule Latapie preferred an elegiac sorrow for lost friendship or an inspiring reminder of everlasting virture. Rather than consider gaping tombs, skulls, and crowded cemeteries, he favored encountering memorials to a cherished or admired spirit in a beautiful pastoral setting. The German garden theorist and moralist Christian Hirschfeld went one step further. He preferred the temples at Stowe—the Temple of Ancient Virtues, the Temple of British Worthies, and the Temple of Friendship—to the urns of the Leasowes, for the former inspired only noble thoughts while the latter still reminded one of death.

At Stowe, De Paule Latapie found death under the old and new guises. Just north of the Elysian Fields were the ancient parish church and cemetery. Although totally hidden from view by thick plantings of evergreens, this presence of gruesome death in the garden shocked the French visitor. The old graveyard at Stowe antedated the creation of the gardens, but De Latapie associated it with the cemeteries that he had seen in other English landscape gardens. Inspired by the black poetry of Edward Young, James Hervey, and Robert Blair, these macabre scenes were intended to horrify the visitor and hence to serve as *memento mori*. The degree to which French attitudes toward death had changed might be inferred from De Paule Latapie's complete rejection of such landscapes as inappropriate to the garden.

In advising his compatriots to follow the example of the Elysian Fields, De Paule Latapie helped to foster the ideal of death in the picturesque landscape. One can only speculate about whether Whately or De Paule Latapie would have accepted real graves rather than memorials in such gardens. The joining of the actual cemetery with the garden would take place in the minds of the garden theorists in the succeeding decade, as the burial of Jean-Jacques Rousseau on the Ile des Peupliers in the landscape garden at Ermenonville fused together the example of the English garden with a sentimental pastoral vision found in painting and literature.

# 5
## Death in the Garden (1762–1789)

The French rejection of the traditional image of the cemetery in favor of burial in a landscape garden took place in the decade preceding the revolution. The change came about gradually as wealthy landowners began to provide memorials and sometimes actual graves in their private gardens and as architects designed hybrid schemes that combined aspects of the old and the new. While the English had developed the garden style with the commemorative monument that served as the example, it was left to the French first to propose and then to plant and to build the urban cemetery after this model.

## Gessner and the Weeping Pastoral

The substitution of the actual tomb for the memorial in the garden was largely prepared by the work of the Swiss author Salomon Gessner. To Christian Hirschfeld, Gessner was the greatest pastoral poet of his time. The Abbé Delille went even further. Bury me, he wrote, beside Gessner and far away from Virgil. To his contemporaries, Gessner surpassed Virgil and Theocritus, the Greek poet whom Gessner claimed as his model. A name now generally unknown to those who are not specialists in either eighteenth-century studies or in the authors of the pastoral, Gessner was one of the most widely read writers of the second half of the eighteenth century. His work was particularly popular in France and, according to Paul Van Tieghem, in Paris. In his social history of literary trends, Van Tieghem concluded that Gessner's *Idylls* (*Idyllen*) enjoyed "one of the most rapid, most complete, and most universal successes ever seen in the literary history of Europe." First published in German in 1756, the *Idylls* were translated into French in 1762 and were joined by the *New Idylls* in 1772 with a French edition of 1773.

Van Tieghem's assessment is backed by praise from the major literary figures and artists of France from Gessner's time. Grimm, co-editor of the *Correspondance Littéraire*, was most enthusiastic in his appreciation of Gessner's work. So, too, were the *Journal Encyclopédique*, the *Mercure de France*, and *L'Année Littéraire*. Diderot proposed that the *New Idylls* appear simultaneously in German and French and contributed two of his own stories to complete the edition. Rousseau was an admirer from the time of the first French edition of Gessner's work. Bernardin de Saint-Pierre ranked Gessner among the "vast geniuses" of humanity. Several of the principal French creators of landscape gardens—Watelet, the Prince de Ligne, the Duc de Laborde, and the Marquis de Girardin—not only admired Gessner but paid him the tribute of a visit.

From the most elevated to the lowest literary public, Gessner was widely read and appreciated. His work was excerpted and reprinted in literary magazines on all levels of taste and sophistication. He also had readers of all ages. In the private secondary schools his work followed upon that of Theocritus and Virgil. Children's stories were fashioned from his pastoral tales. Gessner, Van Tieghem relates, was also widely copied: "In France, Gessner was particularly tempting for imitators. His idylls epitomized the tender and sweetly sentimental sensibility that was so popular in the decades of the 1760s and 1770s, and they expressed these feelings in a cadre new enough to prompt numerous imitators."

Gessner's message, in the words of his admirers, was virtue, not heroic virtue but the "virtues of everyday life." His idylls, recounting episodes in the life of the simple country folk of Arcadia, did not preach virtuous behavior but rather inspired it through the feelings that they imparted. The critics were unanimous in maintaining that reading Gessner made one feel a better person. William Coxe, in 1778, summarized Gessner's themes: paternal affection, filial respect, gratitude, thanksgiving, and humanity. Gessner's poetry not only made virtue "pleasant" and "touching" but also brought it into the reach of the ordinary family.

The *Idylls* were filled with exemplary domestic behavior. They portrayed the good father, the good mother, the loving spouses, the good son, and the good daughter. For this complete dramatis personae Gessner was much appreciated. His admirers praised him for extending the genre of the pastoral beyond the ever-recurring shepherd to concentrate on all members of the family. In Gessner the French found moving family scenes with a natural and primitive goodness in harmony with the pastoral surroundings. The sharp feelings of grief, fear, and anxiety that run through the *Idylls* of Theocritus were transformed into a cloying sentimentality. Crude and earthly gestures and expressions were replaced by ethereal feelings. Tears are never bitter in Gessner's *Idylls*. Melancholy is sweet and longing is filled with nostalgia. In all of this, the tomb played a major role in nurturing sentimental and virtuous feelings.

Gessner's *Idylls* gave birth to the cult of making a sentimental visit to the tomb of a loved one. In the 1770s and 1780s, Gessner's influence was largely on theorists of the garden and on several proprietors of the new picturesque landscapes. In the 1790s, his particular vision of the grave became a commonplace in the literature devoted to establishing a new type of cemetery. With Gessner, the tomb in the landscape became inseparable from the Arcadian scene (fig. 149). Gessner's tombs became a type of family altar to which the living often returned to pay homage, shed tears, and commune with the dead. When Bernardin de Saint-Pierre wrote that the tomb stands on the frontier between two worlds, he was capturing the essence of the Gessnerian idyll. Not only did the living find the presence of their departed loved ones there;

*Death in the Garden*

149
Tomb in the
landscape. From
Gessner, *Oeuvres*,
1797 edition.

they also drew moral inspiration from the visit. A brief sampling from several of the *Idylls* (in the French edition) will illustrate these points.

In "Mirtile," a young man watches over his sleeping father: "I will build an altar beside your tomb and every time that I have a favorable day with the opportunity of doing good for some unfortunate soul, I'll pour milk and spread flowers upon your altar!" In "Glicère," the tomb (fig. 150) is the altar itself at which the young virgin reaffirms her vows of purity: "One day, her eyes filled with tears, Glicère went to visit the solitary tomb where her [dead] mother rested. There she poured a cup of pure water and hung crowns of flowers from the branches of the bushes which she had planted around the grave. Seated in this sad shade . . . she said: 'Oh, most tender of mothers, how the memory of your virtues is dear to me! You have just saved by innocence. . . . Accept these garlands, receive my tears! May they penetrate all the way to you! Oh, Mother, listen, listen. By your ashes which rest under these flowers, which my tears have watered so often, by your sacred shadow, I renew my vows of purity and virtue.' "

In "Damète et Milon," the tomb and altar are the countryside itself. Damète's father is buried where he had transformed an unproductive nature into a fertile landscape. "There it is, my friend! Pour the [cup of wine] into this peaceful shade. Everything that you see here is a monument to his virtue." Similarly, in "Amyntas," a good man has fashioned a stream and planted a small grove of shade and fruit trees to provide a refuge for travelers. After his death, his son and daughter-in-law bury him there and surround his tomb with honeysuckle, willows, and creeping ivy, so that the dead Amyntas will receive the benediction of all the tired travelers who find refreshment there.

Finally, there was the story of Palémon, which Elie Fréron, director of *l'Année Littéraire* proposed as the model for future idylls. Palémon's wife, "dear Myrta," has been dead for twelve years, and he knows that soon he will join her. One night he visits the tomb with his children to pour a libation of honey and wine. "Just then, in the midst of their kisses, Palémon was changed into a cypress whose shadow still covers [Myrta's] tomb. The peaceful moon, witness of this event, stopped in its course." In a sense, in each of these idylls, Gessner took the arrested moment of Poussin's *Et in Arcadia ego* and gave it a scene. This is literally what the writer Jean-François Marmontel would do in his own version of Palémon (1792), which begins with several young shepherds and shepherdesses in a grove contemplating "in a religious silence" a tomb for a young woman on which is written: "I also lived in Arcadia."

O la plus tendre des meres...... tu viens
de sauver mon innocence !

*Idylle 42ᵉ*

150
Glicère at her
mother's tomb.
Illustration by J.-M.
Moreau le Jeune
from Gessner,
*Oeuvres*, 1797
edition.

All of these sources—the Leasowes, Stowe, Poussin, and Gessner—came together in France at the estate of the Marquis de Girardin, where Jean-Jacques Rousseau spent the last six weeks of his life and where he was buried in 1778. René-Louis de Girardin prepared one part of his estate specifically for Rousseau as the intimate Elysée, the private garden with murmuring streams, winding paths, "natural" plantings, and vine-covered trees that was Julie's own creation in Rousseau's popular novel *La Nouvelle Héloïse* (1761). Girardin himself called Ermenonville "the Leasowes of France" in tribute to the extended landscape with intimate scenes that had so deeply impressed him during a visit to the Leasowes in the 1760s.

Rousseau's death and Girardin's intention of burying the great author on his estate in the middle of a small island planted with poplars, the Ile des Peupliers, were widely reported and discussed in the press. In these texts, one finds a new attitude toward death and burial. Thiéry, for example, hoped that "the entire lugubrious apparatus" traditionally associated with death would not be present. To Thiéry, moreover, a thick woods with poplars seemed so much more appropriate than the "sad cypress." Rousseau, wrote Thiéry, had sought "to tear away the hideous mask" that had been given to death; thus his grave should be consonant with his lessons. In commenting on Rousseau's grave at Ermenonville (fig. 151), Hirschfeld noted that "there was nothing somber or sad" there, but rather, as *La Gazette Littéraire de l'Europe* had reported, only a feeling of melancholy. According to Hirschfeld, one had the impression that Rousseau was only "sleeping" there. The temporary tomb with a funerary urn was soon replaced by a stone sarcophagus *à l'antique* by Hubert Robert that was widely celebrated for its beauty (figs. 152–153). Not only did Hirschfeld report these successive transformations at the Ile des Peupliers; he also recognized that a significant development had occurred here. How fitting, he concluded, that in the park of Ermenonville, the person "to whom France owed the birth of its [natural taste] in gardens" was given "not simply a monument but an eternal tomb." To Hirschfeld, Rousseau's grave in a funerary bosquet offered the proper alternative to the often decried but long established custom of burying the dead within the city and "even" inside churches.

Girardin's tomb to Rousseau was more than a mark of friendship. It was a monument, as the inscription read, "to the friend of nature and truth." In his first and second *Discourses*, Rousseau had given his contemporaries the image of a natural man in harmony with himself before he had been corrupted by society. In *La Nouvelle Héloïse*, Rousseau had introduced the French to the pleasures of the *Elysée* garden as well as to the exhilaration of the view from a mountaintop. In *Emile*, Rousseau had taught

151
René de Girardin,
Ermenonville.
Rousseau's grave on
the Ile des Peupliers
with the temporary
tomb. View by J.-M.
Moreau le Jeune,
1778.

152
Girardin,
Ermenonville. Ile des
Peupliers with
Rousseau's tomb.
View by Mérigot fils,
1788.

153
Rousseau's tomb on
the Ile des Peupliers,
Ermenonville. Design
by Hubert Robert
with sculpture by Le
Sueur, c.
1780–1785.

*Death in the Garden*

mothers the virtues of natural child rearing, of nursing at the maternal breast, and of throwing away the constricting wraps that were used to bind an infant's limbs. These last two lessons were depicted in bas-relief on Rousseau's tomb along with several mothers praying before a statue of the goddess Nature (fig. 153).

As might be imagined, Rousseau's tomb became a place of pilgrimage. Girardin soon had to forbid visits to the Ile des Peupliers to keep the entire island from being ruined. This still did not keep an anonymous Englishman, overcome by emotion, from swimming to the tomb and weeping upon it. For the best effect, the guidebook to Ermenonville suggested viewing the tomb from the water's edge at a particular spot called the Mother's Bench (fig. 152).

The visitor to Ermenonville found a series of pastoral views, many of them with tombs or memorials in an intimate setting. As the marquis's son, Stanislas-Xavier de Girardin remarked in his guide to the park, Gessner himself could have situated one of his idylls here. Indeed, Hubert Robert painted such a scene, using the Ile des Peupliers as a background.

At Ermenonville, the Marquis de Girardin offered an Arcadian version of Stowe's Elysian Fields. In place of a Temple of Ancient Virtues with busts of Lycurgus, Socrates, Homer, and Epaminondas, Girardin erected a Temple of Modern Philosophy with columns consecrated to Newton (Light), Descartes (Physics), Voltaire (Satire), Penn (Humanity), Montesquieu (Justice), and Rousseau (Nature). With the last column dedicated to Rousseau, this unfinished monument stood as an encitement for future generations to complete the work through further contributions to mankind. Situated on an eminence, this monopteral temple watched over, so to speak, Rousseau's tomb on the island below.

Other monuments included the actual tomb of the painter Georg Friedrich Mayer, buried on another island in the same lake, as well as the factitious Laura's tomb, which was inscribed with elegiac verses from Petrarch and placed over the source of a spring. The beloved King Henry IV, so popular in the Academy's programs for cenotaphs, made an appearance through Gabrielle's Tower. This building was set upon a small island conceived as a *bosquet de l'amour* and was consecrated with a bust of the good Henry. By the door was a monument to Dominique de Vic, a distinguished soldier who purportedly had died of grief after passing along the Rue de la Ferronnerie two days after Henry IV's assassination there. In addition to these real and imaginary tombs, there was also the Altar of Reverie, which marked the spot where Rousseau would often stop to rest, and a red brick obelisk (fig. 154) consecrated to the four poets "who have excelled in presenting the sweet image of nature": Theocritus, Virgil, Thomson,

154
René de Girardin,
Ermenonville.
Obelisk to
Theocritus, Virgil,
Thomson, and
Gessner.

*Death in the Garden*

and Gessner. Nearby and set within a group of alders there was a related memorial with the simple English inscription:

This plain stone
To William Shenstone
In his verses display'd
His mind natural.
At Leasowes he lay'd
Arcadian greens rural.
. . .

Thus, the entire park at Ermenonville was a landscape of illusion intended to transport the viewer into an Arcadian world. When death was encountered it appeared in a peaceful setting fraught with sweet melancholy and nostalgia.

Girardin accompanied his contribution to the growing appreciation of the pastoral setting for the grave with a stinging condemnation of the contemporary urban cemetery both for empoisoning the living and for inspiring disgust and repulsion. While the marquis stopped short of proposing a public cemetery in the form of a garden, he reminded his readers that the ancients had buried their most important citizens in the beautiful countryside. This critique of existing cemeteries added aesthetic and sentimental considerations to the customary hygienic arguments in favor of burials outside the city. For Girardin, only the countryside could establish an appropriate harmony between the grave and its setting. Death should not take on a "lugubrious" aspect as it did in those "depots of cadavers and of putrefaction" in Paris.

Rousseau's tomb at Ermenonville was to be a source of inspiration and a rallying point for various factions in the nearly two decades of reform efforts that preceded the opening of the first cemetery designed as a landscape garden, the Cemetery of Père Lachaise, in 1804. In the immediate future, the illustrious Ile des Peupliers served as a turning point in the development of the French garden. Henceforth, Rousseau's tomb became the touchstone by which the sincerity of feeling of other gardenists was judged. Fake tombs with neither inhabitants nor dedications came under increasing attack. Even the much appreciated "tombs" at the garden of Betz, consecrated to the ancestral couple Thybaud de Betz, who died in the Crusades, and Adèle, who brought his body back to France only to die of grief "at the last cut of the chisel" on his monument, seemed to J.-A.-J. Cérutti like a "phantasm of the theater, an opera setting for a funeral" in comparison with Rousseau's tomb on the Ile des Peupliers.

**The Garden Cemetery**

Rousseau's burial at Ermenonville was followed by three important works that set the stage for a new image of the cemetery: Hirschfeld's five-volume-in-quarto treatise on garden design, published simultaneously in German and French between 1779–1785; the

Abbé Delille's immensely popular didactic poem *Les Jardins* (1782); and Bernardin de Saint-Pierre's equally popular *Etudes de la nature* (1784). All three authors shared a common conviction about the moral force of the pastoral and elegiac landscape garden. None of them could tolerate the *jardin anglo-chinois*, which was becoming so popular in France, with its mixture of scenes from all countries—Greek temples, Christian hermitages, Chinese kiosks and bridges, Gothic ruins, Turkish tents, Egyptian obelisks, and assorted tombs. Delille explicitly condemned gardens that assembled the "four corners of the world into one park." Hirschfeld dismissed as too ornamental the Duc de Chartres's Parc Monceau in Paris (figs. 155–156). There a *bois des tombeaux*, or woods of tombs, stood between an Italian vineyard and an ornamental flower garden. The French, De Paule Latapie had written, were a gay people. Certainly, as Carmontelle, the creator of Monceau made clear, this was to be a garden for the light-hearted *beau monde*. The elegant men and women who promenaded there were actually walking through the equivalent of an outdoor and permanent rendition of a stage set for a popular opera based on the mythological love story of Pyramus and Thisbe. In contrast, the gardens that Delille and Hirschfeld favored were like the Leasowes, with its unified pastoral theme organized around contrasting lively and melancholy scenes, and like Stowe, with its memorials to virtue.

In passing from commentaries upon existing gardens with memorials to proposals for cemeteries in the form of gardens, these authors influenced each other as they developed their ideas over this brief five-year period. The first volume of Hirschfeld's treatise, published in 1779, merely called attention to the Elysian Fields at Stowe for the "singular impression" that they created while providing a translation of Whately's descriptions of Hagley Park, with its octagonal pavilion consecrated to Thomson's memory. The second volume (1780) reproduced Heeley's account of Envil, with its isolated chapel for meditation dedicated to Shenstone. Here, however, there was a new element. In a discussion of the architectural accompaniments to a type of landscape that he designated as a "melancholy bosquet," Hirschfeld suggested using real tombs. These were offered as an alternative to the "barbaric custom" of burying inside cities and within churches. Hirschfeld suggested that those with sufficent property use a park or woods for a family cemetery arranged to stimulate moral thoughts.

At this point Hirschfeld was torn between two orientations. The *bosquet mélancolique*, as it developed under the influence of the poetry of Young, Hervey, and Blair, was to present a somber reminder of the fragility of life. Yet when Hirschfeld proceeded on his sentimental journey to several actual tombs, the somber gave way to a gentle melancholy. In this same volume, Hirschfeld took his reader to Rousseau's tomb, covered with roses and set

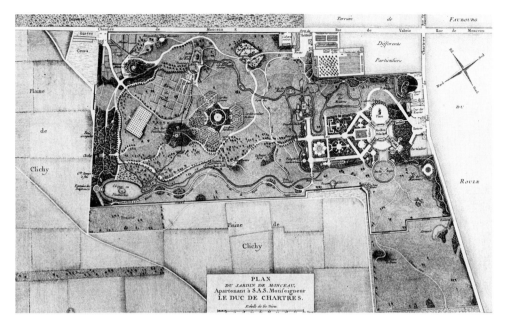

155
Carmontelle, Parc
Monceau, Paris,
1779.

156
Carmontelle, Bois
des Tombeaux, Parc
Monceau, Paris,
1779.

*The Garden Cemetery*

upon a green lawn on the Ile des Peupliers with the tall poplars reflecting in the peaceful waters of the lake. Then the reader accompanied Hirschfeld on a moonlit pilgrimage to a park outside Berlin to visit the tomb of Johann Georg Sulzer, author of *Tableau des beautés de la nature* (1755) and *Allgemeine Theorie der schönen Künste* (1771–1774, second edition 1778–1779) (fig. 157). Hirschfeld had dedicated his first volume to the ailing Sulzer, whom he praised as the first true champion of the landscape garden in Germany. The reader was encouraged to imagine himself leaning on a venerable tree with the moon reflected in the placid waters of the pool and a small rill murmuring at the foot of Sulzer's grave. There was nothing macabre about this "touching" scene, where "the idea of death loses all of its frightfulness." Finally, at a garden in the city of Darmstadt, the reader wound his way down a serpentine path to a thick and "sacred" bosquet sheltering the tomb of the landgräfin. The landgräfin herself had chosen this spot for her grave and had often come here to sit upon a bench and meditate. Now she was buried under "a simple funerary mound covered with ivy" and surrounded by willows, yews, and other dark conifers. In the subsequent three volumes of his treatise, Hirschfeld would continue these visits to other moving scenes.

The third volume (1781) advanced one step further toward the garden cemetery. While praising the Elysian Fields of Stowe as having provided the first instance of an entire area in a garden consecrated to honoring the worthy dead, Hirschfeld remarked that this British example could hardly compare with the memorial park to Danish worthies at Jaegerspris outside of Copenhagen. In 1773–1784, Prince Frederick of Denmark and Norway erected fifty-four monuments, many of them actual tombs, for ancient national heroes as well as recent citizens of merit. The monuments were scattered about this landscape garden; and nearly all were placed in shady sites in situations such as on a slight eminence or under aged oak trees. Many of the monuments, such as those to the famous bishop and captain Absalon and to the astronomer Tycho Brahe (fig. 158), were examples of *architecture parlante*, the forms and decorative elements reflecting the essential nature of the person's virtues or accomplishments. Since Poussin's *Et in Arcadia ego* evoked such satisfying elegiac feelings, then just imagine, speculated Hirschfeld, how much more touching actual tombs in a real garden could be.

Like Hirschfeld, the Abbé Delille, in his poem, *Les Jardins, ou l'art d'embellir les paysages* (1782) took a cue from the "sweet sadness" of Poussin's *Et in Arcadia ego*. "Imitate Poussin," counseled Delille, who rendered *Et in Arcadia ego* as "And I too was a shepherd in Arcadia." Although Delille had no patience for false tombs, it is not clear, as Robert Mauzi has suggested, that

157
Johann Georg
Sulzer's tomb, 1780.

158
Jaegerspris.
Monuments to
Bishop Absalon and
Tycho Brahe. From
Hirschfeld, *Théorie
de l'art des jardins*, 3
(1781).

*The Garden Cemetery*

he required that they be filled so much as that they be sincerely dedicated. If one did not have a loved one to honor, then one might consecrate a tomb to a humble tenant farmer and inscribe it with his virtues: "Here lies the good son, the good father, the good husband." As in an idyll by Gessner, one would find himself drawn to such tombs by "an involuntary charm." There among the "pious" trees, the somber yews, pines, and cypresses, a visitor would hang a garland as an offering and scatter flowers upon the tomb. Like Gessner, Delille understood the emotive power of invoking "the woods, the water, and the flowers" as companions to the tomb. And like Gessner and Hirschfeld, Delille invited the reader not merely to appreciate the tribute of a memorial, as had Dodsley, Whately, and Heeley, but actually to imagine paying a tearful visit to the site of the tomb itself.

Delille ended his poem with a proposal for an Elysium that combined, without naming either, the theme of the memorial park of Jaegerspris with the life-size statues at the Valley of the Norwegians in the royal park at Fredensbourg near Copenhagen, also described by Hirschfeld in his third volume (1781). Delille may also have been thinking of Watelet's earlier proposal for an Elysium (1774), which waxed eloquent with descriptions of white marble statues of the great benefactors of humanity set within an Elysium planted with laurels and myrtles and embellished with slowly moving streams. It is not clear whether Delille's tranquil Elysium, featuring statues of Fénélon, Sully, Henry IV, and the brave English Captain Cook, was to be an actual cemetery or a commemorative garden. The decisive step was taken in the following year (1784) by Bernardin de Saint-Pierre in his *Etudes de la nature*.

Bernardin's text was important on two accounts. It not only advocated an Elysium for the worthy dead as a type of landscape garden; it also proposed a public cemetery arranged according to the same model. In condemning the current practice of burying inside churches for senselessly exposing the living to harmful odors from rotting corpses, Bernardin suggested following the example of the Turks, the ancient Romans, and the Chinese in burying out in the countryside. Paris should have public cemeteries in the environs of the city with bosquets of cypresses and pines mixed with flowering and fruit-bearing trees. The combination of this setting with the memorials would inspire a "profound and sweet melancholy" through the "moral feelings" that they would sustain. In this ambiance, the living would certainly feel that tombs "as I have said elsewhere, are monuments placed on the frontiers of two worlds."

Echoing the reformers' concern that funeral services were disruptive to the activities of the parish church, Bernardin explained how a large sepulchral chapel in a garden cemetery would eliminate this problem. As for graves and memorials in the new landscape cemeteries, "each citizen would be free to lodge himself according to his fantasy." Hence the cemetery would soon appear much as an enlarged version of the Bois des Tombeaux at the Parc Monceau, where monuments of different sizes and forms were scattered throughout the bosquet.

Bernardin was even more explicit in the design of the Elysium for the worthy dead. In a sense, he had to be, for in the cemetery individual tastes and caprice would ensure variety. In a national Elysium, one had to legislate against the ever-present threat of visual monotony. Thus all types of monuments were to be erected here—"obelisks, columns, pyramids, urns, bas-reliefs, medallions, statues, pedestals, peristyles and domes." The tombs and mausoleums would be fashioned from stones of all colors so that they would not seem to have come from the same quarry. True to the aesthetics of the landscape garden, these monuments "would not be crowded together as in a warehouse but spread about with taste." The landscape itself was to be purely of the new picturesque manner, with none of the formal elements of the previous era: "There will be . . . no alignments . . . no bowling greens, no pruned and shaped trees, nothing that resembles our [formal gardens]." The most propitious site for the Elysium would be along the Seine above the Pont de Neuilly on a property about a mile and a half in diameter.

In the view of this champion of nature, the first group of people to be honored here should be naturalists who had introduced new plants into Europe. Their tombs would be placed under the shade of their contributions. There were to be no epitaphs in this Elysium, only suitably characterized monuments as at Jaegerspris, where the forms and sculptural details told all. If, for example, Montgolfier's "aerostatic globe" (hot air balloon) proved useful to humanity, then he would be admitted here and buried under a tomb decorated with his novel machine. Bernardin's Elysium admitted all types of citizens: great generals, illustrious writers, noble statesmen, and virtuous women ("for virtue knows no sex"), remembered mostly for sacrifice and fidelity within their domestic world. Bernardin's vision of a public cemetery and a garden of fame within a picturesque landscape setting was to become a standard point of reference through the remainder of the century.

Hirschfeld provided his own model for a cemetery in the last volume of his treatise, which appeared in 1785. This project had been anticipated at least since 1783, when it appeared in the outline for the remaining volumes of his book. In contrast to the proposals of Delille and Bernardin de Saint-Pierre, the cemetery Hirschfeld envisaged was decidely somber. In many respects it represented an extrapolation of several landscape gardens that

Hirschfeld had visited in Germany, notably the garden at Marienwerder near Hanover. Near the hermitage there Hirschfeld had found a cemetery bordered by somber conifers. The melancholy of the scene was heightened by the ruins of an old Gothic church that had once been part of a cloister.

Both within and without, Hirschfeld's ideal cemetery employed the design aesthetics of the landscape garden. The cemetery was to be surrounded with a "peaceful, solitary, and serious" countryside which psychologically prepared the visitor by removing any distracting influences. A forest of pine trees or a distant waterfall would also contribute to this effect. The cemetery itself was to be visually unified with its surroundings yet protected with either a very low wall, a hedge, or a ha-ha. Well informed about the latest scientific discoveries, Hirschfeld noted that the trees would purify the air. Aromatic plants would even add an enchanting balm.

This would be a spacious cemetery with ample room for covered porticoes, mortuary chapels, and melancholy retreats. The funerary monuments themselves would exhibit great variety in their forms. In their placement, they would also partake of the different types of picturesque situations available to the landscape gardenist: enclosed by a thick bosquet, appearing suddenly around a bend, or viewed in the distance in the midst of some plantings. A solitary birch here and there would direct one's attention to a striking inscription on a neighboring grave.

Hirschfeld anticipated with admirable prescience the most striking and singular effects, the grand and picturesque scenes created by the play of light and shadows over the partially hidden tombs with the white stone contrasting vividly against the dark foliage. The total effect would be "grand, serious, darkened, and majestic but without anything terrible or frightening." In the new cemetery the heart would be filled only with "tender feelings and sweet melancholy." His text, along with those of Delille and Bernardin de Saint-Pierre, had an almost immediate effect upon two cemetery projects that hesitated between the old architectural and the new landscape conceptions of cemetery design.

**Transitional Designs**

In a long entry in the *Encyclopédie Méthodique* (1788) under "Cemetery," Quatremère de Quincy proposed combining the *campo santo* and the picturesque garden. For the former he turned to the famed Campo Santo of Pisa; for the latter, he lifted verbatim long passages from Hirschfeld's article of 1785 on cemetery gardens without any reference to its author. Quatremère's discussion began with the observation that there is a close analogy between words and things. No word could better convey the "infectious dumping grounds," the "hideous depots of cadavers and skeletons" that constituted the cemeteries of Paris than the term *charnier*, or charnel house. *Cemetery*, on the other hand, came from the Greek *coimeterion*, meaning "place where one sleeps." Quatremère's aim was to re-establish a correspondence between "les mots" and "les choses" by proposing a model for a modern cemetery worthy of the name.

The ancient Romans, Quatremère recalled, buried their dead outside their towns and urban centers in what constituted veritable cities of the dead. Two of these "funerary cities," at Pozzuoli in Italy and Arles in France, had been given the name Elysian Fields. The second volume (1782) of the Abbé de Saint-Non's description of Naples and Sicily had included an illustration of the Italian Elysian Fields, whose fertile countryside, mild climate, and sumptuous tombs had misled travelers into believing that they had indeed found Virgil's paradise. As for the Alyscamps at Arles, Chateaubriand was to say of this Gallo-Roman cemetery: "In my travels, I have never encountered a site which tempted me to die as much as the cemetery at Arles." Quatremère described the Alyscamps as a vast plain strewn with the ruins of sarcophagi, cippi, and other funerary monuments, the whole ensemble recalling a once magnificent city of the dead.

For Quatremère, though, the cemetery needed bounds, and more particularly, a building. Rather than adopt the open Roman model, he preferred the Pisan Campo Santo (fig. 27), which he described as the most beautiful monument of its kind. Here Quatremère admired the white marble façade, the exquisitely patterned marble floors, the blind Byzantine arches to the exterior, and the "demi-Gothic" arcades to the interior. To Quatremère the Gothic "tint" enhanced the character of the place. The frescoes covering the walls, the antique tombs, the modern mausoleums, the inscriptions of all types, and the effigies of great men honored by the republic of Pisa made these galleries into something of a "museum." Herein Quatremère found a nearly perfect program for a modern cemetery.

Quatremère was particularly moved by the tombs erected in honor of people of merit, the most recent being the "renowned" Francesco Algarotti, the great patron of the arts for whom Frederick the Great had built a sumptuous wall mausoleum. Even the sepulchral vaults dug under the floor seemed a sensible idea as long as they did not detract from the erection of mausoleums, cenotaphs, and other types of monuments. As for the open land in the middle of the Campo Santo, it could be divided into three hundred sixty-five communal graves, one for each day of the year after the example of the cemetery of Naples. There would also be individual graves for those who could afford them.

At this point in his description Quatremère de Quincy proposed planting somber trees in the manner advocated by Hirschfeld. Evidently Quatremère envisaged a cemetery considerably larger than the long and narrow Pisan Campo Santo, which could hardly accept a garden, especially if there were to be three hundred sixty-five communal graves as well. Quatremère appreciated the use of isolated cypresses and yews. He made a particular point of emphasizing that dark foliage of a brownish tint would augment the "sacred melancholy" of the place. Bosquets with tombs of the worthy dead, isolated seats with inscriptions, in short, all the apparatus of Hirschfeld's ideal cemetery were proposed here with the exception of the larger landscape features, the covered porticoes, and chapels. Whereas Quatremère had no room for these inside his cemetery; he envisaged the *campo santo* itself as a *fabrique* within a larger landscape. Taking Hirschfeld's three ways of siting a monument, he imagined that the cemetery itself could be presented in the countryside outside the city in one of these ways: enclosed within thick and somber plantings, occurring suddenly around the bend of some solitary road, or appearing in the distance within groups of trees.

As a transitional project proposed at a transitional moment, Quatremère de Quincy's design for a cemetery united many aspects of the reform movement. Like the Abbé Laugier, Quatremère welcomed the removal of all somber images from the church; like Bernardin de Saint-Pierre, he also advocated eliminating those monuments to vanity that cluttered it; along with the Abbé Porée and the curé Desbois de Rochefort, he savored the isolation and unique purpose of the cemetery where nothing would distract the visitor from his meditations; and like Hirschfeld, he anticipated the cemetery that offered nothing repulsive, only scenes that would inspire a "sweet and profound melancholy." Finally, he saw the new cemetery as one whose message would be "rest" and "eternity."

A cemetery project by the architect Alexandre-Louis de Labrière, published without a date but reviewed in the press in January 1787, also presented a hybrid plan (figs. 159–160). Labrière's project combined a vast complex of buildings with a picturesque garden. His proposed methods of burial ranged from the traditional mass graves to the newly vaunted Elysium. The siting of Labrière's funerary architecture within a densely planted park of "poplars, cypresses, and evergreens of all varieties" intended to hide the view of the buildings may well reflect Hirschfeld's counsel to apply the principles of the landscape garden to cemetery design. Labrière, though, also had experience as a gardenist, for he had just recently in 1785 arranged an English garden for the Duc d'Orléans in the park of Gennevilliers (fig. 161). This *jardin anglais*, with its Tomb of Laura and Petrarch and an earlier Temple of Aurora by Servandoni (1752) was actually a refashioning of an older formal garden whose traces can still be discerned on Labrière's plan.

Avenue decorant l'entré           du Monument

Entrée

159
Alexandre-Louis de
Labrière, cemetery, c.
1787.

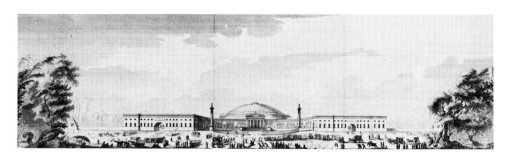

160
Labrière, cemetery, c.
1787.

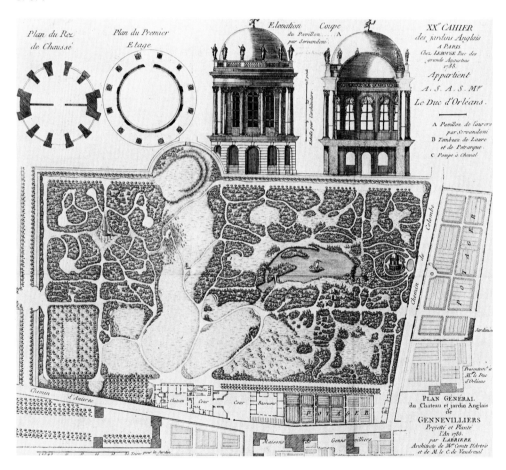

161
Labrière, "English
garden" at
Gennevilliers, 1785.

Projected toward the eve of the revolution and hence at the end of an era, Labrière's cemetery presented in microcosm all three phases of the cemetery under the ancien régime as well as the image that would gain total ascendancy with the revolution. For the poor, Labrière's burial ground still contained large mass graves (11 in fig. 159), which measured 3.6 meters along each side and were four to five meters deep. Adequate space between these thirteen communal graves was left in order to keep the contents from one full grave from tumbling into a newly opened adjacent hole. As in the traditional cemetery, the zone of communal graves was surrounded by a gallery where families and corporations could purchase sepulchral vaults. The architect proposed building only the side and rear walls to enable the clients to complete the entrance as they wished. These galleries (10 in fig. 159) were repeated in the form of concentric half circles to the rear of the cemetery.

At the center of the cemetery, Labrière provided two types of garden spaces. The outer one, which served as a transitional area, consisted of parallel rows of regularly planted trees after the manner of Antoine's cemetery design (fig. 65). Here one would be free to erect a tomb along the central path. These parallels bands of trees, in turn, surrounded a wooded lawn "in the form of Elysian Fields where all those who might have the whim to raise a picturesque tomb could do so . . . by purchasing the necessary terrain." A larger Elysium with winding paths and filled with magnificent tombs surrounded the entire architectural precinct. Labrière proposed gathering together here all of the existing tombs of the great men of France that were at the same time masterpieces by the most famous artists. Presumably these tombs would come from the various parish churches of Paris, where burials were to be forbidden.

The juxtaposition of the old and new images of the cemetery in this project reflects the transitional aspect even of Labrière's thought. The architectural and the landscape settings were given equal prominence, implying that there was no inner compulsion that would make one choose either situation. In a few years, this ambiguity would be unthinkable as architecture ceded to the garden.

Finally, Labrière's cemetery reflected the sublime architecture of the mid-1780s in its gigantic central rotunda destined for royal sepulchers as well as the tombs of princes and the higher nobility. Having heard that the Abbey of Saint-Denis might soon be secularized, Labrière proposed transferring the royal tombs to the central rotunda of his new cemetery. The great men of France would be buried outside around the periphery (9 in fig. 159) just as their statues would crown the drum below the dome. As in the earlier projects sponsored by the Académie Royale d'Architecture, the presence of these worthy citizens was intended to illustrate the glory of the monarchy as much as to honor their personal achievements.

Conceived as a type of French Westminster Abbey, Labrière's design was intended to complement the project initiated in 1774 by the Comte d'Angiviller, Directeur-Général of the Académie de Peinture et de Sculpture, to fill the long gallery of the Louvre with busts of France's great men. Architecturally, Labrière's rotunda owes much to Boullée's project of 1783 for a museum (fig. 162), which had also been conceived as a response to this scheme. In both buildings, the central space consists of a toplit dome with the sun shining down on a hypaethral Temple of Fame. Labrière reinforced the theme of the space of glory and immortality by borrowing the majestic façade proposed by Dufourny in 1778 in his cemetery project (fig. 28), with its complex allusions to death and triumph. While Labrière was proud of the effect obtained by viewing the broad dome through the surrounding trees, a critic writing in the *Nouvelle de la République des Lettres* bemoaned the loss of dignity implied by not isolating the monument. In a sense, the reviewer was a partisan of Boullée's conception of the cemetery, not of Hirschfeld's: "This is not the place to amuse with the picturesque in art and nature, but rather to stupefy through the severity of a building's character and its expansiveness and by the calm and solidity of its foundations." Over the succeeding years, a greater familiarity with the tomb in the landscape garden as well as the violence of the revolution would intensify this debate over the respective merits of stone and greenery as the setting for death and commemoration.

*French Picturesque Gardens*

On the eve of the revolution, Paris had no new cemeteries, but the great French picturesque gardens presented tombs or cenotaphs in the atmosphere of an Elysium. In his garden at Franconville, for example, the Comte d'Albon attempted to rival the Marquis de Girardin with an actual grave for the famous linguist Court de Gébelin (fig. 163). As the author who had unveiled the allegorical language of the primitive world, Court de Gébelin seemed to deserve a more distinguished tomb than his modest place in the Protestant cemetery. His burial at Franconville in 1784 was an act both of friendship for a cherished companion who had enjoyed the gardens there and of homage to a man who was worthy of resting within nature. Four columns suggesting a ruined aedicula consecrated the space around the sarcophagus. The Comte d'Albon likewise contributed an expression of friendship to the Swiss botanist and physiologist Albrecht de Haller. For this famous doctor, he erected a memorial in the form of a mount flanked by four poplars. Finally, the count's illustrious ancestors had their

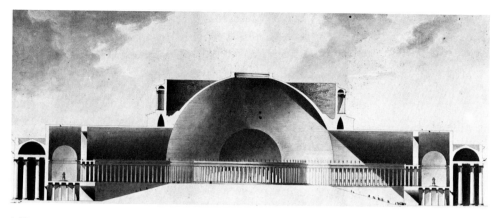

162
Etienne-Louis
Boullée, museum,
1783. Section.

163
Tomb of Court de
Gébelin at
Franconville, 1784.

memorial in a pyramid erected to the memory of Jean and Jacques d'Albon, both *maréchaux de France*.

At the park of Maupertuis, designed by Alexandre-Théodore Brongniart and deemed so beautiful that it earned the epithet *Elysée* or Elysium, the Marquis de Montesquiou erected a tomb (fig. 164) in memory of the brave Admiral Gaspard de Coligny, a Protestant who had been massacred on Saint Bartholemew's Day in 1572 and whose body had hung from the gibbet at Montfaucon. The setting of this tomb by the water's edge and next to a pyramid in ruins was suggestive of a peaceful Elysium.

Equally engaging were the cenotaph to Captain Cook (fig. 165) and the rostral column (fig. 166) at Méréville. In 1786, two of the Duc Jean-Joseph de Laborde's sons, aged twenty and twenty-four, perished in the voyage with La Pérouse as they followed the path of the famous Cook, only to share "his melancholy fate." The rostral column erected to the memory of these two young men was a deep blue marble with bronze rostra and a bronze ball. Situated on a small island at the near side of a lake, the memorial was accompanied by foreign trees planted to evoke a far-off land. Here the duke planted the *épine de mer*, chosen because it grows near the seashore and because its "pale and sad color" seemed appropriate to the site. The engraving shows a weeping willow to one side of the memorial and a poplar to the other.

The monument to Cook was probably designed by Hubert Robert with sculpture by Pajou. Robert was also responsible for the siting, since his original program called for it to be placed within "the most shaded and the most savage" part of the garden. In effect, according to Alexandre de Laborde, the duke's son and successor at Méréville, the memorial was erected in the most solitary part of the garden along the banks of a stream.

Like the tomb for Court de Gébelin at Franconville, the memorial for Cook consisted of an aedicula and a central tomb. The stone canopy, which Robert designed to be about twenty feet tall, was fashioned as a "severe architecture": four channeled Doric columns without bases carrying a heavy roof set upon a platform with three steps. The monument in the middle was composed of an urn *à l'antique* on top of an altar of the type that the ancients consecrated to the manes of the dead.

The contrast between these memorials in the park and the contemporaneous architectural monuments envisaged by the students at the Académie Royale d'Architecture (figs. 76–78) could not have been more extreme. Equally great was the distance between Robert's Egyptian wasteland of 1760 (fig. 84) and his tombs for the parks at Betz, Ermenonville, and Méréville. One notes in passing the seminal role played by Robert in both phases of the changing notions about commemorating the dead.

164
Alexandre-Théodore
Brongniart,
"Elysium,"
Maupertuis.

165
Hubert Robert,
cenotaph to Captain
Cook, Méréville.
Tomb by Augustin
Pajou.

166
Méréville. Rostral
column erected by
Jean-Joseph, duc de
Laborde, in memory
of his two sons who
died on the voyage
of La Pérouse in
1786.

In 1776, Baron Tschoudy, in his article "Bosquet" for the *Encyclopédie*, objected vigorously to the idea of a tomb in a garden. "Was the promenade," he asked rhetorically, "made for melancholy?" By 1789 many Frenchmen were saying yes. They savored the melancholy feelings of a visit to the tomb in the peaceful setting of the garden. They were prepared, moreover, to ask the same of their cemeteries. Perhaps the change in attitudes can be summed up by considering the fortunes of the memorials that had been characteristic features at the Cemetery of the Holy Innocents.

When Baron Tschoudy set down his opinion, the skyline of the Cemetery of the Holy Innocents was punctuated by several obelisks with crosses. In the early 1780s, under the direction of Hubert Robert, a sixteenth-century obelisk from this recently closed urban burial ground was transferred to the totally new context of the Valley of Tombs at Betz. After penetrating an arena of somber trees, the visitor would encounter this memorial along with a type of altar to the dead placed at the center of four poplars. Further on was a "tomb" consisting of a tombstone dating from the time of Francis I, also taken from the former Cemetery of the Holy Innocents. All of this was a prelude to viewing the supposed "tombs" of the twelfth-century knight Thybaud and his lady. The picturesque arrangement of the monuments here, as in the Bois des Tombeaux at the Parc Monceau, suggested a new aesthetic for the cemetery.

The new cemetery would, in a manner of speaking, expand these areas to cover the entire garden. Indeed, in the spring of 1801 this is exactly what Nicolas-Thérèse-Benoist Frochot, Prefect of the Department of the Seine, attempted to do. Since the Parc Monceau was then part of the national domain, Frochot addressed a request to the Minister of the Interior for approval to acquire the park for use as a cemetery. Those landscape features that made the Parc Monceau into such an enchanting garden were precisely the ones that would make it into a perfect burial ground. As Frochot explained: "This solitary place, located at the edge of Paris, has a surface of [46.4 acres] ornamented with the most beautiful plantings. Through the picturesque manner in which it has been arranged, through the irregularity of its forms, the surprise in the movement [of the land and plantings], it offers a delectable Elysium where death would hold sway only in the memory of the living and through the monument which would cover the cherished remains and through the simple epitaph suspended from the foliage of the funerary tree." Not only would this cemetery serve the general public, it would also be a "French historical Elysium." In visiting the site, the prefect's personal secretary, Baron de Norvins, imagined how one could match the character of the landscape to the personality of the celebrities who would be honored there.

For overriding economic as well as other reasons, Frochot was unsuccessful in his request. In 1804, though, the prefect realized his dream by acquiring the magnificent hilltop estate of Mont-Louis, which he opened less than two months later as the Cemetery of Père Lachaise. This burial ground, perhaps the most famous in the West, owes its origins to the eighteenth-century landscape garden, which combined picturesque aesthetics with the commemoration of personal loss and public virtue.

# 6
## The Field of Rest (1789–1804)

One of the paradoxes of the French Revolution was that while it exacerbated the overcrowding in the cemeteries of Paris, it also set the foundations for the successful implementation of a new order in burials. With the expropriation of the church property, the subsequent closing of the churches themselves, the dissolution of the traditional clergy, and the closing of former parish cemeteries, the customary rituals of the funeral were gravely disrupted. The privileged lost the prerogative of a grave inside the church. The traditional funeral procession was gone. Everybody was now buried in mass graves that contained several hundred to over a thousand corpses. All of this took place against a background of revolutionary violence and bloodshed whose traumatizing effects produced, under the Directory and the Consulate, an outpouring of sentiment about dignified funerals and decent cemeteries.

The burial grounds proposed during the revolutionary decade were all conceived as "Fields of Rest." During the period 1794–1799, this phrase, *champs de repos*, along with *lieu de repos* (place of rest), *Elysée* (Elysium), and the more neutral *lieu de sépulture* (place of burial), virtually replaced the word *cimetière* (cemetery), which had lost its etymological meaning of "place where one sleeps" to become synonymous with *charnier* (charnel house), a word that, according to Quatremère de Quincy in 1788, perfectly conveyed the "repulsive" aspect of the burial ground. The new cemetery was to be a garden whose characteristics varied according to the ideologies of the moment. In general, though, its authors abhorred the traditional communal graves which now revolted the contemporary sense of human decency. The Cemetery of Père Lachaise constitutes the final stage in the ongoing debate about how social values and sentiment should be accommodated in the new Arcadian landscapes for the dead.

Before the Terror, little seems to have been done in the way of cemetery reform. Although in 1790 the National Assembly reiterated the often repeated injunction against burials inside the city, proposals to implement this goal, such as the curé Desbois de Rochefort's suggestion to use confiscated church property outside the city to establish new cemeteries, went unheeded. The focus of the government's attention at this time was on honoring heroes of the revolution with special ceremonies and appropriate graves. As a result, the history of the cemetery under the revolution is inseparable from the two consequences of this orientation: the transformation of the Church of Sainte-Geneviève into the French Panthéon and the use of the gardens of Paris to honor people of merit. From time to time, public gardens were consecrated with a memorial or tomb to some great man, thereby momentarily providing a surrogate for the landscape cemeteries, which existed only as projects. One of the earliest of these events took place on August 23, 1790, when a society of naturalists placed a bust of Carolus Linnaeus in the Jardin des Plantes, the botanical gardens of Paris (fig. 167). Since the self-proclaimed purpose of this organization was "to honor the memory of the great men who had advanced the progress of natural history," it may seem that the dreams of the Abbé Delille, Bernardin de Saint-Pierre, and C. C. Hirschfeld were on the way to fruition.

*Architecture or Nature?*  With the nation mourning the death of Mirabeau, the National Assembly decreed on April 4, 1791, that the Church of Sainte-Geneviève be converted into a pantheon to receive the bodies of the great men of the nation. The founding of the French Panthéon brought into focus conflicting beliefs about the proper setting for the dead. By advocating a natural setting, first as a pantheon and then later as a public cemetery, the critics, like the landscape theorists before them, were returning to first principles. As Pierre Trahard has justly observed: "for the revolutionaries, nature is not only the world of forms and colors, of odors and sounds. It partakes of the majesty of the principle which is . . . the origin of beings and things, from which issue the sources of happiness, law, education, politics, and religion." While the debate centered on the honors due the great men of France, the arguments adduced applied to ordinary citizens as well. Often critics would couple their suggestions for both categories of citizens in the same letter or essay.

Champions of the National Assembly's decree on the French Panthéon included the *Journal de Paris*, which praised the decision to convert what was universally recognized as the most magnificent modern church in Paris into a French Westminster Abbey. As Charles Villette had explained a year earlier on the occasion of the twelfth anniversary of the death of Voltaire, the magnificent Corinthian columns of this edifice would be a proper setting for a "Temple of Glory." The architect Antoine-Laurent-Thomas Vaudoyer, though, recently returned from Rome, where he had gone as the Grand Prix laureate of 1783, and filled with memories of the Via Appia, protested vehemently. It was well known, he argued, that Parisians never visited the military tombs at the Invalides or Richelieu's tomb at the Church of the Sorbonne. A pantheon in the Church of Sainte-Geneviève would suffer a similar fate. Vaudoyer proposed following the example of the ancient Romans by transforming the popular promenade of the Champs-Elysées into a *voie de l'honneur* bordered on both sides with mausoleums of the great citizens of France. Both the name and the plantings of the Champs-Elysées evoked an idea of the peace that the virtuous dead were imagined to enjoy. How moved visitors would be as they glimpsed the shaded mausoleums through the trees along this grand route. Even the linear character of the promenade could serve a pedagogical end, with the tombs of

167
Monument to
Carolus Linnaeus,
Jardin des Plantes,
Paris, 1790.

*Architecture or Nature?*

Voltaire and Rousseau, the nominal fathers of the revolution, placed at the head.

While Vaudoyer was describing the attractions of the Champs-Elysées, others were proposing the site of the recent civic Festival of Federation (July 14, 1790). The Champ de Mars, recently renamed the Champ de la Fédération, could be transformed into an Elysium to honor the great men of France. Here the space of the euphoric festival of national unity would be used to consecrate the memory of those who had died for the revolution. The earthen amphitheater that had held the spectators on July 14 could be rebuilt in stone with vaulted underground corridors to house the tombs of the most illustrious Frenchmen. As in Vaudoyer's project, Voltaire and Rousseau were to occupy the place of honor, with their graves at the entry to the circus. People who merited lesser recognition would be buried under the parallel rows of trees that bordered the amphitheater to either side. At the far end of the field in front of the Ecole Militaire, where the dignitaries had sat, there would be statues of the great men of France. As the author of this project reminded his readers, the ancients buried their dead not inside their temples but rather outside in the countryside.

To the opponents of the Panthéon who favored an outdoor Elysium, Charles Villette responded that the weather of Paris was neither that of Naples nor of Athens. In spite of their differences about this issue, however, observers such as Villette and Vaudoyer agreed that the contemporary Parisian cemetery was a repellent place. "What could be more revolting," exclaimed Villette, "than our hideous cemeteries! They do not inspire a religious impression but rather a physical repugnance, or at the very least, indifference." It was time, insisted Vaudoyer, to suppress everything related to the "frightful" ideas of graves and skeletons. Against the "hideous" figure of Death as a skeleton carrying an hourglass and a scythe, Villette evoked the Greek custom of portraying Death as sleep.

Quatremère de Quincy was virtually alone, though, in describing what a public cemetery might be like. Using the occasion of the debate over the Panthéon, he addressed a letter to the *Moniteur Universel* (April 13, 1791), where he observed that there were many worthy people not destined for the Panthéon who deserved private marks of homage but who had little chance of receiving them in the actual cemeteries. Paris, proposed Quatremère, needed cemeteries after the model of the Pisan Campo Santo. In reproducing excerpts from his earlier article in the *Encyclopédie Méthodique*, Quatremère transformed the "renowned Algarotti" into "the Voltaire of Italy" in order to make his point. One notes that Quatremère's new description of an ideal cemetery omits the garden passages that he had once borrowed from Hirschfeld. At this time, then, Quatremère decidedly favored an architectural over a landscape vision of the proper burial ground.

## An Elysium for the Panthéon

The dichotomy between a stark architectural setting for death and a peaceful natural cadre entered into the very conception of the Panthéon. One fanciful engraving (fig. 168) decided the issue by simply erasing all of Paris between the Théâtre Français (today, the Odéon) and the Panthéon so as to portray the latter as situated in the countryside. Quatremère de Quincy, charged with the transformation of the former church into a pantheon, had his own vision of the monument in a natural setting. In his first report of August 1791, Quatremère stressed that an Elysium would be planted to isolate the building from the noise and commotion of the city. As a result, the "silent shadows" of a "sacred woods" would provide the occasion for "philosophical" promenades as well as instilling suitable feelings of veneration in visitors. In a second report of November 15, 1792, Quatremère explained that the projected garden could be used for the tombs of citizens of lesser merit than those buried inside the Panthéon itself.

In a memorandum dated April 15, 1793, Quatremère outlined three possible strategies for a square and garden around the Panthéon. This document reveals that his interests in finishing the surroundings of this building were primarily architectural. Quatremère favored a proposal that was slightly more ambitious than that put forth by J.-G. Soufflot, the architect of Sainte-Geneviève, for a square defined by two curved façades and preceded by a wide street extending to the Rue Saint-Jacques. An anonymous drawing in the Musée Carnavalet (fig. 169) conveys the spirit of Quatremère's plan to enclose the space around the Panthéon in an architectural framework. This new construction would serve as a type of spine for the future addition of amphitheaters where civic festivals could take place. Then the Panthéon could be the focal point for an entire panoply of public activities in which virtue, patriotism, and public service would be honored with ceremonies and prizes. The space between the Panthéon and the square around it would be planted, its narrow dimension ensuring that the view of the Panthéon would not be lost in the trees. The third option, planting a vast Elysium that would include the garden of the Abbey of Sainte-Geneviève, Quatremère dismissed as too costly and as vitiating the effect of the principal monument with too vast a space. Since no Elysium was ever planted, the Panthéon stood at the center of a naked and formless open space through the remainder of the revolution.

The tension between architecture and nature in the early years of the revolution was encapsulated in the popularity of Jean-Paul Marat's tomb, placed temporarily in the garden of the former Cordeliers' Monastery (fig. 170) before his subsequent burial in

168
Anonymous,
idealized view of
Paris near the
Panthéon.

169
Anonymous, project
for a square with
meeting halls around
the Panthéon, Paris.

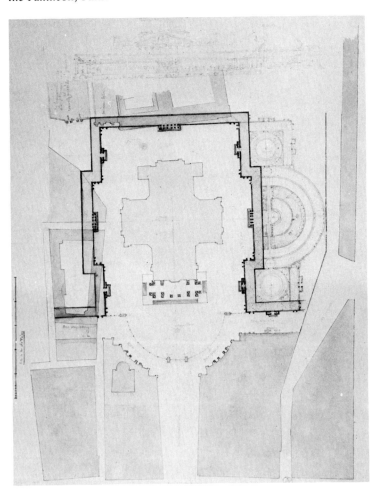

*The Field of Rest*

170
Marat's tomb in the
garden of the former
Cordeliers'
monastery, Paris,
1793.

the Panthéon. After his assassination on July 13, 1793, Marat rested in a "picturesque tomb," as it was called, in the garden where he used to harangue his fellow citizens. This funerary bosquet both reflected and strengthened the conviction that for heroes and martyrs such as this "friend of the people," nature provided the most suitable place of burial.

As time passed, criticism of the Panthéon continued, its tone becoming progressively more strident. Architecture was cast in a negative light in contrast to the splendors of the countryside. Moreover, Quatremère's success in making the Panthéon's interior more "mysterious" by walling up the side windows only made the edifice more forbidding to its detractors (fig. 171). To Jean-Charles Laveaux, editor of the *Journal de la Montagne*, the Panthéon hid the great men of France away from the eyes of the multitude in somber underground vaults and between cold masses of stone. For Laveaux, the true pantheon belonged under the trembling poplars surrounding the Champ de la Fédération. As for ordinary citizens, each family should be given a piece of ground or garden for its own burials. This property would serve as an altar at which all domestic promises, oaths, and contracts would be sworn. For Louis de Saint-Just too, the dead were to be buried in the "cheerful countryside." Each family would be given a "small field" for its burials; and children would scatter flowers over the tombs there. In June 1794, just one month before Laveaux's article, the National Convention had decided that the property confiscated from the *émigrés* as well as common lands would be divided into small shares for wide distribution. For social theorists such as Laveaux and Saint-Just, death had an integral place in these family parcels.

## The First Arcadian Dreamlands

The cemetery in the form of a "Field of Rest" was officially born under the Terror. Partaking of the "dechristianization" and egalitarianism of the times, this new burial ground became a "Garden of Equality." Through a double substitution, the old religious signs were replaced with new civic markers and the social distinctions in burial were leveled to make funerals the same for all classes.

On October 12, 1793, Joseph Fouché, special emissary sent by the National Convention to the Department of Nièvre, issued his famous Arrêté ordering the elimination of religious signs from the cemeteries under his jurisdiction. Not only were all burial grounds to be located far away from dwellings; they were also to be planted with trees and watched over by a statue representing Sleep. The entry would be inscribed: "Death is an eternal sleep." As a result of this Arrêté, the Commune of Beauvais, for example, voted on 22 Brumaire, year II (November 3, 1793) to remove the cross from its cemetery and to inscribe upon the door: "Your souls sleep in this tomb."

171
Pierre-Antoine De
Machy, view of the
Panthéon with a
projected statue of
Fame, mid-1790s.

*The First Arcadian Dreamlands*

Chaumette, the procureur-syndic of Paris, had the city government approve the principle of Fouché's decree on October 16. Three days later he proclaimed that henceforth the funerals of the rich and the poor would be the same. Chaumette, moreover, rejected a report on cemeteries by the Administration of Public Works for promulgating traditional signs of mortality. As reported by the *Moniteur Universel*, Chaumette admonished that the new cemetery should "inspire less somber and more tender feelings. 'I want Elysian Fields where previously the hypocrisy of the priests had us encounter only skulls and bones.'" The administrators were instructed to "replace the images of sadness and despair with sweeter, more philanthropical ideas."

As has been shown by the various comments on the public cemetery from the time of Rousseau's burial in the park at Ermenonville until the Terror, the dictum that death is an eternal sleep was not, as François-Alphonse Aulard has argued, an obscure philosophical opinion arbitrarily imposed by Fouché and Chaumette upon the French people. The concept of death as a sweet rest, known through the funerary art and inscriptions of the ancient Greeks and Romans, gave form to an emerging feeling about mortality that rejected the macabre aspects of the Christian and Baroque tradition. Chaumette's attack on the *memento mori*, which he dismissed as clerical hypocrisy, echoed sentiments expressed even before the revolution. The 1788 guidebook to Ermenonville, for example, had described the hermitage there as happily free of the customary monastic trappings "ranging from the hourglass to the death's head, objects which present only the disgusting tableau of ignorance and superstition."

The second report on the burial grounds of Paris by the Administration of Public Works reflected these new attitudes by condemning the gaping mass graves not only for their insalubrity but also for offering "the disgusting spectacle of putrefaction." Read to the Commune on 21 Nivôse, year II (January 10, 1794) by Jean-Baptiste Avril, this document proposed four new cemeteries for the city to be located in isolated, rural settings. The *Champ de Repos* or Field of Rest, as Avril's version of the cemetery was called, literally turned the image of the cemetery as previously imagined by Jacques-François Blondel upside down and inside out. Both approaches used the design of the burial ground to foster a particular understanding about human mortality. In the Field of Rest, though, everything was calculated to eliminate the terror of death.

Whereas Blondel, following a tradition dating from the late Middle Ages, had enclosed the burial ground with *charniers* to provide a self-contained world of death with graphic reminders of mortality, Avril opened the cemetery to the countryside. The beauties of nature had no place amidst Blondel's charnel houses;

yet to Avril, the natural world held the key to the meaning of death: "How expressive and touching is its language." Conceding that the traditional gallery around the cemetery would certainly impart an air of grandeur as well as a convenient shelter in times of inclement weather, the Avril report rejected this feature in favor of an unimpeded view of the "cheerful" countryside. To assure this visual continuity and yet to protect the burial grounds, the entire cemetery was to be surrounded by a ha-ha, with a vertical masonry wall to the interior and a sloping, grass-covered counterscarp to the other side. In this manner, a most important if not the determining feature of the landscape garden was appropriated by the cemetery. Hirschfeld had proposed using the ha-ha for the garden cemetery; the Avril report applied it in a particular way.

Since it was universally believed that for hygienic reasons the southern exposure of a cemetery needed the most ventilation, this side was not even planted but rather left almost entirely open. The sole entry to the cemetery would be located here and controlled by two small guardhouses. The other three sides were to be planted with a double row of poplars. To the exterior where the counterscarp met the level ground there would be a low hedge. Thus, from within, the Field of Rest would seem to partake of an expansive natural setting, the grass-covered counterscarp effecting a smooth visual transition outward and the poplar trees serving as a type of natural demarcation along the way.

Whereas Blondel and his successors once wanted to have the visitor walk down into the ground as a reminder of his mortality, the Avril report strove to achieve an opposite effect. By slightly elevating the terrain and planting it with grass and trees, the architects of the Field of Rest hoped to make the view of the interior more "pleasing" to the approaching visitor. Just one year earlier, Cérutti, who had no taste for the "horrifying aspects of death," had lauded the so-called Valley of Tombs at the garden of Betz for being situated on a "raised esplanade." As for the vegetation in the cemetery, traditional signs of melancholy—cypresses, yews, weeping willows, and poppies—were to be combined with fragrant plants and flowering bushes whose perfumes would inebriate the visitor so as to fill him with a sense of calm. Soon you will forget the loss that you have sustained, mused Avril, and before you realize it, you will find yourself envying the dead.

In the Field of Rest there would be no mass graves, only orderly rows where the corpses would be buried side by side. After six to ten years the graves would be reopened. During this period, calculated for the body to undergo a complete decomposition, the dead would enjoy an individual grave. The bodies would be buried only one deep with no superimposition of corpses permitted.

Hence, friends and relatives would know where to find a loved one and could focus their affections on his or her precise grave.

No sumptuous mausoleums, so offensive to the principle of equality, would be permitted here. The only distinctions would be the funerary honors accorded at an annual festival for the dead when orators would eulogize worthy citizens. Those who received public approbation would have their names inscribed on the base of the central monument under the category of their particular virtues: "filial piety, *bienfaisance*, heroic courage, devotion, patriotism, humanity, arts, sciences, literature, extraordinary talent, legislature." The monument itself would present an allegory teaching that virtue confers immortality. The message would be reinforced with plantings suggestive of longevity or honor, such as laurels, oaks, olive trees, and flowers called immortals.

The Avril report was a pivotal document in the history of the cemeteries of Paris. Because the National Convention accorded neither permission nor funds to purchase the land for the four new burial grounds, the project did not come to immediate fruition. The vision of the cemetery, though, based on burial in rows rather than in mass graves and planted with grass and trees became the basis of all future planning. The text of the report was also to serve as the working document for succeeding municipal administrations.

The Avril report also linked the planning efforts of the prerevolutionary era to those of the revolutionary period. Without mentioning earlier projects, the Avril report implicitly concurred with several plans as to the number of cemeteries and their locations. The closest projects were those by François-Victor Pérard de Montreuil (c. 1772–1777) and the Abbé Patry (1787), which proposed burial grounds located to the north on the Plaine de Clichy, to the east by the Barrière du Trône, to the southeast on the Plaine d'Ivry, and to the south on the Plaine de Montrouge.

The Plaine d'Ivry had been proposed as early as 1765 in the Parlement's Arrêt of May 21, which named a total of eight locations for new cemeteries. The actual site chosen under the revolution by the commissioners working with the Avril report became the cause of much litigation in the second and third decades of the nineteenth century as recalcitrant property owners opposed the city's efforts to open a burial ground there. The project was finally abandoned in 1832.

The southwestern site was centered on the relatively new cemetery of the Hôpital de la Charité (1785). This area was enlarged to become the Cemetery of Montparnasse (1824). To the north of Paris, a municipal cemetery was opened on the Plaine de Clichy in 1798 as the "Cemetery under Montmartre." After several years of service it was closed and then reopened a few years later as the enlarged Cemetery of Montmartre (1825). A cemetery to the east located along the route to Vincennes beyond the Barrière du Trône (today, Place de la Nation), remained a goal until 1804, when the Cemetery of Père Lachaise was opened, slightly to the north (fig. 172).

Given the importance of the Avril report, one is tempted to speculate about how the commissioners from the Administration of Public Works intended to marry a regular disposition of graves with a beautifully planted terrain. With a little imagination it is possible to understand how this was to be achieved by looking at the Cemetery of Montparnasse, the only Parisian cemetery actually located on the exact site foreseen in the Avril report (fig. 173). It may even be possible that the plan of this cemetery was derived from the Avril report, from accompanying documents, or from a subsequent interpretation of its provisions. It is striking that the writer of a guidebook to the cemeteries of Paris published in 1816 was thoroughly perplexed as to why toward 1810 the city had prepared a vast terrain at this very location by digging a large *fossé* or ha-ha more than fourteen feet wide rather than erecting walls as found at the Cemetery of Père Lachaise. Although the Cemetery of Montparnasse was opened in 1824 as a walled enclosure, the earlier arrangement suggests an effort to create a Field of Rest as outlined in the Avril report.

In the early days, the Cemetery of Montparnasse must have looked much like the burial ground that Avril and his colleagues had envisaged. Today one can still feel the solemn but elevating effect imparted by the upward slope of the land from the point of the old entrance to the central square. Were the allegorical monument envisaged in the Avril report placed here, it would make a striking impression from the entrance. The tombs around the central circle are arranged in a slight amphitheater, most pronounced in the quadrant that includes an old mill, for there is the greatest slope. Beyond the circle, the land begins to rise again. In this cemetery, the graves are all in orderly rows. If the early plan is accurate, it would appear that they always have been. Hence the Cemetery of Montparnasse provides a plausible and interesting interpretation of the intentions expressed in the Avril report.

The geometrical rigor and simplicity of the plan of Montparnasse may suggest a dryness and a monotony to the layout. While this cemetery lacks the picturesque quality of Père Lachaise, the upward slope of the land, the contrasts between the dark plantings along the footpaths and the lighter but noble foliage bordering the major allées, the abundance of mature trees throughout, as well as the mausoleums (which the Avril report had forbidden), make the Cemetery of Montparnasse a unique and engaging landscape.

In the interplay between Panthéon and Elysium, the publication of the Avril report seems to have prompted an ambitious project

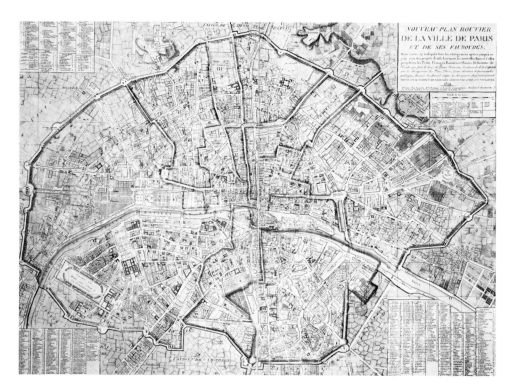

172
Paris, 1809.

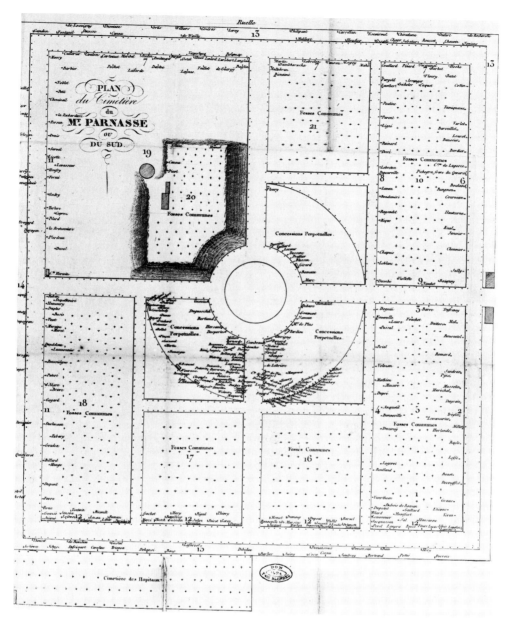

173
Cemetery of
Montparnasse, Paris,
1829.

by the self-proclaimed urbanist, the "disinterested citizen" Maille Dussausoy. On 25 Ventôse, year II (March 15, 1794), just ten days after his first visit to the Panthéon, Dussausoy submitted a proposal for an extensive Elysium around the Panthéon: "J'ai vu ce projet en grand." Thinking big, as he said, Dussausoy imagined a garden on all sides of the Panthéon that would extend, for example, all the way to the Rue (Saint) Jacques to the west. The entire garden would not even be surrounded by a grill, which would block one's sight, but only by a waist-high parapet. This wall was to be crowned with a balustrade of the Doric order, chosen because Dussausoy had read in Scamozzi that the Doric was suited to honoring heroism. Pedestals located around the wall would be inscribed with accounts of heroic actions, and allegorical figures would flank the two entries, which would always remain open. As in the Avril project, the interior would be fully visible from the outside, and the ground would be raised. A broad path beginning at the entrance would gently rise to the level of the principal terrace, which would be at the same height as the top of the circumferential wall. Planted with cypresses, oaks, laurels, and poplars, covered with a green lawn with flowers growing everywhere, and bordered with box, this garden would receive the statues of the great men and women of France. Beyond this Elysium there would be a broad, sand-covered terrace extending up to and surrounding the Panthéon. This vast esplanade would accommodate the crowds during the ceremonies at the Panthéon. Finally, all sides of the Panthéon were to be planted with "the most beautiful flowers." The entire ensemble would form a nodal point for four irradiating streets which would reach out far into the city. Within the Elysium, all visitors would find touching and inspiring civic lessons in this "realm of peace and of eternal rest." One could not ask for a more complete transposition of the Avril Field of Rest into an urban context.

The terms of the Avril report were to have a far-reaching effect on the image not only of the cemetery but generally on that of any funerary precinct dedicated to the martyrs of the revolution. At the Festival for the Supreme Being (June 8, 1794) in Franconville, for example, Cadet de Vaux proposed to the commune a funerary altar conceived in this spirit and consecrated to the memory of those who died in combat for the cause of liberty. The general assembly of citizens voted that this monument would be crowned with an obelisk and placed at the entry to the town in a square that would be surrounded by a dry ditch bordered with a hedge and decorated to the interior with cypresses, laurels, oaks, and assorted evergreens. The drawing of the project, it should be noted, had been obtained from an architect in Paris. If this proposal had been realized, it would have created a miniature version of the Field of Rest.

The Terror bequeathed to the successive stages of the revolution two visions of how the dead might be buried: either on private property out in the country or in municipal and egalitarian cemeteries. Under the Directory, these two orientations would clash as each found its champions and detractors. The underlying premises behind the debate, though, would change when a more conservative conception of the social order replaced the radical ideas of the Terror. Egalitarian visions for the redistribution of land were replaced by an acceptance of the status quo through which property ownership became the prerequisite for voting. The call for burial in one's own field or on one's own estate was directed now toward a privileged bourgeoisie. At the same time, the proponents of municipal cemeteries saw these institutions as a means of fostering social cohesiveness and of promulgating illusions of an equality that did not exist in either an economic or political sense. Since life in society was characterized by "vast inequalities in wealth," it seemed advisable to place civil ceremonies such as birth, marriage, and death under an egalitarian banner and to use the emotive power of these events to cement allegiance both to the individual family and to the larger society. While these controversies were being argued, the Department of the Seine, with the active cooperation of the Minister of the Interior, pursued both courses of action. The Directory was characterized by vigorous efforts both to establish new cemeteries outside the city and to facilitate burials on private property.

Between the Terror and the Directory, the period of the Thermidorian Reaction (July 28, 1794–October 26, 1795) was relatively quiet for the history of the cemetery. There were two important events, though, which primed the arguments heard under the Directory. One focused on the dichotomy between the Panthéon and the countryside. The other was directed toward the deplorable state of the Parisian cemeteries.

## Two Lost Souls

In his report of September 15, 1794, to the National Convention on behalf of the Committee on Public Instruction, Joseph Lakanal conveyed the committee's uneasiness about consigning Rousseau to the vaults of the Panthéon. Rousseau's admission to the "temple of great men" should be provisional, pending the planting of the "vast" and "august" woods around this monument. At that time, the "friend of the countryside and of nature" should be taken outside and his grave surrounded by the poplar trees that had become "inseparable" from his tomb. In that manner, all feeling people (les âmes sensibles) would be reminded of the groves at Ermenonville.

With the projected Elysium in the planning stages, the committee came upon a solution that might satisfy in part the desire to keep Rousseau in nature and evoke, if only temporarily, his final abode in the park of Ermenonville. As part of the ceremony in bringing Rousseau's corpse to Paris, it was decided that the sarcophagus be placed on a stepped platform in the round basin of the Tuileries gardens (fig. 174). Here Rousseau rested on a miniature Ile des Peupliers on October 10–11, 1794, before being taken to the Panthéon. Rousseau's displacement from Ermenonville was soon to become a rallying point for the advocates of burial on private property who sought to maintain close bonds, both physical and psychological, with the dead.

On the somber side, a certain Delamalle published a small brochure in the year III, probably in the early spring of 1795, calculated to spur the authorities to rectify the breakdown of funeral ceremonies and the disarray of the cemeteries of Paris. The author purported to describe the loathsome burial of his mother in a cemetery by the Barrière Blanche. (It is not clear whether this was the abandoned quarry first used to receive the victims of August 10, 1792, or the cemetery of Roch, which had been opened in 1782 after the grave diggers had been caught stealing shrouds from the corpses in the parish's previous burial ground.) Perhaps the most remarkable aspect of Delamalle's text is that he felt compelled to make a case for a respectful funeral and a respected grave as "sacred and solemn institutions among all civilized peoples."

Delamalle's narrative is a tale of desolation. With neither friends nor family arriving on the day of the funeral, Delamalle and his father's steward proceeded toward the cemetery with one civil commissioner and the porters who bore the coffin. The procession, if one could call it that, had little dignity, since the porters dragged the coffin more than they carried it as they dodged heedless passersby. Those who unwittingly knocked into the funeral party were obliged to take notice. Otherwise, the public was indifferent. Toward the end of the journey the cortege was joined by a filthy woman in rags who shook her keys and conversed with the porters for the remainder of the trip. What purpose the keys served is a mystery, for suddenly the commissioner informed Delamalle that they had arrived. The incredulous narrator found himself in the middle of the street beside an empty lot covered with mud. In spite of the functionary's admonitions that it was useless to proceed, Delamalle and the faithful servant persevered across the impracticable terrain. Reaching their destination, Delamalle found a "narrow plot encumbered in the middle by an enormous pile of earth and debris bordered by a path covered with a foot of mud over which a wretched plank had been laid to provide a means of access." The coffin was put down in the mud, and the tricolor flag was removed along with the straps which held the coffin together. The funeral was over. Seeing that Delamalle would not leave, the grave diggers threw a shovelful of mud on the

174
Hubert Robert, view
of Rousseau's
temporary tomb in
the Tuileries gardens,
Paris, October
10–11, 1794.

*Two Lost Souls*

coffin. To one side, Delamalle noticed a wooden scaffolding covering a deep pit which disgorged a cadaverous odor. "I turned away. A feeling of horror made me doubt for a moment that man has an immortal soul and that this body, so marvelously organized, is the work of a god."

In reading this tale of horror one wonders to what extent it exaggerated actual conditions of funerals and cemeteries. A report read to the Institut National on the funeral procession and burial of the architect Charles De Wailly on November 3, 1798, at the Cemetery under Montmartre, the successor to both Roche and the Barrière Blanche, leads one to conclude that the element of fiction was slight indeed. One also wonders whether the prerevolutionary parish cemeteries appeared any different after several days of rain.

It was the total absence of a ceremony as well as of any demarcations between the cemetery and its surroundings at a time when people shuddered at both the thought and the sight of a communal grave that made this experience so traumatic for Delamalle and his responsive readers. One of them, Charles-Joseph Trouvé, was moved to insert an article in the *Moniteur Universel* of 26 Germinal, year III (April 15, 1795) deploring the thoughtlessness, contempt, and impiety of current burials. Commenting on how sensibilities had been brutalized by the Terror, Trouvé echoed Delamalle's plea for encouraging respect for the dead and for reinstituting decent funerals. Like the removal of Rousseau's body to the Panthéon, the indifference to the funeral and the unacceptable state of the cemeteries acted as a time bomb that would explode under the Directory.

As a public outcry, Delamalle's pamphlet and Trouvé's letter constituted isolated events. Yet that summer, the Commission of Public Works was especially attentive to the salubrity of the cemeteries of Paris. Inspectors paid monthly visits to ensure that the mass graves were well maintained, meaning primarily that the corpses were adequately covered with quicklime and earth. This was the only way to prevent, reduce, or eliminate the noxious odors. As one document explained, the Commission's policy was merely a holding action. The high cost of materials and labor were cited as preventing the establishment of new cemeteries: "We must limit ourselves to diminishing the problems of those which we are now using."

**Facing the Abyss**    Under the Directory, in the spring of 1796, the Department of the Seine launched a new and comprehensive program to reform the entire system of burials. The first issue that it addressed was the funeral procession. At this time, the Minister of Police was complaining about the public's indifference to the funeral. As a result, on 3 Germinal, year IV (March 23, 1796), the city of Paris instructed its arrondissements that the municipal Arrêté of 1 Frimaire, year II (November 21, 1793) requiring the presence of a civil commissioner for each funeral all the way to the place of burial was to be faithfully executed. In its Arrêté of 23 Germinal, year IV (April 12, 1796), the Department of the Seine, noting that funerals in Paris lacked suitable decency, went a step further. Borrowing features from the Avril report, the Department decreed that four uniformed porters would carry the coffin from the home to the cemetery. The cortege was to be led by a uniformed inspector carrying a plaque admonishing all passersby to respect the dead. All traffic, whether pedestrian, horse, or carriage, had to yield so as not to interrupt the movement of the funeral party. Porters, grave diggers, and inspectors were also instructed to behave with dignity in the exercise of their functions. In this same Arrêté, the Department affirmed that all citizens had the right to bury their family and friends wherever they wished so long as they selected a spot outside the city. This provision opened the way for burials on private property.

In the following month on 11 Prairial (May 30) and hence immediately preceding the summer, the Department submitted a report to Minister of the Interior Benezech, requesting that the existing cemeteries of Paris be replaced by four new burial grounds located outside the city. The entire report consists of a reiteration of the project submitted by Avril in the year II. Although the Avril report had once been favorably received, the Department of the Seine now worried that the "artists" who wrote the report might not have made sound choices in so important and, in many respects, so technical a subject. It seemed advisable that the Minister of the Interior have the Council on Public Buildings verify all earlier decisions as well as finish any uncompleted matters.

The image of the cemetery that emerged from the requested reports retreated from the radically new proposals of the Avril project. While the double row of trees around the cemetery was maintained for hygienic reasons, the idea of a wide ditch or haha was deemed unsuitable and too expensive. A simple stone wall inside the plantings seemed more appropriate. As health officers, Antoine Cadet de Vaux and Michel-Augustin Thouret modified the proposal to bury the dead in individual graves placed in a row by permitting a stacking of corpses three or four bodies deep. Only the four sites for the cemeteries were retained, with the addition of another burial ground exclusively for the hospitals.

Three days after the first report was submitted, a second report to the Minister of the Interior outlined a provisional reorganization of burials which could be followed until the new cemeteries were opened. On the north side of Paris, the cemeteries of Nicolas-des-Champs, Paul, and Roch would be closed; to the south, the cemeteries of Marcel, Jacques-du-Haut-Pas, Geneviève, Victor, and Gros-Caillou would also be closed. This left five cemeteries to serve the entire city. They were among the most recently opened and the farthest from the center. To the north there were the prerevolutionary, former parish cemeteries of Laurent and Marguerite. The latter burial ground, cited as an ideal cemetery in 1763, was now "saturated" with corpses, but the city could not do without it. There was also a Cemetery of Monceau, located adjacent to the park of that name and at the entrance of the village of Monceau. This burial ground had been opened as a provisional cemetery in 1793. To the south of Paris there were the cemeteries Catherine, opened by the Sisters of Sainte-Catherine in 1783 adjacent to the Cemetery Clamart, and Vaugirard, which had been opened in 1784 for the parish of Saint-Sulpice. Upon the recommendation of the Council on Public Buildings, the Minister of the Interior approved this reorganization toward the end of July. In addition to these five cemeteries, the burial ground for the Hôpital de la Charité was to continue to be used for the indigent who died in that establishment.

In closing Roch in favor of the continued use of Monceau, the Minister of the Interior opened a Pandora's box of complaints that led to two years of controversy between the two communities where the cemeteries were located. Each side won temporary victories as Roch was subsequently reopened and then closed again. This embroilment impelled the Department of the Seine to seek a solution by purchasing property to open a new cemetery on the Plaine de Clichy. By late summer 1798, burials were taking place in the new Cemetery under Montmartre, the first municipal cemetery outside of Paris opened expressly for the purpose of establishing a new order in burials.

The Department's initial actions at the Cemetery under Montmartre were to enclose part of the land with planking and to construct a shelter to house the grave digger so that he could guard against grave robbers. Then the Department pleaded with the Minister of the Interior to approve expenditure of additional funds to make the burial ground into a true Field of Rest. Herein resided the vindication of the Avril report. In spite of differences about particular features, there was no returning to the charnel houses and mass graves of the traditional burial ground:

It is urgent to enclose the terrain with walls, to surround it with trees, to fill it with balsamic plants, to construct a simple and solid home both to lodge the concierge and to receive in a decent manner those who accompany deceased family members or friends, and finally to take all measures to prevent this cemetery from having the sad and hideous aspect of those which we have seen for too long a time now in the middle of Paris.

In retrospect there is a poignancy about this unsuccessful request. It was not a comprehensive proposal for a nonexistent cemetery but rather an attempt to dignify an actual burial ground in which the local government was placing its hopes, a plea for funds after years of inaction on the part of the central government and at a time when one could hardly expect anything else.

Paris received its new cemetery only because the Department of the Seine, in desperation about "fetid and cadaverous vapors" from the Cemetery of Roch, which seemed to threaten the entire neighborhood, broke all the rules and cut through all the red tape. It even went so far as not to bother to obtain prior permission from the legislature, let alone formal approval from the central administration. For nearly a year afterward, the Minister of the Interior repeatedly admonished the Department to regularize the situation according to the legal formalities or face the prospect of having its actions declared null and void.

In the end, the Cemetery under Montmartre differed little from its predecessors. In many respects it could have been the scene of Delamalle's lament. In 1812 the Emperor Napoleon accidentally came upon this burial ground and was so shocked that he ordered his architect Fontaine to prepare plans for four new cemeteries for Paris. Because of the frightful conditions there, this cemetery, sometimes wishfully called the Champ de Repos, was closed for several years over the course of the first two decades of the nineteenth century. During 1818–1824 adjacent properties were acquired to more than double its size and thereby facilitate its reopening in 1825 as the Cemetery of Montmartre. Several views of the cemetery dating from 1824, particularly of the entry and of the commmunal grave (figs. 175–176), capture the ambiance of this burial ground, which had prompted the mayor of the first arrondissement to write to Prefect of the Seine Frochot in 1802: "This is not a cemetery, it is an abyss."

## The New Theologians

The spring offensive in 1796 by the Department of the Seine and the Minister of the Interior was accompanied by a public outcry against conditions in the cemeteries of Paris and throughout France. This protest was most intense during the summer of 1796, tapering off through the fall and winter and reappearing intermittently in the following year. In Prairial, year IV, several voices were raised condemning the disgraceful treatment of corpses and the general disrespect for tombs. A legislator named Bontoux published a denunciation of the violence under the Terror along with a plea for a proper respect for the dead. Emmanuel Pastoret, in a report before the national Council of Five Hundred, lamented the current mistreatment of dead bodies as well as the violation of the grave. In the name of the Commission on the Classification and the Revision of Laws, he called for a law to punish these acts. Other legislators felt that this was not enough. As a consequence, a special commission was established to determine a

175
Cemetery of
Montmartre, Paris.
View by Schaal of
the entrance in 1824.

176
Cemetery of
Montmartre, Paris.
View by Schaal of
the communal grave
in 1824.

*The Field of Rest*

suitable mode of burial. Before this new document was delivered on November 11, numerous citizens, several of considerable stature, outlined their own vision of a decent funeral and an appropriate cemetery: Pierre-Louis Roederer, in a speech at a public session of the Institut National on July 3; François-Valentin Mulot in an address at the Lycée des Arts on August 2; J.-M. Coupé, member of the Council of Five Hundred, in an essay published in Thermidor (late July–early August); A. Jourdan in a letter to the *Moniteur Universel* of July 6; and the poet Gabriel-Marie Legouvé in a reading of his verses before the Institut National on October 6.

Considered together, these documents reveal that the image of an open and verdant cemetery had become a common vision. Furthermore, the discourse at this time was characterized by a heightened degree of sentimentality about death and burial. The recurring theme was illusion: the illusion of passing into a state of sweet rest; that the dead live on and that their presence can be sensed in the gentle movements of the natural world, the rustling leaves, the murmuring streams; and that the dead as well as the living would be comforted by carefully tending the grave, by planting flowers there, and by providing a comforting shade.

*L'âme sensible* took to heart Bernardin de Saint-Pierre's dictum that the tomb stands on the frontier between two worlds, subscribing to it with an intensity unknown in previous years. Roederer spoke of the intimate need of the imagination to feel that the bond between the living and the dead was maintained and sustained through a communication at the grave. Jourdan shuddered at the thought of throwing quicklime over a corpse, as if the earth itself did not separate the living from their loved ones all too soon.

The private grave was seen as a bulwark against the potentially irreparable rupture caused by death. After citing the examples of Rousseau in the park of Ermenonville and of Court de Gébelin at Franconville, Jourdan imagined his own grave on his property. It would be a "truly sweet consolation" to know that after his death, his body would be buried on the land which he had cultivated, that friendly hands would cover him with grass and plant his favorite flower over a simple earthen mound. The thick and somber shade of the cypress and thuja would serve to "concentrate" the regrets of his friends who came to visit him. "Happier after my death than I had been in life, I would not be separated from all that was dear to me. Oh! He who sleeps in the midst of all that he loves must enjoy a truly sweet peace." Legouvé rendered these same feelings in verse whose full import can be felt in a short extract from a very long poem:

Through the charm of this site, called toward their faded
    remains

We will come to mourn those whom we cherished
We will imagine seeing their attentive shades float about
We will imagine that to our plaintive souls
Their voices respond in saddened tones
In the voice of the winds sighing around them
. . .
In the flowers, in the woods, escaping fate
Our parents will return to converse with us.

To these new theologians, the desire for immortality was actually a wish to remain with the family physically as well as in its memory. To Mulot, the private grave was an inalienable right. Rousseau should never have been taken away from Ermenonville, from the tomb consecrated by the hands of friendship. To Roederer, the simple column erected where Turenne lost his life was much more moving than his elaborate tomb in Saint-Denis. To Coupé, the Panthéon should contain only the statues of great men. Their remains should rest where they died. All agreed that a woods, with its majesty and silence, was the most desirable place for burial. Flowers, birds, and a murmuring stream would complete the scene.

For those not fortunate enough to have property for a private burial, there should be vast cemeteries with the same types of plantings. There were to be none of those "horrible" communal graves where vice and virtue lay piled together, where it was impossible to find a friend or a loved one, and where the disgusting mass of putrefying corpses could only make you shudder. Whether in the cemetery or in the private garden, the monument should not be the sumptuous and arrogant mausoleum of the wealthy as under the ancien régime but rather a humble memorial doubly expressive of republican simplicity and heartfelt tenderness.

## The Space of Ignominy

The sense of direct rapport between physical scenes and emotional states that characterized the theory, design, and experience of Neoclassical architecture and of the picturesque landscape gardens of the second half of the eighteenth century reached its height during the revolution. To writers on death, physical surroundings impinged immediately and forcefully on the viewer, as they determined response through an irresistible visceral reaction. In considering the Paris morgue, for example, Avril could not stop himself from imagining that the unfortunate victims there had been the criminals themselves: "If we wished to make them guilty of the crime by which they perished, would it have been possible to choose a more foul and disgusting place?"

In a speech to the Institut National in 1796, Roederer proposed using this manner of reaction to instil virtue and to discourage vice. To this end, he suggested pairing contrasting cemeteries. One would be an Elysium whose resplendent landscape held forth a promise of happiness to those who led a moral life. Nearby would be a burial ground for executed criminals, fashioned as sepulchral caverns cut into "terrifying, arid rocks" over which vultures ("symbols of remorse") would hover. Roederer's fantastic vision of a criminals' burial ground appears to have been directly inspired by William Chambers's much publicized description of the scenes of "terror" in the so-called Chinese gardens which he popularized in his writings. "Bats, owls, vultures, . . . gibbets, crosses, wheels, . . . dismal recesses, . . . deep caverns, brushwood, and brambles" were the principal ingredients in this phantasmagoria of terror, whose principal use for Chambers was to contrast with the "pleasing" scenes which preceded or followed. Remembering how criminals under the ancien régime were hung from the gibbet and how they were then thrown into the refuse dump at Montfaucon, Roederer sought to revive this custom by allying it to a cemetery designed according to the precepts of the new *jardin anglo-chinois*.

Roederer's proposal for paired cemeteries was soon elaborated upon by Pierre Giraud, architect for the prisons of the Department of the Seine. Giraud's cemetery for executed criminals did not partake of the splendid mysteries of Roederer's caverns but rather was a refuse dump sunk into the ground and bordered by a low wall so that it could be seen. At the center was a large cauldron where the bodies were to be burned together, their remains then unceremoniously dumped into large communal graves. In this manner, the horrors of decomposition were to be magnified while also being associated with the shameful stigma of a criminal's end.

Across the way from this cemetery was the special Elysium intended for the remainder of the population. Here Giraud drew upon the contemporary fascination with an idea popularized by the German chemist Johann Joachim Becker (*Physica subterranea*, 1669, 1734, 1768) that human remains could be saved from the horrors of putrefaction by being transformed into a beautiful, imperishable, luminous glass. By conferring immortality through a transmutation of human bones into everlasting, diaphanous glass, the Elysium was, in Giraud's mind, the logical counterpart to the treatment of the criminals' remains. It should be remembered that no less a personage than Jean-Jacques Rousseau had been equally fascinated by Becker's proposition.

In the same year in which Roederer spoke before the Institut National, a founder named Gautier presented Becker's ideas to a public assembly at the Lycée des Arts. According to Mulot, a chemist named Dufourni attempted the experiment. Dufourni or some other enthusiast imagined forming a family "gallery of busts" for the cemetery, where the vacant pedestal, signifying "the honors of vitrification denied," would be like the ancient Roman practice of engraving T. N. (*tacito nomino*) on the grave to discourage crime. Giraud, inspired either by Gautier's lecture or by Mulot's published observations on these events, combined the idea of the glass bust with the paired cemeteries.

By the fall of 1798, Giraud completed his drawings of the Elysium, which depict a circular gallery oriented to the four cardinal points (fig. 177). The interior is densely planted and at the center is a pyramid, which houses the furnaces. Here the bones would be separated from the flesh so that they could be transformed into a bust or urn of translucent glass. These would be taken home to be placed on the family mantel, where they would inspire youth to emulate ancestral virtues as well as to discourage any potential miscreants from crime. The unclaimed skeletons would be used to fashion the columns and sarcophagi of the peripheral gallery in the cemetery, eventually to form a diaphanous ring of immortality.

With these two projects by Roederer and Giraud, the Enlightenment concept of the space of emulation underwent a radical transformation. The space of ignominy became the touchstone by which all were to be judged. No longer the worthy but rather the reprobates were singled out from the undifferentiated masses. Here we find the triumph of the Gessnerian vision of domestic virtues. As Cérutti had written about the tombs at Betz, the proposed cemeteries were touching because they eternalized the memory of love rather than that of grandeur. As Roederer would add: "In a republic, we should direct the citizen's attention not to the honors of apotheosis but to the sweetness of grateful, respectful, and tender memories." With Roederer and Giraud, virtue became the condition of each individual as his descendants would remember him. The central chapel, once the space par excellence for the recognition of superior accomplishments, was now the way to immortality through vitrification for all but the excluded few.

Roederer and Giraud certainly showed little restraint in their vivid schemes for promoting virtue, but they were not alone. In the following years (1797–1798), the Institut National posed the question: "What are the institutions proper for founding the memory of a people?" In the responses, this august body was told that the solution consisted in erecting stigmatizing columns in the public squares and engraving these columns with the names of criminals. Then, in 1800, when the Institut asked what types of funerals and cemeteries should be established, the idea of paired burial grounds reappeared in many of the responses. In the last years of the eighteenth century, people were haunted by what François-Antoine Daubermesnil, in the report of November 11, 1796 by the Special Commission on Burials, termed "this involuntary impression that we feel, that unshakable repugnance at our annihilation." The greatest bulwark against this nothingness

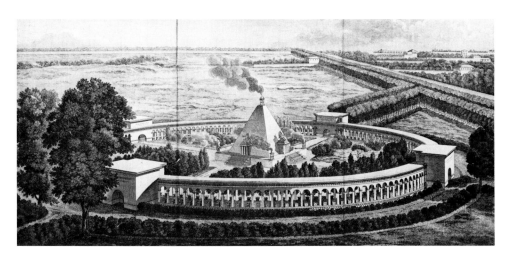

177
Pierre Giraud, "Field
of Rest" for the
Champs-Elysées, the
Butte-Chaumont, or
Montparnasse, Paris,
1798–1801.

was the individual grave and the cherished memory. Social thinkers attempted to profit from this obsession by denying the outlaw the solace of either.

## Private Burials or Public Cemeteries?

Laws were not enough to fashion a new society. Legislators argued that a people's character was formed through institutions. Among these the funeral and the cemetery held a privileged place. La Revellière-Lépeaux encapsulated the social philosophy of the Directory when he wrote: "Make man loving and you will make him good." To the Special Commission on Burials, tender feelings were best nurtured over the grave on one's own property. Once again Rousseau became the rallying point for the advocates for private burials. In 1796 renewed concern about the structural safety of the Panthéon only served further to chill the heart of the sensitive observer. Continued weakening of the supports for the dome seemed to portend imminent collapse. Why am I so moved at the Ile des Peupliers, asked Daubermesnil, and left so cold at the Panthéon? Yet in advocating private graves, Daubermesnil did not intend to reintroduce the "haughty" mausoleums of the ancien régime. The republic had to prevent the emergence of a new aristocracy. Hence the grave was to be planted with a tree and marked by a stone inscribed solely with the name of the deceased. For the less fortunate who did not have property for a private burial, there were to be municipal cemeteries planted with trees.

The Daubermesnil report sparked a heated debate. Sébastien Mercier shuddered at the abuses that the provision for private cremation or inhumation would allow. Mulot wanted to make sure that the "trenches" in the municipal cemeteries would not be those deep communal graves which "only painted the rapacity of death rather than its sweet rest." As for the question of the mausoleum, certainly the nation should have the exclusive right to erect elaborate memorials to the worthy dead, but was it not a matter of individual liberty to erect a monument in a family garden to honor domestic virtues? Mulot found no danger but only positive value in inscriptions with such consoling words as, "he was a good husband and a good father."

La Revellière-Lépeaux, member of the ruling Directory, and J.-B. Leclerc of the Council of Five Hundred thoroughly disagreed. While sensitive to the appeal of private burials, these leaders believed that all the principal rites of passage—birth, marriage, and death—had to be regulated by the government in an egalitarian manner. In that way the wealthy would be prevented from an offensive, ostentatious display and the poor would be rescued from a scandalous indifference. Domestic and social bonds would be fortified and the lesson of equality before the law would be made manifest. Furthermore, burial on private property or within a cemetery belonging to a sect was risky since there was no guarantee that the land would not be sold in the future. To satisfy the desire for an individual grave, La Revellière-Lépeaux and Leclerc evoked the country burial ground as a model even for the urban center. To La Revellière-Lépeaux this meant establishing spacious and isolated cemeteries where each person could be buried separately and "where we could go to cry over their tombs as we spread flowers there.'" Leclerc stressed the importance of allotting land in the cemetery to each family where it could group its graves together yet without any apparent signs. To assure absolute uniformity throughout the cemetery, all tombstones would have to be the same and could be inscribed only with the name, age, and profession of the deceased.

The Administration of the Department of the Seine was not impressed with this reasoning. While continuing its efforts to provide Paris with new municipal cemeteries, the Department delivered two new Arrêtés on the subject of graves on private property. The Arrêté of 22 Floréal, year V (May 11, 1797) sought expressly "to facilitate in every way possible" such burials. Whereas the previous Arrêté of 23 Germinal, year IV had excluded private graves from within the city, now they would be permitted "in gardens, courtyards, cultivated lands, and other vast and aerated locations" within the faubourgs themselves. This provision was reiterated in the Arrêté of 28 Frimaire, year VII (December 18, 1798) and liberalized even further for the smaller communities within the Department. This last Arrêté constitutes a remarkable social document because its preamble invoked all the major arguments in favor of private burials ranging from considerations of natural rights to fostering bonds of affection and to promoting virtue as well as removing the hideous aspect of death. In a spirit reminiscent of Bernardin de Saint-Pierre, the Arrêté encouraged proprietors to plant over the grave a foreign tree which would yield a useful product. Sepulchral monuments would be permitted, but had to be approved by the Department, which presumably would guard against marks of heraldry.

*A Funerary Bosquet*

Given the support for the right to private burial, seconded by the departmental rulings, it should not surprise to learn that Gessner's *Idylls* were immensely popular under the Directory and the Consulate. Readers found in them a mirror to their sentimental values in various aspects of domestic relations, and particularly those involved in death. The grave designed by the architect Michel-Barthélemy Hazon, for example, was thoroughly imbued with the spirit and the ceremonial gestures of the contemporary idyll. A former member of the defunct Académie Royale d'Architecture, Hazon produced an extensive series of annotated drawings for this project. Perhaps it is fitting to note that Hazon was the father-in-law of Alexandre-Théodore Brongniart, the architect who several years later would be called upon to design the Cemetery of Père Lachaise.

Toward the end of the revolution, Hazon drew up a project to convert a bosquet in his park of Cantiers in Normandy into a funerary grove. This *bosquet religieux*, as the architect called it, was consecrated to the future burial of Hazon and his wife. A view of the first project (figs. 178–179) shows an irregular clearing, closed by dense plantings and preceded by a rusticated gate. The inscriptions on both sides of the entry explain why this area was termed a religious bosquet. The interior one repeated the Golden Rule and advised that death is frightening only to the wicked, because "the body perishes but the soul is immortal."

This was a religous enclosure not only for theological reasons but also because it was to serve as a type of family altar. The inscription to the exterior proclaimed, after the manner of the idylls, that here was the final resting place of two spouses who had passed a life of love with children, family, and friends. Dedicated "to filial piety," the bosquet beckoned coming generations to reaffirm their moral fortitude through respectful visits to their parents and ancestors.

Wishing to remain married in death as in life, Hazon and his wife conceived of a tomb under an earthen pyramid, planted with grass and covered with a tree growing up through the center. A symbolic ring suspended from the tree was inscribed with the words "united forever." Below this hung a medallion with the couple's busts in bas-relief. The simple grass-covered mound and the tree above the grave incarnated the type of memorial that Daubermesnil and others had been proposing as the ideal touching monument. These elements are also reminiscent of the décor of so many revolutionary festivals and predecessors in the folklore of the ancien régime where the planting of a tree constituted an act of sanctifying some event and its decoration was a joyous celebration of the special occasion. The same sacral character is found here in Hazon's *bosquet religieux*, where the tree has been planted by the couple and dedicated "to posterity."

This symbol of a living and enduring marriage, along with Hazon's invocation to the sky—"Spread your nourishing dew over its branches"—recall stories such as Pierre-Silvain Maréchal's pastoral tale, "The Marriage Tree." In this story, the young shepherd Lycias proposes on the day of his marriage to the shepherdess Myrthe that they plant together "with our own hands in the most pleasant spot" by their house a young tree which Lycias has been tending for this occasion. The tree will grow with their love and would serve as "its witness, its guarantor, and its glory." Eventually

178
Michel-Barthélemy
Hazon, *Bosquet
Religieux*. Project for
a private grave in the
architect's own
garden. c.
1800–1801.

179
Hazon, *Bosquet
Religieux*, entrance
gate, c. 1800–1801.

*A Funerary Bosquet*

the couple will enjoy the shade of this tree with their numerous children; and even later the tree will live on to perpetuate the memory of the "faithful couple's tender love." Here their descendants will learn of the happiness of their distant ancestors.

The horror of being separated in death from friends and family prompted the Hazons to invite their relations to "keep them company." To the right of the pyramid is a simple grave surmounted by a bust for their friend the painter Voiriot. "Dear Voiriot has already reserved his place . . . (may he live a long time before he has to occupy it)." So strong was this desire to gather all dear ones around in death that the Hazons abandoned the circumscribed and irregular bosquet in favor of a veritable private cemetery. Hazon's revised project from the year IX (1800–1801) was a regular enclosure twenty-eight meters wide in its narrowest dimension (figs. 180–183). A Neoclassical portal flanked by pavilions for gardeners and guardians has replaced the rusticated gateway. To the interior the space is organized around an elaborate sequence of places aligned along major and minor axes. The entry is followed by a small square defined at the four corners by truncated columns surmounted with funerary urns. Straight ahead within a heart-shaped lawn is the couple's pyramid, shorn of its tree. Behind the pyramid and facing the other direction toward a large open square is a monument dedicated to *recueillement* and meditation (fig. 182). Reminiscent of so many garden "seats," this pavilion was intended as a memorial "to the memory of those who were dear" to Hazon and his wife. Here Hazon displayed his skill as a Neoclassical architect who used horizontal striations of space to impart symbolic meaning. The lower portion of the edifice has a bench for visitors and has moral reflections inscribed on the wall. Above, the symbolic dome of heaven has been aligned with the upward thrust of the pyramidal trees.

Beyond this pavilion, the space widens out, and in the center is an altar for placing the coffin during the funeral ceremonies. The entire site has places for tombs outlined to either side of all the paths. Evidently, this was not enough to satisfy Hazon's desire to provide for all of his friends. To the far side of the square is a building called the "catacombs" (fig. 183). The exterior recalls the upper cascade at the Vale of Venus in the garden of Rousham. Did Hazon know that this grotto marked the tomb of a favorite hunting dog with a mock-heroic epitaph? Inside the catacombs, coffins could be placed in three tiers to either side of the central aisle as well as under the floor. An explanatory note for the catacombs could serve as an epigram for this entire second project: "to be extended as needed."

In this revised design, the picturesque warmth of the initial bosquet has been sacrificed to a formal plan which has no end. Yet,

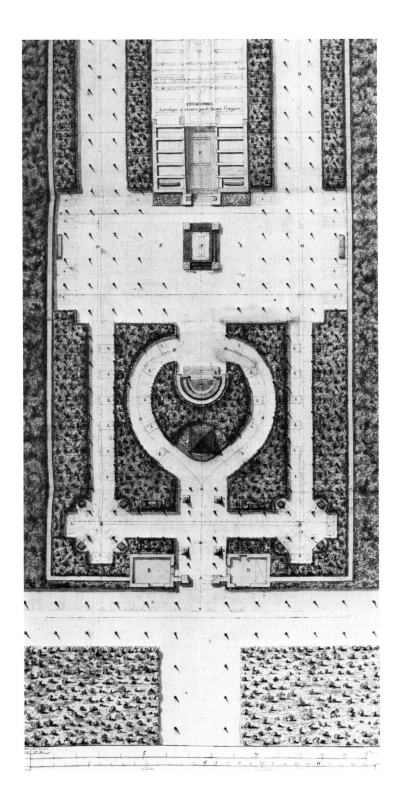

180
Hazon, *Bosquet
Religieux*, second
project, year IX
(1800–1801).

181
Hazon, *Bosquet
Religieux*, second
project, year IX
(1800–1801).
Entrance.

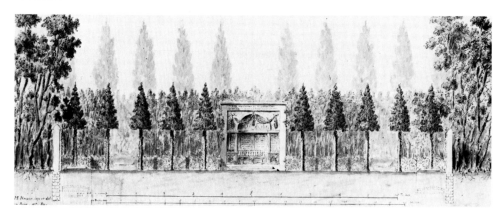

182
Hazon, *Bosquet
Religieux*, second
project, year IX
(1800–1801).
Temple of
Meditation.

183
Hazon, *Bosquet
Religieux*, second
project, year IX
(1800–1801).
Catacombs.

no matter how long the catacombs became, the entire precinct would remain visually and symbolically unified through the heart-shaped lawn. Just as the pyramid serves as the initial and central focus from the entry, so does the temple of meditation tie the linear catacombs to the "heart" of the cemetery. This is achieved geometrically through the alignment of the straight façade of the temple of meditation with the entry to the catacombs, while the rounded back of the seat serves to anchor the long and extendible axis as it moves farther away with succeeding generations of the dead.

## Formal Garden or Picturesque Landscape?

Hazon's hesitation between the formal garden and the picturesque landscape typified the tension that existed between two equally plausible approaches to designing an Elysium toward the end of the eighteenth century. Regular alignment of trees along with subtle orchestration of allées and squares lent an air of dignity that was much appreciated at this time. Thus, in Frimaire, year VI (November–December 1787), Arsenne Thiébaut proposed that the busts of the great men of France be placed in a public garden planted with orderly rows of trees, shrubs, and flowers. The Tuileries, by virtue of its location at the heart of Paris and because of "its regular arrangement, its expanse, and its order" seemed an ideal place to establish this outdoor space of commemoration and civic virtue. In contrast, La Revellière-Lépeaux, in a critique of the Panthéon also published in Frimaire, year VI, argued that the illustrious dead belonged "under the vault of the sky, within the majesty of the forest, . . . that is, in a picturesque setting that has both variety and tranquility." Making reference to Bernardin de Saint-Pierre's project for an Elysium, La Revellière suggested a more secluded site whose slightly greater distance from Paris would protect it from becoming the haunt of idle revelers and miscreants. In the combined woods of Meudon and Clamart, La Revellière found a perfect topography whose august trees and variegated terrain lent itself to this purpose. Tombs characterized by "a certain rustic simplicity" would be scattered about and discovered almost by chance as one wandered along the winding paths. Whatever the aesthetic conception of the funerary garden, it seemed important that all of the parks and even many of the vast open spaces of Paris be converted into some manner of Elysium.

Of the various projects considered at this time, the only one that was realized was the Elysée at the former convent of the Petits-Augustins. In 1791 Alexandre Lenoir was charged with the task of rescuing from destruction the artistic patrimony of France. By 1794 he opened the Elysée in the convent's garden (figs. 184–185) as part of the new Musée des Monuments Français.

184
Hubert Robert, view
of Lenoir's Elysium
Garden, Paris, c.
1800.

185
Alexandre Lenoir,
Elysium Garden with
the tomb of Abélard
and Héloïse, Paris, c.
1800.

*Garden or Landscape?*

This Elysium was much appreciated for its peaceful ambiance and for the tombs of the renowned Frenchmen gathered here. Hubert Robert's painting, in which the mausoleums of Turenne, Boileau, Molière, and Descartes were clearly labeled, indicated that this was not merely a collection of great works of art but also an Elysium of great men. As Lenoir explained: "An Elysium seemed to suit the character which I gave to my establishment, and the garden offered me all the necessary means to execute my project. In this calm and peaceful garden, you find more than forty statues. Tombs, placed here and there on a grass lawn, rise with dignity in the midst of silence and tranquility. Pine trees, cypresses, and poplars accompany them. *Larvae* and cinerary urns positioned upon the walls help establish within this place of happiness a sweet melancholy which speaks to the sensitive soul." The monument most conducive to that sweet melancholy, the Gothic tomb of Abélard and Héloïse, was Lenoir's prize treasure. According to René Schneider, "all of elegiac Paris flocked" there to weep at the tomb of the unfortunate lovers.

Even Lenoir's Garden of French Monuments, though, did not escape criticism. The *Décade Philosophique*, for example, which on 10 Nivôse, year VII (December 30, 1798) had faulted the Panthéon as an inappropriate place for an Elysium, now on 10 Floréal, year VII (April 29, 1799), found even the walled cloister at the Petits-Augustins too confining. Only the expansive terrain and "majestic trees" of the Champs-Elysées could furnish a worthy Elysium.

On 10 Nivôse, year VIII (December 31, 1799), the *Décade Philosophique* was pleased to report that the Consuls had decided in favor of transforming the vast esplanade in front of the Invalides into an Elysium. Not only were the former church and courtyards of the Invalides to be decorated with statues of France's military heroes, but the esplanade was to be planted with trees which would shelter their tombs. The painter David, the sculptor Moitte, and the architect Legrand were collaborating on the design. Although approved by the Consuls, the project was not executed.

Likewise, in the year VIII, Guy de Gisors won a prize for a design to finish the Church of the Madeleine as a national library, which he surrounded with a promenade in the form of an Elysium with statues of great men sheltered under the trees. Another citizen suggested using the Luxembourg palace for a national library, its garden to be made into an Elysium with statues honoring the most illustrious men of science. In the year X, Pierre Chaussard directed the public's attention once again to the Champs-Elysées, which he would have transformed into a "sacred way" with meandering streams and statues of dead heroes and altars to "unknown" virtues.

The ideal of transforming the public garden into an Elysium came full circle with the funeral of the naturalist Louis Daubenton in the Jardin des Plantes in Paris. On 11 Nivose, year VIII (January 1, 1800) at 10:00 in the morning, nine hours after the death of Daubenton, the professors of the National Museum of Natural History met in a special session to determine the honors for the man who, along with Buffon, had been responsible for the development and success of this institution. For sixty years Daubenton had lived and worked on its grounds, and it was decided that he would be buried in the gardens.

Daubenton's grave was to be marked by a column carrying his bust and surrounded by cypress trees and ornamented with flowers. With the help of the architects Molinos and Legrand, the professors chose a site on the eastern exposure of the same hill where Linnaeus had been honored. The column was erected amid a number of evergreens and near the famous and magnificent cedar of Lebanon, "emblems of Daubenton's long life, of his numerous and useful works, and of his immortality" (fig. 186). Neither the symbolism of the evergeens nor the orientation were lost on the artists who depicted the memorial, often shown lit by the rising sun.

The funeral took place on January 4, 1800, the new greenhouse serving for the preliminary service. Among the tapestries hung for the occasion was one of Raphael's *School of Athens*, which was used as the backdrop. In this manner, Daubenton was associated with the august philosophers of antiquity. The contrast between the verdant setting for this temple of fame and Boullée's earlier architectural rendition on the same theme (fig. 162) could not be more explicit.

After the ceremonies, the cortege proceeded slowly through the garden. In addition to friends, family, and colleagues, there were representatives from all the civil, legislative, judicial, and military bodies. Each member of the cortege held a cypress branch. The sarcophagus, of red porphyry, was carried by twenty men to the accompaniment of softly rolling drums. The pathways and the slopes of the two hills in the garden were covered with silent spectators. According to the *Décade*, five hundred people attended the funeral. Fourcroy, director of the museum, delivered a eulogy at the grave. "The tone of the orator's voice, the religious ceremony which terminated his speech, the picturesque setting where it was pronounced, the emotions felt by all those present gathered under the open sky, all of this disposed those listening to feelings of a tender sadness." At the end of the ceremony each member of the cortege placed his cypress branch at the foot of the tomb.

After years of indignant outcries against the neglect of both the ceremonies for the funeral and the ambiance of the place of burial, Daubenton's funeral seems to have served as a focal point

186
Tomb of Louis
Daubenton, buried in
the Jardin des
Plantes, Paris,
January 4, 1800.

for a reaffirmation of moral values. The massive attendance probably owed much to the recent success of the funeral of the architect Charles De Wailly, in which a large cortege from the Institut National created a deeply moving spectacle as it proceeded solemnly through the streets of Paris to the Cemetery under Montmartre. Thanks to Baudin's public address to the Institut National we have a vivid contemporary account which captures the mood at De Wailly's funeral on November 3, 1798:

Over the long distance and through the most heavily traveled streets, at a time of day when traffic was at its height, you saw passersby interrupt their course to gaze upon your own, and carriages turn out of the way, slow down, or even stop to permit you to pass. Workers, merchants, and citizens of all conditions came out of their stores and homes, took off their hats in a spontaneous gesture of respect, and asked among themselves who was the deceased and where had such a numerous cortege come from. . . . As they asked you these questions you heard these simple men and women . . . exclaim: "It's been such a long time since we've seen anything like this." "Finally, here's somebody who has found his relatives and friends." . . . These expressions, and many others like them, are sure signs of an invaluable feeling which we would call a thirst for morals.

Baudin proposed that to attract the public's attention in the future, the Institut could not merely name a delegation to the funerals of its members but had to participate in great numbers to form an impressive cortege. Apparently Daubenton was the first beneficiary of this new hope in the regeneration of a system of dignified funerals and decent burials.

In a second report delivered at the Institut, Baudin described the frightful state of the Cemetery under Montmartre in much the same terms that Delamalle had used a few years earlier about its predecessor near the Barrière Blanche. The new cemetery at the foot of Montmartre was too small for its purpose. Surrounded by ill-fitted boards, it offered for access only a narrow dirty path which, at the time of De Wailly's funeral, had been rendered impassable by two days of rain. The bodies were buried too close to the surface, too close together, and without adequate earth above them. Although the sky was clear and the weather cold, "an insupportable mephitism" choked those present. Baudin, though, was optimistic about the future because according to Aubert's report to the Council of Five Hundred (2 Fructidor, year VI/August 19, 1798) money had been allocated to replace " 'those frightful cloacae called *cemeteries*' " with " 'eight vast and commodious enclosures' " envisaged by the Department of the Seine.

The Institut National ratified the two reports by Baudin and sent them to the Directory. Thus the funeral for Charles De Wailly and the events that it prompted constituted a turning point in the history of the Parisian cemetery.

At this time the attention and emotions of France's leaders were once again directed to the need for new burial grounds for Paris. In the spring of 1799 the city was using five cemeteries—Montmartre, Marguerite, Charité, Vaugirard, and Clamart. When former Minister of the Interior Benezech instituted this reorganization in the spring of 1796, it was reported that over the previous years many of the mass graves had held 1200–1500 bodies. Now, three years later, with all the other cemeteries closed, it was claimed that the number of corpses in a grave had risen to 2000–2500. A new departmental Arrêté of 28 Germinal, year VII (April 17, 1799) expressed a deep concern both about the insalubrity of these burial grounds and about the total absence of a suitable ambiance. It therefore decreed that six new cemeteries be established according to a model that amounted to an embellished version of the Avril Field of Rest. The ha-ha was reintroduced, with the difference now that the inner masonry wall was to be terminated by a low planter filled with balsamic shrubs serving as a type of balustrade. Next would come a double allée of acacia trees bordered to the other side by another planter with more balsamic shrubs. As the shallow trenches used for burials were filled, the land would be planted with bushes and flowers. At all times the entire cemetery was to be covered with flowers. A magnificent obelisk large enough to be seen far away would be placed at the center. This obelisk was to be dedicated to the sun, "principle of reproduction." Everything about the design was consistent with this theme.

One week later on 6 Floréal, year VII (April 25, 1799), the Institut National des Sciences et des Arts announced that the subject for the Grand Prix in architecture would be "an Elysium or public cemetery." The three sections of the Institut's Classe de la Littérature et des Beaux-Arts responsible for defining the program—architecture, painting, and sculpture—conceived it in much the same terms as the departmental Arrêté. Yet as the inheritor of an academic tradition, the Institut National promulgated a concept of the open cemetery mediated by a certain grandeur. The contestants were to select a site "in a pleasant location." The cemetery was not to be enclosed by walls "which obstruct the view but by terraces with plantings" providing shade for a promenade. Elevated topographies such as Menilmontant and Montmartre and locations by the water such as along the Seine or the Bièvre were recommended. All contestants were instructed to create an ambiance devoid of anything repulsive in favor of inspiring respect and peaceful contemplation (*recueillement*).

On September 27, 1799, the Minister of the Interior, Lucien Bonaparte, wrote to the Institut proposing that it sponsor a public competition on the themes of the two Baudin reports. The competition was opened on March 17, 1800, and received an enthusiastic response: forty official entries plus a few late arrivals. Two first prizes and five honorable mentions were accorded to the competitors who had most successfully addressed the two questions: "What ceremonies should there be for funerals? What rules should be adopted for the place of burial?" Several of the essays were published, as was the Institut's own report, which combined the best features from all.

The numerous projects for cemeteries proposed in the years 1799–1800 were grouped into two categories by contemporary observers. There were the grandiose designs of 1799, which were immediately ridiculed by a new conservative spirit that emerged in 1800 and that produced cemeteries modest in size and appearance. In a sense history seemed to be repeating itself as the terminologies and dichotomies of the ancien régime reemerged in the debate. The grandiose cemeteries were divided, in turn, according to whether they favored the free expression of social inequalities or whether they stressed virtue as the only acceptable basis for the hierarchical organization of space. As under the ancien régime, the lines were drawn between the entrepreneurs and the academicians. As for the new simple cemeteries, which eschewed both elaborate architecture and extensive landscaping, their authors reintroduced the traditional mass grave, which was now justified with arguments about economy, yet accompanied by elaborate provisions to hide the horror of this mode of burial from the public's view.

|                        |                                                                 |
|------------------------|-----------------------------------------------------------------|

**Architecture Is Devouring Us**

The cemetery designed as a picturesque garden where all citizens could commemorate their dead as they chose was introduced at this time by a former administrator of the Department of the Seine, Jacques Cambry, in collaboration with Jacques Molinos, Architect and Inspector of Civil Buildings for the same department. On 14 Floréal, year VII (May 3, 1799), the Department approved the Molinos-Cambry project; and on 2 Frimaire, year VIII (November 23, 1799) it ordered the printing and distribution of a sumptuous book complete with a learned and sentimental text on burials by Cambry and beautiful engravings of Molinos's design (fig. 187–194). Although the proposal was published under the aegis of the Department of the Seine, its authors were entrepreneurs working with a company that hoped to build and manage the cemetery for the city.

Gone were any pretenses even of the appearance of equality in burials that had characterized the notion of the cemetery since the Terror. Now the social climate permitted an apology for the visible expression of socioeconomic differences: "Allow everybody, then, the freedom to act according to his taste and desire. You modest people, be content with a simple urn; you wealthy

187
Jacques Molinos,
"Field of Rest"
(project for
transforming the
quarries of
Montmartre into a
cemetery), Paris,
1799.

188
Molinos, "Field of
Rest," Paris, 1799.
Plan.

*The Field of Rest*

*Elévation Géométrale de la Pyramide et du Mur d'Enceinte.*

189
Molinos, "Field of Rest," Paris, 1799. Pyramidal chapel with crematorium.

190
Molinos, "Field of Rest," Paris, 1799. Section through the central chapel with crematorium.

*Coupe de la Pyramide ?.*

*Architecture Is Devouring Us*

191
Molinos, mortuary
depot, Paris, 1799.

*The Field of Rest*

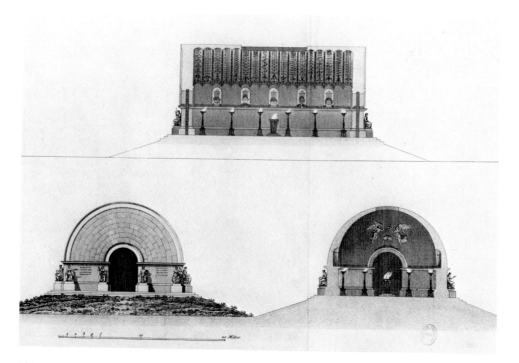

192
Molinos, mortuary
depot, Paris, 1799.

*Architecture Is Devouring Us*

193
Molinos, mortuary
depot, Paris, 1799.

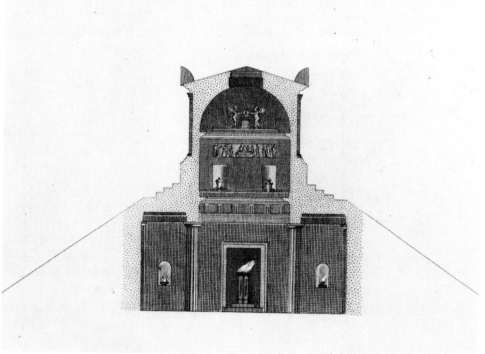

194
Molinos, mortuary
depot, Paris, 1799.

ones, raise tombs that nourish the architect, the painter, and scores of workmen whom you employ. . . . All wills, all whims should know no limit. . . . Ah! Who would deprive a free man of the right to dispose of his ashes and to use a part of his fortune to shelter them from the ravages of accidents and storms. . . ?" Thus, the space of equality would be abandoned in favor of a delight in the contrasts between humble memorials for the poor and magnificent mausoleums for the rich. Frochot would say as much in 1801 when he would try to secure the Parc Monceau for a municipal cemetery. To Quatremère de Quincy the cemetery was both to become the visible expression and to offer the ultimate vindication of social differences. As Quatremère explained to the Conseil Général of the Department of the Seine on August 3, 1800: "No doubt death equalizes all men, but it is precisely the injustice of this leveling that should be rectified." To permit mausoleums in the cemetery, even those erected "out of vanity" would counter the natural egalitarianism of death.

The cemetery designed by Molinos, called the Field of Rest, was to be located on the eminence of Montmartre. This project grew out of the controversy around the new Cemetery under Montmartre. Cambry was an administrator with the Department at this time, when the Department was attempting to secure more funds from the Minister of the Interior to improve this burial ground. The minister, in turn, was insisting that the Department legalize its ad hoc behavior in purchasing and opening the cemetery. Out of this situation came the idea for a new and comprehensive project, large enough to serve all of Paris. The luxurious publication was intended to impress the legislative and executive branches of the government so as to secure approval and financing.

Molinos's *Champ de Repos* was designed as a picturesque garden with meandering paths and funerary monuments of all types scattered among the variegated plantings. Since the cemetery was to be built over former quarries, it would be possible to fashion underground catacombs, decorated with paintings and sculpture, where the wealthy would also be buried. The entire site was to be circular in shape and would be surrounded by a high wall. At the center would be a pyramid twenty-three meters tall. Four entry portals at the periphery of the cemetery would be on axis with the pyramid, although there were to be no direct routes to the center. The four doors were consecrated to the four ages of man—childhood, youth, adulthood, and old age. The central pyramid was conceived as the "image of the last stage of life."

Molinos's cemetery presents a modified version of the allegorical labyrinth of the four ages of man as represented in Ripa's *Iconologia* (fig. 25), now rendered as a picturesque garden. The outer circle can also be considered an abstraction of the medieval wheel of Fortune, but with emphasis as much on the repetitive cycles as on the successive stages of life. The four ages that consecrate the four entries recall the numerous projects for and realizations of revolutionary festivals in which this theme served to stress some positive aspect of the human condition: the child who was close to nature, the innocence of youth, the virility or beauty of the adult, and the wisdom of old age. Certainly this cemetery as picturesque garden served to evoke the latter image, which re-affirmed life and life-giving forces more than it did the older tradition of the *memento mori*.

The pastoral aspect of the cemetery was to be extended into the city through the construction of four mortuary depots where the dead would be collected before being transported to the cemeteries (figs. 191–194). The idea of such intermediary chapels dated back to the Arrêt of May 21, 1765, issued by the Parlement of Paris. When the Avril commission renewed the concept, it had stressed that these *repos*, as they were to be called, were to have an architectural character appropriate to their designation—the ideal for such projects throughout the revolution. Molinos's designs certainly fulfilled this charge.

In their individual forms and taken together as an ensemble, the way stations for the dead are reminiscent of the architectural follies in landscape gardens of the period. These mortuary chapels reflected the willingness to use the picturesque forms of the garden *fabrique* within a functional context much the way Ledoux made houses and workshops for the denizens of his ideal town of Chaux out of symbolic garden pavilions. The variety of Molinos's forms also echoes that of the *barrières* designed by Ledoux and constructed as part of the tax wall erected just before the revolution by the Fermiers Généraux. In a sense, these oversized tax buildings were like so many garden *fabriques* ringing Paris and mediating between the city and the country. Likewise, the mortuary depots designed by Molinos took the message of the cemetery as a landscape garden into the city itself. The simple geometries, the varied forms, the cosmological symbolism, and the traditional images of immortality, such as the butterfly that hovers over the entry, all combined to reassure the citizens of Paris that death was indeed a sweet rest, a journey to immortality, and that the cemetery was the home of tender feelings and sentimental memories.

As might be imagined, the magnificent tombs and the beautiful catacombs in Molinos's cemetery were only for the wealthy. People with less money would either be buried in long trenches two bodies deep or cremated in the furnaces of the central pyramid. The success of the entire project hinged upon the public's willingness to accept this latter alternative, one that was totally alien to the traditions and sensibilities of the times. As an inducement, Cambry proposed to offer inexpensive cinerary urns at one franc eighty centimes along with assurances that the ashes of each corpse would be scrupulously kept separate in the chemical furnaces built within the central pyramid. To avoid the appearance of any macabre operations, not only were the furnaces kept out of sight, but the public spaces inside the pyramid were decorated with columbaria to contain the remains of the illustrious dead. In this manner, the pyramid would appear in the most benign light, its imagery inspired by the great Roman burial chambers known through the engravings of Piranesi and Barbault.

Given both the form of the central pyramid with its flaming beacon and the program for a chemical reduction of the corpses, one can understand Giraud's charge of plagiarism. Neither architect, though, had to worry about the success of his competitor's project. No sooner was Cambry's report published than it came under scathing attack. "Architecture is devouring us," complained the *Décade Philosophique*. The republic needed schools, canals, healthier prisons, larger and better equipped hospitals, not elaborate pyramids and catacombs. Burials should be decent but not extravagant. As for the cremation of the poor, the *Décade* could only mock Cambry's assurances that these hidden cremations would truly respect both the rights and the feelings of the families involved. Cambry had produced a beautiful book, with its expensive paper and impressive engravings. But the hospitals lacked food and medicines. . . .

*The Gazette de France* was also merciless in its attack. How touching that citizen Cambry, who anticipated the time when "she who was the happiness of his life will rest softly beside him" in the Field of Rest, was proposing to cremate the majority of his fellows and sell them cheap funerary urns. Cambry's erudition was extraordinary, yet with his talk of Egypt, Athens, and Assyria, Paris would still lack decent cemeteries.

**The Grand Prix of 1799**

The program for the Grand Prix in architecture for the year VII continued the tradition of a cemetery consecrated to honoring and inspiring great deeds and accomplishments. The program stipulated that a grand but simple monument at the center of the plan would be surrounded by porticoes to shelter monuments to the illustrious men of the republic. Nothing in this or any of the other terms for the competition foreshadowed the enthusiastic development of the idea of a space of emulation which was to permeate most if not all of the designs. In adhering to the academic tradition of the grand architectural complexes and by using grandiose classical structures as their models, the architecture students surpassed Molinos in the elaborateness of their designs.

The Mausoleum of Augustus (fig. 195) provided the basis for Jean-Nicolas Jomard's design (fig. 196), which placed seventh among the eight sketch projects chosen for further development in the second stage of the competition. In contradistinction to

MAVSOLÆVM AVGVSTI
*Hodie uiuntur uestigia ad* S. Rochum.

195
Mausoleum of
Augustus, Rome, 28
B.C. From Lauro,
*Antiquae urbis
splendor,*
1612–1628.

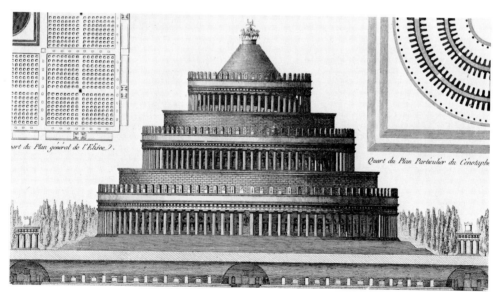

*...art du Plan général de l'Elisée .*

*Quart du Plan Particulier du Cénotaphe*

196
Jean-Nicolas Jomard,
"Elysium or Public
Cemetery," Paris,
design for the Grand
Prix of 1799.

*The Grand Prix of 1799*

Jean-Jacques Lequeu, who used the same Roman tomb for his undated mausoleum for great men (fig. 197), Jomard emphasized the architectural aspects of the model (fig. 198) by emphasizing the tiers of columns rather than trees. Both architects, though, developed the *amortissement* at the top into a conical pyramid. As a result, the mausoleum appears to be composed of two interpenetrating forms with a pyramid rising up through the stacked cylindrical drums.

Jomard set his cenotaph within a field of cypress trees that bordered allées sloping upward to the central building. Along the way one would find monuments to people of lesser talent who did not merit the honors of the central temple. The entire burial ground is divided into eight quadrants with numerous shallow graves, each section dominated by an obelisk inscribed with accounts of the great achievements and virtues of those buried in the cemetery. The three tiers of a somber baseless Doric order that surrounds the central building carry rounded cippi, based on ancient tombstones, which display emblems of the principal professions honored within. At the top is the figure of Immortality showering the illustrious with crowns. The contrast to the figure of Death above the central chapel of Desprez's (fig. 22) or Fontaine's (fig. 70) earlier designs could not be more complete.

Inside the monument, the worthy dead are classified according to profession and arranged in a symbolic manner. Forming the base or support of society, and hence placed on the bottom floor, are the warriors who occupy the outer ring. The same level has two inner rings for magistrates and legislators. Above them are the men of learning, followed by the artisans. Finally, on the fourth and highest level are the poets and the artists.

There are two large rooms within this mausoleum, the lower one domed and distributed in the form of a vast amphitheater. Here the populace would gather to participate in the various ceremonies and festivals patterned in the manner of Quatremère de Quincy's projects for the Panthéon, to excite emulation. To intensify the feelings of veneration, Jomard imagined, after the manner of Boullée's cenotaph to Newton (fig. 105), introducing a mysterious lighting in the form of stars. One significant difference between the two designs was that Boullée had sought accurately to depict the nighttime sky, thereby placing Newton in the bosom of nature, whereas Jomard directed his stars toward the center of the dome in a symbolic manner. The latter approach, a stylization intended to portray the realm of immortality, was also adopted by Jean-Baptiste Guignet in his second-prize Grand Prix design (fig. 199). In describing Jomard's project to readers of the *Athenaeum*, Louis-Pierre Baltard was so moved by the idea of the star-filled dome, that he was sure that the audience would feel itself transported there through the enchantment of the décor.

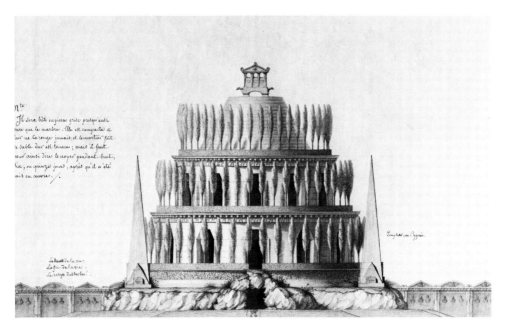

197
Jean-Jacques Lequeu,
mausoleum for great
men to be built in
the woods near The
Hague.

198
Mausoleum of
Augustus, Rome, 28
B.C. From Androuet
Du Cerceau, *Livre
des édifices antiques
romains*, 1584.

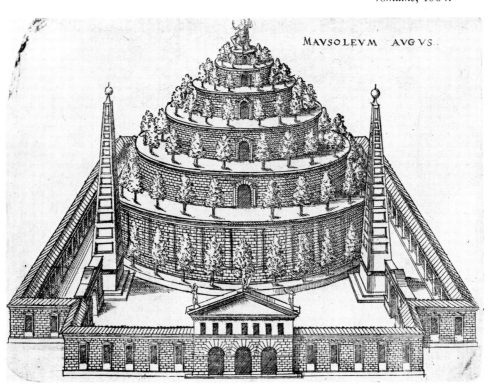

Another student used the cosmological imagery of the sphere, in the manner of Ledoux's cemetery project for the town of Chaux (fig. 101) and Boullée's proposed cenotaph to Newton of 1784 (figs. 103–105). Here (fig. 200), the artist has divided the interior horizontally with a frieze whose bas-relief encapsulates the building's theme: figures in a cortege, with uplifted arms, point to the heavens. The space below this frieze contains the amphitheater where funerary honors are bestowed. The space above represents the realm of immortality where the ashes of the worthy are kept in columbaria.

This spherical monument was placed at the center of an elevated field of honor (fig. 201) reminiscent of Dufourny's *prix d'émulation* of 1778 (fig. 29). In both projects the peripheral arcade derives its grandeur from the projecting rooms as found in the Baths of Diocletian (fig. 31). In the cemeteries, these chambers have become sepulchral vaults. The 1799 design displays an austerity in the treatment of the closed inner wall of the gallery with its heavy "sepulchral" portico by each door after the manner of Moreau's Grand Prix of 1785 (fig. 73).

Several of the designs, including the three winning projects, adhered to the stipulation that the cemetery present a view of planted terraces rather than enclosing walls. Here the architecture students took the Temple of Fortuna at Praeneste (Palestrina) as their model. Their interpretation of this grandiose, stepped temple complex may have been colored by a free adaptation drawn by Boullée ostensibly as a redesign of Mont-Valérien, the favorite site for the Parisian cortege on Corpus Christi Day. In Boullée's interpretation, this religious festival became a pantheistic celebration of nature. His project (fig. 202) consists of a series of low, horizontal terraces that serve as a base for the mountain, now incorporated into the composition as a natural pyramid. It is possible that Boullée may have changed the designation of this project to a "monument of public recognition and thanksgiving" conceived as an Elysium with hanging gardens. It is difficult to imagine what other project Madame Brongniart could have been referring to when she wrote about her enthusiasm for Boullée's cemetery, which conveyed only "calm and rest." Since the subject of the Grand Prix was announced shortly after Boullée's death, it would seem that the projects that drew inspiration from Boullée's design were conceived in homage to this master (fig. 203).

Of all the designs submitted for the Grand Prix of 1799, perhaps none surpassed Auguste-Henri-Victor Grandjean de Montigny's in the elaborate development of a space of emulation (figs. 204–205). Here spatial sequences and geometric forms have been subtly manipulated to create a highly differentiated place of burial that captures the intimacy of the private bosquet within the context

*The Field of Rest*

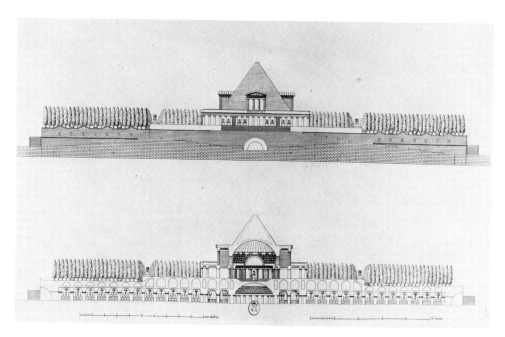

199
Guignet, "Elysium or
Public Cemetery,"
Paris, second prize,
Grand Prix of 1799.

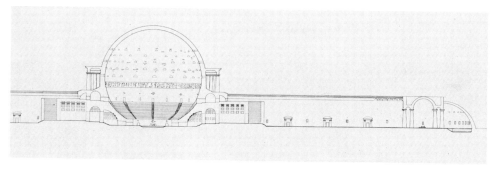

200
Anonymous,
"Elysium or Public
Cemetery," Paris,
design for the Grand
Prix of 1799.

*The Grand Prix of 1799*

201
Anonymous,
"Elysium or Public
Cemetery," Paris,
design for the Grand
Prix of 1799. Plan
for fig. 200.

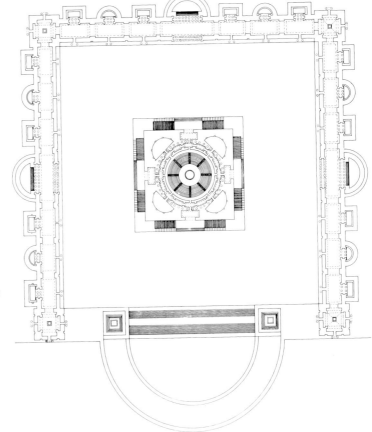

202
Etienne-Louis
Boullée, "Monument
to the Supreme
Being," or cemetery,
Paris.

203
Anonymous,
"Elysium or Public
Cemetery," Paris,
design for the Grand
Prix of 1799.

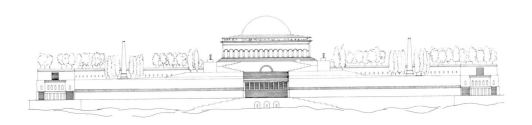

*The Field of Rest*

204
Auguste-Henri-Victor
Grandjean de
Montigny, "Elysium
or Public Cemetery,"
Paris, second first
prize, Grand Prix of
1799. Plan.

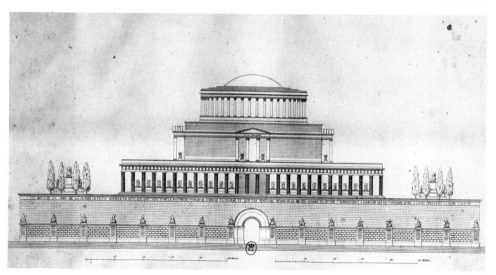

205
Grandjean de
Montigny, "Elysium
or Public Cemetery,"
Paris, second first
prize, Grand Prix of
1799. Central
chapel.

289      *The Grand Prix of 1799*

of a large public cemetery. The axial development of the plans, moreover, is not merely a formal organizational device, but rather provides the basis for a processional space rich in symbolic meaning.

Grandjean's cemetery presents many different worlds within one world. A circumferential canal within the confines of the burial ground isolates the major square land mass from a peripheral buffer zone. Access to the magnificent chapel elevated on a vast esplanade is established through a sequence of broad steps, terraces, and wide bridges. The path around the canal, though, is severely reduced in scale to impart a more intimate character to the promenade. Bridges one-third the width of those in the front link the two land masses along the sides with exedrae terminating their movement to either side. These outdoor exedrae would hold monuments to illustrious people while the thickly wooded areas would shelter the graves of private citizens.

The central monument, a free interpretation of Hadrian's tomb, is consecrated to the virtues by which one can be honored in this Elysium. A frieze across the base is inscribed: "Here in the bosom of glory rest the few who have lived for posterity. Traveler, stop for a moment and learn from the venerable ashes of these illustrious men to become worthy of the rewards due their virtues and their talents." At the center of this building is a star-covered, domed amphitheater to house the special ceremonies in honor of the worthy dead. The catacombs that surround this space are destined for the sepulchers of great men. The second domed space crowning the monument serves as a Temple of Memory.

Behind the central terrace, the outdoor semicircular amphitheater repeats the principal dimensions of the central building while forming the nucleus for the circular and radial geometries of the upper half of the site. The entire composition pivots on the tribune, where orators would extol the merits of the deceased to the assembled populace who would judge whether to accord the honors of the Temple of Virtues.

The public cemetery occupies the large semicircular zone around the amphitheater. Along the diagonal and to either side are terraced semicircular clearings sheltered by laurel trees where the military heroes of France would be buried. A square esplanade bridging the canal and arranged with subtle changes of level and columnar screens to tie the two land masses and the canal back together again precedes the Temple of Virtues, whose apse extends outside the cemetery as if it were reaching toward something beyond.

*A Truly Simple Plan*

The designs submitted for the Grand Prix suffered the same criticism as Molinos's Field of Rest. Impressed with the critique of the latter project, F.-G.-J.-S. Andrieux published his own mocking attack on the former along with a counterproposal. The contestants had certainly produced "beautiful and vast plans displayed in large format with lovely washes. There are columns, pyramids, vaults, and ornaments which would cost a fortune to execute. The students showed talent, they say, since the prize was awarded. But this competition will not give us any cemeteries."

To Andrieux, only the wealthy had sensibilities attuned to the consolations of a beautiful tomb surrounded by cypresses. For the generally dull-minded masses it would be enough to provide simple and decent burial grounds. Twelve seemed a good number, each with four communal graves capable of holding four hundred bodies. If care were taken, individual graves could also be permitted there. A small house for the concierge and a modest building in the center for funeral services were all the constructions needed. The principal difference between this type of cemetery and those proposed at the beginning of the reform movement was that this one was not to be surrounded by walls but rather by a dry ditch or ha-ha and bordered by hedges. Furthermore, and most important, the cemetery was to be planted with fruit trees.

The heart of Andrieux's project came with the cortege. Leaving the city in evening when everything was "more somber and more tranquil," the funeral would unite numerous families to form an impressive train of forty to sixty people proceeding through the darkness. The orderly march, the torches, the funerary chariot in the form of a tomb, the "sepulchral" music, and the silence in the streets would combine to make a touching scene. Finally, the families who found themselves together on this final voyage would not only form an inspiring image of social harmony, but would also share their feelings of tenderness and loss with each other.

At the cemetery the cortege would take leave of the dead after the services were finished in the central chapel. No longer would the funeral party accompany the body to the grave. While the communal grave was to be reintroduced for efficiency and economy, its horrors were to be concealed from the public's view.

Andrieux's project, published in two newspapers soon after Lucien Bonaparte's proposal for the 1800 competition had become known, anticipated both the spirit and the details of the numerous essays that soon would be submitted to the Institut National. The question of his influence on many of these contestants is of less importance than the consensus that emerged in favor of a modest cemetery. "Let's stop this war on and with words," wrote one author. "I do not propose to change the word 'cemetery,' which others have wanted to replace with 'field of rest' or 'Elysian Fields.' We should accept those words which, although adopted under the ancien régime, perfectly express the nature of their use." As with words, so with things. All the projects presented, whether accompanied by drawings (figs. 206–208) or merely described with words, were designs of which Quatremère de Quincy would

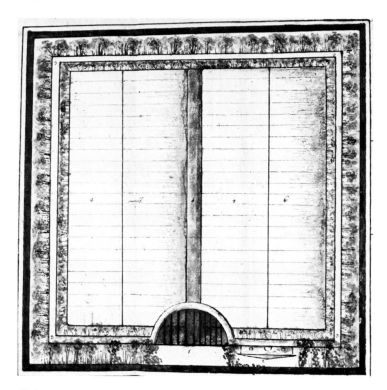

206
Godineau, cemetery,
1800.

*The Field of Rest*

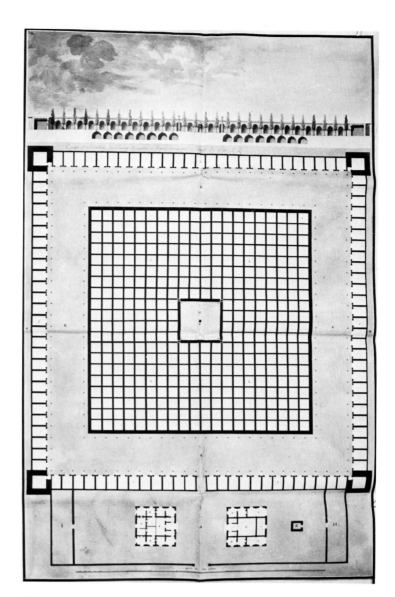

207
François-René-Jean
de Pommereul,
cemetery, 1800.

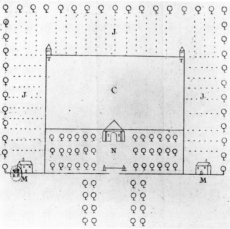

208
Jacques-Michel
Coupé, cemetery,
1800.

*A Truly Simple Plan*

have said that the economist had prevailed over the artist. Amaury-Duval, who was awarded one of the two prizes, was speaking for everybody when he wrote: "You will find this plan truly simple and in effect, it has nothing dazzling. I raise no pyramids, no porticoes. . . . " While the other prizewinner, Mulot, admired the picturesque arrangement of tombs in Lenoir's Elysée (figs. 184–185), he observed that this would not be possible in the new cemeteries where any tomb would have to be aligned along the walls.

In these projects, the sentimental feelings about the individual grave as a bulwark against the separation caused by death were not gone, but rather compromised. "You will never establish the cult of the dead," wrote Amaury-Duval, "when a son does not know where his father is buried." Yet virtually all the contestants, Amaury-Duval included, could propose nothing more satisfying than trenches for small communities and larger mass graves for the cities. Everybody shuddered at the thought of the pure virgin's dead body lying under that of the dissolute roué. Yet the best proposal which could be adduced was to bury men and women in separate trenches, a concept that forms the basis of the bipartite division of Godineau's plan (fig. 206).

The most architectural proposal was submitted by General Pommereul, who based his design on the model of the Campo Santo (fig. 207). In contrast to the severe dignity of this scheme, there were the Arcadian plans. Godineau, for example, surrounded his cemetery with a garden of lilacs, roses, jasmine, and myrtle. In springtime the flowering bushes, he explained, would attract nightingales and warblers whose songs were to make the cemetery into a pleasant bosquet. J. Girard expatiated on the tender melancholy of a walk along the shaded paths beside "murmuring streams" that crossed his ideal cemetery. The "trembling leaves" of the poplars and cypresses and the drooping branches of the weeping willows would form a setting sympathetic to a visitor's reveries. "Pyramids and catacombs might impress the eye," observed Girard, "but never speak to the heart."

In the architect Athanase Détournelle's cemetery, the mass graves would eventually all become earthen mounds. When the cemetery was filled, the walls would be torn down and the fields planted with grain. This provision reflected a common desire to use plantings not only to establish a suitable pastoral ambiance but also to make the cemetery useful for agriculture. For the same reason Coupé insisted that the cemetery be surrounded with fruit trees and its walls be planted with vines and shrubs (fig. 208). In his essay Détournelle anticipated the effect of the soft profiles of the pyramidal mounds covered with wheat and rye as passersby recognized and appreciated the final resting place of their cherished ancestors. Détournelle was the only contestant who did not envisage periodically displacing the dead from their graves (figs. 209–211).

To avoid what Pommereul termed the "unpleasantness" of holding a funeral at the side of the open grave, the various contestants envisaged different strategies. Pommereul and Coupé placed the funeral chapel outside the cemetery proper. Chambon envisaged a pastoral "vestibule" at the entrance to the cemetery. Here dense plantings of yews, cypresses, and poplars would hide the interior of the cemetery, as the deceased disappeared down a diagonal path which obscured their destination. The contestant Ronèsse would not even allow the cortege to proceed beyond the "funerary temple" located in the city. On the other hand, Détournelle took the funeral party up to the edge of the grave but hid the gaping hole with a "cheerful" blue tent (fig. 211). Thus, while the inscriptions and statuary that consecrated these projects proclaimed that death is an eternal rest, there was little about the funeral or the burial ground that would have truly satisfied such claims.

**An Energetic Prefect**

On 15 Vendémiaire, year IX (October 7, 1800), the Institut National awarded its prizes and then published its report. The two prizewinners (Amaury-Duval and Mulot) and three of the five contestants who received an honorable mention (Coupé, Girard, Pommereul) published their essays, as did five others, including the architect Détournelle. The architects Pierre Giraud and Pierre Patte had not participated in the contest, but they too published long essays with illustrations.

This was the context in which Nicolas-Thérèse-Benoist Frochot, the newly appointed first Prefect of the Department of the Seine, pressed for the realization of the reforms in burial customs and cemeteries which, in their general outlines, reached back to mid-century and, in their sentimental features, were characteristic of the revolutionary epoch. Frochot's Arrêté of 21 Ventôse, year IX (March 12, 1801) called for three municipal cemeteries to the north, east, and south of Paris. The most immediate effect of this Arreté was the reform of the funeral. The *bière banale*, or communal coffin, which was used over and over to transport the poor to the cemetery was effectively proscribed. Henceforth even the pauper would have the dignity of his own shroud and coffin, purchased with the proceeds from the inhumations of the wealthy. Frochot was also able to introduce a common mode of transport for all classes, which consisted of a chariot drawn by two horses. The distance from the home to the church and then to the cemetery was too long for the porters who carried the coffin by hand or in a litter. Even for the conscientious, the journey from the Ile

209
Athanase
Détournelle,
cemetery, 1800.
Communal grave (fig.
1). Entrance (fig. 2).

*The Field of Rest*

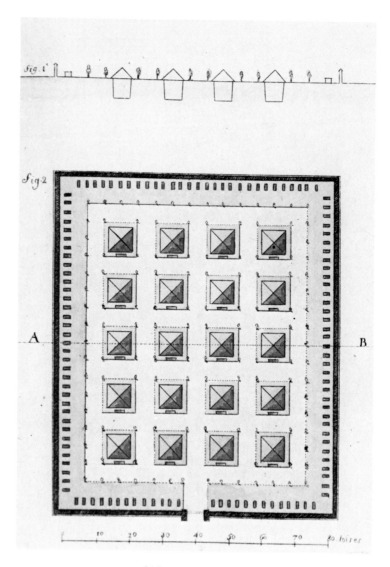

210
Détournelle,
cemetery, 1800.
Section and plan.

*An Energetic Prefect*

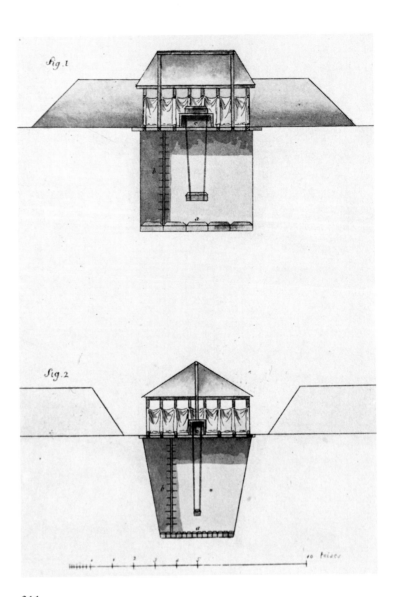

211
Détournelle,
cemetery, 1800.
Section through the
communal grave.

*The Field of Rest*

de la Cité to the cemetery of Sainte-Catherine, for example, necessitated three intermediary stops. Evidently, the sight of a coffin momentarily placed in front of a tavern while the porters fortified themselves for the next stage of the journey was not uncommon in Paris. The horse-drawn chariot abolished this abuse.

Frochot was quite clear about the type of cemetery which he wanted. By the same Arrêté, he revealed himself a partisan of burials on private property by maintaining the provisions already in force. In the public cemetery, citizens would be permitted to honor the memory of the dead with mausoleums.

On March 15, 1801, Frochot wrote to the Minister of the Interior requesting a law to authorize the city to purchase 60 *arpents* (51.5 acres) for public use which would be situated about one kilometer from its walls. Since the legislature would soon recess, it was imperative, argued the prefect unsuccessfully, that the minister act immediately. During the interim before the legislature would convene again, Frochot came upon another idea to furnish Paris with a ready-made cemetery that not only would add substantially to the space available for burial, but would also furnish an appropriate setting. In a long memorandum to the Minister of the Interior, Frochot proposed that the Parc Monceau (figs. 155–156), currently a property within the national domain, be sold to the city for use as a cemetery.

Although Frochot's plans for the Parc Monceau were never realized, the prefect was successful in establishing a framework for three municipal cemeteries and for acquiring the property that he transformed into the Cemetery of Père Lachaise. There already were beginnings on the north of the city with the Cemetery under Montmartre and on the south with the Charité. Through their deliberations of 29 Frimaire and 6 Germinal, year XI (December 20, 1802, and March 27, 1803), the Conseil Général of the Seine designated these two burial grounds for use as municipal cemeteries along with a third property to the east of Paris on an eminence known as Mont-Louis. The law of 17 Floréal, year XI (May 7, 1803) authorized the Commune of Paris to acquire the estate of Mont-Louis as well as land contiguous to the Charité. The purchase of Mont-Louis took place on March 21, 1804. By an Arrêté of 22 Floréal, year XII (May 12, 1804), Frochot designated this property as the Cemetery of the East, or, as it was popularly called, the Cemetery of Père Lachaise, and the burial ground was inaugurated on May 21. That the topography of the estate was so well suited to being transformed into a landscape garden must have endeared it to the prefect as much as its availability as a large piece of land situated just beyond the city's walls.

Less than one month later, on 23 Prairial, year XII (June 12, 1804), Napoleon issued the Imperial Decree on Burials, which reiterated the terms of the entire sixty-year reform movement.

Burials in closed places of worship and within the city were henceforth forbidden. In 1874, Ferdinand Hérold, chairman of a commission on cemeteries and future mayor of Paris, would declare that the Imperial Decree had been the fundamental law on burials for the nineteenth century.

The specific provisions of Napoleon's Decree maintained a balance between the more sentimental advocates of the Elysium and the hard-headed and hard-hearted planners who wanted inexpensive and efficient burial grounds. In helping to prepare the Decree, the Ministry of the Interior argued that both decency and salubrity required proscribing the communal grave. Each person should be buried separately. The official Decree concurred with this position and stipulated individual graves with a prescribed interval between them: thirty to forty centimeters to the sides and thirty to fifty at the head and feet. Ordinary graves would be reused after five years, but in the meantime one was free to erect a tombstone or other marker. If the cemeteries had adequate space, land could be sold for permanent graves marked by tombstones or mausoleums or fashioned as sepulchral vaults for individuals or families. Burials on private property outside the city or town were also permitted.

As for the question of vegetation, Minister of the Interior Chaptal was imbued with the old belief that trees blocked the circulation of the air deemed so necessary to sweep away the dangerous miasmata. The Ministry of the Interior protested vigorously against his proposed ban on trees. Modern science had shown that trees were necessary "to absorb the cadaverous miasmata." Furthermore, trees provided a "somber and religious veil" that diminished the horror of the cemetery while contributing to its salubrity. The government should not only permit trees but should even order that the cemeteries be planted. The result was a compromise. The new cemeteries were to be established on elevated sites, preferably exposed to the north winds. The property would be enclosed with walls and there would be plantings arranged so that they would not hinder air circulation.

Shortly after the Imperial Decree was issued, Napoleon's minister, Champagny, sought to close the cemeteries of Marguerite, Clamart, and Catherine. He also instructed Frochot to press on with the enlargement of the Cemetery under Montmartre and the Charité. Thus, in the opening years of the nineteenth century, the reform movement was one step away from the full realization of its dreams. Over the course of sixty years, the image of what a cemetery should be had undergone several radical transformations. Now, in 1805, Quatremère de Quincy boasted that the new Père Lachaise was going to become the first "true cemetery."

At that time Quatremère could only anticipate the developments which would enable the architect Janniard to declare in 1843 that Père Lachaise was "the cemetery par excellence." Quatremère had no way of knowing how extensive its influence would be throughout Europe and America, as Père Lachaise became the touchstone for all future discussions about the nature of the cemetery. Repeatedly invoked in the United States as a model that justified a departure from the obscure and hideous *intra muros* burial grounds, eventually Père Lachaise helped to create a second generation of cemeteries, which, in the eyes of their champions, far surpassed the beauties of the original.

The Cemetery of Père Lachaise was the first and has been the most renowned western cemetery designed as a picturesque landscape garden. The following lines (written in French), found penciled on a terrace wall in 1813, convey the feelings of comfort and solace which can still be experienced there today:

At this peaceful site, amid trees and flowers,
Sorrows and laments come to cry their tears:
Here they can find a sympathetic shade:
Death hides from their eyes its hideous scythe.
As it spreads its subjects throughout a vast garden;
For the home of the dead has become a new Eden.

Landscapes, especially public ones that have endured for years and which have been much frequented, tend to become self-evident, as if they had always been the way they are. Few visitors to Central Park in New York City, for example, realize that it was created out of a wasteland. While Père Lachaise did not undergo the major transformations involving elaborate draining, considerable movement of earth, and extensive plantings needed to make Central Park, it was nevertheless a considerable product of human creativity. Modern histories err, though, in maintaining that the architect Alexandre-Théodore Brongniart had little more to do than repair the wall around the former garden and widen and firm up the allées. The evidence of both eighteenth-century maps and early nineteenth-century chronicles suggests a different interpretation.

Greeted with the remains of an early eighteenth-century formal garden developed over a highly distinctive topography, Brongniart proceeded to develop a picturesque garden cemetery whose infrastructure exists to this day. Aspects of the earlier garden as well as the slopes and declivities of the land were certainly constraints, but they also offered possibilities that Brongniart used to great advantage. Today, the layout of Père Lachaise seems so natural that it is easy to forget both that it is a designed landscape and that it could have been designed quite differently.

## La Folie Regnault

The beautiful hill situated at the junction of three villages, Belleville, Menilmontant, and Charonne, had been appreciated for many centuries. In the fifteenth century, a wealthy merchant built a country home there. According to legend, he lavished so much upon this house that the people gave it the name of La Folie Regnault, a designation that still appeared on Jouvin de Rochefort's map of 1675 (fig. 212). In 1626 the estate was purchased by a friend of the Jesuits who offered it to them as a retreat for their aging and convalescent members. It has been said that the site was renamed Mont-Louis in honor of Saint-Louis, patron saint of the Jesuits. Others have maintained that the name was changed in honor of Louis XIV's visit on July 2, 1652, when he watched Turenne battle the frondeurs below in the Faubourg Saint-Antoine.

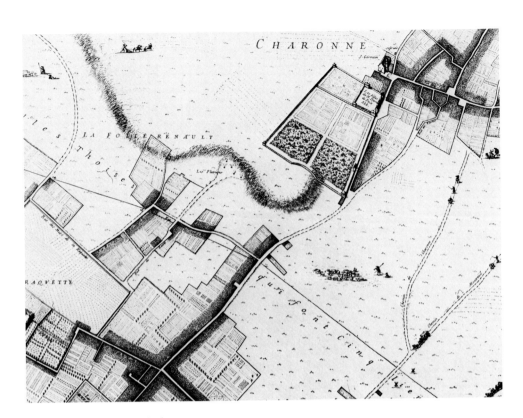

212
La Folie Regnault.
Detail from the 1675
Jouvin de Rochefort
plan of Paris.

In any event, the house was used as a residence by the Jesuit François d'Aix de la Chaise, confessor to Louis XIV, who lived there from 1675 until his death in 1709. By virture of his relationship to the king, Père La Chaise, as he was known, received visits from numerous dignitaries at this country estate. Whether for personal or political reasons or both, Louis expanded both the house and the gardens.

When the Jesuits' estate first appeared on the maps of Paris (figs. 213–214), it was shown oriented with a view toward the city and an entrance from the opposite side. Situated at the crest of the hill (fig. 215), the house overlooked a series of stepped terraces with dense plantings to either side of the principal parterres. This vegetation gave an edge to the space as well as a retreat into the cool shade. At the bottom of the hill and on nearly level land was the kitchen garden. Above this was a long terrace sloping upward and decorated with elaborate *parterres de broderie*. The circular basin with shooting fountain united this terrace in plan and elevation with the next two, which rose rapidly to form the hilltop. To the lower right in the plans but not shown in Perelle's drawing was a long oblong building serving as an orangery.

The land continued to rise above the house, and where it became almost level, a transverse allée was planted. Between the house and the allée the property seems to have been divided into three open bosquets, each with a basin of a different size and shape. Above the allée, the flat land was used again for cultivation. The house had a splendid view of Paris to one side (fig. 216) and of the country to the other. Its orientation ensured sunlight throughout the day; and according to its last owner, the property was so well protected against north winds there were never problems with frozen plants. When the property was extended to comprise nearly fifty-two arpents, or about thirty-five acres, the gardens were made even more magnificent (fig. 217). The estate was provided with numerous fruit trees, exotic plants, and rare flowers. An axis was established above the house to the northeastern entrance to the estate. This allée was regularly planted on either side. The old transverse allée reaching across the upper part of the estate became a true cross axis, extended to the edge of the hill, where a clearing was opened. The old arrangement of basins was changed so that the *bassin* and *grand canal* were apparently combined into one piece and two orthogonal basins were added to the east. To the immediate right of the house the estate was extended down the slope and subdivided into somewhat regular quadrants with diagonal cross paths and a clearing in the center of each area. Below the orangery a series of courtyards with service buildings were added. There was now an entry from Paris along the Rue Saint-André through one of these courtyards. This new orientation gave primacy to the allée along the right side of

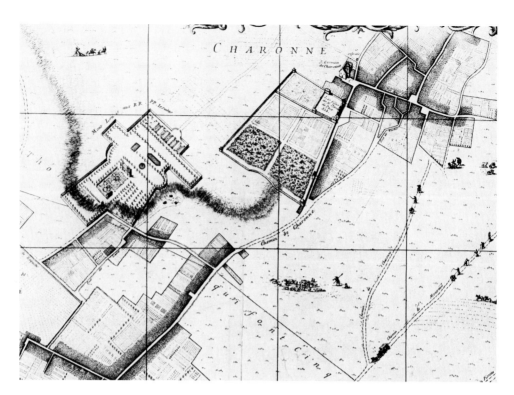

213
Mont-Louis. Detail
from the 1714
Jouvin de Rochefort
plan of Paris.

*A New Eden*

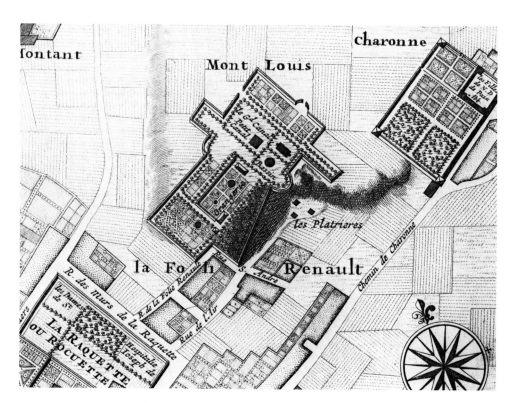

214
Mont-Louis. Detail
from the 1707
Nicolas de Fer plan
of Paris.

*La Folie Regnault*

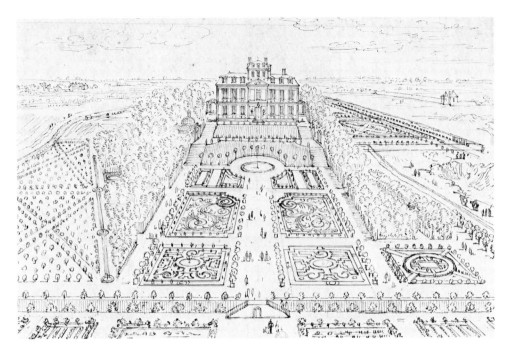

215
Mont-Louis, Paris.
Drawing by Perelle
of the Jesuits' estate.

216
Mont-Louis, Paris.
Engraving by Rigaud
showing view over
Paris, 1752. Detail.

*A New Eden*

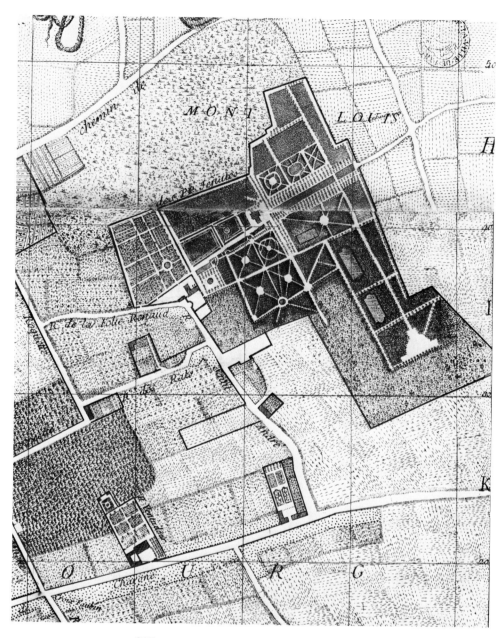

217
Mont-Louis. Detail
from the 1728
Delagrive plan of
Paris.

the principal parterres, which began behind the orangery and led up to the house. There was also a path or allée from the entrance cutting directly across the estate to the uppermost boundary. All of these features were to play an important role in the future development of the cemetery.

After the death of Père La Chaise the Jesuits continued to use the estate as a country retreat until their expulsion from France in 1762. On August 31, 1763, the Parlement of Paris ordered the sale of Mont-Louis to satisfy the Jesuits' creditors. Over the next few decades, the new owners were obliged to put much of the property into culture. Two plans from the mid-1770s suggest that the gardens were gone and that the land was largely subdivided for farming. Both Jaillot's plan of 1773 and Crépy's plan of 1775 reveal that the principal allées were largely intact. Verniquet's plan of 1790 (fig. 218) shows more of a garden just above the house and an elaborate bosquet to the right, which was absent from the two previous plans. The 1804 map of Paris by Picquet virtually reproduces the features of this latter plan.

It is ironic that in 1763 the Parlement of Paris launched its crusade against the cemeteries within the city and in a seemingly unrelated action obliged the sale of Mont-Louis. The first event eventually led to the establishment of new cemeteries for the city and the second set the conditions for the eventual decline and resale of the property. The two sets of circumstances came together in 1804 when Frochot acquired the property and turned it over to Alexandre-Théodore Brongniart in his capacity as Chief Inspector General of the Second Section of Public Works for the Department of the Seine and the City of Paris to develop as a cemetery.

## Designing Père Lachaise

In addition to working with a site and a budget, Brongniart had to accommodate the program devised by Frochot along with the Municipal Council, dominated by the energetic Quatremère de Quincy. By a prefectorial Arrêté of 15 Ventôse, year XIII (March 6, 1805), Frochot outlined four different modes of burial and suggested generally where they were to occur within the cemetery. It is not known to what extent Brongniart may have been consulted on this matter. For the poor, there were to be "public cemeteries" within Père Lachaise located along the "plains" of the estate. Enough land was to be set aside to permit six years to pass before the graves were reopened.

Temporary memorials would be permitted here so long as they did not hinder the prescribed exhumations. The next category was for individual graves of long but not permanent duration. These, explained Quatremère to the Municipal Council, were intended for people of modest means who, in paying a fee of

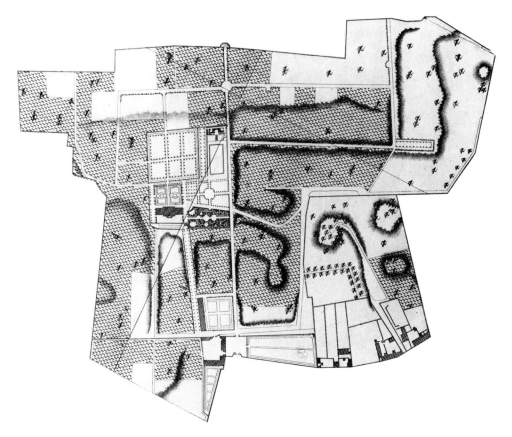

218
Mont-Louis. Detail
from the 1790
Verniquet plan of
Paris.

*Designing Père Lachaise*

fifty francs, could avert the separation caused by death by having a separate grave that could be marked with a monument. According to Frochot's original conception, these were individual graves which apparently could be kept as long as they were maintained. Once they were abandoned, the land would revert to the city. This idea, though, was soon changed. By 1825, the temporary concession had become a five-year renewable contract. These types of graves were to be assigned to the allées and pathways of the cemetery as well as to any of the lower portions of the estate not used for the public cemeteries.

The highest category of grave was the concession in perpetuity. These were divided into two classes. According to Schneider, it was Quatremère who suggested to Frochot that the wall around the cemetery be developed with a covered gallery, much in the manner of a *campo santo*. The land was to be given to individuals or families on the condition that they construct a portion of a uniform peristyle. In this manner the cemetery would eventually be surrounded by a majestic arcade at no expense to the city. Quatremère must have been thinking of his cherished Pisan Campo Santo when he described the continuous covered walkways. For these arcades, Frochot and Quatremère hoped to secure from Lenoir's Elysium the art treasures that were also tombs of illustrious French men and women (figs. 184–185). These were the natural and legitimate heritage, they argued, of the new cemeteries. The arcades were also to shelter the tombs of contemporaries whom the government chose to honor here. The arcades, though, were never built.

The second class of *concessions à perpétuité* were to be located within the garden, which occupied most of the space in the cemetery. For these graves the land would be sold at the rate of one hundred francs a square meter. Whenever additional burials took place in the family or corporate vaults, situated either under the arcade or in mausoleums within the garden, an additional fee would be levied. The Municipal Council approved the Arrêté. Brongniart, the city's architect, was given one month to present a plan for the terrain as well as to prepare drawings for the peripheral arcade.

In the posthumous edition of Brongniart's works, there is a note on the plan for Père Lachaise stating that the architect had been obliged to adjust his project to the existing plantings as well as to the form and movement of the terrain. What exactly were the givens with which Brongniart had to work? First, there was the hill, which rose twenty-seven meters from the boulevard to its crest. Brongniart chose to orient the cemetery around the hilltop, which would be crowned by a majestic chapel in the form of a pyramid (figs. 219–220). Whereas the previous gardens had merely used the slope for their formal parterres, now Brongniart envisaged

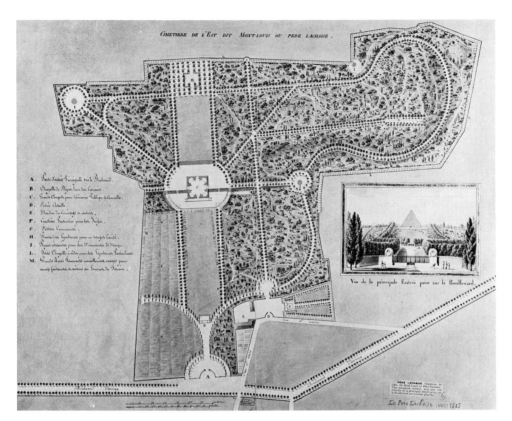

219
Alexandre-Théodore
Brongniart, Cemetery
of Père Lachaise,
Paris. First project, c.
1812.

220
Brongniart, Cemetery
of Père Lachaise,
Paris. First project, c.
1812. View of the
proposed entrance
and chapel.

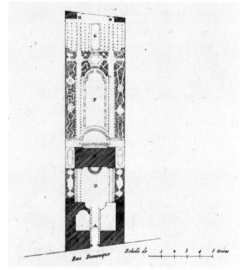

221
Brongniart, Hôtel de
Monaco, Paris,
1774.

*A New Eden*

a magnificent entry with the pyramid rising above a sloping grass lawn bordered on either side by allées of lime trees. To arrange this he had to fashion a portal at the bottom of the former kitchen garden and obliterate the line of demarcation between this area and the terrace above it. This he achieved by creating a type of verdant entry vestibule terminated by a low structure, reminiscent of so many garden seats, but now of a funerary genre and intended to serve as depot and chapel for the funeral parties. Above this point the land rises to the top of the hill where the pair of existing steps were to be supplemented with curved *cordonate* which defined the lower half of a terrace around the pyramid. The slope up the hill already had an allée of linden trees to the right and was to be given matching plantings to the other side.

The broad swath of lawn was to be extended above the pyramid as the ground continued to rise until it met the transverse allée of chestnut trees. At this point the remainder of the way was to be planted in a quincunx with a monument in the middle of the clearing. Brongniart used the quincunx to terminate the upward movement of the lawn as it met the allée of chestnut trees. To have left the space open would have revealed the limits of the property, vitiated the effect of the transverse allée, and given no formal termination at all. Simply to have continued the dense foliage of the irregular garden would have been to provide too abrupt an ending. With the quincunx, the open lawn above the pyramid was given a true edge while the axis was permitted to continue and to resolve itself in the regular plantings. The chestnut allée functioned not only as a cross axis at this point but also as the generating line of the quincunx. Finally, the quincunx served the additional function of mediating between the formal, open greensward and the dense "natural" garden to either side.

In establishing this sequence of spaces, Brongniart had recourse to his earlier experience in site planning, dating back to the 1770s, when he built several private Parisian mansions with gardens. Brongniart's strategy at Père Lachaise resembles most particularly his plan for the Hôtel de Monaco along the Rue Saint-Dominique (fig. 221). In both designs, a central allée leads up to a forecourt or parterre, where it splits to either side. Silvestre de Sacy has noted that at the Hôtel de Monaco, Brongniart departed from the customary practice of lining the forecourt with service buildings by substituting a garden. Beyond the central structure, which is the house at the Rue Saint-Dominique and the pyramidal chapel at Père Lachaise, there is a long parterre or lawn, bordered by a regular allée to each side, which is terminated by a transverse allée and followed by a regular quincunx with a clearing in the center of the grove. Between the walls bounding the sides of the Princess of Monaco's property and the allées defining the parterre, Brongniart fashioned a *jardin anglo-chinois* with the irregular meanderings, twistings, and turnings that were becoming so modish at the time. With the development of a more "natural" type of movement in the 1780s, fostered in large part by Brongniart himself as creator of the famed Elysée at Maupertuis (fig. 164), the earlier tortured lines at the Hôtel de Monaco gave way to more gentle meanderings when Brongniart designed Père Lachaise. Brongniart's recent success with the gardens that he had fashioned in 1802 at Romainville for Madame de Montesson and at Villemomble for Monsieur de Sivri had given him ample opportunity to renew his contact with a genre from which he had been so isolated throughout much of the revolution.

At Père Lachaise the pyramid at the top of the hill not only dominated the entry; it also served, as a contemporary guidebook noted, as the central point of a regular composition that anchored the diverse parts of the irregularly shaped terrain together. The oblong shape of the central plaza defined by the *cordonate* below permitted the creation of diagonal allées extending from the top of the terrace as well as a transverse allée along the lower edge of this terrace, which passes figuratively through the middle of the pyramid. This formal, irradiating pattern linked the central pyramid to the other major allées within the cemetery.

To tie the entire site together within a unified and simple circuit, Brongniart fashioned a peripheral carriage path, which respected the principal contours of the terrain. This road was designed so that it could eventually begin at the new entry on axis with the central chapel but in the meantime would start from the old entrance to the right and wind up along the periphery of the estate to a major *rond-point*. From the *rond-point*, the carriages could proceed left to the central chapel or continue to the right along the lower edge of the heights and then around a large loop, rising upward and around the hill to join the long transverse allée, which passed across a relatively flat terrain. Finally, this long allée was terminated at another *rond-point*, which was linked back to the pyramid by a diagonal route. The diagonal to the right was added not only to maintain symmetry from the upper central terrace but also to intersect with two existing allées, which Brongniart chose to integrate into his plan. One was the direct route through the site leading from the old entry; the other was a transverse allée that terminated in a bosquet called the Bosquet du Dragon. Brongniart's new diagonal allée joined the two others at their point of intersection, thereby linking them formally and visually to the central pyramid. In looking at the Verniquet plan (fig. 218), it is interesting to see which allées Brongniart did not use. The ascending allée that began at the Bosquet du Dragon and another located to the left of the house had no place within his project and were abandoned.

This ligature was strengthened in elevation by the use of vertical accents which both terminated views and provided markers seen across the site. Each of these monuments served a different purpose. The monument at the *rond-point* (fig. 222) was necessary to make the clearing visible to the people at the chapel, for the land fell rapidly, descending eight meters along the transverse allée. In contrast, the memorial at the second *rond-point* (fig. 223) crowned a small eminence. Finally, the third monument (fig. 224) seemed destined to hide a sharp corner as well as to help the curved allée swing around to meet the straight transverse allée, which stretched across the property. In both their siting and their dedication to people of distinction, these three monuments recall the obelisks and columns in gardens such as those at Castle Howard and Stowe (figs. 147–148). As for the straight allée beginning at the existing entry, it already had a small exedra at its end, just waiting for a monument. Brongniart terminated the diagonal that intersected this allée with a mausoleum for the De Greffult family in the form of a small Gothic chapel (fig. 225). Although this tomb was privately owned, by virtue of its form it served a public function. The Greffult mausoleum recalled the many similar chapels in British and French landscape gardens, which elicited prayer, solitary meditation, and reflections on divinity as well as on the ends of human mortality.

Brongniart's plan matched the terrain to the different types of burial as set forth by the Prefect of the Seine and the Municipal Council. To the left of the entry on the plain of the former kitchen garden and then on the slope above were the *fosses communes*, the graves for communal burial. Here people were buried without charge. According to a special commission on cemeteries reporting in 1874, the provision in Napoleon's Imperial Decree of 1804 stipulating separate graves for everybody had never been applied in Paris. In order to utilize the land "judiciously," at first the coffins were superimposed and then later aligned side by side in long rows without the required space between them. Considering that the major portion of the cemetery was reserved for the isolated tombs and mausoleums of the permanent concessions, the limited space accorded these burials of the lowest order was the result of a conscious policy decision. The layout of Père Lachaise effectively reversed the terms of the Imperial Decree, which would have permitted the more opulent sepulchers only to the degree that space remained.

The two principal areas for the *concessions à perpétuité* were the valley to the right of the lower greensward and the hill located above the *rond-point* and within the curving allée. While the tree-lined allées provided carriage access throughout the site, the terrain itself was covered with winding footpaths, which gracefully followed the movement of the landscape. In the posthumous edition

222
Brongniart, Cemetery
of Père Lachaise,
Paris. Second project,
c. 1812. View of the
main *rond-point* with
proposed
mausoleum.

223
Brongniart, Cemetery
of Père Lachaise,
Paris. Second project,
c. 1812. View of the
secondary *rond-point*
with proposed
mausoleum.

224
Brongniart, Cemetery of Père Lachaise, Paris. Second project, c. 1812. View of proposed mausoleum with obelisk.

225
Brongniart, "Gothic Chapel" (the Greffult family tomb), Cemetery of Père Lachaise, Paris.

*Designing Père Lachaise*

of Brongniart's works, the architect's son remarked that on the plan the straight allées and regular bosquets might seem out of place with the serpentine paths. Yet, he added, the expansiveness of the site resolved any possible conflict between the regular and irregular systems. Furthermore, the formal allées were the parts that seemed to reflect man's presence within a savage nature; and it was precisely along these allées that the first tombs had begun to gather. Brongniart's view of the cemetery along with his drawing of the plan show modest tombstones and like monuments lining the two allées leading up to the projected pyramid as well as the base of the pyramid and the wall to the left of the communal graves. This arrangement is verified by descriptions in the early guidebooks. The key to the plan indicates that these graves were concessions of limited duration.

As for the need to establish a separate burial ground for a Jewish cemetery, Brongniart decided to convert the walled garden to the right of the old entry into a type of *campo santo*. Capitalizing on the splayed outer wall, which followed the Rue Saint-André, the architect envisaged creating an identical condition on the opposite side. The result would have been to augment the size of the area both in fact and in the imagination.

The gallery that was to surround the entire cemetery (fig. 231, K) does not appear to have the continuous walkway Quatremère de Quincy had envisaged. Rather it was to be composed of repetitive bays fashioned as so many individual aedicules. In this manner each person, family, or corporation would have its own identifiable sepulchral vault. The succession of pediments recalls the Temple of British Worthies at Stowe (fig. 144), an evocation that would have been greatly appreciated by the proponents of this arcade. Yet Brongniart created a graceful and continuous flow of alternating ascending and descending lines to impart a lively movement to the design, much as he had with the topiary at the Hôtel de Monaco.

Neither Brongniart nor his son had any need to apologize for the formal ligature, which contrasted so sharply on the plan with the winding paths. In 1825, even one of the cemetery's most enthusiastic supporters had to admit that the irregularities of the terrain and the meanderings of the footpaths made it difficult to find the tombs one was seeking. In effect, the carriage ways and the tall vertical monuments were the least that could be done to help orient the visitor. While the guidebooks of the late teens and early twenties repeatedly referred to Père Lachaise as a picturesque garden, this was a landscape garden put to a new use. By 1825 there were over 26,000 monuments. Aids to orientation within the vast domain were certainly welcomed.

The marriage of regular and irregular elements at Père Lachaise accorded with both the theory and the practice of landscape gardening. Brongniart's design fit within the category of "park," which Whately described as showing a "high degree of polish" within a more expansive "wildness." With respect to the formal approach to the pyramid, one is reminded of Sir William Chambers's dictum that straight lines and regular allées provided a most suitable approach to a prominent mausoleum intended to inspire august feelings. Hirschfeld noted that winding paths were out of place on a flat plain and that distant perspectives called for grandly planted allées. As for gardens consecrated to a "sweet melancholy," the tall trees of formal allées provided a "mysterious shade" that contributed an appropriate ambiance. Hirschfeld explained that as the branches joined overhead they recalled the vaults of ancient convents and Gothic churches, which further disposed the spirit to serious meditations. The "sinuous" paths that wound through the remainder of the cemetery were perfect for encouraging tranquility, as well as for leading the eye from one scene to another.

There are at least three variants of Brongniart's design for Père Lachaise. The project with the large cippi at the entrance (figs. 219–220) presents a plan whose major outlines appeared on Picquet's 1812 map of Paris. This will be referred to as project I. The project published in 1814 in the posthumous edition of Brongniart's works (he died June 5, 1813) differs slightly in plan yet has a totally different entry. This will be called project III (figs. 230–231). The link between the two is a project (figs. 226–229) that introduces the new entrance gate as well as an alternative design for the smaller chapel or depot at the bottom of the hill.

In all three cases, the plan was basically the same. With respect to the carriage paths, however, the curving allée that reached into the area of the communal graves was deleted from projects II and III as was the cut-off (in project III only) in front of the *rond-point* to the upper left. In project II the change in land level through the central terrace by the pyramid was shifted downward. In project III, it was eliminated altogether in favor of presenting a unified esplanade. Also, in the second and third projects, the monument in the formal quincunx was shifted down so that the allée of chestnut trees intersected the clearing (project II) and then the monument itself (project III).

In Brongniart's first design, the cemetery was to present a visually open entry. The curved walls, inflected inward from the street, were to provide a preliminary vestibule. Two giant cippi of antique form and reminiscent of the entry constructed in 1772 for the Cemetery Saint-Sulpice (fig. 232) were to flank the entry proper, which was closed by a metal grill. In Brongniart's second project the architect substituted a more monumental and more massive

226
Brongniart, Cemetery
of Père Lachaise,
Paris. Second project,
c. 1812.

227
Brongniart, Cemetery of Père Lachaise, Paris. Second project, c. 1812. View of the proposed entrance and chapel.

228
Brongniart, Cemetery of Père Lachaise, Paris. Second project, c. 1812. View of the proposed mortuary depot.

229
Brongniart, Cemetery of Père Lachaise, Paris. Second project, c. 1812. View of the proposed chapel.

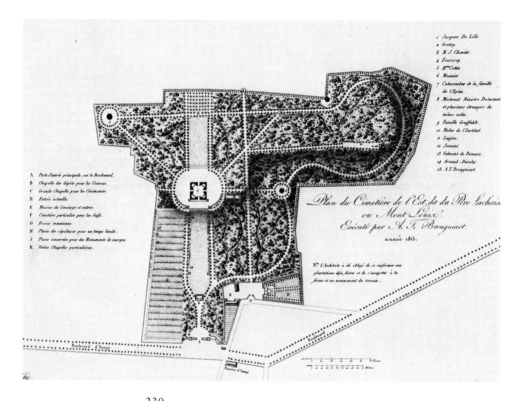

230
Brongniart, Cemetery
of Père Lachaise,
Paris. Third project,
1813.

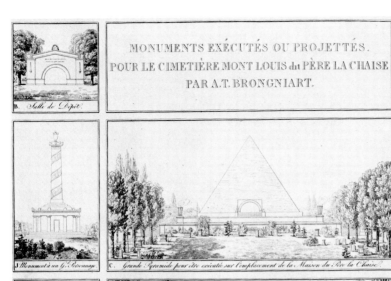

231
Brongniart,
"Executed or
Projected
Monuments for the
Cemetery of Père
Lachaise," c.
1812–1813.

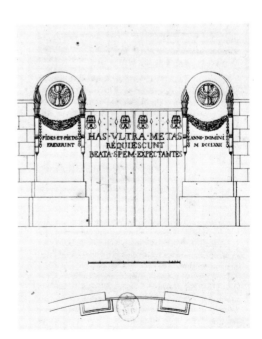

232
Cemetery of Saint-
Sulpice, Paris.
Entrance, 1772.

*Designing Père Lachaise*

gateway (fig. 226), somewhat like Boullée's cemetery entrance (fig. 88) yet rendered in a more picturesque manner. With this new design, Brongniart split the visitor's attention in two directions and into two successive stages. For the approaching funeral party, the entry would have been dominated by the giant pyramid (fig. 227) in a more forceful manner since the new gateway would have obscured the mortuary depot at the foot of the hill. This smaller chapel (fig. 228) would have appeared at the point when the cortege passed through the gateway. This second design for the entrance to Père Lachaise seems to have been the one that Brongniart preferred since it is reproduced in his published works (fig. 231).

All the public monuments in project II have been given a grander aspect than in the first project. The pyramid (fig. 229) now rises above a series of terraced plinths and is flanked by smoking cassolettes. The form of the depot (fig. 228) is now simpler and more somber. The three *monuments de marque*, as Brongniart termed them, which had been indicated only schematically on the first plan, have been developed into circular mausoleums crowned with a vertical accent. The towers for the two *rond-points* (figs. 222–223) are similar in form but arranged hierarchically, and a greater monumentality has been given to the one for the major *rond-point* to the right of the pyramid. The tower with its flaming beacon would have been visible from the terrace of the central chapel. The monument at the sharp corner to the upper right of the plan served a different visual purpose and hence was given a totally different form (fig. 224). The new designs were consecrated to people of merit and would have provided appropriate facilities for the government to bestow special honors on outstanding citizens.

Brongniart's designs for the two *rond-points* recall Ennemond-Alexandre Petitot's "funerary column destined for a queen's sepulcher," a *capriccio* designed in Rome toward 1748 (fig. 233). Petitot's composition consisted of a broad base in the form of a type of chapel carrying a massive column, which in turn was crowned with a sculptural grouping related to its theme. Not only the form but also the siting of Brongniart's monuments bear a strong resemblance to Petitot's prototype. The young *pensionnaire* had placed the mausoleum in the center of a circular clearing in a countryside filled with tombs of architectural distinction. In many respects the view from the column to the pyramid beyond anticipated the effect which Brongniart was to seek a half-century later.

Yet neither Brongniart's column nor the pyramid was ever executed. The closest they came to reality was François-Joseph Bélanger's decorations for the ceremonial transfer of the remains

233
Ennemond-Alexandre
Petitot, funerary
column to serve as a
tomb for a queen,
Rome, c. 1748.

of Louis XVI and Marie-Antoinette on January 21, 1817, to Saint-Denis. For this occasion Bélanger covered the church's twelfth-century façade with a giant pyramid flanked by massive funerary columns and accompanied by smoking cassolettes, all elements that owed much to Brongniart's unrealized dreams for Père Lachaise.

## The Architecture of Père Lachaise

Brongniart was succeeded as architect for Père Lachaise by Etienne-Hippolyte Godde, who was responsible for the entrance and the chapel, which both exist to this day. By 1820, the construction of the entryway according to Brongniart's plans was well under way, with the work reaching over two meters high. At that point Godde argued that it would be financially disastrous to continue. Instead, he proposed an entirely new construction based upon the entry at Saint-Sulpice. Guy de Gisors, Inspector General of the Council on Civil Buildings, objected that Godde's accusations were unproven and that his "inferior" project had eliminated the shelter for the concierge, which Brongniart had arranged in his own design. Since it appeared that the Council would permit Godde to proceed with the proposed demolition and new construction, Gisors adapted Godde's ideas to the existing foundations in three alternative sketches intended as models for the architect to follow in his own composition (fig. 234). The two flanking drawings most closely approximate Godde's project, while the middle solution attempts to retrieve the monumentality of Brongniart's final design.

In 1819, a sizeable gift to the city for the construction of a Catholic oratory prompted the adoption of plans for a chapel to replace the old ruined house at the crest of the hill. Guy de Gisors pointed out that such a construction would violate the spirit of the law, which admitted all religions to the cemetery and which favored none. As a consequence, he proposed an alternative design using the foundations of the existing house. Gisors's project consisted of a central vestibule with a Catholic chapel to the rear and Jewish and Protestant chapels to the sides (fig. 235). The visual effect of this structure would certainly have been better proportioned to the height of the hill and the distance from the entrance than the narrow chapel which Godde constructed after the house was torn down in 1820. By 1825 both the new entry and the chapel were in place (fig. 236). As one of the guidebooks remarked, neither was immune from criticism.

Since the pyramid had become so intimately although not exclusively linked to the image of the cemetery by the beginning of the nineteenth century, it may not be possible or even necessary to attempt to discern the inspiration for Brongniart's design. Instead one might consider the evolving tradition by which the pyramid had become a form that contemporaries would have recognized

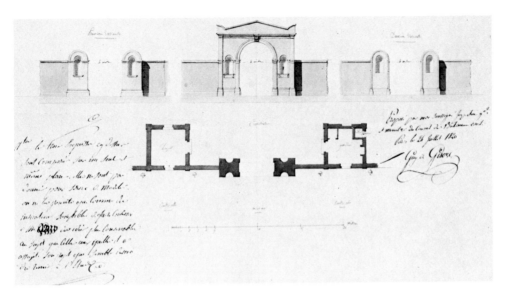

234
Guy de Gisors,
alternative designs
for the entrance to
the Cemetery of Père
Lachaise, Paris,
1820.

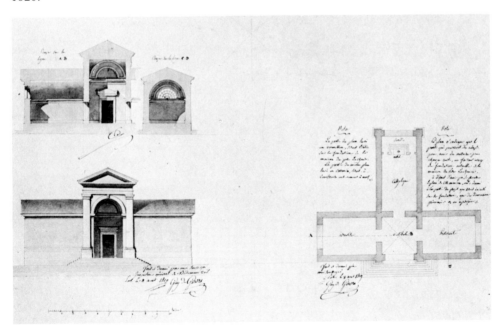

235
Gisors, alternative
design for the chapel
at the Cemetery of
Père Lachaise, Paris,
1819.

*The Architecture of Père Lachaise*

236
Cemetery of Père
Lachaise, Paris,
1848.

as befitting its subject. The effect of proceeding up a slope toward a pyramid whose front plane tilted even farther away had already been explored by Brongniart's teacher Boullée (fig. 86). The principal difference between these two designs, other than the obvious contrast in settings, was that Boullée provided a direct approach on axis while Brongniart followed a picturesque principle by taking the axis only so far and then proceeding along the sides of the greensward.

Closer in spirit as well as in time to Brongniart's design were the pyramids of Louis Gasse's first prize design and Guignet's second prize in the Grand Prix competition of 1799 (fig. 199) and Molinos's contemporaneous cemetery for Montmartre (fig. 187). The frontispiece to F.-A. Rauch's *Harmonie hydro-végétale et métérologique*, published in the year X (1801–1802), features an "Elysium" where a pyramidal chapel at the head of a long lawn is flanked to either side by a row of sumptuous tombs (fig. 237). This was precisely the relationship which Brongniart would adopt at Père Lachaise. In Rauch's Elysium, the cortege proceeds to the pyramid along a central axis only after entering from the side. Brongniart would soon adapt the oblique approach to Père Lachaise. In the year IX (1800–1801), the architect Ercole Silva attempted an Italian counterpart to Hirschfeld's treatise, which included a mausoleum in the form of a pyramid set upon a plinth in a manner that Brongniart would closely follow (fig. 238). Brongniart even envisaged two interior levels of domed chapels as found in the design by Claude-Mathieu de Lagardette. Lagardette's cemetery project (fig. 239) shows a modest chapel with a triangular pediment which may also have provided the inspiration for Brongniart's mortuary depot, also located close to the entrance (figs. 220, 228). Even the contrasts in vegetation in Lagardette's two drawings, one formal, the other picturesque, present two modes of landscaping, which, as we have seen, Brongniart skillfully combined in his design for Père Lachaise.

If anything did actually inspire Brongniart's drawing of the pyramid at Père Lachaise, it might have been the Protestant Cemetery in Rome, which had grown up at the foot of the Pyramid of Cestius (figs. 240–241). We have seen how this ancient Roman funerary monument figured repeatedly in the designs for ideal cemeteries throughout the eighteenth century. Now, in the first two decades of the nineteenth century, the Protestant Cemetery became a popular subject for artists, many of whom circulated their work in the form of engravings. The earliest known burial there dates from 1738. In 1748 this cemetery appeared on the famous Nolli map of Rome. The early nineteenth-century views depict a scene very similar to Brongniart's vision of Père Lachaise, with the variegated monuments clustered at the base of the pyramid. Even today, one can experience something of the effect of

237
*Elysium: Solemnity of Tombs*. Frontispiece from Rauch, *Harmonie hydro-végétale et métérologique*, year X (1801–1802).

*A New Eden*

238
Claude-Mathieu de
Lagardette, cenotaph
or mausoleum. From
Silva, *Dell'Arte dei
giardini inglesi*, year
IX (1800–1801).

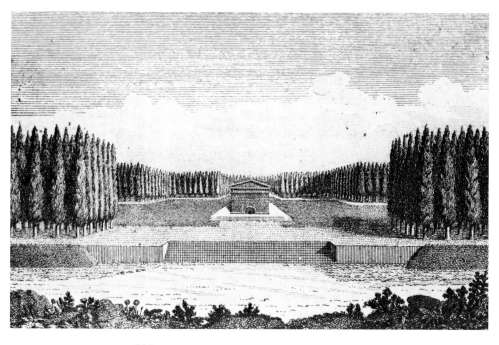

239
Lagardette, cemetery.
From Silva, *Dell'Arte
dei giardini inglesi*,
year IX
(1800–1801).

*The Architecture of Père Lachaise*

240
Protestant Cemetery,
Rome. View by
Pinelli, 1811.

241
Protestant Cemetery,
Rome. Early
nineteenth-century
view.

*A New Eden*

Brongniart's pyramid in the Protestant Cemetery of Rome, which retains the feeling of these early illustrations.

The formal entry at Père Lachaise was too tempting a processional space for architects to leave unbuilt. A guidebook of 1825 mentions a project by Brongniart to precede the colossal pyramid with a broad route bordered by twelve large and identical funerary monuments. A project designed in this spirit had appeared on Maire's 1816 map of Paris (fig. 242). At the Musée Carnavalet, there is a drawing, dated January 1829, of an approved design that would have lined the central allée with a continuous band of sepulchral vaults as well as creating a formal architectural setting around the chapel itself (fig. 243). There is also an undated drawing for an even more elaborate processional space terminating in a crypt cut into the hill (fig. 244). Eventually, family mausoleums came to line the central allée to provide formality without recourse to an unbroken architectural construction (fig. 236). Today the axis is terminated by Bartholomé's Monument to the Dead, which was erected part of the way up the hill in 1899. To terminate the view at this point, a dense screen of vegetation hiding the chapel has been planted just beyond.

## A Terrestrial Paradise

From the beginning the Cemetery of Père Lachaise was favored by the authorities. Frochot's Arrêté of 15 Ventôse, year XIII (March 6, 1805) temporarily limited permanent concessions to this burial ground. In 1813 Frochot's successor Chabrol reiterated this provision, which remained in effect until 1824. The Cemetery of Vaugirard offered little competition. In 1816 a guidebook noted that there were few remarkable tombs in this small and crowded burial ground, serving both a poor working-class neighborhood and the Hôtel-Dieu, which still used large communal graves. On September 24, 1825, Vaugirard was finally replaced by the new Cemetery of the South (Montparnasse) (fig. 173). As for the Cemetery under Montmartre, also called the Champ de Repos, at least one observer in 1816 felt that it fostered more serious reflections than Père Lachaise. The former quarries of Montmartre presented a somber valley of tombs (fig. 245), whose solitude and mysterious light would continue to engage the imagination until its destruction with a landfill in 1843. Yet the overcrowding at Montmartre had forced its closure for a few years. When it was reopened in 1825 (fig. 246) with its area more than doubled, it had lost much of its former prestige. The new land, moreover, had no shrubs or trees but rather appeared as a naked landscape covered with unornamented tombs.

Between 1816 and 1825, however, visitors to Père Lachaise noted a remarkable transformation in the physiognomy of the cemetery. A vogue for more magnificent tombs yielded new memorials that far surpassed even the most splendid ones of the

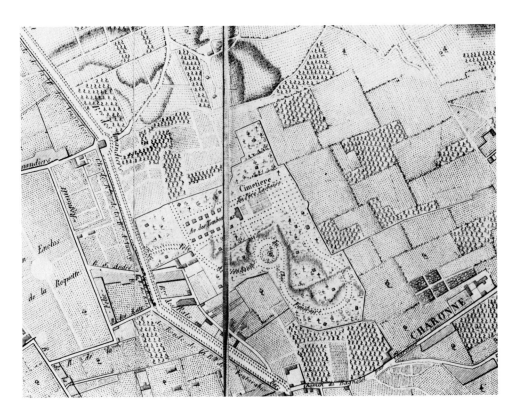

242
Cemetery of Père
Lachaise, Paris.
Project for an
Avenue of Tombs.
Detail from the 1816
Maire plan of Paris.

*A New Eden*

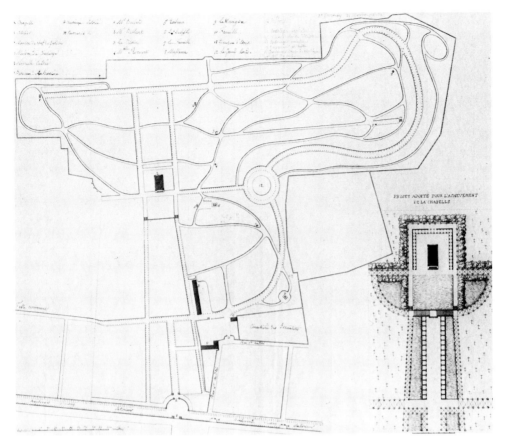

243
Cemetery of Père
Lachaise, Paris.
Project for a central
avenue with
sepulchral vaults,
1829.

244
Cemetery of Père
Lachaise, Paris.
Project for a central
avenue with
sepulchral vaults,
after 1820. Section
and plan.

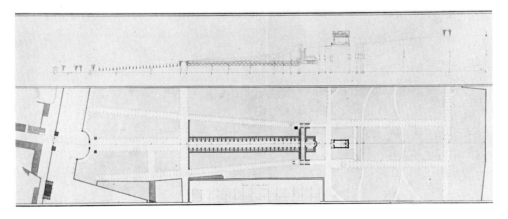

*A Terrestrial Paradise*

245
Cemetery of
Montmartre, Paris.
View by Schaal
showing the Valley
of Tombs in 1824.

*A New Eden*

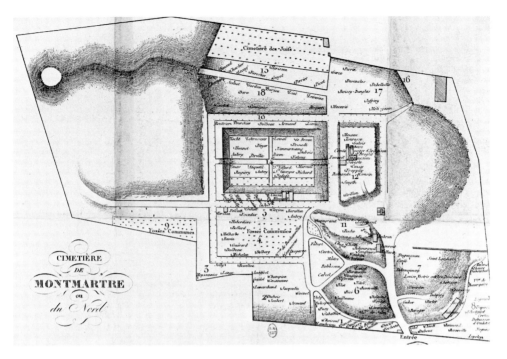

246
Cemetery of
Montmartre, Paris,
1829.

preceding years. Numerous observers commented on this change, which some welcomed as imparting a new grandeur to Père Lachaise and others lamented as a vain display of pomp incompatible with the sweet melancholy of a cemetery. Not only did the memorials become larger, but a new type of tomb, the family sepulchral vault in the form of a substantial mausoleum, became popular. To satisfy the demand for the increasingly popular permanent concession, nearly seven acres were added to expand the cemetery by one quarter of its original size. Rather than take away any of the original garden, the new land to the west was held for temporary concessions and communal graves. This was the policy followed in further expansions over the succeeding decades (fig. 247).

By 1825, the Cemetery of Père Lachaise had reached its most glorious moment. At that point, through its plantings and its tombs, it had acquired all the features that made it into a richly variegated landscape garden of the dead. The American "rural" cemeteries, which would challenge its preeminence, had not yet been formed. In 1825, a popular chronicle of Paris remarked that the beautiful garden of Père Lachaise was attracting crowds of curious visitors. Several guidebooks published maps with itineraries that led the visitor through a tour of several hours, pointing out interesting landscape features as well as the most remarkable tombs and the most illustrious personages. By comparing these maps with those of the Jesuits' estate, it is possible not only to recapture the aspect of Père Lachaise in its most picturesque heyday but also to show how it developed out of the topography of the earlier landscape.

Père Lachaise had all the makings of a successful landscape garden. These are well indicated in a topographic plan of 1815 (fig. 248): the dramatic rise of land up to the crest of the hill where Brongniart hoped to build his pyramid, the valley to the right which sloped up to a steep escarpment with a gracefully rounded top, and a variety of incidents that would furnish intimate bosquets. The only major feature on Hirschfeld's checklist of the attributes of a well-furnished park that was missing was water. While the old fountain, La Fidèle, faithfully continued to supply water for the gardener to care for the flowers, bushes, and trees, the Cemetery of Père Lachaise was never given the still or flowing bodies of water that contributed to the impression of Rousseau's and Sulzer's tombs (figs. 151, 152, 157).

If this early topographic map is accurate, it reveals that by 1815 the major outlines of Brongniart's plan had been realized. Two maps from 1820 (fig. 249) show the general initial strategy still intact, with the winding paths now firmly established. Those to the valley on the right and on the escarpment above closely followed Brongniart's plan (fig. 222). On the other hand, to the left

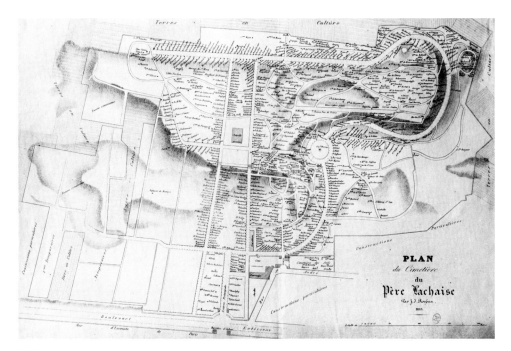

247
Cemetery of Père
Lachaise, Paris,
1839.

248
Cemetery of Père
Lachaise, Paris.
Topographic map of
1815.

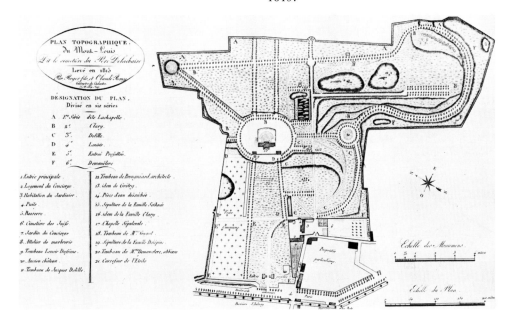

*A Terrestrial Paradise*

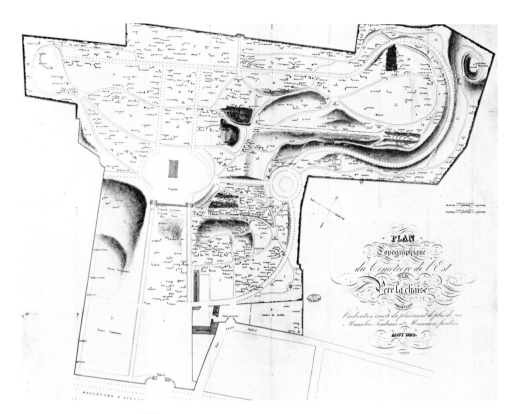

249
Cemetery of Père
Lachaise, Paris.
Topographic map of
August 1820.

*A New Eden*

of the chapel, the diagonal allée leading to the eminence in the upper corner of the cemetery had been replaced by a series of sinuous routes, two of which were permitted to cross over the area directly above the chapel.

With a terrain that rose and fell in elevation as much as these walkways meandered in plan, the Cemetery of Père Lachaise presented the type of landscape where one always anticipated something new around a bend or over a ridge. The skillful use of this topography along with the benefits of an expansive site made Père Lachaise into a world of its own. As the Abbé Delille had written about the landscape garden in general, "where the eye can anticipate no more, the charm disappears." If Père Lachaise appeared as a new Eden, it was largely because its gardens could sustain the illusion of a vast and unbounded park with an inexhaustible degree of variety. For the purpose of analysis, rather than follow any of the guidebooks in a particular tour through the cemetery, the landscape will be considered according to its characteristic areas.

From contemporary descriptions, it is possible to reconstruct the plantings along the main avenues, which provided an overriding sense of order throughout the grounds. From the new entrance, the esplanade sloping up to the chapel was flanked by paths bordered with lime trees. These double rows of limes continued beyond the chapel to meet the grand transverse allée of chestnut trees. The carriage path which looped around the lower right corner of the cemetery was planted with poplars. This Allée des Peupliers, as it was called on a map of 1820, terminated in the large *rond-point*, a true *salle de verdure* with an interior ring of poplar trees. From here the carriage path continued to the right as the Allée des Acacias, which ascended around the edge of the escarpment until it met the Grande Allée des Marronniers.

While it would be difficult to prove the precise degree to which vegetation, first around tombs in the eighteenth-century landscape garden, and then in the early nineteenth-century cemetery, was appreciated for its emblematic or expressive value, the written evidence seems to confirm John Dixon Hunt's observation that sensibilities shifted from favoring the former to the latter in the 1740s. Now contemporaries seemed more interested in the *caractère*, or expressive aspect, of the trees than in their iconographic meaning. Thus, in his manuscript treatise on landscape gardens (1775), the Duc d'Harcourt made no mention of the fable of Cyparissus, who was changed into a cypress by Apollo, thereby consecrating this tree for the tomb. Rather, D'Harcourt observed that the cypress and the yew had a universally recognized character that was "sad and funereal." At Père Lachaise, the lime trees, poplars, and chestnuts were probably appreciated primarily for similar reasons. According to Hirschfeld, the dark, thick foliage of these trees was well suited to creating a somber and "mysterious" shade, suggestive of the "compassion" and "sweet melancholy" that one would want in a funerary garden.

With the infrastructure of the cemetery thus considered, we can now focus on the various sections. One of the guidebooks published in 1825 explained that, although the new monumental portal had been finished, the previous allocation of permanent concessions in the adjacent area prevented its use except for exceptional ceremonies. Visitors to the cemetery still arrived through the old entry, dating from the times when the estate belonged to the Jesuits. The former orangery (on the left in fig. 250) now housed a stonecutter who prepared and displayed his work there. Both Courvoisier's view from the tomb of the Abbé Delille (fig. 251) on the hill above this entryway and two maps from 1820 reveal that the former straight allée had been given a softer contour. This illustration by Courvoisier is particularly valuable because it gives a sense of the flatness of the land at the entry and then its steep slope as one approaches the foreground. The area to the left of the scene is the "romantic" valley whose "solitude" called forth "sweet reveries."

On Brongniart's plan, at the point where the allée of poplars curves around the lower edge of the valley, there is a footpath that forms a small loop into the area between the allée and the Jewish cemetery. There, in 1817, the tomb of Abélard and Héloïse was transferred along with their remains from the recently closed Museum of French Monuments (fig. 185). Here the famed lovers found their final and permanent home, as their tomb (figs. 252–253) became the sentimental focal point of the cemetery. If the two views are accurate in their depiction of both tombstones and vegetation, then one can ascertain the rapidity of change at Père Lachaise between the teens and the early twenties as the stones became more monumental and the vegetation more profuse. The scene in fig. 252 is particularly valuable for conveying a sense of the height of the hill.

Brongniart's intention of providing the *rond-point* with the mausoleum of a great person was realized by the construction of a tomb through public subscription for Casimir Perier, a major political leader under Louis-Philippe, who died in 1832. The extreme elevation given to the base of the monument served to make the statue visible from the esplanade in front of the chapel (fig. 254). As was mentioned earlier, from this point the land falls off sharply to the *rond-point*. From there it begins to rise again as it encircles the rounded escarpment.

One of the features of a park, according to the theory of the landscape garden, was that its views were generally oriented to some other part of the estate and only infrequently to the exterior. At the heights of Père Lachaise the scene opened up to provide

250
Courvoisier, *View of
the Cemetery of Père
Lachaise Taken from
the Entrance*, c.
1817.

251
Courvoisier, *View of
the Cemetery of Père
Lachaise Taken from
the Tomb of the
Abbé Delille*, c. 1817.

*A Terrestrial Paradise*

252
Tomb of Abélard
and Héloïse,
Cemetery of Père
Lachaise, Paris, c.
1817–1818.

253
Tomb of Abélard
and Héloïse,
Cemetery of Père
Lachaise, Paris. From
Marchant de
Beaumont, *Vues
pittoresques*, 1821.

*A New Eden*

254
Cemetery of Père
Lachaise, Paris. Mid-
nineteenth century
view showing the
tomb of Casimir
Perier at the *rond-
point* and the
carriage path that
rises around the
escarpment.

*A Terrestrial Paradise*

a spectacular panorama of the city. These extended views could be had from the esplanade in front of the chapel; from the rounded slope of the escarpment, which provided a picturesque foreground (fig. 255); and finally, from the plateau along the allée of chestnut trees near the so-called Gothic Chapel (fig. 256). As these illustrations show, the tombs at Père Lachaise were carefully tended little garden plots surrounded by low fences and filled with shrubs and flowers. Sometimes a bench was provided for visitors to sit and meditate.

In the 1820s the base of the escarpment bordered by the encircling carriage path underwent a major transformation as majestic sepulchral vaults were built into the side of the hill (fig. 257). Soon the entire way was lined with these mausoleums with their proud—banal, according to one critic—inscriptions: "family sepulcher," "permanent concession." Here, from the allée of acacias, one could look down into the valley or up to the top of the hill with the obelisk to Maréchal Masséna standing out against the sky. Masséna's tomb was located at the heights of Père Lachaise, where France's military heroes were buried. This area was called the Rendez-vous des Braves or the Champ des Braves. In fig. 258, which depicts the funeral of General Collaud on November 11, 1819, Maréchal Lefebvre is shown selecting the site for the grave that he would soon occupy beside Masséna.

The escarpment was also the place for numerous bosquets whose enclosed, intimate settings contrasted sharply with the view upward to the terraced slopes and with the expansive panorama of the city. The Bosquet du Dragon (fig. 259), where, according to one guide, "everything is romantic," developed out of a formal bosquet dating back to the times when Baron Desfontaines owned the estate (fig. 218). Above this bosquet and at the top of the looping carriage road was a densely planted area said to occupy the site of a belvedere constructed by the Jesuits. Here the Protestants clustered their tombs together in a bosquet called La Charmette, shown to the left of quadrant 36 in the map of 1820 (fig. 249). The topographic map of 1815 (fig. 248) depicts two areas just above the allée leading to the Bosquet du Dragon as shallow hollows. Although irregular in form, these depressions correspond through their position to the two basins from the second phase of the Jesuits' gardens (fig. 217). At Père Lachaise these gentle cavities developed into intimate sunken bosquets that can still be visited today. Farther to the left, as indicated on the topographic map of 1820, are two thickly planted bosquets, which developed around and above the basin from the final gardens. Duplat's view (fig. 260) shows a scene in the upper bosquet, often called the Bosquet Clary.

While the last two bosquets developed in spite of Brongniart's plan, whose diagonal marched straight across the dried-out basin,

255
Paris from the
escarpment at the
Cemetery of Père
Lachaise, 1829. View
by Civeton.

256
Paris from the upper
plain at the Cemetery
of Père Lachaise,
view by Courvoisier,
c. 1817. To the right
is the Greffult family
tomb, or "Gothic
Chapel," by
Brongniart.

257
View of the early
family tombs
(1817–1818) along
the escarpment and
above them the
Rendez-vous des
Braves, Cemetery of
Père Lachaise, Paris.
From Marchant de
Beaumont, *Vues
pittoresques*, 1821.

258
*"The Heroes' Last
Rendez-vous"*:
*Maréchal Lefebvre
Selecting His Final
Resting Place by
Maréchal Masséna*
during the funeral of
General Collaud,
November 11, 1819.
From Marchant de
Beaumont, *Vues
pittoresques*, 1821.

259
*View of the Bosquet du Dragon*, Cemetery of Père Lachaise, Paris. From Marchant de Beaumont, *Vues pittoresques*, 1821.

260
Bosquet Clary,
Cemetery of Père
Lachaise, Paris. From
Marchant de
Beaumont, *Vues
pittoresques*, 1821.

the Delille bosquet, the "most picturesque" section of the cemetery, figured prominently in Brongniart's scheme. As mentioned earlier, both the Verniquet plan of 1790 (fig. 218) and the Picquet plan of 1804 show a bosquet to the right of the house with its entrance from the allée to the side of the terrace. In project I of Brongniart's design (fig. 219), a straight path through the center of the bosquet is bordered by tombs in verdant niches and terminated by a major sepulcher. In project II, the niches are unoccupied except for two, which are identified in project III as containing the tombs of Brongniart himself and the Abbé Delille. Brongniart's project for the tomb of Jacques Delille, as well as a view of his own sarcophagus, was published posthumously with his works (fig. 231). According to Silvestre de Sacy, Brongniart had designed the tomb for Delille after an initial drawing by Hubert Robert. The design is based upon the same classical precedent used by Robert for the tomb of Jean-Jacques Rousseau at Ermenonville (fig. 153).

Delille died May 1, 1813, and Brongniart followed on June 5. The Municipal Council accorded Brongniart a tomb in the same bosquet close to his literary friend. Over the next decade, this bosquet became one of the most famous areas of the cemetery as numerous literary and artistic figures chose to be buried there.

The guidebooks of the 1820s reveal not only the sense of identity that the different areas of Père Lachaise acquired through the cemetery's topography and through its burials, but also how friends or kindred spirits were grouped together. In 1817, the tombs of Molière and La Fontaine were transferred to Père Lachaise and placed beside each other. Next to Delille lay his close friend Dureau de la Malle. The architect Bélanger was buried beside Brongniart. Close to the tomb for Cadet de Vaux one can still find the grave of his fellow chemist Parmentier. These are just a few examples selected from the more famous dead. For those who could afford this final gesture, the public Cemetery of Père Lachaise offered an ideal opportunity to realize the vision of a union in death that individuals such as Hazon had so ardently sought in their own private funerary bosquets.

*First Impressions*

The most eloquent testimonials about Père Lachaise came from the American and European travelers who had neither direct emotional attachments to the cemetery nor, unlike the guidebook writers, any prospect of pecuniary gain. While their published observations on travel abroad had a commercial basis, these visitors, who often were relating their "first impressions," were as quick to criticize as they were to praise. When Marianne Baillie crossed the Channel in the summer of 1818, she found herself repulsed by the narrow, crowded streets of Paris, with their "inconceivably filthy effluvia" and the "inconceivable variety of horrible smells." Yet she was deeply moved by Père Lachaise:

"Nothing can be more striking and more affecting to the imagination, than this place of burial." The American Nathaniel Carter arrived in Paris in 1825 during General Foy's funeral, as the cortege proceeded in the rain all the way from Notre-Dame to Père Lachaise. To Carter, who visited the cemetery before exploring the city, Père Lachaise "reflects infinite credit upon the city, as well as upon the character of the French people. In all respects it very far surpasses anything of the kind I have ever seen, and the design strongly recommends itself to the imitation of all great cities." When Carter's compatriot Wilbur Fisk visited Paris in 1838, he intended to give Père Lachaise "but a passing glance, yet the interest of the place held us there from morning till nightfall; and even then, but for the fatigue of the visit, its interest would scarcely have been abated, much less destroyed." Until the emergence of the American "rural" cemeteries in the 1830s, Père Lachaise would enjoy the virtually unqualified praise of such travelers who, although briefer in their descriptions of the topography than the French guidebooks, expatiated more fully upon the sentimental, moral, and cultural significance of the cemetery.

At Père Lachaise the expansive estate, with its varied landscape and its luxuriant vegetation, repeatedly impressed these visitors. They were sensitive to the picturesque quality of the site, "so broken and diversified, as to embrace a great variety of natural scenery—rocks, hills, and deep vales." Among the trees, the "mournful" cypresses and yews were especially noticed, as were the numerous acacias. At the summit of Mont-Louis, everybody remarked upon the splendid view of Paris extending to the towers of Notre-Dame and then on to the gilded dome of the Invalides.

All of the texts under consideration here, covering the period 1818–1838, noted how well kept virtually all the graves were. Almost every plot was surrounded by a railing of wood or iron and planted with shrubs and fragrant flowers. The tombstones themselves were hung with wreaths of leaves and flowers, and wild trailing vines were abundant. "Neatness," "elegance," and "delicacy of taste" were the most popular terms used to characterize both the plots and the memorials. These visitors were dazzled by what they considered to be the beauty of the tombs, their seemingly inexhaustible variety, and their contrast with the "lively verdure." The most remarkable monument, both for its architecture and its associations, was the "light Gothic temple" serving as the sepulcher for Abélard and Héloïse. Yet the most moving aspect of the cemetery were the carefully tended graves. Marianne Baillie recorded several of the "affecting" inscriptions found on the humbler tombs:

To the memory of my best friend—he was my brother!
Here lies P—— N——: In losing him his wife loses the most

tender of her friends and his children, a model of virtue. Here lies our beloved son.

These expressions of loss, reminiscent of Gessner's idylls, reflected the sentimental ties within the family that historians have noted were developing in this period. As Baillie observed: "[E]verything marked the existence of tender remembrance and regret: it appears to me as if in this place, alone, the dead were never forgotten." To Carter, the extreme care given to the graves seemed to establish a "medium of communication between the living and the dead." In this new Eden, Parisians were living out the terms of Legouvé's poem about communing with the dead in and through nature as well as giving reality to Bernardin de Saint-Pierre's famous dictum about the tomb standing on the frontier between two worlds.

Finally, as Fisk observed, "in addition to the architectural beauty, and monumental magnificence, and vegetable verdure and fragrance, and picturesque scenery of Père Lachaise, there is this one most interesting and instructive feature in this marble city of the dead." The cemetery presented a vivid "biographical dictionary" of the illustrious men and women of France. Visitors were held "spellbound" as they entered into an "immediate communion" with the works, deeds, and character of the famous people buried here. The great men of letters, such as Molière, La Fontaine, Delille, Chénier, and Bernardin de Saint-Pierre; the great generals, Masséna, Davoust, Lefebvre, Decres, Pérignon, Beauharnais, and Ney; and the scientists and explorers, such as the pioneering mineralogist Haüy, the chemist Fourcroy, the astronomer Delambre, the naturalist Sonini, and the aeronaut Madeleine-Sophie Blanchard, provided the most elevating moments in this encounter with the spirits of the dead. At Père Lachaise, history seemed almost palpable to the sensitive imagination.

If, as Alberto Tenenti has argued, Christianity has always had difficulty in describing heaven, in a sense the problem was solved at Père Lachaise. While some observers praised the Christian intimations of immortality that the ambiance of the cemetery seemed to suggest and the inscriptions upon the portal promised, the cemetery provided a more immediate bliss, which had little place for questions of sin, grace, or redemption. The graves at Père Lachaise offered a sense of immortality by suggesting the sweetness of death and by sustaining the illusion of a continuing presence which bound the dead to their attentive survivers. All of this had little in common with Christian theology. As Wilbur Fisk astutely observed, "the excessive attention to the graves and adorning of the sepulchers of the dead . . . is an effort to transform the valley of bones into a terrestrial paradise." Fisk's observations are worth citing in full, for they capture the essence of what made the Cemetery of Père Lachaise into a new Eden:

[A]nd although there is an enchantment about it which for a moment almost takes away the gloom of the grave, and makes one willing, he hardly knows why, to lay himself down in the marble temple over which the honeysuckle wreathes its fragrant blossoms, and around which the rose and the hyacinth diffuse their redolent dew—where friends record their virtues on the enduring tablet, and adorn their sepulchers with circling garlands, that at once betoken the warmth and the perpetuity of their love; yet it is an earthly enchantment after all, and only tends to call off the mind from the paradise above, and the awfully interesting realities of the spiritual world.

Such misgivings were rare among the general enthusiasm, which saw in Père Lachaise a prototype for a new kind of cemetery. To John Griscom, Père Lachaise offered the appropriate alternative to the "lugubrious images of death and desolation" found in the traditional parish burial grounds in New York. Griscom's book appeared in New York in 1823 at a moment when several voices were publicly urging the closing of the graveyards located within the city. The yellow fever epidemic of 1822, which had killed 16,000, was linked in the minds of the reformers to the miasmata from the cemeteries. Nathaniel Carter was certain that if he could transport all the inhabitants of New York en masse to pay a single visit to Père Lachaise, they would immediately decide in favor of a similar mode of *extra muros* interments.

### The American Rural Cemeteries

These hopes were soon satisfied as cemeteries in the Anglo-Saxon world underwent a reform movement in the late 1820s and the 1830s very similar to that experienced in Paris in the preceding century. Overcrowding, miasmata, at times desecration of graves, at other times an epidemic, and finally, a new desire to commune with the dead in a beautiful, natural setting—all of these factors combined to usher in a new order in burials in America and Great Britain. In Great Britain, Liverpool led the way with Low Hill General Cemetery (1825), which was followed by St. James Cemetery, developed in 1825–1829. The Glasgow Necropolis (1832) has been termed the most spectacular in Britain. At the time of its inception, it was said to have been modeled on Père Lachaise. London began its new cemeteries with All Souls Cemetery at Kensal Green (1833), to be followed by numerous others, the most famous of which was Highgate Cemetery (1839). In the United States, the first of the "rural" cemeteries, as they were called, was Mount Auburn outside Boston (1831), with Laurel Hill of Philadelphia (1836) and Greenwood in Brooklyn (1838) soon following. By 1849, Andrew Jackson Downing could write in *The Horticulturalist* that there was scarcely a city of note in the whole country "that did not have its rural cemetery." Philadelphia alone had nearly twenty of these new institutions, which generally were formed as joint stock companies. Forest Hills,

Massachusetts, claimed the honor of having opened the first municipal rural cemetery in 1848.

For those who argued in favor of opening *extra muros* burial grounds where nature would elevate the mourner's feelings, reduce his sorrow, promote religious meditations, and foster a sweet melancholy, the Cemetery of Père Lachaise offered eloquent testimony to what might be accomplished. Thus, in addressing the question of establishing a new type of cemetery for the citizens of Boston, the keynote speaker at the second annual festival of the Massachusetts Horticultural Society in September 1830 could find no better way to present his ideas than by reference to Père Lachaise: "I refer to the establishment of a public cemetery, similar in its design to that of Père Lachaise in the environs of Paris, to be located in the suburbs of this metropolis."

Enthusiasm for the Parisian prototype reached its highest point in Philadelphia in 1837, when it was proposed that a new "rural" cemetery be named the "American Père Lachaise." After an initial flurry of excitement in the press over the idea and the name, patriotic critics soon argued in favor of an American theme. In response, the founders changed the name to Monument Cemetery to reflect the lapidary honors to be bestowed upon great Americans who had "rendered blessings to mankind." Although Monument Cemetery was actually to carry, albeit briefly, the name of Père Lachaise, Mount Auburn at this time was often characterized as "the Père Lachaise of America." Americans could imagine no higher form of praise for their new rural cemeteries than to compare them to the first and most illustrious predecessor.

This analogy, though, would soon be reversed, with the American cemeteries gaining an ascendancy over their French counterpart. Although the rural cemeteries such as Mount Auburn and Greenwood resembled Père Lachaise in the sensitive use of winding roads to follow the contour of the variegated terrain, there were also major differences. First, there was the question of size. Père Lachaise had fifty-seven acres when Mount Auburn opened in 1831 with seventy-two. By 1835 Mount Auburn had expanded to comprise a total of one hundred ten. Greenwood opened in 1842 with one hundred eighty-five compared to Père Lachaise's sixty-three. Within ten years Greenwood doubled in size, while Père Lachaise expanded virtually to its current boundaries in 1850 with a total of one hundred seven acres (fig. 261).

While Père Lachaise was planted as a picturesque landscape garden, many of the American rural cemeteries began as untrammeled wilderness. Both Mount Auburn and Greenwood (figs. 262–268) were thickly wooded sites whose sylvan ambiance was much appreciated by contemporaries. The topography of these two cemeteries also differed from that of Père Lachaise. The American examples presented a series of undulating hills and dales

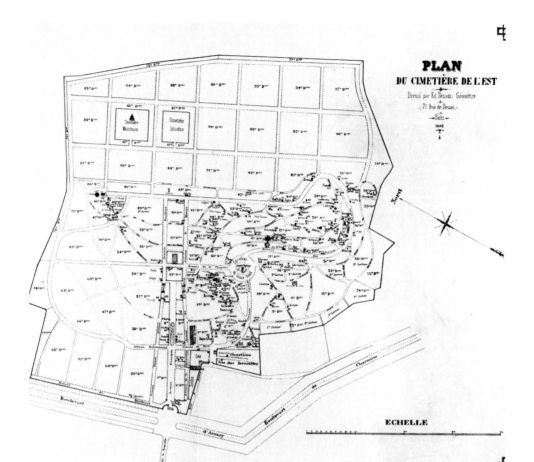

261
Cemetery of Père
Lachaise, Paris,
1862.

*A New Eden*

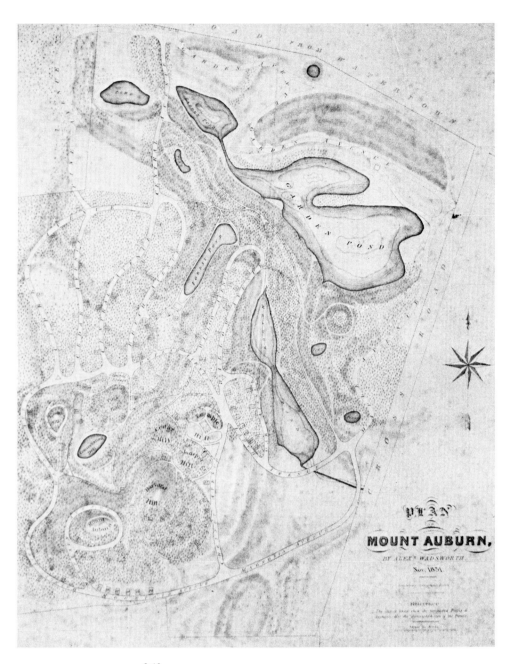

262
Mount Auburn
Cemetery,
Cambridge,
Massachusetts. First
official plan,
November 1831,
drawn by Alexander
Wadsworth.

263
Pilgrim's Path,
Mount Auburn
Cemetery,
Cambridge,
Massachusetts. From
Walter, *Mount
Auburn Illustrated*,
1847.

264
Forest Pond, Mount
Auburn Cemetery,
Cambridge,
Massachusetts. From
Walter, *Mount
Auburn Illustrated*,
1847.

*A New Eden*

265
View over
Consecration Dell,
Mount Auburn
Cemetery,
Cambridge,
Massachusetts. From
Walter, *Mount
Auburn Illustrated*,
1847.

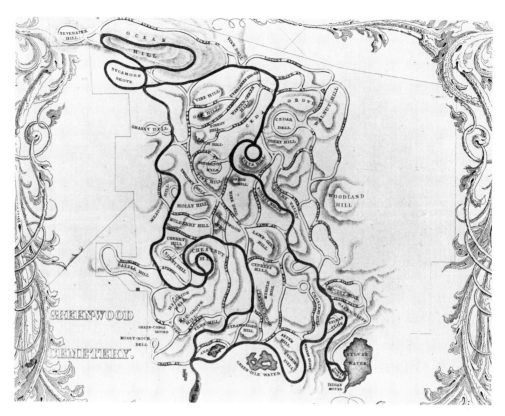

266
Greenwood
Cemetery, Brooklyn.
From Cleaveland,
*Green-Wood
Illustrated*, 1847.

267
"Keeper's Lodge at
Entrance,"
Greenwood
Cemetery, Brooklyn.
From Cleaveland,
*Green-Wood
Illustrated*, 1847.

268
"Lawn-Girt Hill,"
Greenwood
Cemetery, Brooklyn.
From Cleaveland,
*Green-Wood
Illustrated*, 1847.

*The American Rural Cemeteries*

not found in their French counterpart. At Greenwood the many hillocks were surrounded by a maze of winding carriage paths that provided access to all parts of the burial ground.

Although Mount Auburn was originally similar in size to Père Lachaise and presented a comparable degree of unity in its plan, the two cemeteries differed profoundly in layout and effect (fig. 262). Whereas Père Lachaise was organized around the formal esplanade leading up to the chapel at the crown of the hill, Mount Auburn presented a more informal scheme. The Boston cemetery was arranged with numerous winding paths that made their way indirectly to Mount Auburn, the highest landscape feature on the site, located at the far corner of the property. Although one can look through the Egyptian entrance gate to the tower on top of the far mount, one can never proceed directly toward it.

The carriage paths at Mount Auburn ride the crest of the long north-south ridges while footpaths meander through the intervening vales. Mount Auburn itself is preceded by a cluster of hillocks cascading down to the northeast, where they meet the carriage path, which has gathered together the finger-like avenues. Indian Ridge, which runs diagonally from the north to the east just south of Garden Pond, separated the cemetery from the land originally destined as an arboretum for the Massachusetts Horticultural Society, the founder of Mount Auburn Cemetery. The cemetery proper had several smaller ponds (fig. 264), another feature that distinguished it from Père Lachaise. If Père Lachaise wore its chapel like a crown, then Mount Auburn cherished within its bosom the secluded Consecration Dell, sheltered at the northern foot of the Mount (fig. 265). Here nearly two thousand people gathered on September 24, 1831, for a deeply moving transcendentalist ceremony to consecrate the new burial ground.

## A Metropolis of the Dead

From the 1840s onward, as foreign visitors continued their pilgrimages to Père Lachaise, comparisons with the new cemeteries of the Anglo-Saxon world were inevitable. While Père Lachaise was losing much of its greenery as it filled up with more and more tombs, cemeteries like Mount Auburn and Greenwood were having problems with too dense a growth of foliage. American travelers had little appreciation of the closely crowded monuments in the form of miniature chapels that were becoming so popular in French cemeteries. American cemeteries, in contrast, sought to maintain their "rural" character by restricting the size and number of monuments as well as eliminating the low iron railings that cut up the landscape into so many little parcels.

In 1845 an American tourist such as Dr. John W. Corson could still be "deeply" moved by Père Lachaise although it seemed "that in diversified scenery and general natural embellishments," the

French cemetery was surpassed by several in his own country. Travelers' dissatisfaction increased with the years, reflecting the ever-changing aspect of Père Lachaise. In 1850, Père Lachaise annexed more than forty-three acres of relatively flat terrain divided into regular quadrants whose monotony only exacerbated the stultifying effects of the overcrowding in the rest of the cemetery (fig. 261). Thus by 1871, an American traveler would write: "Père Lachaise is one of the disappointments of Paris. There are many cemeteries in the United States superior to it. Indeed, the famous place has very little to recommend it, and reminds one of a brick-yard over a hill. The monuments generally are neither handsome nor in good taste. There are no walks or groves worthy of the name; and you marvel how such a cemetery ever gained a reputation."

To enthusiasts for the American rural cemeteries, Père Lachaise was "looking more like a town or village than a cemetery." With its monuments "huddled too closely together," lining the narrow walks as well as the wider avenues in a way which is still alien to Mount Auburn and Greenwood, Père Lachaise seemed to be a veritable "metropolis of the dead." Yet today, for all the differences, even the giants among the American cemeteries have lost their initial wooded quietude. With their beautiful trees rising above carefully tended lawns, Mount Auburn and Greenwood have become more like parks. Perhaps only Mount Auburn's Consecration Dell, with its dark reflecting pool and its wild forest trees and ground cover, retains a sense of the original.

The story of Père Lachaise as an influential landscape continued in America as the rural cemeteries spurred the development of a public system of parks. A. J. Downing repeatedly invoked the popularity of the cemeteries with leisure-seeking visitors as evidence of the need for true public gardens: "Judging from the crowds of people in carriages, and on foot, which I find constantly thronging Greenwood and Mount Auburn, I think it plain enough how much our citizens, of all classes, would enjoy public parks on a similar scale."

In France the continuing significance of Père Lachaise resided in the new role of the cemetery in the spiritual life of the community. As early as 1825, Nathaniel Carter remarked how on All Souls' Day, "immense crowds perform a solemn pilgrimage to Mont Louis, bearing garlands and decorations of every description, to be strewed upon the graves of their departed relatives, recollections of whom are annually revived. ⊤ . ." As Philippe Ariès has observed, the nineteenth century was the era of the visit to the grave. On All Saints' Day of 1866, one hundred eighty thousand mourners visited the Cemetery of Montmartre. At this time, the three Parisian cemeteries, Père Lachaise, Montmartre, and Montparnasse, were thought by some to threaten the city as had the parish burial grounds of the eighteenth century. The annexation in 1860 of the communes around Paris placed the three famous cemeteries within the new city limits and thus in contravention of the law of 23 Prairial, year XII. The cemeteries themselves were becoming overcrowded with graves; and Baron Haussmann's engineers determined that the water passing through the subsoil of these cemeteries was polluting both the city's wells and the Seine. Haussmann's proposal to close these cemeteries in favor of opening a new one at Méry-sur-Oise, accessible only by rail, prompted a widespread and vehement protest: *pas de cimetière, pas de cité*. Without the cemetery, Paris would lose its soul. A "workers' petition" to the emperor published in *Le Temps* attested to the importance of the funeral on foot as well as the periodic visit to the grave. In face of the stiff opposition, Haussmann's projects as well as those put forth in 1881 by the Prefect Duval were abandoned.

From the early eighteenth century to the late nineteenth century, public opinion had come full circle. In the beginning, the cemetery was banished from the city as having no physical and only a limited spiritual place among the living. At the close of the cycle, the city did not seem to be a viable social organism without the proximity of the cemetery. This reversal, so aptly noted by Philippe Ariès, was due to simultaneous changes in the image of the cemetery and in its social and spiritual purposes. It would be wrong, however, to push this comparison too far. From the vantage of our current indifference toward the cemetery, which stems largely from taboos of openly discussing death and providing for the dead, the two previous centuries emerge as having remarkable unity. Despite all of the transformations in form and use, the cemetery in those times always furnished a landscape, either architectural or horticultural, as well as metaphysical, which reflected the underlying bonds and tensions of social and individual life.

| | Status | Location |
|---|---|---|
| **Parisian Cemeteries in 1763** | | Ile de la Cité and Ile Saint-Louis |
| | Approved by commissioners and parish council | Saint-Landry |
| | Condemned by commissioners but approved by parish council | Saint-Denis-du-Pas and Saint-Jean le Rond Saint-Louis-en-l'Ile |
| | Condemned by commissioners and parish council | |

*Secondary burial ground.

| Center | Toward the Boulevards | Beyond the Boulevards |
| --- | --- | --- |
| Saint-Hilaire | Saint-Sulpice* | Saint-Eustache |
| Saint-Etienne-du-Mont | Saint-Symphorien | Saint-Roch |
| | Saint-Jacques Saint-Philippe du Haut Pas | Notre-Dame de Bonne-Nouvelle |
| | Saint-Médard | Sainte-Marie Madeleine de la Ville l'Evêque |
| | Saint-Martin and Saint-Hippolyte | Saint-Laurent |
| | | Sainte-Marguerite |
| | | Le Gros Caillou |
| | | Les Invalides |
| Saint-Séverin | Saint-Paul | |
| Saint-Cosme and Saint-Damien | Saint-Sauveur | |
| Saint-Nicolas du Chardonnet | Saint-Nicolas-des-Champs | |
| Saint-Sulpice | | |
| Saint-André-des-Arts | Hôpital de la Charité | Sainte-Marie Madeleine de la Ville l'Evêque* |
| Saint-Gervais | Saint-Eustache* | |
| Saint-Jean-en-Grève | | |
| Saint-Benoît | | |
| Saints-Innocents | | |

## Abbreviations

**Acad. Roy. Arch.**

*Procès-verbaux de l'Académie Royale d'Architecture 1671–1793.* Ed. Henri Lemonnier. 10 vols. Paris, 1911–1929.

**A.N.**

Archives Nationales

**Arch. Acad. Inscriptions et Belles-Lettres**

Archives de l'Académie des Inscriptions et Belles-Lettres held by the Archives de l'Institut de France

**A.S.**

Archives de la Seine

**B.N.**

Bibliothèque Nationale, Paris

**B.N. Est.**

Bibliothèque Nationale, Cabinet des Estampes

**B.N., Joly de Fleury**

Bibliothèque Nationale, Manuscrits, Joly de Fleury

**Gannal: 2**

Dr. Félix Gannal, *Les Cimetières depuis la fondation de la monarchie française jusqu'à nos jours: histoire et législation . . . tome premier. Les Cimetières avant la Révolution.* Paris, [1884]. Part 2: Documents.

**Gannal 5021**

Dr. Gannal's handwritten copies of documents pertaining to the cemeteries of Paris. Bibliothèque Historique de la Ville de Paris, Ms. 5021.

# Notes

*Preface*

Leslie Stephen, *History of English Thought in the Eighteenth Century* (New York, 1927), 2 : 329.

*1*

*A New Heaven and a New Earth (1711–1785)*

### The Parish Cemetery

*Memento mori, charniers,* Dance of Death, *Vanitas, écorchés,* Baroque funerals: Huizinga, *Waning,* 138–151. Ariès, *L'Homme,* 62–67. Dufour, "Le Cimetière;" *La Danse macabre.* Chastel, "Le Baroque." Sterling, *La Nature morte,* 11–13, passim. Tenenti, *La Vie,* 9–40; *Il Senso,* 139–184. Silvestre de Sacy. *Le Quartier des Halles,* 22–23. Marle, *Iconographie,* 2 : 376ff.

History of the Cemetery of the Holy Innocents and Pilon's statue of Death: A.N., L 570. Du Breul, *Le Théâtre,* 618–622. Félibien, *Histoire,* 1 : 204–209. Sauval, *Histoire,* 1 : 358–359, 497–499. Brice, *Nouvelle,* 1 : 481–485, 491–494. Le Rouge, *Les Curiositez,* 1 : 223. Dezallier d'Argenville, *Voyage,* 208. Piganiol de la Force, *Description,* 3 : 294, 301–307. Thiéry, *Almanach,* 202. Dulaure, *Nouvelle* (1787), 2 : 136–141. Le Roux de Lincy, *Description,* xl, 21–22, 64. For other sixteenth-century French statues of Death, see Marle, *Iconographie,* 2 : 365–366.

Burial inside parish churches: Porée, *Lettres,* 13–15. Desbois de Rochefort, "Cimetière," 579. Bernard, *La Sépulture,* 16–28. Ariès, *L'Homme,* 37–47. For Amiens and Dijon: Le Bras, "L'Invasion," 191.

*Cimiterium*: Bernard, *La Sépulture,* 29–40. Duparc, "Le Cimetière." Ariès, *L'Homme,* 58.

Burial at the Cemetery of the Holy Innocents: A.N., L 570. B.N., Joly de Fleury 1317, fols. 72–76v.

Saint-Séverin: B.N., Joly de Fleury 1208, fols. 4–5v, 7–9v.

### Urban Hygiene

Mercier: Jean-Louis Vissière, "Pollution et nuisances urbaines d'après le *Tableau de Paris* de Sébastien Mercier," in *La Ville au XVIII<sup>e</sup> siècle,* 107–112.

The parish and its cemetery: Cole, *Journal,* 301. Ariès. *Essais,* 146–147. For the locations of the various parish cemeteries, see the inquest of 1763, listed below. See also Etlin, "The Cemetery," 572–574 (annotated map).

Policing the Cemetery of the Holy Innocents, 1711–1762: B.N., Joly de Fleury 1317, fols. 3–4v, 43–47, 61–80, 100, 108v–138v. A.N., L 570, n° 30 bis, 38. For a discussion of this issue, see Etlin, "The Cemetery," 78–97.

The Cemetery of the Holy Innocents and the markets of Paris: Martineau, *Les Halles,* 9–23, 45–46. Boudon, "L'Aménagement." Mâle, *Religious Art,* 144–145.

Corrupted air: Godart, "Septicologie," 326. Coulet, in *La Ville au XVIIIe siècle,* 276. See also Etlin, "L'Air."

Dechristianization: Ariès, *Essais; L'Homme.* Bertrand, "Une Contribution." Chaunu, *La Civilisation*; "Mourir." Lebrun, *Les Hommes.* Roche, " 'La Mémoire.' " Vovelle, "Les Attitudes"; *Mourir; Piété.*

Reform movement: Porée, *Lettres,* 23–24. First published in 1743, this book was reissued in 1745 and 1749 along with *Observations sur les sépultures dans les églises.* . . . Louis, *Lettres,* 162. Voltaire, "Babouc," in *Recueil,* 99. D'Alembert, "Genève," (1757), 7 : 577. Sobry, *De l'Architecture,* 132–133. See also, D'Alembert, "Air," in *Encyclopédie* (1751), 1 : 233, and "Exhalaison," in *Encyclopédie* (1756), 6 : 253.

### The Pure and the Impure

Defiling the church: Sobry, *De l'Architecture,* 132. See also Porée, *Lettres,* 21; Desbois de Rochefort, "Cimetière," 583; Laugier, *Observations,* 173–174, 236–237; Dehorne, *Mémoire,* 6; Quatremère de Quincy, letter in the *Moniteur Universel,* April 13, 1791; Ariès, *Essais,* 148.

The new parish church: Blondel, *Cours,* 2 : 312–315, 345; 3 : 382–393. Ledoux, *L'Architecture,* 155–156. *Une architecture terrible:* Blondel, *Cours,* 1 : 426–427. Quatremère de Quincy, "Cimetière," in *Encyclopédie méthodique* (1788), 1 : 682.

### The Parlement's Intervention

Arrêts of Parlement: *Arrest de la cour du Parlement, extrait des registres du Parlement du 12 mars 1763* (Paris, 1763). *Arrest de la cour de Parlement, extrait des registres du Parlement de 21 mai 1765* (Paris, 1765). Both documents are conserved in B.N., Joly de Fleury and are reproduced in Gannal, 2 : 44–55. For an earlier draft of the Arrêt of May 21, 1765, see B.N., Joly de Fleury 1207, fols. 27–31v.

Inquest of 1763: with related papers, in B.N., Joly de Fleury 1207–1209; A.N., L 570, n° 38; Y 12612, 15827. See also Lemoine, "Les Cimetières," and Etlin, "The Cemetery," 97–125.

Godart, "Septicologie," 326–327.

Response to the Arrêt of May 21, 1765: B.N., Joly de Fleury 1207, fols. 15–21, 105–105v; 1208, fols. 46 (Saint-Jean-en-Grève), 149–151, 158, 174–174v, 204.

Lubersac de Livron, "Programme générale ou Exposition abrégée des matières contenues au second volume devant faire suite d'un ouvrage portant pour titre *Discours sur les monumens publics . . .* " B.N., Est. Ye 157. fol. 2v. In "Lubersac" (p. 108), Guillerme and Harouel suggest that this prospectus was written in 1776. See also *Lettres du baron,* 5–6.

Porée, *Lettres,* 38–42; Desbois de Rochefort, "Cimetière," 580.

### Rethinking the City

Laugier, *Observations,* 168–175.

Patte, *Monumens,* 212–229.

Mechanical ventilation: Genneté, *Purification.*

"Reservoir" of air: Oliver, *Sépultures,* xi, quoted approvingly in *Mémoires sur les sépultures hors des villes,* 68. See also Audin-Rouvière, *Essai,* 14.

Fountains: Peyre, *Oeuvres,* 25.

Competitions: *Acad. Roy. Arch.,* 7 : 228, 265.

Projects: Patte, *Mémoires sur les objets . . .* Delafosse, *Mémoire pour une boucherie.* Petit, *Mémoire.*

1769: Louis-Pierre Moreau, *Plan général du cours de la rivière de la Seine et ses abords dans Paris, avec les projets d'embellissement.* B.N. Est. Ve 36. Plan and text reproduced in Bardet, *Naissance,* 294–308. *Edit du*

*Roi qui ordonne la démolition des maisons construites sur les ponts de la ville de Paris, sur les quais et rues de Gêvres, de la Pelletterie, et autres adjacentes des deux côtes de la rivière, conformément au projet arrêté en 1769 . . . septembre 1786.* A.N., K 1028, n° 45. See also Lafont de Saint-Yenne, *L'Ombre*, 64–65.

Canal: Poncet de la Grave, *Projet*, 1 : 77–79.

### The Scientific Contribution

Priestley, *Experiments*. Priestley had delivered his findings at the Royal Society in London in March 1772. A French translation appeared in Abbé François Rozier's *Observations et mémoires sur la physique, sur l'histoire naturelle et sur les arts* (avril 1773), 1 : 292–325.

Lavoisier, *Oeuvres* and "Memoire."

Fontana: Cadet de Vaux, *Mémoire*, 2. Hannaway, "La Fermature," 187–188. For further discussion of this theme and in particular of Lavoisier's work, see Etlin, "The Cemetery," 14–25.

Parlement of Toulouse, Arrêt of September 3, 1774: Gannal, 2 : 58–61.

Loménie de Brienne, Ordinance of March 23, 1775: Gannal, 2 : 62–76.

*Procès-verbal de l'Assemblée*, 106–109, 115, 132.

Royal Declaration on Burials: *Déclaration du Roi, concernant les inhumations. Donnée à Versailles le 10 mars 1776. Registré en Parlement le 21 mai 1776.* B.N., Joly de Fleury 1182, fols. 3–4v and Gannal 2: 77–80.

Lyon: Favre, "Lyon en 1783," 156.

Vicq d'Azyr, *Essai sur les lieux et les dangers des sépultures.*

Menuret de Chambaud, *Essai sur l'action de l'air.*

Ingen-Housz, *Experiments*, xiii.

*Fragment*, 166.

Closing the Cemetery of the Holy Innocents: Cadet de Vaux, *Mémoire*. "Rapport de M$^{rs}$ les Commissaires de la Faculté Médecine de Paris à M. le Lieutenant général de Police . . . " (June 7, 1780), in *Commentaires*, Ed. Pinard, 501–514. A.N., X$^{1b}$ 8975, Lenoir's report to the Premier Président of Parlement, December 5, 1780. Other documents, including the Parlement's action of September 4, 1780 (A.N., X$^{1b}$ 8974) can be found in Gannal, 2 : 96–104. See also Etlin, "The Cemetery," 129–132, Appendix B; and Hannaway, "La Fermature." For Cadet de Vaux's previous use of fire and slaked lime, see *Observations sur les fosses d'aisance*.

Transforming the Cemetery of the Holy Innocents into an herb and vegetable market: A.N., Z$^{10}$ 222, report by the Société Royale de Médecine, November 12, 1785, reproduced in Gannal (2 : 115ff.) along with the Arrêt du Conseil d'Etat of November 9, 1785. Thouret, *Rapport*. Héricart de Thury, *Description*, 163–178.

### The Fountain of the Holy Innocents

Porée, *Lettres*, 41–43; *Observations*, 31–32.

Report on the hygiene of prisons: "Rapport sur les prisons fait à l'Académie Royale des Sciences, le 17 mars 1780," in *Histoire de l'Académie des Sciences, année 1780*, and reproduced in Lavoisier, *Oeuvres*, 3 : 465–498.

Royal Declaration: *Déclaration du roi, concernant les alignements et ouv-*

*ertures des rues de Paris. Donnée à Versailles, 10 avril 1783. Registré en Parlement le 8 juillet 1783*, 1. On this subject, see Le Moine, *Le Parallèle*, 20.

Poyet: Coquéau, *Mémoire*. The reports by the Académie Royale des Sciences are reprinted in Lavoisier, *Oeuvres*, 3 : 603ff. See also Fortier, "La Politique de l'espace parisien," in Fortier et al., *La Politique*, 1–152.

Royal Edict: *Edit de Louis XVI, ordonnant la démolition des maisons construits sur les ponts, 1786*. A.N., K 1028, n° 45.

Dulaure, *Réclamation*.

Report on slaughterhouses: "Rapport des mémoires et projets pour éloigner les tueries de l'intérieur de Paris," in *Histoire de l'Académie des Sciences, année 1787* and reprinted in Lavoisier, *Oeuvres*, 3 : 579–601.

Cadet de Vaux, *Mémoire*, 8.

The original fountain: Brice, *Nouvelle*, 1 : 46–48, 491–494. Antonini, *Mémorial*, 108. Dezallier d'Argenville, *Voyage*, 209. Piganiol de la Force, *Description*, 2: 307.

The new herb market: Dulaure, *Nouvelle* (1787), 2 : 140–141; (1791), 1 : 365–367, 2 : 135–136. Thiéry, *Guide*, 1 : 479, 498. Blanvillain, *Le Pariséum*, 303–304. Chastel, et al. "L'Aménagement," 99–100.

### A New Order in Burials

On the twentieth-century refusal of death, see Ariès, *Essais*, 61–72, 157–163, 180–197, and *L'Homme*, 553–595.

**2**
**Public and**
**Permanent**
**Buildings**
**(1765–1785)**

Public and permanent buildings: Molé, *Lettre*, 22.

### The Academic Tradition

*Prix d'émulation*: Egbert, *The Beaux-Arts Tradition*, 11, 14, 27.

Competitions: *Acad. Roy. Arch.* (1765), 7 : 228; (1766), 7 : 265; (1778), 8 : 365; (1785), 9 : 154–156, 162–163. For 1799: *Procès-verbaux de l'Académie des Beaux-Arts*, 1 : 206, and Archives de l'Institut de France, Rés. 6B 10, fols. 23–28.

Renaissance humanism: Tenenti, *Il Senso*, 21–47.

Civic statuary: Honour, *Neo-classicism*, 83.

Boisguillebert, *Le Détail*.

Vauban, *Projet*.

Porée, *Lettres*, 43–48, and *Observations*, 26.

Civil, military, naval architecture: J.-F. Blondel, *Cours*, 1:4–5. Theater scenes and landscape genres: S. Lang, "The Genesis of the English Landscape Garden," in Pevsner, ed., *The Picturesque Garden*, 16–19.

### Balancing Christian and Humanist Ideals

Desprez: *Acad. Roy. Arch.*, 7 : 265. Desprez, *Ouvrage*.

Blondel, Cours, 2 : 340–346, and *Recueil contenant la description, les plans, les élévations et les coupes du château de Blois, levés par ordre de Monsieur le marquis de Marigny en 1760 . . . avec quelques observations faites sur les divers monuments répandus dans les villes d'Orléans, de Tours, etc.* Bibliothèque de l'Institut de France, Ms. 1046, fol. 2.

Voltaire, *Lettres*, 149.

Campo Santo of Pisa: Titi, *Guida*, 65. See also Martini, *Theatrum*. P. Lasinio, *Raccolta*. G. P. Lasinio, figlio, *Pitture*. Castelli, *Pisa*, 57–60. *Pisa. Tre secoli*.

French Palladianism: Kalnein and Levey, *Art*, 306–308.

### The Ascendancy of the Humanist Vision

Dufourny: *Acad. Roy. Arch.*, 7 : 365.

Sublime and grand architecture: Blondel, *Cours*, 1 : 377–380, 423–424.

Porte Saint-Denis: Blondel, *Architecture*, 3 : 10–13. See also *Cours*, 1 : 380, 424.

Marie-Joseph Peyre: Peyre, *Oeuvres*. *Piranèse*, 266–270.

### The Space of Emulation

Servandoni: Patte, *Monumens*, 210–212.

Pont-Neuf: Ibid.

Laugier, *Observations*, 233–235. Other projects: Dussausoy, *Le Citoyen*, 1 : 145. Jarry, *Vieilles demeures*, 3–4, 8. Mopinot de la Chapotte, *Eloge*, 20–21.

Jardin: *Plans, coupes* . . . ; *Piranèse*, 158–159.

### The Speculative Tradition

Draft for a new Arrêt, 1782: B.N., Joly de Fleury 1182, fols. 49–54. See also, fols. 55–61, 65–65v.

### The Modest Cemetery

Patte: While Patte did not publish his drawings until the year X in his *Mémoires qui intéressent* . . . , the project corresponds to the earlier description of 1769 in *Mémoires sur les objets* . . . (41ff.), just as the style belongs to this earlier period.

Saint-Sauveur and Sainte-Marguerite: B. N., Joly de Fleury 1208, fols. 58, 69.

Pérard de Montreuil: *Mémoire* (manuscript text submitted between August 1772 and July 1773). B. N., Joly de Fleury 1207, fols. 7–12v; *Mémoire* (revised manuscript written sometime after Loménie de Brienne's Ordinance of March 23, 1775, and before the Royal Declaration of March 10, 1776. Gannal published the text (2 : 173–183) along with a letter about this project dated July 19, 1777, from Lenoir to Amelot, *ministre de la maison du Roi*). Three copies of Pérard's project can be found in Joly de Fleury 1182, fols. 10–21, 22–33, 36–46. See also, *Mémoire sur les sépultures, pour le sieur Pérard de Montreuil*. A.S., 1 AZ 10, pièce 48, or B.N., Joly de Fleury 1182, fols. 5–8.

### A Mirror to Society

Delafosse: first cemetery project. Cabinet des Dessins, Musée des Arts Décoratifs, Paris. Second project, Gannal, 1 : 85 (plan, June 2, 1782); 2 : 184–195 (text).

La Guêpière: *Piranèse*, 162–164.

Blondel, *Cours*, 2 : 341.

### The New Catacombs

Procureur Général, 1782: B.N., Joly de Fleury 1182, fols. 49–61, 65–65v.

Capron: A.N., N III Seine 846 (drawings), also contains revised drawings for the chapel, dated August 20, 1783 (see *La Vie*, pl. 5). B.N., Joly de Fleury 1209, fols. 61–63v (text). See also fols. 59–60, 64–67, 73.

### The Naked Cemetery

Proscription of plantings: S. Carlo Borromeo, *Instructiones Fabricae et Suppellectilis Ecclesiasticae* (Milan, 1577). I am indebted to Professor David Coffin for this reference. See also the preparatory notes for the Arrêt of May 21, 1765, B.N., Joly de Fleury 1207, fol. 31. Troyes: Maret, *Mémoire*, 56. Navier, *Réflexions*, 64–78. Vicq d'Azyr, *Essai*, xlvii. Priestley, *Experiments*, 1 : 49–54. Ingen-Housz, *Experiments*, xv–xxxvi.

Antoine: *Mémoire* with annotated plan, B.N., Joly de Fleury 1209, fols. 79–89. Another copy of the plan is conserved in B.N. Est. Gannal (2 : 196–207) published a slightly different version of the *Mémoire* without the plan. See also Antoine's letter of November 25, 1782, to the Premier Président and accompanying memorandum: Joly de Fleury 1209, fols. 94–94v, 73.

Arrêté du Département de la Seine, 28 Germinal an VII. A.S., DZ⁶ carton 3.

## 3
## The Sublime
## (1785)

Boileau: Boulton, "Editor's Introduction" to Burke, *A Philosophical Enquiry*, xlvi.

From More to Addison: Tuveson, "Space." See also Nicolson, *Mountain Gloom*.

Diderot, *Salons* (1767), 3 : 165–166.

### Sublimity and the Academy

Grand Prix of 1785: *Acad. Roy. Arch.*, 9 : 154–156, 162–163.

Fontaine: Biver, *Fontaine*, 14.

Mortimer and West: Ziff, "Mortimer's 'Death.'"

Fontaine denied the first Grand Prix: Hautecoeur, *Histoire*, 5 : 156. *Acad. Roy. Arch.*, 9 : 163, 165.

November 24, 1788: *Acad. Roy. Arch.*, 9 : 236.

### From the Creation to the Creator

Paul Van Tieghem, *Le Sentiment de la Nature dans le préromantisme européen*, chapter 5, "De la création au créateur," 254–263.

Boullée: Pérouse de Montclos, *Boullée*, as well as the abbreviated English-language edition. Etlin, "Boullée." For Boullée's essay on architecture, see Boullée, *Architecture* (ed. Pérouse de Montclos) or Rosenau, *Boullée*, for an English translation.

Boullée's funerary architecture: *Architecture*, fols. 87–87v, 123–128v.

### The Egyptian Wasteland

Roman sojourns of Bellicard, Challe, and Robert: *Piranèse*, 52–55, 69–82, 304–326.

Robert's pyramid in the Smith College Museum of Art: *Piranèse*, fig. 16 bis.

Stones: Praz, *On Neoclassicism*, 95–96.

### An Architecture of Life and Death

Thomson, *The Seasons*. Durling, *Georgic*, 122–123. Chalker, *The English*. Van Tieghem, *Le Sentiment*, 19–67.

Morel: le "patriarche des jardins," characterization by Fontaine (Journal), quoted in Ganay, *Les Jardins*, 243. See also ibid., 195–198, 242–245.

Morel, *Théorie*, 23, 24 (nature), 46–73 (seasons). See also Harcourt, *Traité*, 211–244.

Boullée on the seasons: *Architecture*, fols. 84–87v.

Blondel, *Cours*, 2 : 340–343, and above.

Le Camus de Mézières, *Le Génie*, 1–78, 275–276.

*Caractère*: For a discussion of Boffrand and Blondel, see Etlin, "The Cemetery," 214–218.

Rousseau: Burgelin, *La Philosophie*, 115–190.

### Intimations of Immortality

Chancellor Séguier's funeral: Tapié, *Baroque*, 264–265.

Freemasonry: Lenoir, *La Franche-maçonnerie*, 246. On the diffusion of masonic imagery in the late eighteenth century, see Fay, *La Franc-maçonnerie*; Darnton, *Mesmerism*; and Vidler, "The Architecture of the Lodges."

Norden: *Acad. Roy. Arch.*, 7 : 218–219.

Sobry: Ozouf, "Le Cortège," 902, note 2.

Turenne's funeral: Tapié, *Baroque*, 265–267.

Starobinski, *L'Invention*, 202.

The mountain as a manifestation of Nature's glory: Mornet, *Le Sentiment*, 52–62, 259–286. Le Flamanc, *Les Utopies*, 63–64. Van Tieghem, *Le Sentiment*, 155–198. Stafford, "Rude Sublime," 113–126, and "Toward," 89–124.

Romé de l'Ile and Boullée: Guillerme, "Lequeu."

Witte, "Précis d'un *Essai sur l'origine des pyramides d'Egypte*," in *Magasin Encyclopédique*, 3 (year VII/1798), 338–348. Stafford writes that Witte's conclusions were based on the work of Desmarets, Deluc, and Faujas de Saint-Fond: "Toward Romantic Landscape Perception," 108.

Ledoux, *L'Architecture*, 8, 193–197.

### The Cenotaph to Newton

Cenotaph to Newton: Boullée, *Architecture*, fols. 126v–128v, 138. Letter from Mme. Brongniart to her husband, 19 Prairial, year II (June 7, 1794), in Pérouse de Montclos, *Boullée*, 199, note 2, and Boullée, *Architecture*, 184. See also Nicolson, *Newton*, 14.

Fireworks in the eighteenth-century festival: Gruber, *Les Grands fêtes*.

Faujas de Saint-Fond, *Méthode*; *Description*. See also Pilâtre de Rozier, *Première expérience*.

Balloon flights and the contemporary imagination: Lemas, "La Chute."

Newton and Copernicus: Pérouse de Montclos, *Boullée*, 200, 253.

Bailly: Ibid., 255. Vogt, *Boullées Newton-Denkmal*, 312–314.

The dome and the artificial infinite: Monk, *The Sublime*, 74–74 (John Baillie), and Burke, *A Philosophical Enquiry*, 74–76, 138–142.

*Métropole*: Boullée, *Architecture*, fols. 88–97v.

Rousseau, *Oeuvres*, 1 : 1141.

Chambers, *A Dissertation*, 30–31. See also Wiebenson, *Picturesque Garden*, 57–58.

Seven liberal arts: Marle, *Iconographie* 2 : 203–215.

Rysbrack: Vogt, *Boullée*, 302, 317, fig. 125b.

Campanella, *City*, 33–38.

Berington, *Memoirs*, 168–174.

On the background to Viel de Saint-Maux's Lettres, see Pérouse de Montclos, "Viel," 262ff.

Delespine's Newton cenotaph: Prieur, *Collection*. Delespine, *Marché*.

Prix d'émulation, November 21, 1800: Vaudoyer and Baltard, *Grand Prix*.

Pope: Nicolson, *Newton*, 37.

### From Alchemy to Pantheism

Libavius, "De Lapide Philosophorum," *Commentariorum Alchemiae*, book 4, part 2, pp. 51–56 of *Alchymia*. See also Read, *Prelude*, 88, 119–121, 217–219.

Boullée's library project: *Architecture*, fols. 119–123.

Gay, Cenotaph to Newton, 1800: The description of this project can be found in a series of annotated tracings of the Grand Prix designs at the Cabinet des Dessins, Musée des Arts Décoratifs, Paris. According to Szambien ("Notes," 115), these early nineteenth-century tracings were probably done by Antoine-Marie Peyre.

Celebration of colors: Nicolson, *Newton*, 27, 30. The quotation is from Thomson, "To the Memory of Newton."

Alchemy (Valentin; Mylius; *Cabala*): Van Lennep, *Art*, 89–90, 100.

Ledoux, *Architecture*, 8.

### The Neoclassical World of Death

*Numitor*: See also Pâris's preparatory sketches for the stage set, which show the exterior of the pyramid, as well as the plan and several variants for the view of the interior, Bibliothèque Municipale de Besançon. Reproduced in Etlin, "The Cemetery," fig. 60. On the quest for reality in the design of stage sets and its relationship to Boullée's architecture, see Etlin, ibid., 234–236.

Desprez: See also Jacques Gamelin's "The Last Judgment," published in his *Nouveau recueil d'ostéologie . . .* (1779) and discussed in Pupil, "Aux Sources," 62–63, fig. 4.

Gonzaga: Oenslager, *Stage Design*, 114.

Borsato: Ibid., 147.

Piranesi, "Temple of Vesta" (1743) in *Opere Varie*.

Barberi: Westfall, "Antolini's Foro Bonaparte," and *Crosscurrents*, 26–29. Kaufmann (*Architecture*, 113, figs. 81–82) attributed this project to Giuseppe Valadier. For the Concorso Clementino of 1795, see Marconi, *I disegni*, 1 : 29 and figs. 904–927.

Ancient catacombs: [Villedieu,] *Projet*, 14–16.

Quarries: Héricart de Thury, *Description*, 143–148. See also Fortier, "L'Urbanisme," 5–7.

First day of the Catacombs: Thouret, *Rapport*, 12.

Quatremère de Quincy, "Catacombes," in *Encyclopédie méthodique* (1788), 1 : 545–555.

For the descriptions of the Catacombs as depicted by Cloquet, see Héricart de Thury, *Description*, 283ff. Also see [Détruisard,] *Essai*, 9–10; Aubry, *Le Guide*, 134–135; Marchant de Beaumont, *Le Nouveau conducteur*, 242–246. For a recent history of the formation of the Catacombs, see Hillairet, *Les 200 Cimetières*, 300–308.

## 4
## The Arcadian Landscape (1712–1781)

Landscape gardener: Shenstone, "Unconnected Thoughts on Gardening," in *Works*, 2 : 129, 139.

### A Natural Gardener

Tuveson, "Space." See also Røstvig, *The Happy Man*, 2 : 13–59.

Nourse: Røstvig, *The Happy Man*, 2 : 70–73.

Addison: *Spectator*, no. 414 (1712).

Switzer, *Nobleman*, xii. *Ichnographia*, 1 : xviii–xix; 2 : 201 ("the natural Gardener"); 3 : iii, xv, 3–6, 9, 47. See also Pope, *Windsor Forest*, 1–3. Røstvig, *The Happy Man*, 2 : 75–83. William Brogden, "Stephen Switzer, 'La Grand Manier,' " in *Furor*, 21–30.

Watteau: Adams, *French Garden*, 104–105.

Switzer on terraces: *Ichnographia*, 2 : 150–153, 163–165.

James, *Theory*, 28, 77.

Dezallier d'Argenville, *Théorie*, 73–74.

Ha-ha: Clarke, "Stowe—VIII." Hussey, *English Gardens*, 35–36, 142–143.

Enfilade: Etlin, "Blondel," 139–142.

### Paradise Regained

*Beatus ille*: Røstvig, *The Happy Man*, 1 : 18–21, *passim*; 2 : 17–28, 97–111.

Switzer on Virgil, Milton, Cowley, and the Creation: *Nobleman*, 15, 67, 69, 71, 264. *Ichnographia*, 1 : 19–20, 67, 92, 95–97, 349, 352; 3 : iii. See also Pope, *Windsor Forest*, 12.

### The Elysian Fields of Castle Howard

Wray Wood: Switzer, *Ichnographia*, 1 : 87; 2 : 198. Hussey, *English Gardens*, 123–124.

Lady Irwin: Hussey, *English Gardens*, 114–115, 122–128.

Elysian Fields and the Golden Age: Giamatti, *The Earthly Paradise*, 15–33.

Mausoleum and pyramid at Castle Howard: Hussey, *English Gardens*, 128.

### The Cypress Grove at Twickenham

Pope's garden: "An Epistolary Description of the Late Mr. Pope's House and Gardens at Twickenham" (1747), in Hunt and Willis, eds. *Genius*, 247–253. Mack, *Garden*, 28–31. Hunt, *Figure*, 79–88.

Pope to Spence: Hunt, *Figure*, 80. Brownell, *Pope*, 133.

Walpole, *Essay*, 63.

Hirschfeld, *Théorie*, 3 : 161.

### The Elegiac Shenstone

Elegiac melancholy: Draper, *Elegy*, 13–16.

Shenstone and the Leasowes: Shenstone's letters, nos. 96, 97, in *Works*, 3 : 329–336, and R. Dodsley, "A Description of the Leasowes," in Shenstone, *Works*, 2 : 333–392. See also Shenstone, "A Prefatory Essay on Elegy," in *Works*, 1 : 3–6, passim; "Unconnected Thoughts on Gardening," *Works*, 2 : 125–144. Clark, "Elysiums," 175–177.

The "solemn" urn: Shenstone, *Works*, 2 : 127–128, 134. See also Whately, *Observations*, 170.

The English Virgil: Durling, *Georgic*, 47.

Virgil: Panofsky, "*Et in Arcadia ego*: Poussin and the Elegiac Tradition," in *Meaning*, 297–302, figs. 90–92.

Heeley, *Letters*, 2 : 114–115.

Allen, *Tides*, 2 : 176–177. See also Heeley, *Letters*, 1 : 192–193.

Hagley: Heeley, *Letters*, 1 : 132–228; 2 : 2. See also Pococke, *Travels*, 1 : 223–230. Whately, *Observations*, 197–201.

### Et in Arcadia ego

From Guercino to Poussin: This discussion follows Panofsky's essay "*Et in Arcadia ego*," as well as the refinements to Panofsky's reading of Poussin's famous painting suggested by Steefel, "A Neglected Shadow."

Still life: Sterling, *La Nature morte*, 12–13. Tenenti, *Il Senso*, figs. 3–4.

Dubos, *Critical Reflections*, 1 : 45–46.

Shenstone, Letter of October 3, 1759, to Richard Graves, in *Works*, 3 : 336.

Maria Dolman: The Latin inscription (Shestone, *Works*, 2 : 356) was translated by Heeley in his *Letters*, 2 : 177.

### The Elysian Fields at Stowe

Contemporary guidebooks to Stowe: Seeley, *Stowe*.

Early history: Clarke, "Stowe—IV," 70.

Stowe, 1713–1730: Clarke, "Stowe—VII." Willis, *Bridgeman*, 107–112. Hussey, *English Gardens*, 93–97. On Cowley and the Whigs in 1713–1714, see Røstvig, *The Happy Man*, 2 : 21–22.

Gilbert West: Gibbon, "Stowe—IX." Willis, *Bridgeman*, 113–119.

Elysian Fields: Clarke, "Stowe—X"; "Stowe—XI"; "Stowe—XIII"; "Grecian Taste"; and "William Kent, Heresy in Stowe's Elysium," in *Furor*, 48–56. Willis, *Bridgeman*, 121; Hussey, *English Gardens*, 98–103.

Kent's drawings: S. Lang, "The Genesis of the English Landscape Garden," in Pevsner, ed., *The Picturesque Garden*, figs. 13–15.

Stowe, 1741–1749: Gibbon, "Stowe—XII." Clarke, "Stowe—XIX." Willis, *Bridgeman*, 123–127. Hussey, *English Gardens*, 103–106.

Stowe, 1749–1773: Gibbon, "Stowe—XXI." Michael McCarthy, "Eighteenth Century Amateur Architects and Their Gardens," in Pevsner, ed., *The Picturesque Garden*, 31–55.

Tempe and *Paradise Lost*: Hunt, *Figure*, 74.

Vitruvius, Serlio, Roger de Piles: Lang, "Genesis," 16–19.

Serlio, *Tutte l'opere*, 49–51.

The Elysian Fields as political allegory: Hunt, "Emblem," 229–301. Paulson, *Emblem*, 22–28. Willis, *Bridgeman*, 121–122. Horace Walpole (1753): Willis, *Bridgeman*, 121.

Lady Montagu: *Allen*, 2 : 175–176.

Whately, *Observations*, 219–221.

De Paule Latapie: notes to his translation of Whately, *L'Art de former les jardins*, 201–203, 232–233, and "Description détaillée des jardins de Stowe, par le traducteur," 387–388.

Hirschfeld, *Théorie*, 3 : 89.

Young, Hervey, Blair: Draper, *Elegy*, 27.

**5**
**Death in the**
**Garden**
**(1762–1789)**

### Gessner and the Weeping Pastoral

This account of Gessner's popularity is adapted from Van Tieghem, "Les Idylles de Gessner et le rêve pastoral," *Le Préromantisme*, 2 : 228–292. See also Hibberd, *Gessner*.

The tomb: Bernardin de Saint-Pierre, *Etudes*, 3 : 123.

Gessner, *Oeuvres*: "Mirtile" (1 : 28), "Glicère" (1 : 207–211), "Damète et Milon" (1 : 222–223), "Palémon" (1 : 66).

Fréron: Van Tieghem, *Le Préromantisme*, 2 : 252.

### Rousseau's Tomb at Ermenonville

Rousseau at Ermenonville: Thacker, "Voltaire," 1609–1610. Crocker, *Rousseau*, 2 : 351–352.

Girardin and the Leasowes: Neumeyer, "The Landscape Garden," 196. Thacker, "Voltaire," 1609. Willis, *Bridgeman*, 145–146.

Hirschfeld, *Théorie*, 2 : 71–74; 5 : 302–305.

Hubert Robert: S. de Girardin, *Promenade*, 26.

Visiting Rousseau's tomb: S. de Girardin, *Promenade*, 17, 21–26. See also Villeneuve, *Vues*.

Description of Ermenonville: S. de Girardin, *Promenade*; Villeneuve, *Vues*.

Temple of Ancient Virtue, Stowe: Seeley, *Stowe* (1745), 14–16.

R. Girardin, *Composition*, 109–110.

Garden of Betz: Designed by the Duc d'Harcourt and Hubert Robert. Cérutti, *Les Jardins*, 3–4, 19–23. See also Hallays, *Autour de Paris*, 225–236.

Ganay, *Les Jardins*, 234.

### The Garden Cemetery

*Jardin anglo-chinois*: Delille, *Les Jardins*, 86. Hirschfeld, *Théorie*, 3 : 92–93; 5 : 310.

De Paule Latapie: Whately. *L'Art de former les jardins*, 233, translator's note.

Hirschfeld on the tomb in the garden: *Théorie*, 1 : 64–74; 2 : 47–49, 71–74, 105, 123–124, 194, 201–206; 3 : 89–90, 153–171, 226–237 (Jaegerspris), 263–274; 4 : 94–97, 271, 276; 5 : 131–135, 231, 247, 251–252, 262, 267, 269, 302–305, 401–403. On Jaegerspris, see also the article by Schuhl.

Poussin: Hirschfeld, *Théorie*, 3 : 164–165. Delille, *Les Jardins*, 83.

On Delille: Mauzi, "Delille," in *Delille est-it mort?*, 176.

Delille, *Les Jardins*, 85, 100–101.

Watelet, *Essai*, 111–115.

Bernardin de Saint-Pierre, *Etudes*, 3 : 123, 357–376. See also Circaud, "Projet."

### Transitional Designs

Quatremère de Quincy, "Cimetière," in *Encyclopédie méthodique*, 1 : 677–683.

Saint-Non, *Voyage*, 2 : 216–217.

Chateaubriand: "Cimetière romain à Arles," *Magasin pittoresque*, 29 (1861), 365.

Labrière, *Mémoire*. See also "Plan d'un temple pour la sépulture de nos rois . . . ," in *Nouvelles de la République Universelle des Arts* (January 3, 1787), also reproduced in the *Revue Universelle des Arts*, 20 (1865), 51–54.

D'Angiviller: Dowley, "D'Angiviller's *Grands Hommes*."

### French Picturesque Gardens

Franconville: *Vues des monuments*. Vaquier, "Les Jardins." Ganay, *Les Jardins*, 228. Poisson, *Evocation*, 296.

Maupertuis: Delille, *Les Jardins*, 114. De Laborde, *Description*, 153–160. Silvestre de Sacy, *Brongniart*, 55.

Méréville: Hubert Robert, Letters of August 11, 1786, and February 25, 1788, to Jean-Joseph, duc de Laborde. Photoreproduction from microfilm of manuscript letters, Dumbarton Oaks.

De Laborde, *Description*, 95–113.

Tschoudy: Wiebenson, *Picturesque Garden*, 28.

Parc Monceau: Frochot's letter of 8 Prairial, year IX (May 28, 1801) as well as the other documents on this subject are conserved in A.N., F³ ᴵᴵ Seine 20.

De Norvins, *Mémorial*, 2 : 239–241. See also Biver, *Le Paris*, 138.

*Champ de repos*: For Quatremère de Quincy's prerevolutionary discussion of the words *cimetière* and *charnier*, see "Cimetière," *Encyclopédie méthodique*, 1 : 677–678.

Desbois de Rochefort: Letter in *Moniteur Universel*, June 11, 1790.

Linnaeus: *Chronique de Paris*, August 26, 1790.

### Architecture or Nature?

Panthéon: *Journal de Paris*, April 5, 1791. Villette, Letter of May 30, 1790, in *Chronique de Paris* and reprinted in *Lettres*, 62–67. Vaudoyer, *Idées*. See also Vauthier, "Le Panthéon."

Nature: Trahard, *Sensibilité*, 145.

Champ de Mars: Héron, *Représentation*.

Villette: Letters of April 6, May 3, and May 8, 1791, in *Lettres*, 107–141.

Quatremère de Quincy, *Rapport sur l'édifice dit de Sainte-Geneviève* (1791), 33; *Rapport fait au Directoire du Département de Paris, le 13 novembre 1792*, 18–19; Letter to the Procureur Syndic, April 15, 1793. A.N., F¹³ 333a.

Laveaux, "Sur les sépultures des grands hommes, et celles des autres citoyens," *Journal de la Montagne*, July 19, 1793.

Saint-Just, "Fragments sur les institutions républicaines," in *L'Esprit*, 170.

### The First Arcadian Dreamlands

Fouché: Aulard, *Le Culte*, 26–29. Dommanget, "La Décristianisation," 181–188.

Chaumette: *Moniteur Universel*, October 21, 1793. Aulard, *Christianity*, 102.

Ermenonville: [S. de Girardin], *Promenade*, 37.

Avril, *Rapport*. See also *Moniteur Universel*, January 13, 1794. On the fate of this report, see A.N., F¹³ 330.

Cérutti, *Les Jardins*, 21 (note 22).

Pérard de Montreuil: B.N., Joly de Fleury 1182, fols. 5–46; 1207, fols. 7–12v. A.S., 1 AZ 10, pièce 48.

Patry, *Mémoire concernant l'établissement de quatre cimetières hors des murs de Paris*, 12 juillet 1787. A.N., F¹⁴ 187ᴮ. See also the anonymous project, *A nos Seigneurs les députés aux Etats-Généraux* (1789). A.S., 3 AZ 240.

Plaine d'Ivry: A.N., F³ ᴵᴵ Seine 18. Gannal 5021. Des Cilleuls, *Histoire*, 2 : 95–96.

Cemetery of Montparnasse: P. de St.-A., *Promenade* (1816), 76–77. See also the second edition (1825), 1 : 147.

Dussausoy, *Projet d'accessoires du Panthéon français*. Paris, 25 Ventôse, year II [March 15, 1794]. A.N., F$^{14}$ 187$^B$.

Cadet de Vaux: Vaquier, "Un Philanthrope," 428.

"Vast inequalities": La Revellière-Lépeaux, *Réflexions*, 30–31.

### Two Lost Souls

Lakanal, *Rapport*, 11–12.

Delamalle, *L'Enterrement*.

Cemetery at the Barrière Blanche: Hillairet, *Les 200 Cimetières*, 316.

Cemetery inspections, 1795: A.N., F$^{13}$ 888, 908. For 1793–1794, see A.N., AF$^{II}$ 139, n° 1088, pièces 34–35. A.S., DZ$^6$ carton 3.

### Facing the Abyss

Suitable funerals: Letter of 3 Germinal, year IV, in Gannal 5021. Arrêté of 23 Germinal, year IV. A.S., DL$^1$ 2.

Four new cemeteries (1796–1798): A.N., F$^{13}$ 908. See Etlin, "The Cemetery," 143–145.

Provisional use of old cemeteries: A.N., F$^{13}$ 908, 987; F$^3$ $^{II}$ Seine 20. A.S., DL$^1$ 2; DZ$^6$ carton 3; VD* 424, 2244, 2247, 2248.

Roch-Monceau controversy: Principal documents in A.N., F$^{13}$ 908 and A.S., DL$^1$ 2. See also A.N., 333$^b$–334. A.S., VD* 311, 338, 424, 3533–3542, 3544–3547.

Cemetery under Montmartre: Report of 8 Fructidor, year VI (August 25, 1798) by the Department of the Seine to the Minister of Interior. The request for balsamic plants is repeated in the Report of 9 Vendémiaire, year VII (September 30, 1798). A.N., F$^3$ II Seine 18 n° 8. See also other documents in this file, as well as A.S., DL$^1$ 2, VD* 3553, and the earlier Report of 6 Floréal, year V (April 25, 1797) by the Conseil des Bâtiments Civils, which is signed by the architects Brongniart, Legrand, Vaudoyer, Rondelet, and Peyre. A.N., F$^{13}$ 908.

Napoleon: Biver, *Le Paris*, 146. Lemoine, "Les Cimetières," 99. A.N., F$^3$ $^{II}$ Seine 20.

Fontaine, *Journal*, entry for April 6, 1812. Bibliothèque Marmottan.

Abyss: Letter of 26 Nivôse, year X (January 16, 1802). A.S., VD* 386, quoted in Lemoine, "Les Cimetières," 97.

### The New Theologians

On the literature discussed in this section, see Sozzi's excellent study, "I 'Sepolcri.' "

Bontoux, *Des Devoirs*.

Pastoret, *Rapport*. See also Pénière's response in *Moniteur Universel*, 1 Messidor, year IV (June 19, 1796).

Roederer, *Des Institutions*.

Mulot, *Discours sur les funérailles*.

Legouvé, "La Sépulture," in *Oeuvres*, 2 : 159–171. Compare these lines (pp. 166–167) to Hirschfeld, *Théorie*, 5 : 267.

Coupé, *Des Sépultures*.

### The Space of Ignominy

Avril, *Rapport*, 15–16.

Roederer, *Des Institutions*, 5, 11, 13.

Chambers, *Dissertation*, 36–37. See also Whately, *Observations*, 111–115, and Hirschfeld, *Théorie*, 1 : 220.

Giraud, *Essai*, 5–12, and *Les Tombeaux*, 17–23.

Rousseau: *Annales J.-J. Rousseau*, 12 (1918–1919), 16–17. Starobinski, *Rousseau*, 303.

Gautier, Dufourni: Mulot, *Discours sur les funérailles*, 11, and *Vues*, 8–11.

Love: Cérutti, *Les Jardins*, 22 (note 22).

Tender memories: Roederer, *Des Institutions*, 12.

Institut National (1797–1798): Ozouf, "La Fête," in Le Goff and Nora, eds., *Faire de l'Histoire*, 3 : 260.

Institut National (1800): Etlin, "The Cemetery," 362–363.

Annihilation: Daubermesnil, *Rapport*, 8.

### Private Burials or Public Cemeteries?

La Revellière-Lépeaux, *Réflexions*, 21–22.

Special Commission on Burials: Daubermesnil, *Rapport*, 9–10, 13–14.

Mercier, *Opinion*.

Mulot, *Vues*, 11–20, 28.

Rites of Passage: La Revellière-Lépeaux, *Réflexions*, 29–33. Leclerc, *Rapport*, 41–43, 57, 71, and *Règlement*.

Department of the Seine. Arrêté of 23 Germinal, year IV; 22 Floréal, year V; and 28 Frimaire, year VII. A.S., DL[1] 2.

### A Funerary Bosquet

Gessner: Van Tieghem, *Le Préromantisme*, 2 : 239.

Hazon: I am grateful to Monique Mosser for making it possible for me to review the documents, which are held in a private collection. Two of Hazon's drawings, along with a brief notice, were published in the exhibition catalogue *Jardins*, 148–149.

The tree: Ozouf, "Symboles," 591–592, and *La Fête*, 280–316.

Pierre-Silvain Maréchal, "L'Arbre des noces," in *Bibliothèque pastorale*, 4 : 116–120.

### Formal Garden or Picturesque Landscape?

Thiébaut, *Réflexions*.

La Revellière-Lépeaux, *Du Panthéon*.

Elysium garden, Musée des Monuments Français: Lenoir, *Description*, 17, 363–367, and *Musée*, 18–20. Landon, *Annales*, 1 : 12. Mulot, *Disours qui a partagé le prix*, 84. *Décade Philosophique*, 20 (10 Nivôse, year VII/December 30, 1798), 51; 21 (10 Floréal, year VII/April 29, 1799), 246. Schneider, *Quatremère de Quincy*, 186. *Jardins*, 149.

Les Invalides: *Décade Philosophique*, 23 (20 Frimaire, year VIII/December 11, 1799), 493–495; 24 (10 Nivôse, year VIII/December 31, 1799), 52. De Norvins, *Mémorial*, 2 : 233–234. Biver, *Paris*, 138–139, 250–251. Although approved by the Consuls, the project was never executed. The church, though, now called the Temple of Mars, was the scene of French funeral ceremonies on February 18, 1800, honoring George Washington as liberator of the New World. Washington had died December 14, 1799.

Chaussard, *Monuments*.

Luxembourg Gardens: Velye, *Considérations*.

Gisors Guy de: Landon, *Annales*, 1 : 137–138.

### A Thirst for Morals

Daubenton: *Extrait des registres du Muséum National d'Histoire Naturelle* . . . , and *Décade Philosophique*, 24 (20 Nivôse, year VIII/January 9, 1800), 109–110.

De Wailly: Baudin, "Rapport."

Cemetery under Montmartre: Baudin, "Second Rapport."

Department of the Seine, Arrêté of 28 Germinal, year VII. A.S., DZ[6] carton 3.

Grand Prix, 1799: "Programme pour les Grands Prix de l'an 7ᵉ, donné par l'Institut." Archives de l'Institut de France, Réserve 6B 10. An excerpt of the program was published in Vaudoyer and Baltard, *Grands prix*. See also *Décade Philosophique*, 21 (10 Floréal, year VII/April 29, 1799), 246–247.

Institut National: "Rapport contenant le programme d'un prix sur les sépultures" (26 Ventôse, year VIII/March 17, 1800), in *Magasin Encyclopédique*, 6 (year VIII), 530–535.

1800 competition: Désessartz, *Rapport*, 22–23. The manuscripts are in the Archives de l'Institut de France under Archives de l'Académie des Inscriptions et Belles-Lettres, 1H 5–1H 7.

### Architecture Is Devouring Us

Cambry, *Rapport*, i–ii, 13.

Quatremère de Quincy, *Rapport fait au Conseil-Général*, 24, 28.

Cemetery under Montmartre: A.N., F³ ᴵᴵ Seine 18.

Symbolism of Molinos's design: Cambry, *Rapport*, 65.

Wheel of Fortune: Marle, *Iconographie*, 2 : 191–202.

Circle of life and the revolutionary festival: Ozouf, "Symboles," 583–585.

Ledoux's *barrières*: Braham, *Architecture*, 191–197. Ironically, to William Beckford, Ledoux's custom houses exhibited a "sepulchral character" (quoted, p. 193).

Plagiarism: Giraud, *Les Tombeaux*, 43–46. See also the letter of 16 Ventôse, year IX (March 7, 1801), from Fournier, former Administrateur du Département de la Seine, to Fourcroy, Conseiller d'Etat and Directeur du Muséum d'Histoire Naturelle, which is bound with Giraud's *Essai*, B.N., Rp. 6141. Fournier sides with Giraud and explains that he received a copy of this architect's *Essai* in the year VI and the drawings at the beginning of the year VII.

*Décade Philosophique*, 24 (20 Pluviôse, year VIII/February 9, 1800), 280–285. "l'Architecture nous dévore" (284).

*Gazette de France*, 27 Pluviôse, year VIII (February 16, 1800), 586–587.

### The Grand Prix of 1799

I am grateful to Mme. de Garry, Conservateur of the Cabinet des Dessins, Musée des Arts Décoratifs, Paris, for showing me the tracings of both the designs for the Grand Prix of 1799 and for the *prix d'émulation* of November 21, 1800, for a cenotaph to Newton.

Jomard: Baltard, "Projet d'un Elysée, ou monument sépulchral," in *Athenaeum*, 1807.

Anonymous designs: It can be deduced by process of elimination that the architects were Vincent, Augustin Famin, C. Gay, or Pinault. "Admission définitive des huits concurrents aux Grands Prix d'architecture, le 7 floréal, an VII" (April 26, 1799). Archives de l'Institut de France, Rés. 6B 10. The vote on the *esquisse* was as follows: Gasse (14), Grandjean (14), Guignet (13), Vincent (12), Famin (12), Gay (10), Jomard (9), Pinault (9).

Mont-Valérien: Fournel, *Les Rues*, 143, 154–155. Hillairet, *Evocation*, fig. 32.

Mme. Brongniart's letter of 19 Prairial, year II (June 7, 1794), to her husband Alexandre-Théodore Brongniart, in Boullée, *Architecture*, 183–185.

Grandjean de Montigny: Vaudoyer and Baltard, *Grands prix*.

### A Truly Simple Plan

Andrieux's letter was published both in the *Décade Philosophique*, 20 (20 Ventôse, year VIII/March 11, 1800), 541–549, and *Le Mois, journal historique, littéraire et critique*, no. XII, year VIII, 311–321.

War on words: Ronèsse, *Projet*, 26. Quatremère de Quincy, "Cimetière," in *Encyclopédie méthodique*, 1 : 680.

Simplicity: Amaury-Duval, *Des Sépultures*, 43. Mulot, *Discours qui a partagé le prix*, 84.

Amaury-Duval, *Des Sépultures*, 48–52, 74–75.

Godineau l'aîné: Arch. Acad. Inscriptions et Belles-Lettres, 1H 7, n° 39.

Girard, *Des Tombeaux*, 111–112.

Agriculture: Coupé, *De la Moralité*, 9–10. Détournelle, *Des Funérailles*, 50. Désessartz, *Rapport*, 20.

Unpleasantness: Pommereul, ms. in Arch. Acad. Inscriptions et Belles-Lettres, 1H 6, n° 16. See also his *Mémoire*. Coupé, *De la Moralité*,

24–26. Chambon, 1H 5, n° 5. Détournelle, *Des Funérailles*, 23, 47.
Ronèsse, *Projet*, 23–26, 29.

### An Energetic Prefect

"L'impulsion énergique de Frochot": Lemoine, "Les Cimetières," 96.
See also Passy, *Frochot*, 229–234, 237–240, 245–247, 440–446.

Institut National: Désessartz, *Rapport*.

Giraud, *Les Tombeaux*.

Patte, *Mémoires qui intéressent particulièrement Paris*.

Arrêté of 21 Ventôse, year IX–March 12, 1801: *Préfecture du Département de la Seine. Commune de Paris. Arrêté du Préfet du Département de la Seine, concernant les inhumations*. Paris, n.d. A.S., DZ⁶ carton 3.

Funeral reform: Frochot, *Extrait du Rapport du 21 Fructidor, an XII adressé . . . à son Excellence le Ministre des Cultes* (September 8, 1804) and Report of 6 Germinal, year II (March 26, 1794) by Guigot Sainte-Hélène, *commissaire de police de la Section de la Cité*, to the *administrateurs des travaux publics*. A.S., DZ⁶ carton 3.

Parc Monceau: Frochet, Letter of 8 Prairial, year IX. A.N.,F³ ¹¹ Seine 20.
See above.

Sixty *arpents*: Frochot's letter of 24 Ventôse, year IX (March 15, 1801).
A.N., F³ ¹¹ Seine 20. See also Frochot's letters of 8 Prairial, year IX (May 28, 1801), and 9 Nivôse, year X (December 30, 1801), the latter accompanied by his *Rapport au Conseil Général du Département de la Seine faisant fonctions de Conseil Municipal de la Ville de Paris . . . sur la nécessité d'acquérir pour la Commune de Paris 60 arpents (mesure nouvelle) de terrain à consacrer au service des inhumations*. A.N., F³ ¹¹ Seine 18, n° 11. For the authorization to purchase the requested sixty *arpents*, see *Conseil d'Etat. Extrait du Registre des délibérations*, séance du 28 Brumaire year X (November 19, 1801). A.N., AF^{IV} 49, dossier 278, pièce 22. See also, Carret, *Rapport*.

Conseil Général: *Rapport au Gouvernement*, from the Minister of the Interior to the First Consul. 1 Floréal, year XI (April 21, 1803). A.N., F³ ¹¹ Seine 18.

Purchase of Mont-Louis: Paul-Albert, *Histoire*, 34.

Arrêté of 22 Floréal, year XII (May 12, 1804). A.S., VD⁴ 2871.

Imperial Decree on Burials: *Décret impérial sur les sépultures. Au palais de Saint-Cloud, le 23 Prairial an XII (12 juin 1804)*. A.S., DZ⁶ carton 3. Hérold, *Rapport*, 1.

Ministry of the Interior: Louis-Philippe, comte de Ségur, *Rapport fait au Conseil d'Etat dans la séance du 9 prairial, an XII [May 29, 1804] sur les sépultures*. A.S., DZ⁶ carton 3.

Compromise: *Le Ministre de l'intérieur, au Préfet du département d . . .* ,
8 messidor, year XII (June 27, 1804). A.S., DZ⁶ carton 3.

Champagny: Lemoine, "Les Cimetières," 99.

Quatremère de Quincy: Paul-Albert, *Histoire*, 38.

1843: Janniard, "Coup d'oeil," 252.

"[U]n nouvel Eden": Arnaud, *Recueil*, 16.

### La Folie Regnault

La Folie Regnault and Mont-Louis: Marchant de Beaumont, *Itinéraire*, 4–6. Saint-A., *Promenade* (1816), 33–34. Acquier and Noel, *Les Cimetières*, 2–4. *De Belleville à Charonne*, 29–31.

Brongniart: Silvestre de Sacy, *Brongniart*, 143–144.

### Designing Père Lachaise

Préfecture du Département de la Seine. Arrêté du 15 Ventôse an XIII (March 6, 1805). Paris, [year XIII]. *Arrêté* by Frochot and *Rapport* of 29 Germinal (April 19) by Quatremère de Quincy. A.S., DZ⁶ carton 3.

Temporary concessions: Saint-A., *Promenade* (1825), 1 : 45–47. Marchant de Beaumont, *Vues*, 1 : 125. In 1874, Hérold (*Rapport*, 5) reported that the temporary concessions had been given a duration of six years in 1827 and five years in 1829.

Covered galleries: Schneider, *Quatremère de Quincy*, 69.

Brongniart as garden designer: Silvestre de Sacy, *Brongniart*, 20, 24–26, 28, 55–56, 131–132.

Pyramid: Marchant de Beaumont, *Itinéraire*, 7.

Note: Brongniart, *Plans*, 8.

Orientation: Marchant de Beaumont, *Itinéraire*, 8.

Whately, *Observations*, 183–184.

Chambers, *Dissertation* (1773), 51.

Hirschfeld, *Théorie*, 2 : 161–162; 4 : 96.

Petitot: *Piranèse*, 250–251.

Bélanger: Drawings in the Musée Carnavalet, Paris. See also Stern, *Belanger*, 2 : 320.

### The Architecture of Père Lachaise

Guy de Gisors: *Recueil*. Bibliothèque de l'Institut de France, Ms. 1044, n° 7.

Critique of the entrance and chapel at Père Lachaise: Marchant de Beaumont, *Itinéraire*, 8.

Grand Prix, 1799: Vaudoyer, *Grands prix*.

Silva, *Giardini inglesi*, 255–261, 326–331. Brongniart's drawing of the section through his central chapel is kept in a private collection.

Protestant Cemetery: Beck-Friis, *The Protestant Cemetery in Rome*.

Project for a formal entry: Marchant de Beaumont, *Itinéraire*, 7.

Monument to the Dead: Brown, *Père Lachaise*, 66–67 (photo). Le Clere, *Cimetières*, 87–88.

### A Terrestrial Paradise

Permanent concessions: Arrêté of 15 Ventôse, year XIII, with Report of 29 Germinal (April 19) by Quatremère de Quincy. A.S., DZ⁶ carton 3.

See also Frochot's Arrêté of 22 Floréal, year XII (May 12, 1804). A.S., VD⁴ 2871; Paul-Albert, *Histoire*, 46–47.

Cemetery of Vaugirard: Saint-A., *Promenade* (1816), 76, 81–82; (1825), 1 : 141–148.

Cemetery under Montmartre: Ibid. (1816), 9–11, 36; (1825), 1 : 13–15. Hillairet, *Les 200 Cimetières*, 316–317 (Montmartre), 347–349 (Montparnasse). On the Valley of Tombs, see also Janniard, "Coup d'oeil," 249–251.

Transformation of Père Lachaise: Saint-A., *Promenade*, 1 : 46–47. G. G., *Promenade*, 38–39. On the family tomb as a small chapel, see Etlin, "Landscapes," 22–28, and "Geometry," 136.

Visitors: Dulaure, *Histoire* (1825), 9 : 298.

Hirschfeld, *Théorie*, 1 : 180ff.; 2 : 47–49, 161–162.

Maps of 1820: In addition to fig. 249, see *Plan du Cimetière du Mont-Louis* (1820). B.N., Lk⁷ 7736.

Delille, *Les Jardins*, 21.

Plantings: *Plan du Cimetière du Mont-Louis* (1820). B.N., Lk⁷ 7736. Marchant de Beaumont, *Itinéraire*, 7–8, and *Vues*, 1 : 125. Saint-A., *Promenade* (1825), 1 : 46–48.

Expressive landscape: Hunt, "Emblem." D'Harcourt, *Traité*, 136. De Genlis, *La Botanique*, 31. Hirschfeld, *Traité*, 4 : 96–97.

Entrance: Saint-A., *Promenade* (1825), 1 : 39.

Abélard and Héloïse: Ibid., 50–54. Marchant de Beaumont, *Itinéraire*, 20–23.

"Family sepulcher": G. G., *Promenade*, 38–39.

Rendez-vous des Braves: Marchant de Beaumont, *Vues*, 1 : 185, and *Itinéraire*, 45–52. Saint-A., *Promenade* (1825), 1 : 48.

Bosquet du Dragon: Marchant de Beaumont, *Vues*, 1 : 334. Saint-A., *Promenade* (1825), 1 : 89–90.

Bosquet Delille: Saint-A., *Promenade* (1825), 1 : 47, 61–68. Marchant de Beaumont, *Itinéraire*, 85–93.

Delille's tomb: Silvestre de Sacy, *Brongniart*, 146. Brongniart's tomb: ibid., 154.

### First Impressions

Baillie, *First Impressions*, 34, 42–47.

Carter, *Letters*, 1 : 391–399.

Fisk, *Travels*, 38–41.

Picturesque: Carter, *Letters*, 1 : 393. See also Baillie, *First Impressions*, 42; Fisk, *Travels*, 38; and other texts cited in this chapter.

Biographical dictionary: Fisk, *Travels*, 40. Carter, *Letters*, 1 : 396–397.

Tenenti, *La Vie*, 73.

Fisk, *Travels*, 39.

Griscom, *A Year*, 1 : 277–279.

### The American Rural Cemeteries

On American "rural cemeteries": "Rural Cemeteries," *North American Review* (October 1841), 385–412. Rotondo, "Mount-Auburn" and "The Rural Cemetery Movement." French, "The Cemetery."

On British cemeteries: Collison, *Cemetery Interment*. Curl, *The Victorians* and *Celebration*, 206–264.

Downing, "Public Cemeteries and Public Gardens," *The Horticulturalist*, 4 (July 1849), 9–12.

Forest Hills: *Forest Hills Cemetery*, 10.

Massachusetts Horticultural Society, September 10, 1830: Zebedee Cook, Jr., *An Address*, 27.

Philadelphia: Elkington, *The Monument Cemetery of Philadelphia*.

Mount Auburn as the Père Lachaise of America: *Picturesque Pocket Companion*, 3. Holley, *The Picturesque Tourist*, 298.

Mount Auburn Cemetery: Adams, "Mount Auburn." Bigelow, *History*. Dearborn, *Third Anniversary*, *Mount Auburn*, and *Guide*. Flagg, *Mount Auburn*. "Mount Auburn," *Gleason's Pictorial Drawing-Room Companian* (August 13, 1853), 104–105. *Notes on Mount Auburn*. Walter, *Mount Auburn Illustrated*. Ames, "Mount Auburn's Sixscore Years."

Greenwood Cemetery: Cleaveland, *Green-Wood in 1846* and *Green-Wood Illustrated*. *Rules and Regulations*. *Guide*.

Consecration ceremony, Mount Auburn: Bigelow, *History*, 11–14.

### A Metropolis of the Dead

Comparisons between Père Lachaise and Mount Auburn or Greenwood: Clark, *Glimpses* (1838) 1 : 476–477. Buckingham, *America* (1841), 3 : 390–399. *North American Review* (October 1841), 402–403. Cuyler, "Cemeteries" (1845), 10–12. Corson, *Loiterings* (1848), 61–62. Chowles, *Young Americans* (1852), 198–199. Channing, *A Physician's Vacation* (1856), 457–458. Edwards, *Random* (1856), 71–72. Forbes, *A Woman's First Impressions* (1865), 308–309. Coghill, *Abroad* (1868), 72. Clayton, *Rambles* (1869), 52. Browne, *Sights* (1871), 136. Falk, *Trans-Pacific* (1877), 148. Burnham, *Pleasant Memories* (1877–1878), 53–54. Cook, *A Holiday* (1878), 152–157. Damseaux, *Voyage* (1878), 174–179. Burchard, *Two Months* (1879), 156–157. Blake, *A Summer* (1891), 99–101.

Downing, "A Talk about Public Parks and Gardens," *The Horticulturalist*, 3 (October 1848), 157. See also his "Additional Notes on the Progress of Gardening in the United States" (November 29, 1840), *Gardening in the United States*, 147, and "Public Cemeteries and Public Gardens," *The Horticulturalist*, 4 (July 1849), 11; and Comettant, *L'Amérique*, 120–121.

Carter, *Letters*, 1 : 394.

Méry-sur-Oise: Haussmann, *Mémoires*, 3 : 419 passim. Vafflard, *Notice*, 1–2; *Plus de fosse commune!* Auzelle, "Haussmann." Ariès, *Essais*, 150–152, and *L'Homme*, 531–540. Etlin, "Landscapes," 29–30.

All Saints' Day, 1866: Chenel, *Note*, 10.

Taboos about death: Ariès, *Essais*, 61–72, 157–163, 180–197, and *L'Homme*, 550–595.

# Archival Sources

**Archives de la Seine**
1 AZ. 10, pièce 48
3 AZ. 240
DL$^1$2
DZ$^6$ carton 3
VD$^4$ 2871
VD* 311, 331, 338, 424, 2149, 2205, 2243, 2244, 2247–2249, 2260, 3533–3555, 6770

**Archives de l'Institut de France**
Réserve 6B 10
1H 5–1H 7 (Archives de l'Académie des Inscriptions et Belles-Lettres)

**Archives Nationales**
AD$^I$ 25$^A$
AF$^{II}$ 139, pl. 1088, pièces 34–35
AF$^{IV}$ 49, dossier 278, pièce 22
AF$^{IV}$* 216, no. 2506
C 248, pièce 374
F$^{13}$ 330, 333a, 333b–334, 523, 888, 908, 983, 987
F$^{14}$ 187$^B$
F$^{3II}$ Seine 18
F$^{3II}$ Seine 20
L 570
N$^{III}$ Seine 87, 846
O$^1$ 500, fol. 223; 1694
Z$^{10}$ 222
Y 12612, 15827
X$^{1b}$ 8975

**Bibliothèque Doucet**
Cartons 32, 62

**Bibliothèque de l'Institut de France**
Ms. 1044–1046

**Bibliothèque Historique de la Ville de Paris**
Ms., C.P. 5017–5024 (Collected papers of Dr. Félix Gannal)

**Bibliothèque Marmottan**
Fontaine, Pierre. *Journal.*

**Bibliothèque Nationale, Estampes**
Collection Deloynes
Ye 157

**Bibliothèque Nationale, Manuscrits**
Fonds français 9153
Joly de Fleury 584, 1182–1183, 1317, 1207–1209

**Dumbarton Oaks, Garden Library**
Letters from Hubert Robert to Jean-Joseph, duc de Laborde, 1786–1804 (photoreproduction from microfilm of manuscript letters)

# Bibliography

## Primary Sources

Acquier, Hippolyte, and Noel, Albert. *Les Cimetières de Paris, ouvrage historique, biographique et pittoresque.* Paris, 1852.

Adams, Nehemiah. "Mount Auburn," *The American Quarterly Observer,* 3 (July 1834), 149–172.

Alembert, Jean le Rond d'. *Discours préliminaire de l'Encyclopédie.* 1763; reprint Paris, 1965.

Alembert, Jean le Rond d'. "Air," "Exhalaison," "Genève," in *Encyclopédie ou Dictionnaire raisonné des sciences, des arts et des métiers.* 17 vols. Paris, 1751–1765.

Amaury-Duval. *Des Sépultures. Ouvrage couronné par l'Institut National.* Paris, year IX.

Andrieux, F.-G.-J.-S. "Lettre aux auteurs de la Décade," *La Décade Philosophique, Littéraire et Politique,* 20 Ventôse, year VIII/March 11, 1800, 541–549.

Androuet Du Cerceau, Jacques. *Livre des édifices antiques romains.* n.p., 1584.

*A nos seigneurs les députés aux Etats-Généraux.* Avignon, Paris, and Versailles, 1789.

Antonini, Abbé A. *Mémorial de Paris et de ses environs, à l'usage des voyageurs.* Nouvelle édition. Paris, 1744.

Arnaud, C.-P., and Laurens l'aîné. *Recueil de tombeaux des quatres cimetières de Paris.* Paris, 1813.

Arouet, François-Marie. See Voltaire.

Aubry, A. *Le Guide des étrangers aux monuments publics de Paris.* Paris, n.d.

Audin-Rouvière, Joseph-Marie. *Essai sur la topographie physique et médicale de Paris, ou dissértation sur les substances qui peuvent influer sur la santé des habitants de cette cité, avec une description de ses hôpitaux.* [Paris], year II [1794].

Avril, Jean-Baptiste. *Rapport de l'Administration des Travaux Publics sur les cimetières, lu au Conseil-Général par le citoyen Avril* [21 Nivôse, year II/January 10, 1794]. N.p., n.d.

B., H. L. "Père La Chaise," *The Knickerbocker, or New-York Monthly Magazine,* 9 (March 1837), 285–286.

Baillie, John. *An Essay on the Sublime* (1747). Introduction by Samuel Holt Monk. The Augustan Reprint Society, No. 43. Los Angeles, 1953.

Baillie, Marianne. *First Impressions on a Tour upon the Continent in the Summer of 1818.* London, 1819.

Baltard, Louis-Pierre. *Athenaeum, ou Galerie française des productions de tous les arts, ouvrage périodique, entrepris par une société d'hommes de lettres et d'artistes, et publié par M. Baltard.* Paris, 1807.

Barbault, Jean. *Les plus beaux édifices de Rome moderne.* Rome, 1763.

Barbault, Jean. *Recueil de divers monumens anciens répandus en plusieurs endroits de l'Italie.* Rome, 1770.

Barrière, Dominique. *Villa Aldobrandina Tusculuna sive Varii illius hortorum et fontium prospectus*. Rome, 1647.

Baudin, P.-C.-L. "Rapport fait . . . au nom de la Commission composée des citoyens Laplace, Fourcroy, Cels, Naigeon, Fleurieu, Baudin, Camus, Mongez et Vincent, chargée par l'Institut National d'examiner comment, au décès de ses membres, il doit leur rendre les derniers devoirs. Lu à la séance général du 5 frimaire an VII [November 25, 1798]," *Mémoires de l'Institut National des Sciences et Arts. Sciences Morales et Politique*, 2 (year VII/1799), 681–694.

Baudin, P.-C.-L. "Second rapport fait . . . au nom de la Commission chargée d'examiner quelle part l'Institut doit prendre aux funérailles de ses membres, sur l'état actuel des lieux de sépulture de la commune de Paris. Lu à la séance générale du 5 frimaire an VII [November 25, 1798]," *Mémoires de l'Institut National des Sciences et Arts. Sciences Morales et Politique*, 2 (year VII/1799), 695–699.

Beguillat, E.; La Borde, J.-B. de; and Guettard, J.-E. *Voyage pittoresque de la France*, vol. 10. Paris, 1792.

Berington, Simon. *The Memoirs of Signor Gaudentio di Lucca*. London, 1737.

*Bibliothèque pastorale, ou cours de littérature champêtre, contenant les chefs-d'oeuvre des meilleurs poètes pastoraux, anciens et modernes, depuis Moyse, jusqu' à nos jours*. 4 vols. Paris, year XI/1803.

Bigelow, Jacob. *A History of the Cemetery of Mount Auburn*. Boston and Cambridge, 1860.

Blake, Elizabeth Mary. *A Summer Holiday in Europe*. Boston, 1891.

Blanvillain, J.-F.-C. *Le Pariséum, ou Tableau actuel de Paris*. Paris, 1807.

Blondel, François. *Cours d'architecture enseigné dans l'Académie Royale d'Architecture*. Paris, 1675–1683.

Blondel, Jacques-François. *Architecture françoise*. 4 vols. Paris, 1752–1756.

Blondel, Jacques-François. *Cours d'architecture ou Traité de la décoration, distribution et construction des bâtiments; contenant les leçons données en 1750 et les années suivantes*. 9 vols. Paris, 1771–1777.

Boffrand, Germain. *Livre d'architecture.* . . . Paris, 1745.

Boisguillebert, Pierre le Pesant de. *Le Détail de la France*. N.p., 1695.

Bontoux, P.-B.-F. *Des Devoirs à rendre aux morts, question envisagée sous le rapport politique et morale.* . . . Paris, year IV [1796].

Boullée, Etienne-Louis. *Architecture, essai sur l'art*. Ed. Jean-Marie Pérouse de Montclos. Paris, 1968.

Bretez, Louis. *Plan de Paris commencé in 1734*. Paris, 1739.

Brice, Germain. *Nouvelle description de la ville de Paris*, 8th ed. 4 vols. Paris, 1725.

B[rongniart], A[lexandre]. *Plans du palais de la Bourse de Paris, et du cimetière Mont-Louis, en six planches, par Alexandre-Théodore Brongniart, architecte; précédés d'une Notice sur ces plans et sur quelques autres travaux du même artiste*. Paris, 1814.

Browne, Junius Henri. *Sights and Sensations in Europe*. Hartford, 1871.

Bruhier d'Ablaincourt, Jacques-Jean. *Dissertation sur l'incertitude des signes de la mort et l'abus des enterrements, et embaumements précipités, par M. Jacques Benigne-Winslow . . . traduite et commentée par Jacques-Jean Bruhier, docteur en médecine*. Paris, 1742.

Buckingham, James S. *America, Historical, Statistic, and Descriptive*. 3 vols. London and Paris, 1841.

Burchard, Oscar Roger. *Two Months in Europe. A Record of a Summer Vacation Abroad*. Syracuse and New York, 1879.

Burke, Edmund. *A Philosophical Enquiry into the Origins of Our Ideas of the Sublime and Beautiful*. Ed. J. T. Boulton. Notre Dame, 1968.

Burnham, Sarah Maria. *Pleasant Memories of Foreign Travel*. Boston, 1896.

Cadet de Vaux, Antoine. *Mémoire historique et physique sur le Cimetière des Innocents . . . lu à l'Académie Royale des Sciences en 1781. Extrait du Journal de Physique, Juin 1783*. N.p., n.d.

Cambry, Jacques. *Rapport sur les sépultures, présenté à l'Administration Centrale du Département de la Seine, par le citoyen Cambry, administrateur du Département de la Seine. . . .* Paris, year VII.

Campanella, Tommaso. *La Città del Sole*. Ed. Adriano Seroni. Milan, 1981.

Camus, Armand-Gaston, et al. "Rapport contenant le programme d'un prix sur les sépultures," *Magasin Encyclopédique*, 6 (year VIII/1800), 530–535.

Carmontelle (Louis Carrogis). *Jardin de Monceau, près de Paris, appartenant à . . . Monseigneur le duc de Chartres*. Paris, 1779.

Carret. *Rapport . . . sur un projet de loi tendant à autoriser la commune de Paris à acquérir soixante hectares de terrain pour les inhumations*. Tribunat, séance du 21 frimaire, an X [December 12, 1801]. Paris, year X [1801].

Carter, Nathaniel Hageltine. *Letters from Europe, Comprising the Journal of a Tour through Ireland, England, Scotland, France, Italy, and Switzerland in the Years 1825, '26, and '27*. 2 vols. New York, 1827.

*A Catalogue of Proprietors in the Cemetery of Mount Auburn Together with an Appendix, Containing the Charter, Regulations, . . . with a Plan of the Grounds*. Boston and Cambridge, 1855.

Cérutti, Joseph-Antoine-Joachim. *Les Jardins de Betz*, 2d ed. Paris, 1792.

Chadwick, Sir Edwin. *A Report on the Results of a Special Inquiry into the Practice of Interment in Towns. Made at the Request of Her Majesty's Principal Secretary of State for the Home Department*. Philadelphia, 1845.

Chambers, Sir William. *A Dissertation on Oriental Gardening*. London, 1772.

Chambers, Sir William. *Traité des édifices . . . des Chinois . . . compris une description de leurs temples, maisons, jardins, etc*. Paris, 1776. Published as the 5th *cahier* of Lerouge, *Détail des nouveaux jardins. . . .*

Channing, Walter. *A Physician's Vacation; or, A Summer in Europe*. Boston, 1856.

[Chappotin de Saint-Laurent, Michel]. *Projets ou plutôt idées de fêtes à exécuter pour le prochain mariage de Monseigneur le Dauphin, ou, si elles sont déjà déterminées, pour ceux de Monseigneur le comte de Provence, de Monseigneur le comte d'Artois, dans le temps, ainsi que pour les naissances à venir de Monseigneur le duc de Bourgogne et autres princes, à espérer de leurs augustes alliances.* Vienna and Paris, 1770.

Chappu. "D'une part, sécurité dangereuse, ou de l'autre, alarmes mal fondées," *Mercure de France*, octobre 1748, 93–97.

Charron, Joseph. *Translation de Voltaire à Paris, et détails de la cérémonie qui aura lieu le 4 juillet, arrêtés par le Directoire du Département de Paris.* . . . Paris, 1791.

Chaussard, Pierre. *Monuments de l'héroïsme français: nécessité de ramener à un plan unique, et de coordonner à ceux déjà existants, les monuments qu'on propose d'élever à Paris sur l'étendue comprise entre les Tuileries et l'Etoile, considérations et projet.* [Paris, year X].

Chenel. *Note sur les nouveaux cimetières de Paris.* Paris, 1868.

[Chowles, John Overton]. *Young Americans Abroad; or, Vacation in Europe. Travels in England, France,* . . . Boston, 1852.

"Cimetière romain à Arles," *Magasin pittoresque*, 29 (1861), 363–365.

Clark, John A. *Glimpses of the Old World, or Excursion on the Continent, and in Great Britain.* 2 vols. London, 1840.

Clayton, Thomas J. *Rambles and Reflections. Europe from Biscay to the Black Sea.* . . . Chester, 1892.

Cleaveland, Nehemiah. *Green-Wood Illustrated.* New York, 1847.

Cleaveland, Nehemiah. *Green-Wood in 1846.* New York, 1846.

Cleaveland, Nehemiah. *Hints Concerning Green-Wood; Its Monuments and Improvements.* New York, 1853.

Coghill, J. Henry. *Abroad. Journal of a Tour Through Great Britain and on the Continent.* New York, 1868.

Cole, Reverend William. *A Journal of My Journey to Paris in the Year 1765.* Ed. Francis Griffin Stokes. New York, 1931.

Collison, George. *Cemetery Interment: Containing a Concise History of the Modes of Interment Practised by the Ancients; Description of Père La Chaise, the Eastern Cemeteries, and those of America; the English Metropolitan and Provincial Cemeteries.* London, 1840.

Comettant, Jean-Pierre-Oscar. *L'Amérique telle qu'elle est. Voyage anecdotique de Marcel Bonneau dans le Nord et le Sud des Etats-Unis. Excursion au Canada par Oscar Comettant.* Paris, 1864.

*Commentaires de la Faculté de Médecine de Paris, 1777 à 1786 publiés sous les auspices du Conseil de l'Université.* Ed. Adolphe Pinard et al. 2 vols. Paris, 1903.

Cook, Joel. *A Holiday Tour in Europe. Described in a Series of Letters Written for the Public Ledger during the Summer and Autumn of 1878.* Philadelphia, 1879.

Cook, Zebedee, Jr. *An Address Pronounced before the Massachusetts Horticultural Society in Commemoration of its Second Annual Festival, the 10th of September, 1830.* Boston, 1830.

Coquéau, Claude-Philibert. *Mémoire sur la nécessité de transférer et reconstruire l'Hôtel-Dieu, suivi d'un projet de translation de cet hôpital, proposé par le sieur Poyet.* . . . N.p., 1785.

[Coquéau, Claude-Philibert]. *Réflexions sur le projet d'éloigner du milieu de Paris les tueries des bestiaux et les fonderies des suifs.* London, 1788.

Corson, John W. *Loiterings in Europe; or Sketches of Travel in France, Belgium,* . . . New York, 1848.

Coupé, Jacques-Michel. *De la Moralité des sépultures et de leur police.* Paris, year IX.

Coupé, Jacques-Michel. *Des Sépultures en politique et en morale.* [Paris], year IV [1795].

[Coyer, Abbé Gabriel-François]. *Etrennes aux morts et aux vivants, ou projet utile partout où l'on est mortel, en deux chapitres.* A la vallée de Josaphat, 1768.

Crucé, Emery. *Le Nouveau Cynée, ou Discours d'estat représentant les occasions et moyens d'establir une paix générale et la liberté du commerce par tout le monde. Aux monarques et souverains de ce temps.* Paris, 1623.

Cuyler, Theodore Ledyard. "The Cemeteries of Paris and London," *Godey's Magazine and Lady's Book,* 30 (January 1845), 10–12.

Damseaux, Emile de. *Voyage dans l'Amérique du Nord.* Paris, 1878.

Daubermesnil, François-Antoine. *Rapport fait au nom d'une Commission spéciale, sur les inhumations.* Corps législatif, séance du 21 brumaire, an V [November 11, 1796]. Paris, year V [1796].

David, Jacques-Louis. *Rapport sur la fête héroïque pour les honneurs du Panthéon, à décerner aux jeunes Barra et Viola.* Convention nationale, séance du 23 messidor an II [July 11, 1794]. [Paris], n.d.

Dearborn, Nathaniel. *A Concise History of, and Guide through Mount Auburn.* Boston, 1843.

Dearborn, Nathaniel. *Guide through Mount Auburn.* 2d ed. Boston, 1848. 3rd ed., 1849.

Dearborn, Nathaniel. *Third Anniversary Festival of the Massachusetts Horticultural Society.* Boston, 1831.

Dehorne, Jacques. *Mémoire sur quelques objets qui intéressent plus particulièrement la salubrité de la ville de Paris.* Paris, 1788.

"Delabrière," *Revue universelle des arts,* 20 (1865), 51–54.

Delafosse, Jean-Charles. *Mémoire pour une boucherie et tuerie générale, servant à la consommation de la ville de Paris, laquelle tuerie serait placée dans l'Ile des Cignes.* N.p., [1766].

Delamalle, Gaspard G. *L'Enterrement de ma mère, ou réflexions sur les cérémonies des funerailles et le soin des sépultures, et sur la moralité des institutions civiles en général.* [Paris], year III.

Delespine, Pierre-Jules. *Marché des Blancs-Manteaux . . . suivi du Tombeau de Newton.* Paris, 1827.

Delille, Abbé Jacques. *Les Jardins, ou l'art d'embellir les paysages,* 4th ed. Paris, 1782.

Deparcieux, Antoine. "Mémoire sur la possibilité d'amener à Paris, à la même hauteur à laquelle y arrivent les eaux d'Arcueil, mille à douze cents pouces d'eau, belle et de bonne qualité, par un chemin facile et par un seul canal ou aqueduc," in *Histoire de l'Académie Royale des Sciences avec les Mémoires de Mathématiques et de Physique, pour la même année, tirés des registres de cette Académie. Année 1762*, 147–159, 337–401. Paris, 1764.

Desbois de Rochefort, Eléonore-Marie. "Cimetière," in *Encyclopédie méthodique, Economie politique et diplomatique, partie dedié et présentée à Monseigneur le baron de Breteuil, ministre et secrétaire d'état, etc. par M. Démeunier*, vol. 1, 575–587. Paris, 1784.

*Description du mausolée pour . . . Princesse Marie Josephe Albertine de Saxe, Dauphine de France, fait à Paris dans l'Eglise de Notre-Dame le 3 septembre 1767 . . . sur les desseins du sieur Michel-Ange Challe. . . .* [Paris], 1767.

Désessartz, Jean-Charles. "Essai sur la topographie médicale du canton de Paris," *Moniteur Universel*, July 4, 1807, 724–726.

Désessartz, Jean-Charles. *Rapport fait par les citoyens Hallé, Désessartz, Toulongeon, Reveillère-Lépaux [sic], Leblond et Camus, commissaires chargés par l'institut National des Sciences et Arts, de l'examen des mémoires envoyés au concours proposé par le gouvernement, sur les questions relatives aux cérémonies funéraires et aux lieux des sépultures. Jugement porté par l'Institut et proclamation du prix.* Paris, n.d.

Deshayes. *Observation sur les salles de spectacles.* [Paris], n.d.

Desprez, Louis-Jean. *Ouvrage d'architecture des sieurs Desprez et Panseron.* Paris, 1781.

Détournelle, Athanase. *Des Funérailles . . . Mémoire qui a concouru pour le prix de l'Institut, en vendémiaire an IX.* Paris, year IX.

[Détruisard, J.]. *Essai sur les catacombes de Paris.* Paris, 1812.

Dezallier d'Argenville, Antoine-Nicolas. *La Théorie et la pratique du jardinage où l'on traite à fond des beaux jardins de propreté.* Paris, 1709.

Dezallier d'Argenville, Antoine-Nicolas. *The Theory and Practice of Gardening.* Trans. John James. London, 1712.

Dezallier d'Argenville, Antoine-Nicolas. *Voyage pittoresque de Paris . . . par M. D\*\*\*.* 3rd ed. Paris, 1757.

Diderot, Denis. *Encyclopédie ou Dictionnaire raisonné des sciences, des arts et des métiers, par une société de gens de lettres.* 35 vols. Paris, 1751–1780.

Diderot, Denis. *Salons*, vol. 3 (1767). Ed. Jean Seznec and Jean Adhémar. Oxford, 1963.

Dolivier, Pierre. *Essai sur les funérailles.* Versailles, year IX.

Downing, Andrew Jackson. "Public Cemeteries and Public Gardens," *The Horticulturalist*, 4 (July 1849), 9–12.

Downing, Andrew Jackson. "A Talk about Public Parks and Gardens." *The Horticulturalist*, 3 (October 1848), 157.

Dubos, Jean-Baptiste. *Critical Reflections on Poetry and Painting.* Trans. Thomas Nugent. 2 vols. London, 1748.

Du Breul, Jacques. *Le Théâtre des antiquités de Paris.* Paris, 1639.

Dulaure, Jacques-Antoine. *Histoire civile, physique et morale de Paris,* 3rd ed. 10 vols. Paris, 1825.

Dulaure, Jacques-Antoine. *Nouvelle description des curiosités de Paris.* 2 parts. 2d ed., Paris, 1787; 3rd. ed., 1791.

Dulaure, Jacques-Antoine. *Réclamation d'un citoyen, contre la nouvelle enceinte de Paris, élevée par les Fermiers-Généraux.* N.p., 1787.

Durand, Jean-Nicolas-Louis. *Précis des leçons d'architecture données à l'Ecole Polytechnique.* 2 vols. Paris, year XIII/1805.

Dussausoy, Maille. *Le citoyen désintéressé, ou diverses idées patriotiques, concernant quelques établissements et embellissements utiles à la ville de Paris, analogues aux travaux publics qui se font dans cette capitale, lesquels peuvent être adaptés aux principales villes du royaume et de l'Europe.* 2 parts in 1 vol. Paris, 1767–1768.

Edwards, John Ellis. *Random Sketches and Notes of European Travel in 1856.* New York, 1857.

Elkington, John A. *The Monument Cemetery of Philadelphia (Late Père La Chaise) Containing General Scientific Essays on the Subject of Rural Cemeteries.* Philadelphia, 1837.

*Extrait des registres du Muséum National d'Histoire Naturelle, sur la fête funéraire relative à l'inhumation du corps du citoyen Daubenton, dans le jardin de cet etablissement.* [Paris], n.d.

Falda, Giovanni Battista. *Le Fontane di Roma nelle piazze e luoghi publici della città.* 2 vols. in 1. Rome, c. 1690.

Falda, Giovanni Battista. *Li Giardini di Roma.* Rome, [1680].

Falk, Alfred. *Trans-Pacific Sketches. A Tour through the United States and Canada.* Melbourne, Sydney, and Adelaide, 1877.

Faujas de Saint-Fond, Barthélemy. *Description des expériences de la machine aérostatique de mm. de Montgolfier.* Paris, 1783.

Faujas de Saint-Fond, Barthélemy. *Méthode aisée de faire la machine aérostatique . . . et la relation des voyages aériens de Mrs. Pilâtre de Rozier, Giroud-de-Villette, du marquis d'Arlandes, et de Mrs. Charles & Robert.* Liège, 1784.

Félibien, Michel. *Histoire de la ville de Paris, composée par D. Michel Félibien, rev., augm. et mise au jour par D. Gut-Alexis Lobineau.* Paris, 1725.

Fischer von Erlach, Johann Bernhard. *Entwurff einer historischen Architectur.* Vienna, 1721.

Fisk, Wilbur. *Travels in Europe,* 4th ed. New York, 1838.

Flagg, Wilson. *Mount Auburn: Its Scenes, Its Beauties, and Its Lessons.* Boston, 1861.

*Fondation de la chapelle funéraire de Picpus. . . .* Paris, 1814.

Forbes, E. A. *A Woman's First Impressions of Europe. Being Wayside Sketches Made during a Short Tour in the Year 1863.* New York, 1865.

*Forest Hills Cemetery: Its Establishment, Progress, Scenery, Monuments, etc.* Roxbury, Mass., 1855.

Fournel, Victor. *Les Rues du vieux Paris: galerie populaire et pittoresque.* Paris, 1879.

*Fragment d'une correspondance flamade et rochelloise, au sujet de la translation des cimetières hors de l'enceinte de la ville.* N.p., 1779.

[G., C.] *Dissertation sur l'architecture française, qui par des parallèles puisés dans la France et dans l'antiquité la plus reculée, tend à démontrer que la nation française a atteint le même point de perfection dans la pratique des arts, que les Grecs et les Romains. . . .* The Hague and Châlons-sur-Saône, 1762.

G. G. *Promenade sérieuse au cimetière du Père La Chaise, ou de Mont-Louis près de Paris.* Paris, 1826.

Galli da Bibiena, Giuseppe. *Architettura & prospettive.* Augusta, 1740.

Gauthier-Lachapelle, A. *Des Sépultures.* Paris, year IX/1801.

Genlis, Stéphanie-Félicité, comtesse de. *La Botanique historique et littéraire.* 2 vols. Paris, 1810.

Genneté, Léopold de. *Purification de l'air croupissant dans les hôpitaux, et les vaisseaux de mer, par le moyen d'un renouvellement continuel d'air pur et frais. . . .* Nancy, 1767.

Géraud, Mathieu. *Essai sur la suppression des fosses d'aisance, et de tout espèce de voiries, sur la manière de convertir les substances qu'on y renferme, etc.* Amsterdam and Paris, 1786.

Gessner, Salomon. *Oeuvres.* 4 vols. Paris, 1795.

Girard, J. *Des Tombeaux, ou de l'influence des institutions funèbres sur les moeurs.* Paris, year IX/1801.

[Girardin, Stanislas-Xavier, comte de.] *Promenade ou Itinéraire des jardins d'Ermenonville, auquel on a joint vingt-cinq de leurs principales vues, dessinées et gravées par Mérigot fils.* Paris, 1788.

Girardin, René-Louis de. *De la composition des paysaqes, ou des moyens d'embellir la nature autour des habitations champêtres.* Geneva and Paris, 1777.

Giraud, Pierre. *Essai sur les sépultures . . . composé en l'an IV et déposé au Département de la Seine le 11 nivôse an VII avec les plans, coupes et élévations du monument projeté.* Paris, [year VII].

Giraud, Pierre. *Les Tombeaux, ou essai sur les sépultures. Ouvrage dans lequel l'auteur rappelle les coutumes des anciens peuples; cite sommairement celles observées par les modernes; donne les procédés pour dissoudre les chairs, calciner les ossements humains, les convertir en une substance indestructible, et en composer le médaillon de chaque individu: seconde édition, revue, augmentée, et accompagnée des plan, coupe et élévation d'un monument sépulchral à construire pour le Département de la Seine et les environs.* Paris, year IX/1801.

Godart, Guillaume-Lambert, et al. *Dissertations sur les antiseptiques, qui ont concoru pour le prix proposé par l'Académie des sciences, arts et belles-lettres de Dijon, en 1767.* Dijon, 1769.

Gondoin, Jacques. *Description des Ecoles de chirurgie.* Paris, 1780.

Grasshoff, Johann. *Dyas chymica tripartita.* Frankfurt am Main, 1625.

Griscom, John. *A Year in Europe Comprising a Journal of Observations in England, Scotland, Ireland, France, . . . in 1818 and 1819.* 2 vols. New York, 1823.

Goulet, Nicolas. *Observations sur les embellissements de Paris et sur les monuments qui s'y construisent.* Paris, 1801.

*Greenwood As It Is.* New York, 1901.

Harcourt, François-Henri, duc d'. *Traité de la décoration des dehors, des jardins et des parcs.* Ed. Count Ernest de Ganay.

Haussmann, Georges-Eugène. *Mémoires du Baron Haussmann,* 3rd ed., vol. 3. Paris, 1893.

Heeley, Joseph. *Letters on the Beauties of Hagley, Envil, and the Leasowes, with Critical Remarks and Observations on the Modern Taste in Gardening.* 2 vols. London, 1777.

Héricart de Thury, Louis. *Description des Catacombes de Paris précédée d'un précis historique sur les catacombes de tous les peuples de l'ancien et du nouveau continent.* Paris and London, 1815.

Hérold, Ferdinand. *Rapport présenté par M. Hérold, au nom de la deuxième Commission sur le projet de création d'un cimetière parisien à Méry-sur-Oise.* Conseil Municipal de Paris. Annèxe au procès-verbal de la séance du 11 avril 1874. [Paris, 1874].

Héron, Louis-Julien-Simon. *Représentations d'un citoyen à la nation.* [Paris], 1791.

Hirschfeld, Christian Cay L. *Théorie de l'art des jardins, traduit de l'allemand.* 5 vols. Leipzig, 1779–1785.

Holley, O. L. *The Picturesque Tourist; Being a Guide through the Northern and Eastern States and Canada.* New York, 1844.

Home, Henry (Lord Kames). *Elements of Criticism. The Sixth Edition with the Author's Last Corrections and Additions.* 2 vols. Edinburgh, 1785.

Horace. *The Odes and Epodes.* Trans. C. E. Bennett. Cambridge, Mass., 1964.

Iberti. *Observations générales sur les hôpitaux, suivies d'un projet d'hôpital par M. Iberti, docteur en Médecine, avec des plans détaillés, rédigés et dessinés par M. Delannoy, architecte, et ancien pensionnaire du Roi, à Rome.* London, 1788.

Ingen-Housz, John. *Experiments upon Vegetables, Discovering their Great Power of Purifying the Common Air in the Sun-shine, and of Injuring it in the Shade and at Night, to which is Joined, a New Method of Examining the Accurate Degree of Salubrity of the Atmosphere.* London, 1779.

Institut National. *Séance publique du 15 vendémiaire an VII au palais national des sciences et des arts.* [Paris], n.d.

Janniard, H. "Coup d'oeil sur les cimetières de Paris," *Revue générale de l'architecture et des travaux publics,* 4 (1843), cols. 241–265.

Jardin, Nicolas-Henri. *Plans, coupes et élévations de l'église royale de Frédéric V. Monument de la piété de ce monarque dédié au roi.* N.p., 1769.

Kip, Johannes. *Brittania Illustrata or Views of the Queens Palaces and also of the Principal Seats of the Nobility and Gentry of Great Britain.* 2 vols. London, 1709.

Kip, Johannes. *Nouveau théâtre de la Grande Bretagne.* 5 vols. London, 1714–1716. 4 vols. London, 1724–1729.

Krafft, Jean-Charles, and Ransonnette, N. *Plans, coupes et élévations des plus belles maisons et des hôtels construits à Paris et dans ses environs entre 1771 et 1802.* Paris, 1802.

Laborde, Alexandre-Louis-Joseph, comte de. *Description des nouveaux jardins de la France et de ses anciens châteaux.* Paris, 1808.

Labrière, Alexandre-Louis de. *Mémoire sur la nécessité de mettre les sépultures hors de la ville de Paris, présenté à M. de Calonne, ministre d'Etat, conseiller au conseil royal, contrôleur général des finances, commandeur, grand-trésorier de l'ordre du Saint-Esprit, par le Sieur Labrière, architecte de Monseigneur le comte d'Artois.* N.p., n.d.

[Lafont de Saint-Yenne]. *L'Ombre du grand Colbert, le Louvre et la Ville de Paris, dialogue.* The Hague, 1749.

Lakanal, Joseph. *Rapport sur J.-J. Rousseau, fait au nom du Comité d'instruction publique . . . dans la séance du 29 fructidor . . . suivi des détails sur la translation des cendres de J.-J. Rousseau au Panthéon français.* [Paris], year III [1794].

Lambert, Charles. *Paris tel qu'il a été, tel qu'il est, et tel qu'il sera dans dix ans. . . .* Paris, 1808.

Landon, Charles-Paul. *Annales du Musée et de l'Ecole moderne des Beaux-Arts, Recueil de gravures au trait. . . .* 20 vols. Paris, 1800–1809.

La Revellière-Lépeaux, Louis-Marie de. *Du Panthéon et d'un théâtre national.* Paris, year VI [1797].

La Revellière-Lépeaux, Louis-Marie de. *Réflexions sur le culte, sur les cérémonies civiles et sur les fêtes nationales. . . . Lu à l'Institut le 12 floréal an V [May 1, 1797] . . . dans la séance de la classe des sciences morales et politiques.* Paris, year V [1797].

Lasinio, G. Paolo, figlio, and Rossi, Giuseppe. *Pitture a fresca del Camposanto di Pisa.* Firenze, 1832.

Lasinio, Paolo. *Raccolta di sarcofagi, urne e altri monument di scultura del Campo Santo di Pisa intagliati.* Pisa, 1814.

Laugier, Abbé Marc-Antoine. *Essai sur l'architecture, nouvelle édition, revue, corrigée, et augmentée; avec un dictionnaire des termes, et des planches qui en facilitent l'explication.* Paris, 1755.

Laugier, Abbé Marc-Antoine. *Observations sur l'architecture.* The Hague and Paris, 1765.

Lauro, Giacomo. *Antiquae urbis splendor.* Rome, 1612–1628.

Lavoisier, Antoine Laurent de. "Mémoire sur les altérations qui arrivent à l'air dans plusieurs circonstances où se trouvent les hommes réunis en société," *Histoire de la Société Royale de Médecine 1782–1783 avec les Mémoires de médecine et de physique médicale, pour les mêmes années, tirés des registres de cette Société.* Paris, 1787.

Lavoisier, Antoine Laurent de. *Oeuvres de Lavoisier publiées par les soins de S. Exc. le Ministre de l'Instruction publique.* 6 vols. Paris, 1864–1893.

Le Brun, Corneille. *Voyage au Levant, c'est-à-dire, dans les principaux endroits de l'Asie Mineure.* Paris, 1714.

Le Camus de Mézières, Nicolas. *Le Génie de l'architecture, ou l'analogie de cet art avec nos sensations.* Paris, 1780.

Leclerc, Jean-Baptiste. *Rapport fait . . . sur les institutions relatives à l'état civil des citoyens.* Corps législatif, séance du 16 brumaire an VI [November 6, 1797]. Paris, year VI [1797].

Leclerc, Jean-Baptiste. *Règlement proposé . . . à la suite du Rapport sur les institutions civiles.* Corps législatif, séance du 17 brumaire an VI [November 7, 1797]. Paris, year VI [1797].

Ledoux, Claude-Nicolas. *L'Architecture considérée sous le rapport de l'art, des moeurs et de la législation.* Paris, 1804.

Legouvé, Gabriel-Marie. *Ouevres complètes.* 3 vols. Paris, 1826.

Le Moine, P. J. *Le Parallèle du Paris de la République, avec le Paris des rois.* Paris, year II.

Lenoir, Alexandre. *Description historique et chronologique des monuments de sculpture, réunis au Musée des Monuments Français,* 5th ed. Paris, year VIII.

Lenoir, Alexandre. *La Franche-maçonnerie rendue à sa véritable origine, ou l'antiquité de la Franche-maçonnerie prouvée par l'explication des mystères anciens et modernes.* Paris, 1814.

Lenoir, Alexandre. *Musée des monuments français, ou description historique et chronologique des statues en marbre et en bronze, bas-reliefs et tombeaux des hommes et des femmes célèbres, pour servir à l'histoire de France et à celle de l'art. . . .* Paris, year IX/1800.

Le Rouge, Georges-Louis. *Les Curiositez de Paris, de Versailles, de Marly.* 2 vols. Nouvelle édition. Paris, 1733.

Le Rouge, Georges-Louis. *Détail des nouveaux jardins anglo-chinois à la mode.* Paris, 1776–1788.

Le Roux de Lincy. *Description de la ville de Paris au XV^e siècle par Guillebert de Metz, publiée pour la première fois d'après le manuscrit unique.* Paris, 1855.

Le Roy, David. *Les Ruines des plus beaux monuments de la Grèce considérées du côté de l'histoire et du côté de l'architecture,* 2nd ed. 2 vols. Paris, 1770.

Le Roy, J.-B. "Précis d'un ouvrage sur les hôpitaux," *Histoire de l'Académie Royale des Sciences avec les Mémoires de mathématiques et de physiques, pour la même année, tirée des registres de cette Académie* (1787), 585–600. Paris, 1789.

*Lettres du baron de ***, à son ami, sur l'affaire des cimetières, avec des observations sur les arrêts de la Cour, du 3 septembre 1765, et 4 septembre 1780.* N.p., 1781.

Libavius, Andreas. *Alchymia.* Frankfurt, 1606.

Longinus. "On the Sublime," in *Classical Literary Criticism.* Trans. T. S. Dorsch. New York, 1965.

Loudon, J. C. "Remarks on Laying Out Public Gardens and Promenades," *Gardener's Magazine,* 11 (December 1835), 644–669.

Louis, Antoine. *Lettres sur la certitude des signes de la mort, où l'on rassure les citoyens de la crainte d'être enterrés vivants, avec des observations et des expériences sur les noyés.* Paris, 1752.

Lubersac de Livron, Charles-François, abbé de. *Discours sur les monuments publics de tous les âges et de tous les peuples connus, suivis d'une description du monument projeté à la gloire de Louis XVI et de la France, terminé par quelques observations sur les principaux monuments de la ville de Paris et plusieurs projets de décoration et d'utilité publique pour cette capitale.* Paris, 1775.

Marchant de Beaumont, François-Marie. *Itinéraire du curieux dans le Cimetière du P. La Chaise, ou l'Indicateur de ses plus beaux monuments et de ses plus beaux souvenirs; accompagné d'un plan sur leguel est tracée la route à suivre pour y visiter, dans une seule promenade, 250 monuments funèbres les plus remarquables, et jouir de ses plus beaux points de vue et de ses plus riches aspects.* Paris, 1825.

Marchant de Beaumont, François-Marie. *Le Nouveau conducteur de l'étranger à Paris en 1819.* Paris. 1819.

Marchant de Beaumont, François-Marie. *Vues pittoresques, historiques et morales du Cimetière du P. La Chaise, représentant ses aspects, ses sites, ses points de vue, les plus magnifiques, les scènes les plus touchantes. . . ,* vol. 1. Paris, 1821.

Maret, Hugues. *Mémoire sur l'usage où l'on est d'enterrer les morts dans les églises et dans l'enceinte des villes.* Dijon, 1773.

Maret, Hugues. "Cimetière," in *Supplément à l'Encyclopédie, ou Dictionnaire raisonné des sciences, des arts et des métiers, par une société des gens de lettres,* vol. 2, 428–430. Amsterdam, 1776.

Maret, Hugues. "Mémoire sur la construction d'un hôpital, dans lequel on détermine quel est le meilleur moyen à employer pour entretenir dans les infirmeries un air pur et salubre," in *Nouveaux Mémoires de l'Académie de Dijon, pour la partie des Sciences et Arts* (1782), 25–68. Dijon, 1783.

Martini, Joseph. *Theatrum Basilicae Pisanae.* Rome, 1705; 2d ed., 1728.

Marulli, Giacomo. *Su l'Architettura e su la nettezza della città.* Florence, 1808.

Mason, George. *An Essay on Design in Gardening.* London, 1768.

Maundrell, Henry. *Voyage d'Alep à Jerusalem, à Pâques en l'année 1697. Traduit de l'anglais.* Utrecht, 1705.

*Mémoire pour le doyen, chanoines et chapitre de l'Eglise royale, collégiale et paroissiale de Saint-Germain l'Auxerrois, à Paris. Intimez contre les marguilliers de l'oeuvre et fabrique de l'Eglise des Saints-Innocents, appellants.* Paris, 1737.

*Mémoire sur les sépultures, pour le sieur Pérard de Montreuil.* Paris, 1778.

*Mémoires sur les sépultures hors des villes; ou recueil de pièces concernant les cimetières de la ville de Versailles.* Versailles and Paris, 1774.

Menuret de Chambaud, Jean-Jacques. *Essai sur l'action de l'air dans les maladies contagieuses, qui a remporté le prix proposé par la Société Royale de Médecine.* Paris, 1781.

Menuret de Chambaud, Jean-Jacques. *Essais sur l'histoire médico-topographique de Paris, ou Lettres à M. d'Aumont . . . sur le climat de Paris, sur l'état de la médecine, sur le caractère et le traitement des maladies, et particulièrement sur la petite vérole et l'inoculation.* Paris, 1786.

Mercier, Louis-Sébastien. *L'An deux mille quatre cent quarante, rêve s'il en fut jamais.* Ed. Raymond Trousson. Bordeaux, 1971.

Mercier, Louis-Sébastien. *Opinion . . . sur les sépultures privées.* Corps législatif. Conseil des Cinq-Cents, séance du 18 frimaire an V [December 8, 1796]. [Paris, 1797?]

Mercier, Louis-Sébastien. *Tableau de Paris.* New ed., 4 vols. N.p., 1782.

Meyern, Conrad and Rudolf. *Die menschliche Sterblichkeit unter dem Titel Todten-Tanz in LXI. Original-Kupfern.* Hamburg and Leipzig, 1759.

[Molé, Guillaume-François-Roger]. *Lettre de M. M*** a M. J***, sur les moyens de transférer les cimetières hors l'enceinte des villes.* N.p., [1776].

Mopinot de la Chapotte, A. R. *Eloge historique de Pigalle . . . suivi d'un mémoire sur la sculpture en France, avec son portrait.* London and Paris, 1786.

Morel, Jean-Marie. *Théorie des jardins.* Paris, 1776.

"Mount Auburn," *Gleason's Pictorial Drawing Room Companion* (August 13, 1853), 104–105.

Mulot, François-Valentin. *Discours qui a partagé le prix proposé par l'Institut National de France, au nom du Gouvernement, et décerné le 15 vendémiaire an IX . . . sur cette question; Quelles sont les cérémonies à faire pour les funérailles, et le règlement à adopter pour le lieu de la sépulture?* Paris, year IX.

Mulot, François-Valentin. *Discours sur les funérailles et le respect dû aux morts.* Lu, le 15 thermidor, an IV [August 2, 1796], au Lycée des Arts. Paris, year IV.

M[ulot], F[rançois]-V[alentin]. *Vues d'un citoyen, ancien député à l'Assemblée législative, sur les sépultures.* N.p., [year V].

Navier, Pierre-Toussaint. *Réflexions sur les dangers des exhumations précipitées, et sur les abus des inhumations dans les églises; suivies d'observations sur les plantations d'arbres dans les cimetières.* Amsterdam and Paris, 1775.

[Necker, Madame]. *Des inhumations précipitées.* Paris, 1790.

Neufforge, Jean-François de. *Recueil élémentaire d'architecture.* 8 vols. Paris, 1757–1768.

Neufforge, Jean-François de. *Supplément au Recueil élémentaire d'architecture.* 2 vols. Paris, 1772–1780.

Norvins, Jacques-Marquet de. *Souvenirs d'un historien de Napoléon. Mémorial de J. de Norvins.* Ed. Louis de Lanzac de Laborie. 2 vols. Paris, 1896.

*Notes on Mount Auburn Cemetery, Edited by an Officer of the Corporation; Intended to Serve as a Stranger's Guide Book.* Boston, 1849.

*Observations sur les fosses d'aisance, et moyens de prévenir les inconvénients de leur vuidange, par MM. Laborie, Cadet le jeune, et Parmentier, membres du Collège de Pharmacie, etc., etc.* Imprimé par ordre et aux frais du gouvernement. Paris, 1778.

Olivier. *Sépultures des anciens, où l'on démontre qu'elles étaient hors des villes; l'on donne les moyens de revenir à l'ancien usage; et l'on expose les effets de la putréfaction, sur l'air et sur nous. par M. Olivier, docteur en médecine de Montpellier.* Marseille, 1771.

*Paris et ses curiosités avec une notice historique et descriptive des environs.* 2 vols. Paris, year XII/ 1804.

Pastoret, Emmanuel. *Rapport sur la violation des sépultures et des tombeaux, fait au nom de la Commission de la classification et de la révision des lois.* Corps législatif. Conseil des Cinq-Cents, séance du 26 prairial, l'an IV [June 14, 1796]. Paris, year IV [1796].

Patte, Pierre. *Enumération des ouvrages de P. Patte, architecte, adressée aux différents membres de l'Institut national des sciences et des arts.* [Paris, n.d.].

Patte, Pierre. *Mémoires qui intéressent particulièrement Paris.* Paris, year IX.

Patte, Pierre. *Mémoires sur les objets les plus importants de l'architecture.* Paris, 1769.

Patte, Pierre. *Monumens érigés en France à la gloire de Louis XV, précédés d'un Tableau du progrès des arts et des sciences sous ce règne, ainsi qu'une Description des honneurs des monuments de gloire accordés aux grands hommes.* . . . Paris, 1765.

Petit, Antoine. *Mémoire sur la meilleure manière de construire un hôpital de malades.* Paris, 1774.

Peyre, Marie-Joseph. *Oeuvres d'architecture.* Paris, 1765.

*The Picturesque Pocket Companion, and Visitor's Guide, through Mount Auburn.* Boston, 1839.

Piganiol de la Force. *Description historique de la ville de Paris et de ses environs.* 10 vols. Paris, 1765.

Pilâtre de Rozier, Jean-François. *Première expérience de la montgolfière . . . lancée . . . le 23 juin 1784.* 2d ed., Paris, 1784.

Pineau. *Mémoire sur le danger des inhumations précipitées, et sur la nécessité d'un règlement, pour mettre les citoyens à l'abri du malheur d'être enterrés vivants.* Paris, 1776.

*Plan du Cimetière du Mont-Louis dit du Père Lachaise. Avec la liste alphabétique de toutes les personnes qui ont des tombeaux ou des monuments.* Paris, 1820.

Pococke, Richard. *The Travels through England . . . during 1750, 1751, and Later Years,* vol. 1. Ed. James J. Cartwright. London, 1888.

Pommereul, F.-R.-J. *Mémoire sur les funérailles et les sépultures. Question proposée par le Ministère, et jugée par l'Institut, le 15 vendémiaire an IX.* Tours and Paris, year IX.

Poncet de la Grave, Guillaume. *Projet des embellissements de la ville et des faubourgs de Paris.* 3 vols. Paris, 1756.

Pope, Alexander, *Windsor Forest.* London, 1713.

Porée, Abbé Charles-Gabriel. *Lettres sur la sépulture dans les églises à Monsieur de C . . . [and] Observations sur les sépultures dans les églises, et réflexions sur les Lettres écrites à ce sujet.* Caen, 1749.

Poullet, Pierard. *Traicté des tombes et sépultures des deffuncts, par lequel est monstré qu'elles sont en la protection du droict divin et humain.* Paris, 1612.

Priestley, Joseph. *Experiments and Observations on Different Kinds of Air.* 2d ed. 2 vols. London, 1775.

Priestley, Joseph. "Observations et expériences sur différentes espèces d'air; par M. Joseph Priestley, docteur en droit, et membre de la Société Royale de Londres; lues dans les Assemblées de cette Société, les 5, 12, 19, et 26 mars 1772. Traduits de l'anglais," in Abbé François Rozier, *Observations et mémoires sur la physique, sur l'histoire naturelle et sur les arts,* 1 (1773), 292–325.

Prieur, Armand-Parfait, and Van Cléemputte, Pierre-Louis. *Collection des prix que la ci-devant Académie d'Architecture proposait et couronnait tous les ans, gravée au trait, imprimée sur papier propre à être lavé,* vol. 1. Paris, n.d.

*Procès-verbal de la première séance du Jury des Arts, nommé par la Convention Nationale, et assemblé . . . pour juger les ouvrages de peinture, sculpture et architecture mis au concours pour obtenir le prix.* Paris, year II.

*Procès-verbal de l'Assemblée générale du Clergé de France, tenue à Paris, au couvent des Grand-Augustins, en l'année 1775.* Ed. Abbé Du Lau. Paris, 1777.

*Procès-verbaux de l'Académie Royale d'Architecture, 1671–1793.* Ed. Henri Lemonnier. 10 vols. Paris, 1911–1929.

*Procès-verbaux de l'Académie des Beaux-Arts.* Ed. Marcel Bonnaire and Louis Hourticq. 3 vols. Paris, 1937–1943.

*Projet pour la parfaite salubrité de l'air dans la ville de Rouen, proposé aux amis de l'humanité, par le chevalier de . . . , citoyen.* N.p., n.d.

Pugin, Augustus. *Paris and Its Environs Displayed in a Series of Picturesque Views.* 2 vols. London, 1829–1831.

Quatremère de Quincy, Antoine-Chrysostôme. *De l'Architecture égyptienne considérée dans son origine, ses principes et son goût et comparée sous les mêmes rapports à l'architecture grecque. . . .* Paris, year XI/ 1803.

Quatremère de Quincy, Antoine-Chrysostôme. *Dictionnaire d'histoire d'architecture comprenant dans son plan les notions historiques, descriptives, archéologiques . . . de cet art.* 2 vols. Paris, 1832.

Quatremère de Quincy, Antoine-Chrysostôme. *Encyclopédie méthodique. Architecture.* 3 vols. Paris, 1788–1825.

Quatremère de Quincy, Antoine-Chrysostôme. *Histoire de la vie et des ouvrages des plus célèbres architectes du XIe siècle jusqu'à la fin du XVIIIe siècle, accompagnée par la vue du plus remarquable édifice de chacun d'eux.* Paris, 1830.

[Quatremère de Quincy, Antoine-Chrysostôme]. *Rapport fait au Conseil-Général, le 15 thermidor, an VIII sur l'instruction publique, le rétablissement des bourses, le scandale des inhumations actuelles, l'érection de cimetières, la restitution des tombeaux, mausolées, etc.* Paris, n.d.

Quatremère de Quincy, Antoine-Chrysostôme. *Rapport fait au Directoire du Département de Paris, le 13 novembre 1792 . . . sur l'état actuel du Panthéon français, sur les changements qui s'y sont opérés, sur les travaux qui restent à entreprendre. . . .* [Paris], n.d.

Quatremère de Quincy, Antoine-Chrysostôme. *Rapport fait au Directoire du Département de Paris, sur les travaux entrepris, continués ou achevés au Panthéon français, depuis le dernier compte rendu le 17 novembre 1792, et sur l'état actuel du monument, le deuxième jour du second mois de l'an II.* Paris, [1793].

Quatremère de Quincy, Antoine-Chrysostôme. *Rapport sur l'édifice dit de Sainte-Geneviève, fait au Directoire du Département de Paris.* Paris, 1791.

*Rapport des commissaires chargés par l'Académie de l'examen du projet d'un nouvel Hôtel-Dieu. Extrait des registres de l'Académie Royale des Sciences, du 22 novembre 1786.* Paris, 1786.

"Rapport des Mémoires et Projets pour éloigner les tueries de l'interieur de Paris." *Histoire de l'Académie Royale des Sciences* (1787), 19–43. Paris, 1789.

*Rapport sur plusiers questions proposées à la Société Royale de Médecine, par M. l'Ambassadeur de la Religion, de la part de son altesse eminentissime Monseigneur le Grand Maître, relativement aux inconvénients que l'ouverture des caveaux destinés aux sépultures d'une des églises paroissiales de l'île de Malte pourrait occasionner, et aux moyens de les prévenir, dans lequel, après avoir exposé les dangers des inhumations et des exhumations dans les églises, on indique les précautions à prendre dans la fouille d'un terrain suspect.* Lu dans la séance de la Société Royale de Médecine tenue au Louvre le 5 décembre 1780. Malta, 1781.

[Rast de Maupas]. *Réflexions d'un fossoyeur et d'un curé, sur les cimetières de la ville de Lyon.* Lyon, 1777.

Rauch, F.-A. *Harmonie hydro-végétale et météorologique, ou recherches sur les moyens de recréer avec nos fôrets la force des températures et la régularité des saisons, par des plantations raisonnées.* 2 vols. Paris, year X.

Regnault-Warin, J.-J. *Le Cimetière de la Madeleine.* 4 parts in 2 vols. Paris, year IX/1801.

*Requeste signifiée pour les marguilliers de l'oeuvre et fabrique des Saints-Innocents, appellants. Contre les doyens, chanoines et chapitre de Saint-Germain l'Auxerrois, intimez.* Paris, [1737].

Rigaud, Jean. *Stowe Gardens in Buckinghamshire.* London, 1746.

Ripa, Cesare. *Baroque and Rococo Pictorial Imagery. The 1758–80 Hertel Edition of Ripa's Iconologia with 200 Engraved Illustrations.* Ed. Edward A. Maser. New York, 1971.

Robinet. *Paris sans cimetière.* Paris, 1869.

Robinet, Jean-Baptiste-René. *Dictionnaire universel des sciences morale, économique, politique et diplomatique, ou Bibliothèque de l'homme d'état et du citoyen,* vol. 2. London, 1777.

Roederer, Pierre-Louis. *Des Institutions funéraires convenables à une république qui permet tous les cultes, et n'en adopte aucun.* Mémoire lu par Roederer, dans la séance publique de l'Institut National des Sciences et des Arts, le 15 messidor, l'an IV [July 3, 1796]. Paris, year IV [1796].

Roger père et fils. *Le Champ du repos, ou le Cimetière Mont-Louis, dit du Père De La Chaise.* 2 vols. Paris, 1816.

Ronèsse, A.-J. *Projet pour les sépultures, ouvrage qui a concouru pour le prix proposé par l'Institut National, au nom du Gouvernement, sur cette question: Quelles sont les cérémonies à faire pour les funérailles, et le règlement à adopter pour le lieu de la sépulture?* Paris, year IX.

Rousseau, Jean-Jacques. *Essai sur l'origine des langues.* Ed. C. Porset. Bordeaux, 1970.

Rousseau, Jean-Jacques. *Lettre à Mr. d'Alembert sur les spectacles.* Ed. M. Fuchs. Geneva, 1948.

Rousseau, Jean-Jacques. *Oeuvres complètes.* Bibliothèque de la Pléiade, 4 vols. Paris, 1959–1969.

Rousseau, Jean-Jacques. *Les Rêveries du promeneur solitaire.* Ed. H. Roddier. Paris, 1960.

*Rules and Regulations of the Green-Wood Cemetery; with a Catalogue of Proprietors, and Mr. Cleaveland's Descriptive Notes of "Green-Wood Illustrated."* New York, 1848, 1851, 1853.

"Rural Cemeteries," *North American Review* (October 1841), 385–412.

Saint-A., P. de. *Promenade aux cimetières de Paris, aux sépultures royales de Saint-Denis, et aux catacombes.* Paris, [1816].

Saint-A., P. de. *Promenade aux cimetières de Paris avec quarante-huit dessins représentant les principaux monumens qu'on y remarque, et particulièrement les tombeaux des personnages les plus célèbres,* 2d ed. 2 vols. Paris, 1825.

Saint-Just, Louis de. *L'Esprit de la Révolution suivi de Fragments sur les institutions républicaines.* Ed. Robert Mandrou. Paris, 1963.

Saint-Non, Jean-Claude Richard de. *Voyage pittoresque ou Description des royaumes de Naples et de Sicile.* 4 vols. Paris, 1781–1786.

Saint-Pierre, Jacques-Henri Bernardin de. *Etudes de la nature.* Paris, 1784.

Sauval, Henri. *Histoire et recherches des antiquités de la ville de Paris,* vol. 1. Paris, 1724.

Seeley, Benton. *Stowe: A Description of the Magnificent House and Gardens.* London, editions of 1745, 1750, 1763, 1769, 1777, 1788, 1797.

*Sépultures publiques et particulières.* Paris, year IX.

Serlio, Sebastiano. *Tutte l'opere d'architettura.* Venice, 1600.

Shenstone, William. *The Works in Verse and Prose of William Shenstone, Esq; Most of Which Were Never Before Printed.* Ed. R. Dodsley. 2 vols. London, 1764.

Shenstone, William. *The Works in Verse and Prose of William Shenstone, Esq; Volume III Containing Letters to Particular Friends, from the Year 1739 to 1763.* Ed. J. Dodsley. London, 1769.

Silva, Ercole. *Dell' Arte dei giardini inglesi.* Milan, year IX.

Smith, R. A. *Smith's Illustrated Guide to and through Laurel Hill Cemetery.* Philadelphia, 1852.

Sobry, Jean-François. *De l'Architecture.* Amsterdam and Paris, 1776.

Switzer, Stephen. *The Nobleman, Gentleman, and Gardener's Recreation:*

*or an Introduction to Gardening, Planting, Agriculture, and the Other Business and Pleasures of a Country Life*. London, 1715.

Switzer, Stephen. *Ichnographia Rustica: or, the Nobleman, Gentleman, and Gardener's Recreation*. 3 vols. London, 1718.

Tenon, Jacques-René. *Mémoires sur les hôpitaux de Paris*. Paris, 1788.

Thévenot, Jean. *Relation d'un voyage fait au Levant dans laquelle il est curieusement traité des estats sujets au grand seigneur, des moeurs, religions, forces, gouvernemens, politiques, langues, et coustumes des habitants de ce grand empire*. Paris, 1664.

Thiébaut, Arsenne. *Réflexions sur les pompes funèbres*. Paris, year VI [1797].

Thiébaut, Arsenne. *Voyage à l'isle des peupliers*. Paris, year VII.

Thiéry, Luc-Vincent. *Almanach du voyageur à Paris, année 1784*. Paris, 1784.

Thiéry, Luc-Vincent. *Guide des amateurs et des étrangers voyageurs à Paris*. 2 vols. Paris, 1787.

Thomson, James. *The Seasons*. Edition of 1746. Ed. John Beresford. London, 1927.

Thouret, Michel-Augustin. *Rapport sur les exhumations du Cimetière et de l'Eglise des Saints Innocents; lu dans la séance de la Société Royale de Médecine, tenue au Louvre le 3 mars 1789*. Paris, 1789.

Titi, Pandolfo. *Guida per il passaggiere dilettante di pittura, scultura ed architettura nella città di Pisa*. Lucca, 1751.

Trouvé. "Des Honneurs qu'on doit rendre aux morts," *Moniteur Universel*, 26 Germinal, year III/April 15, 1795.

Vafflard, Léon. *Notice sur les champs de sépultures anciens et modernes de la ville de Paris*. Paris, 1867.

Vafflard, Léon. *Plus de fosse commune! Le Cimetière de l'avenir. Méry-sur-Oise*. Paris, 1867.

Vauban, Sébastien le Prestre de. *Projet d'une dixme royale*. N.p., 1707.

Vaudoyer, A.-L.-T. *Idées d'un citoyen français sur le lieu destiné à la sépulture des hommes illustres de France*. Paris, [1791].

Vaudoyer, A.-L-T., and Baltard, Louis-Pierre. *Grands prix d'architecture. Projets couronnés par l'Académie Royale des Beaux-Arts en France*. Paris, 1818.

Velye, Machet. *Considérations importantes sur un des plus précieux monuments de la République française*. Paris, n.d.

Venturini, Giovanni Francesco. *Le Fontane ne' palazzi e ne' giardini di Roma*. (Vol. 3 of Falda, *Le Fontane*.) [Rome], n.d.

Vicq d'Azyr, Félix. *Essai sur les lieux et les dangers des sépultures. Traduit de l'italien (de Scipion Piattoli); publié avec quelques changements, et précédé d'un discours préliminaire. . . .* Paris, 1778.

Vicq d'Azyr, Félix. *Oeuvres de Vicq d'Azyr, recueillies et publiées avec des notes et un discours sur sa vie et ses ouvrages, par Jacques-Louis Moreau. . . .* 6 vols. Paris, year XIII/1805.

Viel de Saint-Maux, Jean-Louis. *Lettres sur l'architecture des anciens et celle des modernes dans lesquelles se trouve développé le génie symbolique qui présida aux monuments de l'antiquité.* Paris, 1787.

[Villedieu]. *Projet de catacombes, pour la ville de Paris, en adaptant à cet usage les carrières qui se trouvent tant dans son enceinte que dans ses environs.* London and Paris, 1782.

[Villeneuve]. *Vues pittoresques, plans, etc. des principaux jardins anglois qui sont en France: Ermenonville.* Paris, c. 1788.

Villette, Charles. *Lettres choisies de Charles Villette, sur les principaux évènements de la Révolution.* Paris, 1792.

Virgil, *Works*. Trans. H. Rushton Fairclough. 2 vols. London and New York, 1916.

Vitruvius. *The Ten Books of Architecture.* Trans. M. H. Morgan. New York, 1960.

Voltaire. *Lettres philosophiques.* Ed. René Pomeau. Paris, 1964.

[Voltaire]. *Recueil de pièces en vers et en prose, par l'auteur de la tragédie de Sémiramis.* Amsterdam, 1750.

*Vues des monuments construits dans les jardins de Franconville-La-Garenne appartenans à Madame la Comtesse d'Albon, gravés d'après ses dessins et ceux de M. de Lussi.* Paris, 1784.

Walpole, Horace. *Essay on Modern Gardening.* Strawberry Hill, 1785.

Walter, Cornelia W. *Mount Auburn Illustrated.* New York, 1847.

Watelet, Claude-Henri. *Essai sur les jardins.* Paris, 1774.

[West, Gilbert]. *Stowe, the Gardens of the Right Honourable Richard Lord Viscount Cobham. Address'd to Mr. Pope.* London, 1732.

Whately, Thomas. *L'Art de former les jardins modernes, ou l'art des jardins anglais, traduit de l'anglais.* Trans. François de Paule Latapie. Paris, 1771. (Contains William Chambers's *Traité des édifices . . . chinois.*)

Whately, Thomas. *Observations on Modern Gardening.* London, 1770.

Wither, George. *A Collection of Emblemes Ancient and Moderne.* London, 1635.

**Secondary Works**     Adams, William Howard. *The French Garden.* New York, 1979.

*The Age of Neo-Classicism.* Exhibition catalogue. The Arts Council of Great Britain. London, 1972.

Agulhon, Maurice. *La Sociabilité méridionale (Confréries et Associations dans la vie collective en Provence orientale à la fin du XVIIIe siècle).* Publications des Annales de la Faculté des Lettres, Aix-en-Provence, Série: Travaux et Mémoires, No. 36. 2 vols. Aix-en-Provence, 1966.

Allen, Beverly Sprague. *Tides in English Taste (1619–1800): A Background for the Study of Literature.* 2 vols. New York, 1958.

Alpers, Svetlana. "Is Art History?" *Daedalus* (Summer 1977), 1–13.

Ames, Oakes I. "Mount Auburn's Sixscore Years," in *Publications of the Cambridge Historical Society* (1951–1952), 77–95.

Ariès, Philippe. *Essais sur l'histoire de la mort en Occident, du moyen âge à nos jours.* Paris, 1975.

Ariès, Philippe. *L'Homme devant la mort.* Paris, 1977.

Aulard, François-Alphonse. *Christianity and the French Revolution*. Trans. Lady Fraser. Boston, 1927.

Aulard, François-Alphonse. *Le Culte de la Raison et le culte de l'Etre suprême (1793–1794). Essai historique*. Paris, 1892.

Auzelle, Robert. "Haussmann et les cimetières. Le Projet de Méry-sur-Oise," in Louis Réau, et al., *L'Oeuvre du Baron Haussmann, Préfet de la Seine (1853–1870)*. Paris, 1954.

Baltrusaitis, Jurgis. "Eighteenth-Century Gardens and Fanciful Landscapes," *Magazine of Art* (April 1952), 172–181.

Baltrusaitis, Jurgis. "Lands of Illusion: China and the Eighteenth-Century Garden," *Landscape*, 11 (Winter 1961–1962), 5–11.

Bardet, Gaston. *Naissance et méconnaissance de l'urbanisme, Paris*. Paris, 1951.

Beck-Friis, Johan. *The Protestant Cemetery in Rome*. Malmö, 1956.

Bernard, Antoine. *La Sépulture en droit canonique du Décret de Gratien au Concile de Trente*. Paris, 1933.

Bertrand, Régis. "Une Contribution à l'histoire du sentiment: cimetières et pratiques funéraires à Marseille du milieu du XVIIIe siècle à la fin du XIXe." *Les Conférences de l'Institut historique de Provence, janvier-février 1970*, 264–267.

Biver, Marie-Louis. *Le Paris de Napoléon*. Paris, 1963.

Biver, Marie-Louis. *Pierre Fontaine, premier architecte de l'empereur*. Paris, 1964.

Bosher, J. F. *French Finances 1770–1795; From Business to Bureaucracy*. Cambridge, 1970.

Boudon, Françoise. "La salubrité du Grenier de l'Abondance à la fin XVIIIe siècle," *Dix-huitième siècle*, 9 (1977), 171–180.

Braham, Allan. *The Architecture of the French Enlightenment*. Berkeley and Los Angeles, 1980.

Brémond, Henri. *Histoire littéraire du sentiment religieux en France depuis la fin des guerres de religion jusqu'à nos jours*, vol. 9: *La vie chrétienne sous l'Ancien Régime*. Paris, 1932.

Brown, Frederick. *Père Lachaise, Elysium as Real Estate*. New York, 1973.

Brownell, Morris R. *Alexander Pope and the Arts in Georgian England*. Oxford, 1978.

Bruegmann, Robert. "Architecture of the Hospital, 1770–1870. Design and Technology." Doctoral dissertation. University of Pennsylvania, 1976.

Buffenoir, Hippolyte. "Les Cendres de J.-J. Rousseau au jardin des Tuileries," *Annales de la Société Jean-Jacques Rousseau*, 7 (1911), 41–46.

Burgelin, Pierre. *La Philosophie de l'existence de J.-J. Rousseau*. Paris, 1952.

Caso, Jacques de. " 'Venies ad tumulos. Respice Sepulcra.' Remarques sur Boullée et l'architecture funéraire à l'âge des Lumières," *Revue de l'Art*, 32 (1976), 15–22.

Cassirer, Ernst. *The Philosophy of the Enlightenment*. Trans. F. C. A. Koelln and J. P. Pettegrove. Boston, 1966.

Castelli, Urano, and Gagetti, Ranieri. *Pisa and Her Artists*. Florence, 1977.

Chalker, John. *The English Georgic. A Study in the Development of a Form*. London, 1969.

Charageat, Marguerite. *L'Art des jardins*. Paris, 1962.

Chastel, André. "Le Baroque et la mort," in *Retorica e barocco: atti del III Congresso Internazionale di Studi Umanistici*, Venice, June 15–18, 1954. Rome, 1955.

Chastel, André, et al. "L'Aménagement du marché central de Paris de la 'Réformation des Halles' du XVIe Siècle à celle du XIXe," *Bulletin Monumental*, 127 (1960), 7–26, 69–106.

Chaunu, Pierre. *La Civilisation de l'Europe des Lumières*. Paris, 1971.

Chaunu, Pierre. "Mourir à Paris (XVIe–XVIIe–XVIIIe siècles)," *Annales: Economies, Sociétés, Civilisations* (janvier-février 1976), 29–50.

Christ, Ivan. *Paris des utopies*. Paris, 1970.

"Cimetière romain à Arles," *Le Magasin Pittoresque*, 29 (1861), 363–365.

Circaud, E. "Projet ou plan d'un Elysée, tracé par Bernardin de Saint-Pierre, qui devait être placé dans une des îles de la Seine, près du pont de Neuilly," *Bulletin de la Commission municipale historique et artistique de Neuilly-sur-Seine*, 8 (1910), 9–10.

Clark, H. F. "Eighteenth-Century Elysiums: The Role of 'Association' in the Landscape Movement," *Journal of the Warburg Institute* 6 (1943), 165–189.

Clarke, George B. "Grecian Taste and Gothic Virtue: Lord Cobham's Gardening Programme and Its Iconography," in *The Splendors of Stowe*, offprint from *Apollo* (June 1973), 26–31.

Clarke, George B. "The History of Stowe—IV. Sir Richard Temple's House and Gardens," *The Stoic* (March 1968), 65–80.

Clarke, George B. "The History of Stowe—VII. The Vanbrugh-Bridgeman Gardens," *The Stoic* (July 1969), 257–264.

Clarke, George B. "The History of Stowe—VIII. Military Gardening: Bridgeman and the Ha-Ha," *The Stoic* (December 1969), 11–15.

Clarke, George B. "The History of Stowe—X. Moral Gardening." *The Stoic* (July 1970), 113–121.

Clarke, George B. "The History of Stowe—XIII. Kent and the Eastern Gardens," *The Stoic* (July 1971), 265–272.

Clarke, George B. "The History of Stowe—XIX. Earl Temple's Gardens: The First Phase," *The Stoic* (December 1973), 265–268.

Coffin, David R. *The Villa d'Este at Tivoli*. Princeton, 1960.

Coffin, David R. *The Villa in the Life of Renaissance Rome*. Princeton, 1979.

*Coins d'autrefois. Gravures anciennes concernant les services de la direction des affaires municipales reproduites pour l'Exposition Universelle de 1900.* [Paris], 1900.

*Country Houses in Great Britain.* Exhibition catalogue. Yale Center for British Art. New Haven, 1979.

Crocker, Lester G. *Jean-Jacques Rousseau.* 2 vols. New York, 1968–1973.

*Crosscurrents: French and Italian Neoclassical Drawings and Prints from the Cooper-Hewitt Museum.* Exhibition catalogue. Washington, D.C., 1978.

Curl, James Stevens. *A Celebration of Death.* New York, 1980.

Curl, James Stevens. *The Victorian Celebration of Death.* Newton Abbot, 1972.

Curtius, Ernst Robert. *European Literature and the Latin Middle Ages.* Trans. Willard R. Trask. New York, 1963.

Darnton, Robert. *Mesmerism and the End of the Enlightenment in France.* New York, 1970.

*De Belleville à Charonne. Promenade historique à travers le XXe arrondissement.* Exhibition catalogue. Musée Carnavalet. Paris, 1979.

*Delille, est-il mort?* Clermont-Fernand, 1976.

Des Cilleuls, Alfred. *Le Domaine de la Ville de Paris dans le présent et dans le passé.* Paris, 1885.

Des Cilleuls, Alfred. *Histoire de l'administration parisienne au XIXe siècle.* 3 parts. Paris, 1900.

Des Cilleuls, Alfred. *Origines et développement du régime des travaux publics en France.* Paris, 1895.

*Deux siècles d'opéra français.* Bibliothèque Nationale, Musée de l'Opéra. Paris, 1972.

Dommanget, Maurice. "La Déchristianisation à Beauvais, les sacrements civiques," *Annales révolutionnaires,* 11 (1919), 160–194.

Dowley, Francis H. "D'Angiviller's *Grands Hommes* and the Significant Moment." *The Art Bulletin,* 39 (1957), 259–277.

Draper, John W. *The Funeral Elegy and the Rise of English Romanticism.* New York, 1967.

Du Camp, Maxime. *Paris, ses organes, ses fonctions et sa vie dans la seconde moitié du XIXe siècle,* vol. 3, 6th ed. Paris, 1879.

Dufour, Abbé Valentin. "Le Cimetière des Saints-Innocents et le quartier des Halles," in F. Hoffbauer, *Paris à travers les âges,* vol. 2, 1–28. Paris, 1882–1885.

Dufour, Abbé Valentin. *La Danse macabre des Saints-Innocents de Paris d'après l'édition de 1484 précédée d'une étude sur le cimetière, le charnier et la fresque peinte en 1425.* Paris, 1874.

Duparc, Pierre, "Le Cimetière, séjour des vivants (XIe–XIIe siècle)," *Bulletin philologique et historique* (1964), 483–504.

Durling, Dwight L. *Georgic Tradition in English Poetry.* Port Washington, N.Y., 1914.

Egbert, Donald Drew. *The Beaux-Arts Tradition in French Architecture, Illustrated by the Grands Prix de Rome.* Ed. David Van Zanten. Princeton, 1980.

Essar, Dennis F. *The Language Theory, Epistemology, and Aesthetics of Jean Lerond d'Alembert*. Studies on Voltaire and the Eighteenth Century, ed. T. Besterman, vol. 159. Oxford, 1976.

Etlin, Richard. "L'Air dans l'urbanisme des Lumières," *Dix-huitième siècle*, 9 (1977), 123–134.

Etlin, Richard. "Architecture and the Festival of Federation, Paris, 1790," *Architectural History*, 18 (1975), 23–42.

Etlin, Richard. "The Cemetery and the City: Paris, 1744–1804." Doctoral dissertation. Princeton University, 1978.

Etlin, Richard A. " 'Les Dedans,' Jacques-François Blondel and the System of the Home," *Gazette des Beaux-Arts*, 91 (1978), 137–147.

Etlin, Richard. "Etienne-Louis Boullée," in *The Macmillan Encyclopedia of Architects*, vol. 1, 262–264. New York, 1982.

Etlin, Richard. "The Geometry of Death," *Progressive Architecture* (May 1982), 134–137.

Etlin, Richard. "Landscapes of Eternity: Funerary Architecture and the Cemetery, 1793–1881," *Oppositions*, 8 (1977), 14–31.

*The Eye of Thomas Jefferson*. Ed. William Howard Adams. Exhibition catalogue. National Gallery of Art. Washington, D.C., 1976.

Favre, Robert. "Du 'médico-topographique' à Lyon en 1783," *Dix-huitième siècle*, 9 (1977), 151–160.

Fay, Bernard. *La Franc-maçonnerie et la révolution intellectuelle du XVIIIe siècle*. New edition. Paris, 1961.

*Les Fêtes de la Révolution*. Exhibition catalogue. Musée Bargoin. Clermont-Ferrand, 1974.

Foisil, Madeleine. "Les Attitudes devant la mort au XVIIIe siècle: sépultures et suppressions de sépultures dans le cimetière parisien des Saints-Innocents," *Revue historique*, No. 510 (avril–juin 1974), 303–330.

Fortier, Bruno. "La Maîtrise de l'eau," *Dix-huitième siècle*, 9 (1977), 193–202.

Fortier, Bruno, et al. *La Politique de l'espace parisien à la fin de l'ancien régime*. Paris, 1975.

Fortier, Bruno. "L'Urbanisme parisien à la fin de l'ancien régime," *Espaces et sociétés*, 13–14 (octobre 1974–janvier 1975), 5–17.

Foucault, Michel. *The Birth of the Clinic: An Archaeology of Medical Perception*. Trans. A. M. Sheridan Smith. New York, 1975.

Foucault, Michel. *Histoire de la folie à l'âge classique. . . .* New edition. Paris, 1972.

French, Stanley. "The Cemetery as Cultural Institution: The Establishment of Mount Auburn and the 'Rural Cemetery' Movement," in *Death in America*, ed. David E. Stannard, 69–91. Philadelphia, 1975.

*Furor Hortensis: Essays on the History of the English Landscape Garden in Memory of H. F. Clark*. Ed. Peter Willis. Edinburgh, 1974.

Ganay, Ernest, comte de. *Les Jardins de France et leur décor*. Paris, 1949.

Gannal, Félix. *Les Cimetières depuis la fondation de la monarchie française jusqu'à nos jours. Histoire et législation par le docteur Gannal. Vol. 1. Les Cimetières avant la Revolution.* Paris, [1884].

Giamatti, A. Bartlett. *The Earthly Paradise and the Renaissance Epic.* Princeton, 1966.

Gibbon, Michael J. "The History of Stowe—IX. Gilbert West's Walk through the Gardens in 1731." *The Stoic* (March 1970), 57–64.

Gibbon, Michael J. "The History of Stowe—XI. Lord Cobham's Garden Buildings, Part I (1715–1737): Vanbrugh, Gibbs, Kent," *The Stoic* (December 1970), 171–182.

Gibbon, Michael J. "The History of Stowe—XII. Lord Cobham's Garden Buildings, Part II: Gibbs (1738—1748); the Question of the Grecian Temple." *The Stoic* (March 1971) 209–215.

Gibbon, Michael J. "The History of Stowe—XXI. The Garden Buildings of Earl Temple and the Marquis of Buckingham," *The Stoic* (December 1974) 121–128.

Goldwater, Robert, and Treves, Marco, eds. *Artists on Art from the XIV to the XX Century.* New York, 1972.

Greenbaum, Louis S. "Health-Care and Hospital Building in Eighteenth-Century France: Reform Proposals of Du Pont de Nemours and Condorcet," in *Studies on Voltaire and the Eighteenth Century.* Ed. T. Besterman, 152 (1976), 895–930.

Gruber, Alain-Charles. *Les Grandes fêtes et leurs décors à l'époque de Louis XVI.* Geneva and Paris, 1972.

Guillerme, Jacques. "Lequeu et l'invention du mauvais goût." *Gazette des Beaux-Arts,* 66 (September 1965), 153–163.

Guillerme, Jacques. "Le Sain et le malsain dans l'économie de la nature," *Dix-huitième siècle,* 9 (1977), 61–72.

Guillerme, Jacques, and Harouel, Jean-Louis. "Lubersac et les infortunes de la dédicace," *Gazette des Beaux-Arts* 94 (1981), 104–110.

Hallays, André. *Autour de Paris.* Paris, 1911.

Hannaway, Owen, and Hannaway, Caroline. "La Fermature du cimetière des Innocents," *Dix-huitième siècle,* 9 (1977), 181–192.

Harouel, Jean-Louis. "Les Fonctions de l'alignement dans l'organisme urbain," *Dix-huitième siècle,* 9 (1977), 135–150.

Harris, John. "Le Geay, Piranesi and International Neoclassicism in Rome 1740–1750," in *Essays in the History of Architecture Presented to Rudolf Wittkower,* ed. D. Fraser, H. Hibbard, and M. J. Lewine, 189–196. London, 1967.

Harris, John. *Sir William Chambers, Knight of the Polar Star.* London, 1970.

Hautecoeur, Louis, *Histoire de l'architecture classique en France,* vol. 5: *Révolution et Empire 1792–1815.* Paris, 1953.

Hazard, Paul. *La Pensée européenne au XVIIIe siècle de Montesquieu à Lessing.* Paris, 1963.

Héron de Villefosse, René. *Prés et bois parisiens.* Paris, 1942.

Hibberd, John. *Salomon Gessner, His Creative Achievement and Influence.* Cambridge, 1976.

Hillairet, Jacques. *Les 200 cimetières du vieux Paris.* Paris, 1958.

Hillairet, Jacques. *Evocation du vieux Paris: les faubourgs.* Paris, 1953.

Honour, Hugh. *Neo-classicism.* Harmondsworth, 1968.

Huizinga, Johan. *The Waning of the Middle Ages.* New York, 1954.

Hunt, John Dixon. "Emblem and Expressionism in the Eighteenth-Century Landscape Garden," *Eighteenth-Century Studies,* 4 (1971), 294–317.

Hunt, John Dixon. *The Figure in the Landscape: Poetry, Painting and Gardening during the Eighteenth Century.* Baltimore, 1976.

Hunt, John Dixon, and Willis, Peter. *The Genius of the Place: The English Landscape Garden 1620–1820.* London, 1975.

Hussey, Christopher. *English Gardens and Landscapes 1700–1750.* New York, 1967.

Hussey, Christopher. *The Picturesque: Studies in a Point of View.* London and New York, 1927.

Ingersoll-Smouse, Florence. *La Sculpture funéraire en France au XVIIIe siècle.* Paris, n.d.

Jacot, R.-S. *Notice historique et descriptive du Cimetière du Père-Lachaise.* Paris, 1864.

*Jardins en France 1760–1820, Pays d'illusion, terre d'expériences.* Exhibition catalogue. Caisse Nationale des Monuments Historiques et des Sites, Hôtel de Sully. Paris, 1977.

Jarry, Paul. *Vieilles demeures parisiennes.* Paris, 1945.

Kalnein, Werd Graf, and Levey, Michael. *Art and Architecture of the Eighteenth Century in France.* Baltimore and Harmondsworth, 1972.

Kaufmann, Emil. *Architecture in the Age of Reason: Baroque and Post-Baroque in England, Italy, France.* New York, 1968.

Kaufmann, Emil. "Etienne-Louis Boullée," *The Art Bulletin,* 21 (1939), 213–227.

Kaufmann, Emil. *Da Ledoux a Le Corbusier: Origine e sviluppo dell'architettura autonoma.* Trans. Claudio Bruni. Milan, 1975.

Kaufmann, Emil. "Three Revolutionary Architects, Boullée, Ledoux, Lequeu," *Transactions of the American Philosophical Society,* 42 (1952), 431–559.

Kiernan, Colm. *The Enlightenment and Science in Eighteenth-Century France,* 2d ed. Studies on Voltaire and the Eighteenth Century, ed. T. Besterman, vol. 59a. Oxford, 1973.

Lankheit, Klaus. *Der Tempel der Vernunft: Unveröffentlichte Zeichnungen von Boullée.* Schriftenreihe des Instituts für Geschichte und Theorie der Architektur an der Eidgenössischen Technischen Hochschule Zürich, No. 2. Basel and Stuttgart, 1968.

Lavedan, Pierre. *Histoire de l'urbanisme,* vol. 2: *Renaissance et temps modernes,* 2d ed. Paris, 1959.

Le Bras, Gabriel. "L'Invasion de l'Eglise dans la cité. Programme de recherche historique sur les rapports de l'urbanisme et du droit canon," in *Urbanisme et architecture. Etudes écrites et publiées en l'honneur de Pierre Lavedan*. Paris, 1954.

Lebrun, François. *Les Hommes et la mort en Anjou aux XVIIe et XVIIIe siècles: Etude de démographie et de psychologie historique*. Paris and The Hague, 1971.

Le Clere, Marcel. *Cimetières et sépultures de Paris*. Paris, 1978.

Lee, Rensselaer W. *Ut Pictura Poesis: The Humanistic Theory of Painting*. New York, 1967.

Le Flamanc, Auguste. *Les Utopies prérévolutionnaires et la philosophie du XVIIIe siècle*. Paris, 1934.

Lemas, Thomas. "La Chute d'une montgolfière à Lacaune en 1785," *La Révolution française*, 27 (1894), 545–547.

Lemoine, Henri. "Les Cimetières de Paris de 1760 à 1825," *Bulletin de la Société de l'Histoire de Paris et de l'Ile-de-France*, 1924, 78–102.

Lemoine, Henri. "Les Quais et les ponts de Paris d'autrefois," *Bulletin de la Société de l'Histoire de Paris et de l'Ile-de-France*, 1925, 30–42.

McCloy, Shelby T. *The Humanitarian Movement in Eighteenth-Century France*. Lexington, Ky., 1957.

McManners, John. *French Ecclesiastical Society under the Ancien Régime: A Study of Angers in the Eighteenth Century*. Manchester, 1960.

McManners, John. *Reflections at the Death Bed of Voltaire: The Art of Dying in Eighteenth-Century France*. An Inaugural Lecture Delivered before the University of Oxford on November 21, 1974. London, 1975.

Mack, Maynard. *The Garden and the City: Retirement and Politics in the Late Poetry of Pope, 1731–1743*. Toronto, 1969.

Mâle, Emile. *Religious Art from the Twelfth to the Eighteenth Century*. New York, 1949.

Malins, Edward. *English Landscaping and Literature, 1660–1840*. London, 1966.

Marconi, Paolo, et al. *I disegni di architettura dell' Archivio storico dell' Accademia di San Luca*. 2 vols. Rome, 1974.

Marle, Raimond van. *Iconographie de l'art profane au Moyen-Age et à la Renaissance et la décoration des demeures*. 2 vols. New York, 1971.

Martineau, Jean. *Les Halles de Paris des origines à 1789. Evolution matérielle, juridique et économique*. Paris, 1960.

Mathieu, Mae. *Pierre Patte, sa vie et son oeuvre*. Paris, 1940.

Mauzi, Robert. *L'Idée du bonheur dans la littérature et la pensée françaises au XVIIIe siècle*. Paris, 1960.

Messerer, Wilhelm. "Zu extremen Gedanken über Bestattung und Grabmal um 1800," *Kunstgeschichte und Kunsttheorie im 19. Jahrhundert*, 172–194. Berlin, 1963.

Michéa, R. "Le 'Plaisir des tombeaux' au XVIIIe siècle," *Revue de littérature comparée*, 18 (1938), 287–311.

Monglond, André. *Le Préromantisme français*. 2 vols. Paris, 1965.

Monin, Hippolyte. *L'Etat de Paris en 1789, études et documents sur l'Ancien régime à Paris*. Paris, 1889.

Monk, Samuel H. *The Sublime: A Study of Critical Theories in Eighteenth-Century England.* Ann Arbor, 1960.

Morawińska, Agnieszka. "Eighteenth-Century 'Paysages Moralisés,' " *Journal of the History of Ideas,* 38 (July–September 1977), 461–475.

Mornet, Daniel. *Le Romantisme en France au XVIIIe siècle.* Paris, n.d.

Mornet, Daniel. *Le Sentiment de la nature de J.-J Rousseau à Bernardin de Saint-Pierre, essai sur les rapports de la littérature et des moeurs.* . . . Paris, 1907.

Mortier, Roland. "Sensibility, Neoclassicism, or Preromanticism?" in *Eighteenth Century Studies Presented to Arthur M. Wilson,* ed. Peter Gay, 155–163. Hanover, N.H. [1972].

Neumeyer, Alfred. "Monuments to 'Genius' in German Classicism," *Journal of the Warburg Institute,* 2 (1938–1939), 159–163.

Neumeyer, Eva Maria. "The Landscape Garden as a Symbol in Rousseau, Goethe and Flaubert," *Journal of the History of Ideas,* 8 (1947), 187–217.

Nicolson, Majorie Hope. *The Breaking of the Circle: Studies in the Effect of the "New Science" on Seventeenth-Century Poetry,* rev. ed. New York, 1962.

Nicolson, Majorie Hope. *Mountain Gloom and Mountain Glory: The Development of the Aesthetics of the Infinite.* New York, 1973.

Nicolson, Marjorie Hope. *Newton Demands the Muse: Newton's 'Opticks' and the Eighteenth Century Poets.* Princeton, 1966.

Oechslin, Werner. "Pyramide et sphère, notes sur l'architecture révolutionnaire du XVIIIe siècle et ses sources italiennes," *Gazette des Beaux-Arts,* 77 (avril 1971), 201–238.

Oenslager, Donald. *Stage Design. Four Centuries of Scenic Invention.* New York, 1975.

Ozouf, Mona. "Architecture et urbanisme: l'image de la ville chez Claude-Nicolas Ledoux," *Annales: Economies, Sociétés, Civilisations* (novembre–décembre 1966), 1273–1304.

Ozouf, Mona. "Le Cortège et la ville: les itinéraires parisiens des fêtes révolutionnaires," *Annales: Economies, Sociétés, Civilisations* (septembre–octobre 1971), 889–916.

Ozouf, Mona. *La Fête révolutionnaire 1789–1799.* Paris, 1976.

Ozouf, Mona. "La Fête sous la Révolution française," in Jacques le Goff and Pierre Nora, *Faire de l'histoire,* vol. 3, 256–277. Paris, 1974.

Ozouf, Mona. "Symboles et fonctions des âges dans les fêtes de l'époque révolutionnaire," *Annales historiques de la Révolution française* (octobre–décembre 1970), 569–593.

Panofsky, Erwin. *Meaning in the Visual Arts.* New York, 1955.

Parmentier, A. "Les Boulevards de Paris au XVIIIe siècle," *Revue du dix-huitième siècle,* 1 (avril–juin 1913), 121–137.

Passy, Louis. *Frochot, préfet de la Seine.* Evreux, 1867.

Paul-Albert N. *Histoire du Cimetière du Père La Chaise: vieilles tombes, vieux souvenirs.* Paris, 1937.

Paulson, Ronald. *Emblem and Expression: Meaning in English Art of the Eighteenth Century.* Cambridge, 1975.

*Secondary Works*

Pérouse de Montclos, Jean-Marie. "Charles-François Viel, architecte de l'Hôpital général, et Jean-Louis Viel de Saint-Maux, architecte, peintre et avocat au Parlement de Paris," *Bulletin de la Société de l'Histoire de l'Art français* (1966), 257–269.

Pérouse de Montclos, Jean-Marie. *Etienne-Louis Boullée 1728–1799, de l'architecture classique à l'architecture révolutionnaire.* Paris, 1969.

Pérouse de Montclos, Jean-Marie. *Etienne-Louis Boullée, 1728—1799: Theoretician of Revolutionary Architecture.* Trans. James Emmons. New York, 1974.

Perrot, Jean-Claude. "Genèse d'une ville moderne: Caen au XVIIIe siècle." 2 vols. Service de reproduction des thèses, Université de Lille III, 1974.

Pevsner, Nikolaus, ed. *The Picturesque Garden and Its Influence outside the British Isles.* Washington, D.C., 1974.

Pevsner, Nikolaus, and Lang, S. "The Egyptian Revival," in *Studies in Art, Architecture and Design*, vol. 1, 213–248. New York, 1968.

Pinkney, David H. *Napoleon III and the Rebuilding of Paris.* Princeton, 1972.

*Piranèse et les Français 1740–1790.* Exhibition catalogue. Académie de France à Rome. Rome, 1976.

*Pisa. Tre secoli di guide.* Exhibition catalogue. Museo Nazionale e Civico di San Matteo. Pisa, 1977.

Poisson, George. *Evocation du grand Paris. La Banlieu nord-ouest.* Paris, 1960.

Poisson, George. *Napoléon et Paris.* Paris, 1964.

Praz, Mario. *On Neoclassicism.* Trans. Angus Davidson. London, 1969.

Proust, Jacques. *L'Encyclopédie.* Paris, 1965.

Pupil, François. "Aux Sources du Romantisme, le XVIIIe siècle et les ténèbres," *L'Information d'histoire de l'art* (mars–avril 1974), 55–65.

Read, John. *Prelude to Chemistry: An Outline of Alchemy, Its Literature and Relationships.* New York, 1937.

Reutersvärd, Oscar. "De 'Sjunkande,' cenotafierna hos Moreau, Fontaine, Boullée och Gay." *Konsthistorisk Tidskrift*, 28 (1959), 110–124.

Reutersvärd, Oscar. "De Sjunkna bågarna hos Ledoux, Boullée, Cellerier och Fontaine," *Konsthistorisk Tidskrift*, 29 (1960), 98–118.

Robiquet, Paul. *Le Personnel municipal de Paris pendant la Révolution. Période constitutionelle.* Paris, 1890.

Roche, Daniel. " 'La Mémoire de la Mort:' recherche sur la place des arts de mourir dans la librarie et la lecture en France au XVIIe et XVIIIe siècles," *Annales: Economies, Sociétés, Civilisations* (janvier–février 1976), 76–119.

Rosenau, Helen. *Boullée and Visionary Architecture.* London and New York, 1976.

Rosenau, Helen. *Boullée's Treatise on Architecture.* London, 1953.

Rosenau, Helen. *Social Purpose in Architecture: Paris and London Compared, 1760–1800.* London, 1970.

Rosenblum, Robert. *Transformations in Late Eighteenth Century Art.* Princeton, 1970.

Røstvig, Maren-Sofie. *The Happy Man: Studies in the Metamorphoses of a Classical Ideal, 1600–1700.* 2 vols. Oslo, 1954–1958.

Rothstein, Eric. " 'Ideal Presence' and the 'Non Finito' in Eighteenth-Century Aesthetics," *Eighteenth-Century Studies,* 9 (1976), 307–332.

Rotundo, Barbara. "Mount Auburn Cemetery: A Proper Boston Institution," *Harvard Library Bulletin,* 22 (July 1974), 268–279.

Rotundo, Barbara. "The Rural Cemetery Movement," *Essex Institute Historical Collections,* 109 (July 1973), 231–240.

Saddy, Pierre. "Le Cycle des immondices." *Dix-huitième siècle,* 9 (1977), 203–214.

Schapiro, Meyer. Review of "The City of the Architect Ledoux", by Emil Kaufmann, *The Art Bulletin,* 18 (1936), 265–266.

Schneider, René. *Quatremère de Quincy et son intervention dans les arts, 1788–1830.* Paris, 1910.

Schuhl, Pierre-Maxime. "Le Mémorial de Jaegerspris," *Gazette des Beaux-Arts,* 85 (February 1975), 49–60.

Sedlmayr, Hans. *Verlust der Mitte; die bildende Kunst des 19. und 20. Jahrhunderts als Symbol der Zeit.* Salzburg, [1948].

Silvestre de Sacy, Jacques. *Alexandre-Théodore Brongniart, 1739–1813. Sa vie, son oeuvre.* Paris, n.d.

Silvestre de Sacy, Jacques. *Le Quartier des Halles.* Paris, 1969.

Souchal, François. *Les Slodtz, sculpteurs et décorateurs du Roi, 1685–1764.* Paris, 1967.

Sozzi, Lionello. "I 'Sepolcri' e le discussioni francesi sulle tombe negli anni del Direttorio e del Consolato," *Giornale Storico della Letteratura Italiana,* 144 (1967), 567–588.

Stafford, Barbara Maria. "Rude Sublime: The Taste for Nature's Collosi during the Late Eighteenth and Early Nineteenth Centuries," *Gazette des Beaux-Arts,* 87 (1976), 113–126.

Stafford, Barbara Maria. "Toward Romantic Landscape Perception: Illustrated Travels and the Rise of 'Singularity' as an Aesthetic Category," *The Art Quarterly,* new series, 1 (autumn 1977), 89–124.

Starobinski, Jean. *1789, les emblèmes de la raison.* Paris, 1973.

Starobinski, Jean. *L'Invention de la liberté, 1700–1789.* Geneva, 1964.

Starobinski, Jean. *Jean-Jacques Rousseau: la transparence et l'obstacle, suivi de sept essais sur Rousseau.* Paris, 1971.

Steefel, Lawrence D., Jr. "A Neglected Shadow in Poussin's *Et in Arcadia Ego,*" *The Art Bulletin,* 57 (1975), 99–101.

Sterling, Charles. *La Nature morte de l'antiquité à nos jours.* Paris, 1952.

Stern, Jean. *A l'Ombre de Sophie Arnould, François-Joseph Belanger, architecte des Menus-Plaisirs, Premier architecte du comte d'Artois.* 2 vols. Paris, 1930.

Stillman, Damie. "Death Defied and Honor Upheld: The Mausoleum in Neo-Classical England," *The Art Quarterly*, new series, 1 (summer 1978), 175–213.

Szambien, Werner. "Notes sur le Recueil d'Architecture privée de Boullée (1792–1796)," *Gazette des Beaux-Arts*, 94 (1981), 111–124.

Tapié, Victor L. *Baroque et classicisme*, 2d ed. Paris, 1972.

Tenenti, Alberto. *Il Senso della morte e l'amore della vita nel Rinascimento (Francia e Italia).* Turin, 1957.

Tenenti, Alberto. *La Vie et la mort à travers l'art du XVe siècle.* Paris, 1952.

Thacker, Christopher. "Voltaire and Rousseau: Eighteenth-Century Gardeners," *Studies on Voltaire and the Eighteenth Century*, 90 (1972), 1592–1614.

Trahard, Pierre. *La Sensibilité révolutionnaire (1789–1794).* Paris, 1936.

Tuveson, Ernest. "Space, Diety and the Natural Sublime," *Modern Language Quarterly*, 12 (1951), 20–38.

Van Lennep, J. *Art et alchimie. Etude de l'iconographie hermétique et de ses influences.* Bruxelles, 1971.

Van Tieghem, Paul. *Le Préromantisme. Etudes d'histoire littéraire européenne.* 3 vols. Paris, 1924–1930.

Van Tieghem, Paul. *Le Sentiment de la Nature dans le préromantisme européen.* Paris, 1960.

Vaquier, André. "Les Jardins du Comte d'Albon à Franconville-la-Garenne," *Mémoires de la Fédération des Sociétiés Historiques et Archéologiques de Paris et de l'Ile-de-France*, 9 (1956), 237–297.

Vaquier, André. "Un Philanthrope méconnu, Cadet de Vaux (1743–1828)," *Mémoires de la Fédération des Sociétés Historiques et Archéologiques de Paris et de l'Ile-de-France*, 9 (1957–1958), 365–467.

Vauthier, Gabriel. "Les Bals d'hiver et les jardins d'été sous le Directoire," *Annales révolutionnaires*, 15 (1923), 146–153.

Vauthier, Gabriel. "Le Panthéon français sous la Révolution," *Annales révolutionnaires*, 3 (1910), 395–416.

Vauthier, Gabriel. "La Statue de Jean-Jacques Rousseau," *Annales révolutionnaires*, 14 (1922), 68–69.

Vidler, Anthony. "The Architecture of the Lodges: Ritual Form and Associational Life in the Late Eighteenth Century," *Oppositions*, 5 (1976), 75–97.

*La Vie quotidienne à Paris dans la seconde moitié du XVIIIe siècle.* Introduction by Guy Duboscq. Exhibition catalogue. Musée de l'histoire France, Archives Nationales. Paris, 1973.

*La Ville au XVIIIe siècle.* Colloque d'Aix-en-Provence, April 29–May 1, 1973. Centre Aixois d'Etudes et de Recherches sur le XVIIIe siècle. Aix-en-Provence, 1975.

Vogt, Adolf Max. *Boullées Newton-Denkmal: Sakralbau und Kugelidee.* Schriftenreihe des Instituts für Geschichte und Theorie der Architektur an der Eidgenössischen Technischen Hochschule Zürich, No. 3. Basel and Stuttgart, 1969.

Vovelle, Michel. "Les Attitudes devant la mort: problèmes de méthode, approches et lectures différentes," *Annales: Economies, Sociétés, Civilisations* (janvier–février 1976), 120–132.

Vovelle, Michel. *Mourir autrefois: attitudes collectives devant la mort aux XVIIe et XVIIIe siècles.* Collection Archives. Paris, 1974.

Vovelle, Michel. *Piété baroque et déchristianisation en Provence au XVIIIe siècle: les attitudes devant la mort d'après les clauses des testaments.* Paris, 1973.

Vovelle, Gaby, and Vovelle, Michel. *Vision de la mort et de l'au-delà en Provence du XVe au XXe siècle.* Cahiers des Annales, No. 29. Paris, 1971.

Westfall, Carroll William. "Antolini's Foro Bonoparte in Milan," *Journal of the Warburg and Courtauld Institutes,* 32 (1969), 366–385.

Weyl, Th., and Weinberg, M. M. *Histoire de l'hygiène sociale.* Trans. Robert André. Paris, 1910.

Whistler, Laurence. *Stowe, A Guide to the Gardens.* London, 1956.

Wiebenson, Dora. "Le Parc Monceau et ses 'Fabriques,'" *Les Monuments Historiques de la France* (1976), 16–19.

Wiebenson, Dora. *The Picturesque Garden in France.* Princeton, 1978.

Willis, Peter. *Charles Bridgeman and the English Landscape Garden.* London, 1977.

Willis, Peter. "Jacques Rigaud's Drawings of Stowe in the Metropolitan Museum of Art," *Eighteenth-Century Studies* 6 (1972), 85–98.

Ziff, Norman D. "Mortimer's 'Death on a Pale Horse,'" *Burlington Magazine,* 112 (1970), 531–532.

## Illustration Credits

Numbers are illustration numbers; names of photographers are given in parentheses.

Archives de l'Institut de France, Paris: 206, 207 (Jean-Claude Vaysse)

Archives Nationales, Paris: 60 (Richard Etlin); 59, 61 (R. Lalance)

Beck-Friis, Johan, *The Protestant Cemetery in Rome* (Malmö: Allhems, 1956): 241 (Joseph Mills)

Bibliothèque Historique de la Ville de Paris: 12, 172, 212–214, 217–218, 242 (Lalance); 209–211 (Vaysse)

Bibliothèque de l'Institut de France, Paris: 234, 235 (Vaysse)

Bibliothèque Municipale, Besançon: 115

Bibliothèque Nationale, Paris: 2–7, 17–19, 21, 22, 40, 41, 54, 65, 73, 76, 85–91, 94–100, 103–106, 109–111, 117, 118, 120, 130, 131, 151, 152, 155, 156, 162, 163, 168, 171, 173, 176, 186–194, 196, 197, 199, 202, 204, 205, 208, 215, 230–232, 236, 237, 246, 248–253, 255, 257–260

Collection Le Fuel, Paris: 55, 129

Columbia University Libraries: 8, 13, 14, 16, 20, 23, 26, 27, 31, 153, 161, 263–268

Cooper-Hewitt Museum of Design, Smithsonian Institution: 121, 123, 125 (Scott Hyde); 126

Dumbarton Oaks, Harvard University: 9–11, 15, 24, 25, 30, 32, 33, 35, 36, 45–48, 50–52, 63, 64, 66–69, 79–81, 83, 92, 93, 101, 102, 107, 132–137, 139–150, 154, 157, 158, 164–166, 195, 198, 216, 238, 239

Gabinetto Comunale delle Stampe, Rome: 240 (Oscar Savio)

Gabinetto Fotografico. Soprintendenza alle Gallerie, Florence: 114

Gannal, Félix, *Les Cimetières depuis la fondation de la monarchie française jusqu'à nos jours. Histoire et législation par le docteur Gannal. Tome premier. Les Cimetières avant la Révolution.* (Paris: Muzard et fils, [1884]): 44 (drawing by Chris Burns)

Inventaire Général des Monuments et des Richesses artistiques de la France: 28, 29, 34, 62, 77, 78 (Corbierre); 56, 57, 70–72, 74, 75 (Emmanuelli)

Library of Congress: 108, 112, 113, 116

Louvre, Paris: 138 (La Réunion des Musées nationaux)

Miscellaneous illustrations: 38, 39, 159, 160, 177 (Vaysse); 49 (drawing by Donna Pennington)

Mount Auburn Cemetery: 262 (Pat Rodgers)

Musée des Arts Décoratifs, Paris: 1, 42, 43, 119, 127, 128 (Vaysse); 200, 201, 203 (drawings by Chris Burns)

Musée Carnavalet, Paris: 222–229 (Etlin); 167, 170, 175, 185, 247, 256, 261 (Lalance); 169, 219, 220, 243–245, 254 (Vaysse)

National Gallery of Ireland: 174

Oenslager, Donald, *Stage Design: Four Centuries of Scenic Invention.* Copyright © 1975 by The Viking Press, Inc.; material reprinted by permission of Viking Penguin Inc.: 122, 124 (Mills)

The Pierpont Morgan Library, New York: 82

# Index